A REVOLUTION IN TASTE

Modern French habits of cooking, eating, and drinking were born in the ancien régime, radically breaking with culinary traditions that originated in antiquity and creating a new aesthetic. This new culinary culture saw food and wine as important links between human beings and nature. Authentic foodstuffs and simple preparations became the hallmarks of the modern style.

Susan Pinkard traces the roots and development of this culinary revolution to many different historical trends, including changes in material culture, social transformations, medical theory and practice, and the Enlightenment. Pinkard illuminates the complex cultural meaning of food in this history of the new French cooking from its origins in the 1650s through the emergence of *cuisine bourgeoise* and the original *nouvelle cuisine* in the decades before 1789.

This book also discusses the evolution of culinary techniques and includes historical recipes adapted for today's kitchens.

Susan Pinkard holds a master's degree and a Ph.D. in modern European history from the University of Chicago. Since 2005, she has been a full-time visiting member of the Department of History at Georgetown University. She spent most of her earlier career as a university administrator, serving as Associate Dean and Director of Undergraduate Studies in the School of Foreign Service, Georgetown University, and as Senior Lecturer in History and Assistant Dean in the Weinberg College of Arts and Sciences, Northwestern University.

TO TERRY

Contents

Illustrations

Preface and Acknowledgments

The history of cuisine is full of legends, and some of the evergreens among them relate directly to the subject of this book. Whenever I mention that I write about the rise of modern French habits of cooking, eating, and drinking, someone always responds with one or more of the following views:

Fine cuisine was introduced to France by the Florentine chefs in the suite of Catherine de' Medici, who married the future Henry II in 1533. In other words, the Italians taught the French how to cook.

The historical role of spices and sauces was to disguise inferior ingredients, especially meat that was rotting or of otherwise poor quality.

Dom Pérignon, a Benedictine monk, invented sparkling champagne.

Foods introduced from the Americas quickly transformed the European diet in the century after 1492.

All of these legends turn out to be just that – beliefs unfounded in fact. The myth that *haute cuisine* was an Italian invention was first articulated in the eighteenth century in the context of polemics about luxury and artifice, which also gave rise to the belief that spicy seasonings and sauces functioned as masks for corruption. (Catherine de' Medici enjoyed a reputation for gluttony and lavish entertaining during her lifetime, but the food served in her household continued a culinary style that had been established at the French court in the late Middle Ages.) Spices are ineffective as preservatives (whereas salting, drying, and pickling are efficient), and in any case they were so expensive in medieval and early modern times that anyone who could afford spices in quantity could easily afford to buy meat and fish of the best quality. Self-carbonated champagne that effervesced in the glass was an unintended consequence of bottling wine for storage, a new technology in the seventeenth century. The American crops that ultimately had the greatest impact on the European diet and cooking (potatoes, tomatoes, and, to some extent, maize) were relatively slow to be accepted as foods for humans. The items that spread rapidly, such as the chili pepper, the turkey, and New World beans and squash, did so precisely because they fit into the culinary patterns that Renaissance Europe inherited from the Middle Ages.

These common misunderstandings raise the question of what *did* account for the fundamental shift in ingredients, aesthetics, and techniques that revolutionized French – or, more precisely, Parisian – cooking in the seventeenth and eighteenth centuries.

Around 1600, the food served on the tables of the elite still reflected the traditions of the pan-European medieval kitchen, the key elements of which merged influences from Roman, Germanic, and Arab sources. The distinction between sweet and savory, so fundamental to modern French taste, did not exist. Sauces for meat or fish typically combined sugar, honey, or other sweet ingredients with sour ones, such as vinegar or citrus juices, and aromatic spices, including cinnamon, ginger, cloves, nutmeg, corian-der, pepper, and saffron. Cooks strove to produce dishes that fused many layers of flavor into a single, unitary whole, rendering individual ingredi-ents unidentifiable to even sensitive palates. The techniques, equipment, and many of the seasonings used to achieve these results had been part of European practice since antiquity or dated, at the latest, from the spread of Muslim influence in the High Middle Ages.

By 1700, this ancient way of doing things had all but disappeared from the kitchens of the nobility and aspiring Parisian bourgeoisie, displaced by what one of its progenitors called "the art of cooking foods delicately." This meant discarding seasonings and techniques that tended to obscure the nat-ural taste and texture of principal ingredients. Mild garden herbs replaced aromatic spices; acidic or sweet-sour sauces were jettisoned in favor of sub-tle, silky ones rich in butter and cream (fats tend to magnify the flavor of the foods they accompany); roasted meats were sauced with their own deglazed juices; vegetables, which had traditionally been boiled into mush, were now served "half cooked," that is, still green and slightly crisp to the tooth. Sugar, which was more plentiful and cheaper than ever (thanks to plantations in the Americas), was now segregated into the dessert course or was consumed between meals in the newly fashionable colonial drinks (cof-fee, tea, and chocolate) and the confections served with them. In the course of a century, all the old culinary rules of thumb had been discarded by Parisian chefs, and the new ones adopted in their place form the foundation of French cooking – and much of modern European and American cook-ing – as we know it today. Whereas medieval culinary practice privileged sharp contrasts of flavor and texture, the new cooking stressed harmonious combinations of natural flavors. "Make it simple" and "let things taste of what they are" are famous dictums of the twentieth-century gastronome

Curnonsky; the aesthetic they express came into its own in the kitchens of the ancien régime.

Given the deep cultural roots and staying power of the medieval culinary tradition – not to mention the fundamental human preference for eating foods that are familiar from an early age – an interesting historical question is, how and why did traditional cuisine lose its place in the daily lives of Europeans (starting with the French) and get replaced with a new approach to cooking that was (and is) in many respects its antithesis? That this transformation took place in a relatively short period of time (three generations, more or less) in a pre-industrial society makes it all the more remarkable. A sufficient answer, I would argue, would necessarily involve both the history of material culture and the social history of ideas.

The chapters that follow touch on a wide range of subjects, from demographic and economic developments to changes in medical theory and from the history of horticulture to Rousseau's ideas about the virtue of simplicity. There is much analysis of recipes, culinary techniques, and equipment, but also of the social context in which these evolved. The ancien régime was an era in which the diets of the rich and poor became even more sharply differentiated than had previously been the case. Among the elites, refinement came to count, along with high birth, as essential to a noble way of life, and a household's cuisine functioned as a marker of distinction for the upwardly mobile as well as the established aristocracy. The century and a half that followed the emergence of delicate cooking in the 1650s was characterized by increasingly radical waves of desire to live in a manner that appeared to be ever closer to nature – simpler, more authentic, less artificial. The historical moment that created the pomp of Versailles also longed for its opposite, a world without ceremony, in which informal manners, sincerity, and friendship ruled. These ideas about what constituted the good life inevitably affected the way people wanted to eat and drink, as well as their behavior at the table. This desire to experience the wonderful variety of the natural world and to live in harmony with it was articulated with increasing clarity and force as the age of Louis XIV gave way to the Enlightenment, and, perhaps more than any other single factor, it confirmed the preference for authentic tastes and simple presentations embodied in the delicate style and its eighteenth-century descendant, the self-described (and original) *nouvelle cuisine*.

I have tried to tell this complex tale succinctly, while presenting details and examples that illuminate the narrative as a whole. However, some readers may wish to focus on sections of the book that address their particular interests. For example, readers who want to learn about historical recipes and culinary techniques will find most of this material concentrated in Chapter 4, Chapter 5 (specifically the sections "Cuisine as a Systematic Art" and "French Cooking in England in the Age of Massialot"), Chapter 6 (*"Nouvelle Cuisine,* circa 1740" and *"Cuisine Nouvelle, Cuisine Bourgeoise"*), and the Appendix. For the social milieu of Paris high society and the royal court in relationship to food and dining, see Chapter 3 ("Feeding Bourbon Paris," "A New Standard of Luxury," and "Dining Without Ceremony") and Chapter 5 ("Delicate Cooking Becomes French" and "Cooking for *la Cour et la Ville*"). The interplay between elite cuisine and the food of the poor is explored in Chapter 2 ("Divergent Diets of Rich and Poor") and Chapter 6 ("Anti-Cuisines"). Developments in horticulture and gardening are discussed in Chapter 2 ("Vegetable Renaissance") and Chapter 3 ("Capturing the Variety of Nature" and "A New Standard of Luxury"). Diet, medicine, and cooking are addressed in Chapter 1 ("Hippocratic Medicine and Dietetics"), Chapter 3 ("The Revolution in Medicine"), and Chapter 6 ("A New Science of Dietetics"). The development of modern taste, which privileges ideas of simplicity and authenticity, is treated in Chapter 3 ("Capturing the Variety of Nature" and "A New Standard of Luxury"), and Chapters 4–7.

ACKNOWLEDGMENTS

As is often the case with projects that take a long time to mature, I have accumulated debts, intellectual and otherwise, to many people, whom I would like to thank here.

William H. McNeill, my teacher at the University of Chicago, was the first person to suggest to me that food might constitute a serious historical subject. In the years since, he has been a source of ideas and information on many topics. More recently, Peter Gay, Sterling Professor of History Emeritus at Yale, encouraged me to quit a career in university administration to return to full-time teaching and writing. Although it took me longer than I would have liked to act on his advice, I was finally able to do so, thanks to Georgetown University and its president, John G. De Gioia. The late Terence Moore of Cambridge University Press urged me to write the proposal for this book, and his confidence in the project helped to sustain me during the long process of research and writing.

I benefited from the expertise and assistance of the librarians and staff members at the following institutions: the Newberry Library, Chicago; the Crerar and Regenstein libraries at the University of Chicago; the Deering Memorial Library at Northwestern University; the Lauinger Library at Georgetown University; the National Gallery of Art, Washington, DC; the Museum of Fine Arts, Boston; the Bibliothèque Nationale, Paris; and the Staatsbibliotek zu Berlin. Dave Klemm of the Georgetown University Medical Center drew the figures. Jill Gubesch, the sommelier at the Frontera Grill and Topolobampo in Chicago, provided insight about pairings of wine and food and assistance with securing examples of unusual wines.

The Weinberg College of Arts and Sciences at Northwestern University allowed me to take an unpaid leave in 2003–2004 for the purpose of working on this book. Among my colleagues in the Northwestern history department, Ken Alder and Sarah Maza offered helpful advice. Eliza Earle, Mary Finn, and Ruth Reingold, colleagues and friends at the dean's office, gave invaluable moral support. At Georgetown, I would like to thank the chair of the history department, John Tutino, as well as colleagues Jim Collins, J. R. McNeill, and Richard Stites for their advice and encouragement.

A number of friends have supported me in carrying out this project in ways that were less direct but no less important: Caroline Fawcett, Douglas Gold, Kitty and Steve Klaidman, Patricia and Art Liebeskind, Madison Powers, Françoise Sauvage, Nicholas Weingarten, and Cynthia Winter. My mother, Suzanne Kadlec (a superb baker), my aunt, Anne Oklepek, and my late grandmother stimulated my interest in food and cooking at an early age.

Terry Pinkard inspired me to write this book, and he also contributed ideas, advice, and practical assistance over the years. Thank you, Terry – this book is dedicated to you.

PART I

Before the Culinary Revolution

CHAPTER 1

The Ancient Roots of Medieval Cooking

THE TASTE FOR COMPLEXITY

This book aims to explain how and why it was that cooking, eating, and drinking in seventeenth-century France took a radically different turn from the standards of wholesomeness and good taste that had dominated European culinary traditions for more than two millennia, creating the foundations of the styles of cooking we know and appreciate today. In order to grasp the scale and scope of this transformation, we must first explore the ideas and practices concerning the preparation and consumption of food that dominated kitchens all over Europe from ancient times to the Renaissance.

As Alberto Capatti and Massimo Montanari have pointed out, the aesthetic of modern European cooking (which first emerged in France and then took root in other parts of the continent and the British Isles) is analytic. That is, it

> tends to *distinguish between* flavors (sweet, salty, tart, sour, or spicy) reserving a separate place for each, both in individual dishes and in the order of courses served at a meal. Linked to this practice is the notion that the cook should respect as much as possible the *natural* flavor of each food: a flavor that is distinct and different should be kept separate from other flavors.[1]

Thus, the modern cook aims to capture the taste, texture, and aroma of principle ingredients and uses sauces and seasonings to compliment these without disguising them. From this point of view, the success of any dish rests primarily on the quality of the main ingredient (whether this is an artichoke, a salmon trout, or a roast of veal), and a good cook's special skill resides in her ability to highlight the character of fine foodstuffs.

---

[1]   Alberto Capatti and Massimo Montanari, *Italian Cuisine: A Cultural History*, translated by Aine O'Healy (New York: Columbia University Press, 2003), p. 86.

The cuisines of the ancient Mediterranean took an approach that was the opposite of this modern one: they revolved around a preference for complex, multi-layered flavors that were achieved through the prolific use of strong seasonings, and they favored modes of preparation and presentation that transformed the taste, texture, color, and shape of principal ingredients. The aim was to turn raw materials of all sorts into confections unlike anything in nature:

> A perfect dish was thought to be one in which *all* flavors were simultaneously present. The cook was expected to perform an intervention on "natural" products by altering their traits, sometimes in a radical way. Cooking was perceived as an art of combination that aimed at modifying and transforming the "natural" taste of foods into something different or "artificial."[2]

Cuisine *was* artifice: perfection was achieved when flavors fused so completely that it was hard to guess what the individual components were.

This idea of cuisine as a transformative art and the love of spicy complexity that went along with it were not unique to the ancient Mediterranean world. Throughout human history most of the great culinary traditions of the world have been marked by their taste for deep, layered flavors that fuse many ingredients and seasonings. We experience and appreciate this culinary aesthetic today in the cuisines of Mexico, North Africa and the Middle East, the Indian subcontinent, southeast Asia, and many parts of China. The quality of cooking in Indian homes is often judged by the subtlety of custom-ground spice mixtures that give each dish a unique taste that cannot be traced to any single seasoning. Mexican kitchen lore claims that if one can identify a recipe's ingredients by smelling the steam rising from the pot, the mixture must cook longer to achieve a perfect blend of flavors.[3]

Fernand Braudel, the great historian of everyday life, pointed out long ago that the dominant taste for spicy complexity is linked to the fact that most people in most of the world have always consumed most of their calories in the form of cereals and legumes. He quoted a Hindu poet as saying, "When the palate revolts against the insipidness of rice boiled with no other ingredients, we dream of fat, salt, and spices."[4] Rice, beans, noodles,

---

2   Ibid., pp. 86–87.
3   Author's conversation with Rick Bayless, cookbook writer and chef-proprietor of Topolobampo and the Frontera Grill in Chicago, January 22, 2002.
4   Fernand Braudel, *The Structures of Everyday Life*, translated by Siân Reynolds, vol. 1 of *Civilization and Capitalism, 15th–18th-Century* (New York: Harper & Row, 1981), p. 220.

porridges, breads, and corn *masa* are bland in themselves, but they make excellent carriers for other flavors. Sauces and condiments concocted from small amounts of meats or fish, vegetables, herbs, spices, and fats transform bland starches into delicious foods of infinite variety. Complex, spicy cooking relieves the monotony of diets dominated by carbohydrates.

The aesthetic preference for strong seasonings in ancient Mediterranean cooking was associated with the dominant role of cereals in the diet: barley, which grew well in Greece; wheat from the region of the Black Sea and Sicily; and millet, chestnuts, and other "minor grains" that varied from place to place according to the topography and climate. As we shall see, medical theory also played a significant role, because it was widely agreed that health was preserved or restored by the calculated modification of basic foodstuffs by seasonings that rendered them easily digestible and amenable to the constitution of the person for whom they were prepared. Finally, culinary practices that strove to transform the fundamental character of principle ingredients were perceived as one of the markers that separated civilized peoples from barbarians. When, in the fifth century BC, the Greek geographer and historian Herodotus tried to convey the otherness of the nomadic tribes who lived beyond the Black Sea, he explained that they drank the milk yielded by their herds (instead of making it into cheese, in the Greek manner) and that they ate huge joints of meat roasted and seasoned only with salt – a practice that recalled the legendary past described by Homer but was foreign to the Greek kitchen of classical times, which featured fish, small cuts of meat and poultry, and vegetarian foods that were often highly seasoned and elaborately sauced.[5] The Greeks of Herodotus's day, like their Persian adversaries and their Roman heirs, ate foods that had been unmistakably altered – and civilized – by the artistry of the cook.

This approach to cooking endured in Europe for a very long time, spanning the rise and fall of Rome, the incorporation of Germanic and Celtic food traditions, the opening of Latin Christendom to the influence of Islamic civilization during the Middle Ages, and even the discovery of the Americas. Patterns of consumption and styles of preparation changed to accommodate various cultural traditions and regional differences, the religious imperatives of Christianity and Islam, and the introduction of many foods that were unknown or at least unfamiliar in the ancient Mediterranean. The pungent, sweet-sour flavors that dominated the kitchens of Greece and Rome carried over into the cooking of Latin Christendom. Aromatic spices paired with sweet ingredients dominated the elite cooking of the High and

---

5   Phyllis Pray Bober, *Arts, Culture, and Cuisine: Ancient and Medieval Gastronomy* (Chicago and London: The University of Chicago Press, 1991), pp. 82–84, 85, 87, and 114.

late Middle Ages. This type of cuisine became even more pronounced in the sixteenth century, when supplies of sugar and exotic seasonings increased in the wake of the voyages of the Portuguese, Columbus, and other explorers. The tables of the High Renaissance combined sweet, perfumed dishes with ingredients believed to have been popular in ancient Rome, including mushrooms, cockscombs, and organ meats. But all of these stylistic variations were the products of the same broad school of thought about what turned foodstuffs into cuisine. In their embrace of complexity and artifice, the cooking of the ancient Mediterranean and of medieval and Renaissance Europe could not have been more different from the approach to cooking that emerged in seventeenth-century France, which aspired to the ideals of naturalness and simplicity.

HIPPOCRATIC MEDICINE AND DIETETICS

From ancient Greece to Renaissance Europe, the culinary aesthetic that privileged artifice and the creation of complex flavors was buttressed by ideas about the role of diet in preserving health and curing disease associated with the Hippocratic school of medicine. Hippocrates was a Greek physician, a native of the island of Cos, whose dates are traditionally given as circa 460–337 BC. The corpus of sixty or so texts on medicine associated with his name were certainly the work of many different authors. Composed in the fifth and fourth centuries BC, they were assembled into single collection around 250 BC in the library of Alexandria, which was the great center of Greek learning in the Hellenic age.[6] Hippocratic ideas and practices spread to Italy via the Greek colonies in Sicily and the southern part of the peninsula, and by the second century BC, émigré Greek physicians had attracted a fashionable clientele in Rome itself and eventually became naturalized throughout the Roman world.[7] Hippocratic attitudes about health, disease, and diet persisted in folk remedies even after learned medicine went into decline in the wake of Germanic migration and settlement. In the eastern Mediterranean, North Africa, and Spain, Muslim and other Arabic-speaking physicians (including

---

[6] On Hippocrates and the Hippocratic corpus, see Henry E. Sigerist, *A History of Medicine,* 2 vols. (New York: Oxford University Press, 1961), vol. 2, pp. 260–295; and E. D. Phillips, *Aspects of Greek Medicine* (New York: St. Martin's Press, 1973), pp. 38–121.

[7] On the reception of Greek physicians and Hippocratic ideas and practices in Rome, see Ralph Jackson, *Doctors and Diseases in the Roman Empire* (Norman, OK, and London: University of Oklahoma Press, 1988), pp. 9–31.

the Jewish rabbi Moses Maimonides) became the principal inheritors of the Hippocratic intellectual tradition, which they refined, reinvigorated, and reintroduced to Latin Christendom beginning in the eleventh century. Half a millennium later, Renaissance humanists revived a series of Hippocratic texts and focused anew on the theory of dietetics that they contained.[8] Thus, ideas about the role of food and cooking in maintaining health and curing disease that originated in ancient Greece continued to shape culinary practices on the cusp of modernity.

The key insight of the Greek physicians associated with the origin of the school was that the human body was ruled by the same laws as the cosmos. At a time when supernatural explanations and magical cures were routinely invoked in matters of health and disease, they insisted that medicine was a rational science, using the same tools of logical reasoning and empirical observation that helped men to understand the natural world.[9] Furthermore, they argued that the body was composed of exactly the same kinds of matter that constituted everything else in the cosmos. The philosopher Empedocles had taught that matter consisted of four elements – earth, air, water, and fire. Hippocratic physicians accepted this idea and theorized that the body was composed of four vital fluids or humors (blood, yellow bile, black bile, and phlegm) that correlated with the four elements (air, fire, earth, and water, respectively) as well as the four seasons of the year (spring, summer, fall, and winter) and the four qualities of moisture, heat, dryness, and cold.[10] (See Illustration 1.)

When the four humors were in equilibrium with each other in terms of strength and quantity and when they were perfectly blended throughout the body, health prevailed. However, if too much or too little of one of the humors was present or if it became separated from the others, illness resulted. Sometimes a humor became concentrated in a single organ or extremity of the body, causing localized pain and inflammation.[11] For example, coughs were caused by a flow of phlegm from the head to the lungs.

[8]   Roy Porter, *The Greatest Benefit to Mankind: A Medical History of Humanity* (New York and London: W. W. Norton, 1997), pp. 106–109 and 168–176; and Nancy Siraisi, *Medieval and Early Renaissance Medicine: An Introduction to Knowledge and Practice* (Chicago and London: The University of Chicago Press, 1990), pp. 7–16.

[9]   Porter, *Greatest Benefit to Mankind*, pp. 55–56.

[10]   Sigerist, *History of Medicine*, vol. 2, pp. 279 and 318–320. On the Empedoclean foundation of the Hippocratic theory of the humors, see Peter Green, *Alexander to Actium: The Historical Evolution of the Hellenistic Age* (Berkeley and Los Angeles: University of California Press, 1990), p. 489.

[11]   Sigerist, *History of Medicine*, vol. 2, pp. 319–321.

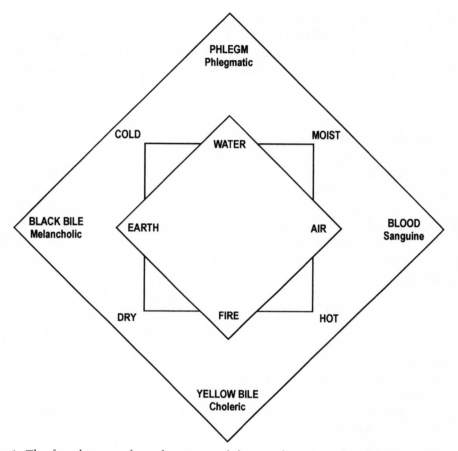

1. The four humors, four elements, and four qualities according to Hippocratic medical theory.

The searing pain and swollen joints symptomatic of gout were the result of the defluxion of humors to the feet. Mental illnesses were also attributed to disequilibrium of various sorts. Mania was caused by an excess of fiery yellow bile in the brain, whereas melancholy resulted from a constitution dominated by earthy black bile.[12] Hippocratic physicians believed that imbalance among the humors could be caused by many different factors, including trauma to the body, unsuitable food or drink, and changes in the weather. It was observed, for example, that cold winter temperatures correlated with an upsurge in diseases caused by phlegm, whereas fevers and diarrhea, which were linked to hot yellow bile, proliferated during the

---

[12]   Ibid., vol. 2, pp. 323–324; and Porter, *Greatest Benefit to Mankind*, pp. 56–57.

summer.[13] Because the humors corresponded to the elements and the cardinal qualities, "it was possible to establish a direct relationship between the macrocosm of the universe and the microcosm of the organism and to link them up with the atmospheric changes due to the seasons."[14] Thus the humors constituted an elegant theory of health and disease, satisfying in its symmetry and ability to fully integrate man into the natural world.

In terms of clinical practice, the theory of the humors gave physicians a means of uniting empirical observations and the case histories of individual patients (a concept invented by Hippocratic physicians) with a causal framework.[15] Furthermore, by conceiving of illness as disequilibrium within the body and pairing humors with opposite qualities (cold phlegm and hot yellow bile, moist blood and dry black bile), the theory also suggested remedies and preventative therapies that could be used to restore or preserve health – an invaluable asset for practicing physicians, whose patients hoped for relief to follow in the wake of diagnosis. Although techniques that aimed to evacuate excess humors (purges, vomits, and bloodlettings) were fundamentals of Hippocratic medicine, physicians preferred to minimize the chances of patients falling ill by prescribing a hygienic regime tailored to the age, sex, and constitution of each individual.[16] Such regimes regulated patterns of sleep, exercise, elimination, sexual activity, and diet in a manner calculated to achieve equilibrium of the humors. Although all these aspects of daily life contributed to the balance that was essential to health, diet was subject to the greatest variation. Food and drink thus became focal points in the care of the self, the single most important branch of treatment as conceived by Hippocratic physicians.

At the heart of the classical theory of dietetics lay the principle "that contraries could be cured by contraries."[17] One offset the phlegm-maximizing effects of cold, wet winter weather by eating foods that were dry, such as roasted meat, and by drinking wine mixed with a minimum of water. Summer heat called for moist and cooling foods, such as thin barley gruel, raw vegetables, and meats and fish that were poached in water.[18] Individuals of melancholy disposition were advised to eat foods that countered black bile because they were light in color or by association – for example, small birds whose flesh was pale and whose natural element was

13 Sigerist, *History of Medicine*, vol. 2, pp. 323–324.
14 Ibid., p. 322.
15 Porter, *Greatest Benefit to Mankind*, p. 58.
16 Phillips, *Aspects of Greek Medicine*, pp. 77–80 and 85–87; and Jackson, *Doctors and Diseases in the Roman Empire*, pp. 20–22 and 70–73.
17 Sigerist, *History of Medicine*, vol. 2, p. 322.
18 Ibid.

the air. Choleric and lustful temperaments could be corrected by diets that omitted most meats – an idea that would outlive Greco-Roman antiquity and flourish in the monastic societies of the Christian Middle Ages.[19] And so on.

Physicians evaluated foodstuffs according to two separate sets of criteria. The first of these categorized foods according to their "strength," that is, the amount of nourishment they provided to human beings. The strongest class of foods included "bread, pulses, the meat of large game and domesticated animals, large birds, 'sea monsters' (including whale), honey, and cheese; to the middle class [belonged] smaller game, birds, fish, and pots herbs whose roots or bulbs were eaten; and to the weakest class vegetables, fruit, olives, snails, and shellfish."[20] Within categories, individual specimens could range in strength according to the qualities of the environment in which they were raised, the age and sex of animals, cuts of meat, processing and cooking methods, and many other factors.[21] People who engaged in physical labor or strenuous exercise were thought to flourish on a diet dominated by strong foods, while intellectuals and the idle rich were advised to eat more ingredients of medium or weak strength.[22]

Foodstuffs were also classified according to their elementary composition: an item was thought to be cold, moist, warm, or dry according to the amounts of earth, water, air, and fire it contained. (See Illustration 2.) For example, partridge and pheasant were perfectly balanced between dry and moist but were warm in the second degree; duck, goose, and peacock were as warm as these game birds, but were two degrees wetter, whereas beef and hare were two degrees drier. Pork was cold to the first degree and moist to the second. The most neutral meats were veal and goat (one degree each of warmth and humidity). Fish and seafood varied enormously according to variety and mode of preparation, from very warm to very cold; counterintuitively, some fish, such as tuna, were considered to be dry. Vegetables and fruits were also all over the chart, ranging from sour cherries (cold in the third degree, dry in the second) to melons (cold in the second degree, moist in the third) to onions (moist in the third degree, hot in the fourth) to garlic (hot in the fourth degree, dry in the third). Fresh milk was the only

---

[19]   Innocenzo Mazzini, "Diet and Medicine in the Ancient World" in *Food: A Culinary History*, edited by Jean-Louis Flandrin and Massimo Montanardi, English edition by Albert Sonnenfeld (New York: Columbia University Press, 1999), pp. 141–152; and Porter, *Greatest Benefit to Mankind*, pp. 57–58.

[20]   Jackson, *Doctors and Diseases in the Roman Empire*, p. 34.

[21]   Ibid.

[22]   Mazzini, "Diet and Medicine in the Ancient World," pp. 146–147.

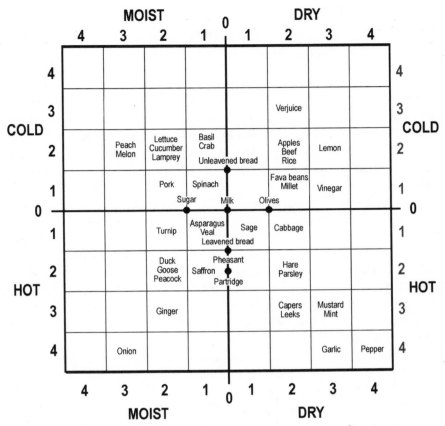

2. The qualities of foodstuffs according to Hippocratic dietetics.

common foodstuff that achieved perfect balance of the elements, although fine white bread and sugar came close. Indeed, many physicians believed that the balanced composition of sugar had a neutralizing effect on other foodstuffs with which it was combined, rendering them nourishing and easy to digest even for the infirm, the very old, or the very young.[23] Herbs and spices were considered to be warming (four degrees for pepper, three degrees for mustard, one degree for sage); with a few exceptions, they were thought to be drying as well.[24] As many generations of Hippocratic

[23]   Sidney W. Mintz, *Sweetness and Power: The Place of Sugar in Modern History* (London and New York: Penguin, 1985), pp. 96–99 and 244–246. See also M. Levy, *Early Arabic Pharmacology* (Leiden: Brill, 1973), p. 74.

[24]   Bruno Laurioux, *Manger au moyen âge: pratiques et discours alimentaires en Europe aux XIVe et XVe siècles* (Paris: Hachette, 2002), p. 140. For additional details see Mazzini, "Diet and Medicine in the Ancient World," pp. 146–147.

physicians enriched this picture with observations drawn from clinical experience, efforts to classify foods according to their elemental properties become increasingly fine-grained. Many schemes differed at the level of detail, even as the overall paradigm remained constant.[25]

From the point of view of Hippocratic dietetics, this broad distribution of foods across elemental categories created an infinite array of therapeutic options. Patients who had fallen ill could be cured by foods that offset the excess humors at the root of the disease. For example, garlic soup (which in its simplest form consisted of a large quantity of garlic boiled in a small amount of lightly salted water until it became a liquid purée) was the ultimate remedy for colds, since the strong heating and drying qualities of the garlic were believed to neutralize phlegm. Spiced, sweetened wine, known as hippocras, was the favorite remedy for ailments caused by excesses of cold, earthy humors.[26] Mixtures of honey and water (hydromel) or honey and vinegar (oxymel) were administered to patients suffering from fevers.[27] When used in this manner to directly attack the manifestations of disease, foodstuffs formed a critical part of the pharmacopoeia.[28]

Even more significant, from the point of view of cuisine, was the idea that foods that might upset the constitution of a healthy person could be rendered safe and wholesome through a judicious choice of cooking methods and seasonings. For example, mustard could be used to balance the elemental properties of pork. Veal could be warmed to the neutral point by cooking it with a little sage. Dangerously cold and moist fish, such as lamprey eel (a surfeit of which was said to have killed Henry I of England), could be transformed by a sauce of pepper, garlic, and marjoram into a delicious and healthy dish. Apicius, the compiler of the sole culinary manuscript to have survived from ancient Rome, gave a recipe for what he called "a harmless salad" – harmless because the cold and damp qualities of the lettuce were neutralized by a dressing made with an infusion of "2 ounces of ginger, 1 ounce of green rue, 1 ounce of meaty dates, 12 scruples of ground

---

[25]   For example, although there was broad agreement that saffron was warming, some authorities thought it was mildly moist, others mildly dry. There was also disagreement about whether beef, a dry meat, was cold or hot. Compare Laurioux, *Manger au moyen âge*, p. 140 and Odile Redon, Françoise Sabban, and Silvano Serventi, *The Medieval Kitchen: Recipes from France and Italy*, translated by Edward Schneider (Chicago and London: The University of Chicago Press, 1998), p. 29; and Jack Turner, *Spice: The History of a Temptation* (New York: Alfred A. Knopf, 2004), p. 122.

[26]   Porter, *Greatest Benefit to Mankind*, pp. 73–75.

[27]   Jackson, *Doctors and Diseases in the Roman Empire*, pp. 22–23.

[28]   Porter, *Greatest Benefit to Mankind*, pp. 79–80.

pepper, 1 ounce of good honey, and 8 ounces of either Aethiopian or Syrian cumin."[29] All of these ingredients were warming and (except for the ginger) drying, too. Because all foods other than milk were thought to benefit from some degree of dietary correction, an enduring partnership between medicine and cuisine was born. The road to health was also the road to complex, highly seasoned cooking.

Surely the staying power of Hippocratic ideas about diet and the corrective role of seasonings was enhanced by the fact that they could be implemented with a huge range of raw materials, many of which were accessible to ordinary people and even to the poor. Doctors' consultations and elaborate regimens were expensive, the prerogative of the well-to-do; however, the basic program of cooking and eating to achieve bodily equilibrium could be pursued by those with modest means. Many of the foods that were thought to be strongly nutritious and relatively well balanced just happened to be cheap and widely accessible. These included leavened and unleavened breads; porridges of barley, millet, chestnuts, and dried legumes; and cheese of many sorts. Conveniently, these sources of inexpensive calories were just what the doctor ordered for the bulk of the diet. Bulk commodities such as olive oil and vinegar and common herbs that grew in gardens and hedgerows were just as effective as expensive imported spices when it came to correcting the elemental properties of vegetables, fish, and meats. For example, a salad dressing of olive oil, vinegar, pounded mustard seeds, and garlic would warm and dry the greens as effectively as Apicius's deluxe infusion, and at a very low cost.

FUSION FOOD: COOKING IN THE MIDDLE AGES

Long before the formal end of the Roman Empire in the West (476 AD), northern peoples of Celtic and Germanic stock had been exposed to – and seduced by – many aspects of classical civilization, fusing them with their own traditions. This was true in cooking, eating, and drinking habits, as it was in art, architecture, and dress. The Gaulish poet Ausonius (310–396 AD) wrote of how porridge made of wheat, in the Roman fashion, had displaced acorns, which had formerly been a staple of the local diet.[30] Pepper, the

---

29   Joseph Dommers Vehling, editor and translator, *Apicius: Cooking and Dining in Imperial Rome*, with an introduction by Frederick Starr (New York: Dover, 1977), p. 86.

30   Maguelonne Toussaint-Samat, *History of Food*, translated by Anthea Bell (Cambridge and Oxford: Blackwell, 1992), p. 370.

favorite seasoning of Roman soldiers, also became very popular among the Germanic troops who joined the ranks of the Roman army. When Alaric, king of the Goths, besieged Rome in 408, he demanded as his price for sparing the city a ransom of 5,000 pounds of gold, 30,000 pieces of silver, 4,000 robes of silk, 3,000 pieces of fine scarlet cloth, and 3,000 pounds of pepper.[31]

Clearly, a merging of culinary practices was well under way prior to the final disintegration of Roman rule. We know that the manuscript of Apicius's *De re coquinaria* continued to be copied during this period – indeed, the text we now have is based on two separate copies dating from the ninth century, one from Tours in France and the other from the monastery of Fulda in central Germany.[32] Manuscripts about cooking and diet that originated in the post-Roman period show remarkable fidelity to the flavor combinations that were popular in classical times. For example, around the beginning of the sixth century, an author named Vinidarius, who appears to have been an Ostrogoth living in northern Italy, attached an addendum to a copy of Apicius in which he mentions all the familiar spices and seasonings.[33] At about the same date, Anthimus, a member of the court established by Theodoric, king of the Ostrogoths, at Ravenna, wrote a book about cooking and diet called *De observatione ciborum*. He gave many recipes for familiar mixtures such as oxymel (which was used as a sauce as well as a drink for the sick) and *garum* (the strong-smelling liquid exuded by the internal organs of fish steeped for days or months in oil, herbs, and salt, more or less resembling the fish sauces of Southeast Asia we know today).[34] Significantly, Anthimus's original recipes made use of the pungent flavorings that were so central to classical cooking and dietetics. For example, his directions for roasted beef called for a sauce spiced with cloves, costus, nard, and no fewer than fifty peppercorns.[35]

One aspect of Anthimus's recipe for this dish was novel: its principal ingredient was beef, a meat that was conspicuous for its rarity on the elite tables of the ancient world. This was certainly due to the fact that cattle were raised primarily as farm animals destined to pull ploughs and carts, and they were slaughtered for the table only when they ceased to be useful for this purpose, at ten or even fifteen years of age. The quality of beef would have improved somewhat during the early medieval period, when it became usual to slaughter cattle that had been used as beasts of burden

---

[31] Turner, *Spice*, pp. 85–86.
[32] Ibid., p. 75.
[33] Capatti and Montanari, *Italian Cuisine*, pp. 88.
[34] Ibid.
[35] Turner, *Spice*, p. 88.

between the ages of three and five years.[36] The willingness to sacrifice draft animals to the stew pot at an age when they still had many working years ahead of them reveals the high value placed on eating meat – even the chewy meat of a middle-aged ox – in the culinary traditions of the Germanic peoples who settled in the old territory of Rome. On the whole, beef was thought to be inferior to wild game, poultry, and the tender meat of young animals, such as lamb and veal. But under the right conditions, ennobled, as it were by Anthimus's costly spices, beef was thought to be a dish fit for a king.

Meat consumption rose during the early Middle Ages and grains continued to be central, but interest in vegetables declined precipitously and did not fully recover until the culinary revolution of the seventeenth century. Indeed, some of the vegetables that had been widely cultivated in Roman times disappeared from the record during the fifth century only to reemerge hundreds of years later. For example, asparagus, which had been common in Roman gardens, seems to have been unknown in Western Europe for almost a millennium. It reappeared in the late fourteenth century in a Tuscan recipe collection, *Il libro della cucina*.[37] By 1469, asparagus was known in northern France, and by 1538 in England, too.[38] Whether it had survived all that time in isolated pockets or had been reintroduced by Muslim gardeners in Spain or Sicily is unknown. Perhaps gardeners who were unfamiliar with the special techniques necessary to produce thick, fleshy shoots were discouraged from growing asparagus. On the other hand, radishes, which are easy to cultivate, seem to have disappeared, too, only to reemerge in France in the twelfth century and in Britain circa 1550.[39]

Such items as continued to be generally available – cabbages, turnips, onions, leeks, and an assortment of leafy green herbs, many of them wild – became linked in the imagination with the monastic diet and with the many days of abstinence from meat and other animal products that the Church imposed on the entire Christian population from the fourth century on. As late as the 1650s, vegetables continued to be associated with penance, self-denial, and the monastic way of life. Even Nicolas de Bonnefons, who did as much as anyone in France to help reverse this long-standing trend, dedicated the vegetable chapter of *Les Délices de la campagne* to the Capuchin order

---

[36] On the archeological evidence that establishes the ages of cows and oxen at slaughter see Massimo Montanardi, "Production Structures and Food Systems in the Early Middle Ages" in Flandrin and Montanari, eds., *Food*, pp. 170–171.

[37] For the recipe for asparagus with saffron from *Il libro della cucina*, see Redon, Sabban, and Serventi, *The Medieval Kitchen*, p. 75.

[38] Alan Davidson, *The Oxford Companion to Food* (Oxford and New York: Oxford University Press, 1999), pp. 37–38.

[39] Ibid., pp. 648–649.

of monks, who nourished themselves exclusively on vegetable foods and cultivated many of the varieties featured in his book.[40]

The synthesis of Germanic and Roman elements we find in Anthimus's sixth-century recipe for beef with peppered sauce would dominate cooking in Latin Christendom for more than half a millennium. The taste for pungent seasonings continued unabated. Even when supplies of Eastern spices were impossible to procure (thanks to the collapse of the economy in the post-Roman West), cooks persisted in using local ingredients, such as garlic, herbs, vinegar, and *garum,* to achieve the sharp, complex flavors and dietary balance that had been sought since antiquity. Then, in the twelfth and thirteenth centuries, we begin to see signs of significant change.

Although pungency would remain a popular taste right through the Renaissance, it ceased to dominate the culinary landscape. The cooking of the High Middle Ages favored a second set of flavors that combined sweet ingredients – honey, grape must, dried fruits, nuts, and a costly new import, sugar – with a profusion of fragrant spices and other perfumed seasonings, such as rosewater, orange water, citrus peels, and juices.

Some of the perfumed spices that rose to such prominence during this time had been known in antiquity: cinnamon, cassia, and ginger. However, their primary culinary application in Greek and Roman times had been to perfume wine. Around 1200 or so, cinnamon, cassia, and ginger began to appear regularly as seasonings in savory recipes, usually in combination with sweet ingredients. Cloves, which were known but rare in the cooking of late imperial Rome, became fashionable, as did a number of new imports to the West, including nutmeg and mace (from the Moluccas and Indonesia), galingale (a relative of ginger that originated in southern China), and "true" cardamom (a very fragrant relative of the cardamom seeds that had been known in Greece and Rome since the fourth century BC). Of the traditional pungent spices, pepper remained important and was frequently used along with the newly fashionable aromatics, although its overall share of the spice trade declined.[41] Saffron, which appeared in only three of the recipes collected in Apicius, became more popular and accessible than ever, as cultivation spread from the Mediterranean to several parts of France, to England (where the town of Walden was renamed Saffron Walden in honor

[40]   Nicolas de Bonnefons, *Les Délices de la campagne,* dedicated to mistresses of households, augmented by the author, 2nd ed. (Paris: Pierre des Hayes, 1656), pp. 97–98.

[41]   Bruno Laurioux, "Spices in the Medieval Diet" in *Food and Foodways I* (1985), pp. 43–76. On the history of Eastern spices and their introduction to Europe, see Toussaint-Samat, *History of Food,* pp. 480–526 and also the individual articles for cardamom, cassia, cinnamon, clove, galingale, ginger, mace, nutmeg, and pepper in Davidson, *Oxford Companion to Food,* pp. 136–137, 143, 186–187, 194, 329, 338, 466–467, 543, and 595.

of its most famous crop), and to Germany, which eventually became the top producer in all of Europe.[42] In addition to adding flavor and aroma, saffron also imparted a golden yellow color to foods with which it was cooked. The juices of fruits and berries were sometimes used to create a whole palette of colors in addition to saffron yellow. By the fourteenth century, a kind of international Gothic culinary style had evolved, dominating elite tables from one end of Europe to the other. Perfumed, sweet, and colorful, it was quite distinct from the sharper, more pungent cooking that Latin Christendom had inherited from Rome. It bore witness to the manifold influence of Arabic-Islamic civilization on Latin Christian culture.[43]

The role of exotic ingredients in the cooking of the high medieval period has long been explained as a consequence of the Crusades. Pilgrims returning from the Holy Land were said to have carried corms of saffron in their staffs.[44] Noble knights who established themselves as rulers of territories in Syria and Palestine cultivated a style of life that was heavily influenced by that of their Islamic peers. The splendid households of men such as Raymond of Toulouse, prince of Antioch, certainly helped to spread Eastern styles of music, dress, and food among other elite Europeans. The

---

[42]   Davidson, *Oxford Companion to Food*, p. 680.

[43]   The subject of Arab influence on the cooking of medieval Europe is a controversial topic in the annals of culinary history. Some scholars, notably Bruno Laurioux and Jean-Louis Flandrin, have argued that use of spices in the High Middle Ages was simply a development within the paradigm inherited from Rome and Hippocratic dietetics. Other scholars, beginning with Maxime Rodinson in the 1940s, have argued that the Arabs reshaped the fundamentals of the medieval kitchen by contributing ingredients, techniques, and flavor combinations that had hitherto been unfamiliar in the West and that these contributions have been ignored or undervalued by historians of Europe. Recently T. Sarah Peterson and Clifford A. Wright have been outspoken proponents of the latter point of view. See Bruno Laurioux, "Spices in the Medieval Diet," pp. 43–76 and "Medieval Cooking" in Flandrin and Montanari, eds., *Food*, pp. 295–301; Flandrin, "Seasoning, Cooking, and Dietetics in the Late Middle Ages" in Flandrin and Montanari, eds., *Food*, pp. 313–315; Maxime Rodinson, "Recheches sur les documents Arabes relatifs à la cuisine" in *Revue des Etudes Islamiques* (1949), pp. 96–165 and "*Romania* and Other Arab Words in Italian" in *Petits Propos Culinaire*, vol. 34 (March 1990), pp. 31–44; and Charles Perry, A. J. Arberry, and Maxime Rodinson *Medieval Arab Cookery: Papers by Maxime Rodinson and Charles Perry with a Reprint of a Baghdad Cookery Book* (Totnes: Prospect Books, 1998). See also T. Sarah Peterson, *Acquired Taste: The French Origin of Modern Cooking* (Ithaca, NY, and London: Cornell University Press, 1994); and Clifford A. Wright, *A Mediterranean Feast* (New York: Morrow, 1999). For a judicious assessment of the debate, see Bernard Rosenberger, "Arab Cuisine and Its Contribution to European Culture" in Flandrin and Montanari, eds., *Food*, pp. 207–223.

[44]   Davidson, *Oxford Companion to Food*, p. 680.

presence of crusaders and pilgrims in the eastern Mediterranean encouraged maritime powers such as Amalfi, Venice, Genoa, and Pisa to expand their activities in those waters, opening the way to a larger volume of trade in luxury goods, including spices and sugar.[45]

It is important to note, however, that the Holy Land was not the only or even the most important point of contact between Muslims and Latin Christians. Southern Italy was a crossroads of cultural exchange before the first crusade was preached in 1095. So were Sicily and Spain, where large Muslim populations had lived in close proximity with Christians for hundreds of years. Interestingly, it was in these regions that many of the foods introduced to the Mediterranean by Muslim gardeners and cooks seem to have made the jump to Christian tables. Thanks to the sophisticated use of irrigation techniques by Arab gardeners, many cities were surrounded by market gardens (which became known as *huertas* in Spain and Sicily and *hortas* in Provence) that produced an array of vegetables that dwarfed what was known elsewhere in Europe, including artichokes, beets, cabbages, cardoons, carrots, cauliflowers, celery root, cucumbers, eggplants, fennel, leeks, melons, onions, radishes, and spinach. Nearby orchards, irrigated by the same water systems, yielded almonds, bitter oranges, blackberries, citrons, lemons, mulberries, peaches, pistachios, plums, pomegranates, walnuts, and even bananas.[46] Hard durum wheat was used to manufacture dried pasta, an Arab specialty, in the vicinity of Palermo for export to both Christian and Muslim countries in the twelfth century or even earlier.[47] Attempts were made to grow sugarcane in Andalusia and Sicily, although cultivation of this crop was truly successful only in the warmer eastern areas of the Mediterranean, such as Cyprus.[48] Over time, trade and other sorts of daily exchanges of products and know-how contributed more than the Crusades

---

[45] By the date of the first Crusade, European economic activity was beginning to rebound from its post-Roman nadir. The classic account of this revival is Robert Lopez, *The Commercial Revolution of the Middle Ages, 950–1350* (Cambridge and New York: Cambridge University Press, 1976). See also the same author's "The Trade of Medieval Europe: The South" in *The Cambridge Economic History of Europe*, translated by M. M. Postan and H. J. Habakkuk (Cambridge: Cambridge University Press, 1952), vol. 2, pp. 257–354; Georges Duby, *The Early Growth of the European Economy: Warriors and Peasants from the Seventh to the Twelfth Century*, translated by Howard B. Clarke (London: Weidenfeld and Nicolson, 1974); and Archibald Lewis, *Naval Power and Trade in the Mediterranean, A. D. 500–1100* (Princeton, NJ: Princeton University Press, 1952).

[46] Rosenberger, "Arab Cuisine and Its Contribution to European Culture," pp. 216–219.

[47] Capatti and Montanari, *Italian Cuisine*, p. 53–54.

[48] J. H. Galloway, "The Mediterranean Sugar Industry" in *Geographical Review*, vol. 67, no. 2, pp. 177–192.

to the growing European taste for foods influenced by the multifaceted culinary traditions of the Islamic world.[49]

Interestingly, many of the new foods that were introduced to Europe via the Arabic-Islamic world arrived in the Middle East by way of Persia. The geographical location of the country astride the major land routes to India and China encouraged exposure to foreign species, and its varied terrain and climate – from the cold, arid north to the warm, marshy areas along the Persian Gulf – made it possible to grow an unusually large number of plants with different horticultural requirements. By the time of the Islamic conquest, Persian farmers had acclimated an array of plants that originated farther east and south, including the banana, bitter orange, eggplant, lemon, rice, sorghum, spinach, and sugarcane. This diversity of foodstuffs created unusually rich possibilities for the development of a sophisticated cuisine.

Persian cuisine was also informed by an ancient courtly tradition that stressed sumptuous refinement and elaborate presentations with a heavy emphasis on visual interest. Meats and vegetables were stuffed with complicated mixtures of nuts, fruits, herbs, and spices and were sometimes formed into fanciful shapes. Pilafs and sauces were endowed with a golden glow by lavish additions of saffron, and, on special occasions, foods were gilded with gold or silver leaf. Fruit juices and syrups were used to stain confectionary and aspics all the other colors of the rainbow. Almond milk was used as a moistening agent in many recipes in which a white color and bittersweet taste were desired. Meat and poultry were often marinated in yogurt or vinegar (a ingredient that continued to be very common, despite the Muslim ban on the wine from which it was made) and then cooked with fruits, yielding a mildly sweet-sour flavor. Pounded almonds, hazelnuts, or walnuts were used to thicken sauces, imparting richness as they adjusted consistencies. Refined white sugar, a Persian invention of the seventh century, appeared in pastries and confections of all kinds, including forerunners of modern sherbets, and it also reinforced the sweetness introduced to savory dishes by the liberal use of fruits and nuts. Aromatic spices, especially cinnamon, cloves, and ginger, were used profusely. More perfume was added in the form of rosewater, an ancient Persian favorite, which was distilled locally in great quantities.[50] Interestingly, some of the characteristics of Persian

49 Andrew Watson, *Agricultural Innovation in the Early Islamic World: The Diffusion of Crops and Farming Techniques, 700–1100* (Cambridge and New York: Cambridge University Press, 1983), pp. 87–102.

50 See the remarks on Persian cooking in Delphine Roger, "The Middle East and South Asia" in *The Cambridge World History of Food*, edited by Kenneth F. Kiple and Kriemhild Coneè Ornelas, 2 vols. (Cambridge and New York: Cambridge University Press, 2000), pp. 1140–1150; and "Iran" and "Roses" in Davidson, *Oxford Companion to Food*, pp. 402–403 and 672–673.

cooking – the fondness for sweet-and-sour flavors, the use of nuts and fruits in forcemeats, and the love of bright colors, trompe l'oeil surprises, and artifice for its own sake are reminiscent of Roman cooking. It would be interesting to know whether these shared characteristics were a matter of coincidence or the result of contact between Persia and the Mediterranean in antiquity.

Between the tenth and thirteenth centuries, dishes featuring Persian ingredients and cooking techniques became popular with elites in many parts of the Arabic-Islamic Empire. Cookery manuscripts originating in Abbasid Iraq and in Syria, Egypt, and Muslim Spain illustrate the diffusion of such foods as spinach, eggplant, rosewater, and sugar. Many recipes bore names derived from Persian roots, and many others used combinations of ingredients and flavorings characteristic of Persian cuisine. Examples include sweets made of almond and sugar paste (an early form of marzipan), chicken served in a vividly colored aspic of plums or blackberries, and *isfidbadj*, a thick, creamy meat pudding cooked with sugar and aromatic spices.[51]

Interestingly, dishes very similar to these eventually became popular on the tables of the elites of Latin Europe and surely provided inspiration for the sweet and aromatic style that became so fashionable in the late Middle Ages. The exact path by which the *isfidbadj* of Arabic-Islamic cuisine became the *blancmange* of medieval Paris, Barcelona, London, and Rome has so far eluded historical reconstruction. But the family resemblance between these two versions of "white food" (the literal meaning of both "*isfidbadj*" and "*blancmange*") is unmistakable. By any name, the dish was prepared by poaching light-colored meat (usually chicken breast, but also very pale, young, milk-fed lamb in at least one variation) in some kind of light-colored liquid (water, almond milk, or stock), shredding the meat, and combining it with pounded nuts (usually almonds), sugar, and a starchy binder (rice, when available, or soaked bread crumbs); the mixture was cooked over a low fire until the desired thickness was achieved and served with sugar, cinnamon, and rosewater sprinkled on top. Already popular in tenth-century Andalusia, *isfidbadj/blancmange* arrived in other parts of Europe during the High Middle Ages, where it continued to be an acclaimed delicacy until the middle of the seventeenth century. Thanks to the large amounts of sugar it contained, it was widely regarded as healthy for people of all ages and constitutions. Even La Varenne, who is generally

---

[51]   Rosenberger, "Arab Cuisine and Its Contribution to European Culture," pp. 209–210, 215–216, and 220.

regarded as the founder of modern French cooking, included a recipe for *blancmange* in his revolutionary cookbook, *Le Cuisinier françois*.[52]

Foods prepared in the sweet, aromatic style of *isfīdbadj/blancmange* must have appealed to elite Europeans for a number of reasons. Certified by the doctors as dietetically correct, such dishes also introduced greater variety to the table when presented in the same course with foods cooked in the familiar pungent style (a combination we see often in medieval banquet menus). The liberal use of coloring agents such as saffron, fruit, and almond milk created foods that were beautiful to look at and added a festive air to the table. And because sugar and spices were expensive and rare, perfumed foods proclaimed the wealth and prestige of the royal, noble, and clerical households that consumed them. Indeed, the high cost of spices in the Middle Ages exposes the weakness of the old myth that their purpose was to disguise inferior and rotting foodstuffs: any kitchen that used spices in abundance was able to afford meat, fish, and other ingredients of the best and freshest quality.[53]

PATTERNS OF CONSUMPTION

By 1300 or so, the principal meal of the day in well-to-do households was served as a sequence of individual courses designed to promote good

[52] Ibid., p. 216. For Italian and Catalan adaptations under the name *"blancmange"* see Redon, Sabban, and Serventi, *The Medieval Kitchen*, pp. 196–199; for French and English versions, see Peterson, *Acquired Taste*, pp. 3–4. As Peterson notes, *Le Ménagier de Paris*, a fourteenth-century Parisian source, gives a kindred recipe under the name *"brouet blanc"*; see *Le Ménagier de Paris*, edited by Georgine E. Brereton and Janet M. Ferrier (Oxford: Clarendon, 1981), p. 217. For an early modern *blancmange* (in versions suitable for fat days and days of abstention), see La Varenne, *Le Cuisinier françois*, edited by Philip and Mary Hyman (Paris: Manucius, 2001), pp. 100, 237, and 300. For a general overview, see "Blancmange" in Davidson, *Oxford Companion to Food*, p. 80.

[53] Flandrin, "Seasoning, Cooking, and Dietetics in the Late Middle Ages," pp. 313–314. Salting, smoking, and drying provided efficient and cheap means of preservation for meats that could not be consumed at once and opened the way to the creation of a huge variety of hams, sausages, and cured foods that came to be recognized as delicacies in their own right. Most items of charcuterie included herbs and spices, but these were used to infuse the cured meats with additional flavor and to render them more easily digestible. Fish of all sorts was also preserved according to these means (as well as pickling), from the herring of the North Sea to the cod of the Atlantic and the sardines, anchovies, and tuna of Mediterranean waters. See Giovanni Rebora, *The Culture of the Fork: A Brief History of Food in Europe*, translated by Arthur Sonnenfeld (New York: Columbia University Press, 2001), pp. 70–85.

digestion. Meals opened with dishes that featured acidity in one form or another: seasonal fruits, such as melons, cherries, strawberries, or grapes, or salads of vegetables and greens dressed with oil, salt, and vinegar. Known as entrées, such foods were thought to "open" the stomach in preparation for the more substantial courses to come.[54]

The second course, the *potage*, consisted of principal ingredients cooked in sauce, a broad designation that included what we would classify today as soups, stews, purées, and pastas. Depending on the ecclesiastical calendar, the season, and the budget and whims of the cook, a *potage* could feature small pieces of meat, fish, vegetables, or legumes. What made a *potage* a *potage* was the technique of boiling the ingredients in liquid: water, bouillon, wine, vinegar, almond milk, or some combination.[55] The moist heat of the cauldron – like that of the stomach itself – began to heat and, therefore, to digest the food even before it was consumed, a process that could be further accelerated by the addition of warming herbs, spices, and other seasonings to the cooking liquid.[56]

Although the *potages* were filling dishes, they were thought to be easier for the body to convert into nourishment than the foods offered in the third course, the *rôt* or roast. This consisted of the largest and most impressive pieces of meat or fish the kitchen could secure (except on the strictest days of abstinence, such as Good Friday, when vegetables or grains were substituted instead). As their name suggests, roasts were typically cooked on a spit in the fireplace, although they could also be grilled, baked, or even boiled. Roasts were accompanied by spicy, condiment-like sauces that were made separately and chosen to correct the dietary properties of the meat or fish.[57] Guests used their fingers to dip small pieces of the roast into the sauce before lifting the morsels to their mouths.

Medieval cooks developed several sorts of sauces that had many variants. *Poivrade* was probably the most popular of them all and was served with robust red meats. It featured black pepper, sometimes reinforced with garlic (an equally hot and dry seasoning), mixed with toasted bread crumbs (which served as a thickening agent), vinegar, or verjuice (the unfermented juice of sour grapes). *Sauce verte* (green sauce) was milder, taking its name from the pounded herbs that colored it. Its heat could be adjusted and its taste refined by adding aromatics such as nutmeg, cloves, and ginger. *Cameline* sauces were medium hot and brown in color, thanks to quantities of cinnamon mixed with cloves, ginger, nutmeg, sugar, and bread crumbs.

[54] Redon, Sabban, and Serventi, *The Medieval Kitchen*, p. 10.
[55] Ibid.
[56] Laurioux, *Manger au moyen âge*, pp. 232–233.
[57] Redon, Sabban, and Serventi, *The Medieval Kitchen*, p. 10.

Jance or *poivre jaunet* used ginger and saffron to achieve the yellow color for which it was named. *Moutarde* (mustard) was usually yellow, although red and violet versions also existed. To make it, the pulverized seeds of *brassica alba,* a common herb, were mixed with vinegar and sweet grape must to produce a fiery, sweet-and-sour flavor. All of these sauces were strongly acidic. Vinegar was omnipresent, but some recipes called for verjuice, white wine, and the juice of lemons or bitter oranges to be added, too.[58] For a modern comparison, think of barbecue sauce, which layers the acidic flavors of vinegar and tomato with garlic, sugar, and spices.

The sauces described above were classics of the medieval table, appearing in many variations in French, English, Italian, and German sources. However, cooks must have also improvised many personal recipes on the basis of familiar dietetic principles and their own aesthetic sense. For example, a single copy of the *Viandier* of Taillevent dating from the fifteenth century includes an unusual recipe for marjoram sauce with ginger, clove, cinnamon, sugar, and white wine. Thin in texture, it was probably used as a dip for pieces of roasted meat.[59] Around the same time, Martino of Como, the celebrated chef who cooked for Cardinal Ludovico Trevasian in Rome, recorded recipes for several fruit-based sauces that were designed to be served with chickens, capons, and other light meats. Less acidic than the norm, they were perfumed with aromatic spices and brilliantly colored with the juice and pulp of blackberries, plums, mulberries, and red grapes. Pounded almonds replaced the usual bread crumbs in several of these recipes, and sugar was sometimes used to soften the acidity of the vinegar, wine, or lemon juice, creating a tart rather than sour taste. These touches echo characteristics of Persian cooking – a fact of which Martino was probably unaware.

After the roast was cleared, the dinner wound down, both aesthetically and dietetically, with two or three courses designed to "close" the stomach and bank its fire for a long, quiet period of digestion.[60] The entremets course consisted of smaller, lighter dishes of many different kinds. This was the place on the menu where a delicacy like *blancmange* was likely to appear. Other dishes appropriate as entremets included cheese, thinly sliced ham and other items of charcuterie, eggs cooked and sauced in many

---

[58]　Versions of all of these sauces collected from French and Italian sources are found in Redon, Sabban, and Serventi, *The Medieval Kitchen,* pp. 169–174 and 177–178. See also the discussion and recipes in D. Eleanor Scully and Terence Scully, *Early French Cookery: Sources, History, Original Recipes and Modern Adaptations* (Ann Arbor: University of Michigan Press, 1995), pp. 111–143.

[59]　Scully and Scully, *Early French Cookery,* pp. 141–142.

[60]　Redon, Sabban, and Serventi, *The Medieval Kitchen,* pp. 10–11.

different ways, foods in aspic, fritters, pastries, and many sorts of pies and tarts, whose fillings typically mingled savory ingredients with sweet ones. The entremets were followed by dessert. Mellow, fresh fruits such as pears and apples; dried fruits, including figs, raisins, and prunes; nuts; and many kinds of preserves were featured in the dessert course, although savory foods, including cheese, also appeared. After dessert came the *issue de table* (departure from the table), which consisted of more sweetmeats and light pastries served with hippocras or sweet wines. Upon leaving the table and moving to another part of the house, guests were offered the *boute-hors:* more wine and confetti (candied spices such as cardamom seeds, coriander, or ginger), which sweetened the breath in addition to aiding digestion.[61]

Menus that followed this basic pattern prevailed not only in France but in England, Italy, and central Europe as well.[62] Indeed, one can still see the progression of acidic entrée, sauced *potage*, roast, and soothing entremets and deserts in the modern Italian menu of antipasti, pasta, and meat or fish followed by cheese and fruit – proof that good culinary ideas can outlive the medical regimes from which they originally sprang. This manner of organizing a meal could be adapted to all sorts of budgets. Rich households could create even more impressive meals on celebratory occasions by multiplying the dishes served in each course or adding subdivisions to the principal courses. For example, the roast might be preceded by a course of boiled meats or fish that were served whole or in large pieces with sauces similar to those presented with the roasted meat – a custom that continued at the French court through the reign of Louis XIV.[63] Of course, one could also trim the number of courses in the interest of economy. For example, the dessert and the *issue de table* could be collapsed into a single service and the *boute-hors* eliminated, while still preserving the principle of ending the meal with foods that soothed the stomach and conserved its heat. Costs could also be controlled by relying on less expensive ingredients, adjusting portions, and limiting the number of dishes presented in each course.[64] An apple and a piece of cheese met the dietetic requirements for entremets just as well as sugared pastry or *blancmange*.

Medieval meals also embodied another kind of pattern, one that reflected the standing of the diners in the household and the wider social world. The

[61] Ibid., p. 11.
[62] Laurioux, *Manger au moyen âge*, pp. 190–196 and 236–238. See also Capatti and Montanari, *Italian Cuisine*, pp. 121–129.
[63] Roland Jousselin, *Au couvert du roi: XVIIe-XVIII siècles* (Paris: Editions Christian, 1998), pp. 72–73.
[64] Redon, Sabban, and Serventi, *The Medieval Kitchen*, p. 11; and Laurioux, *Manger au moyen âge*, pp. 231–236. See the discussion of the menus and household budget of a bourgeois family in *Le Ménagier de Paris*, pp. 539–598.

fundamental inequality of persons and their places in multiple hierarchies both sacred and profane were made tangible at the table in a variety of ways.

The most obvious sign of the status of an individual among a group of diners was the seat he or she occupied at the table. Until the advent of dedicated dining rooms in the seventeenth century, tables in homes of all social levels were usually trestle models of a long and narrow shape that could be taken down or pushed aside as other activities required.[65] Tables were positioned with one of the long sides in front of the fireplace, and the head of the household sat in the middle of the table with his back to the hearth. Other members of the household were seated to either side of the host, in declining order of precedence. In domestic settings this meant that head of the family, usually the father or grandfather, sat in the center, with the other men and boys to his right in order of age and the females, beginning with his wife or mother, seated to the left. Although the youngest children or the retainers who ate with the family (tutors, chaplains, ladies in waiting, for example) sometimes bent around the narrow ends of the table, they were usually not seated opposite their elders and betters. If the group was large, additional tables would be set up at right angles to the head table, forming the horseshoe or U-shape still used today for formal banquets and in the dining halls of certain colleges and schools.[66] Members of the party were seated on the outside edges of the horseshoe, preserving the hierarchical seating plan down to the persons of lowest rank on the two extreme ends. When guests were present, they, too, were integrated into the plan according to rank, with the highest seated to the immediate right of the host. In grand establishments – the court of France, for example, or the household of a bishop or powerful nobleman – the number of people seated in this manner could run to dozens, even hundreds. At this level, the women often dined in a separate room, where the table was arranged to reflect the declining rank of female diners. Or, conversely, women might also be seated along with the men, but according to rank, along one side of the perimeter of the table. It is interesting to note that the principle of hierarchy was so deeply rooted in the medieval imagination that seating according to rank prevailed at all social levels. We find evidence of it in the households of merchants and professional men, among artisans, and even among peasants, where the senior male members and the mother or grandmother were seated with their backs to the fire and served by the younger women and girls.

---

[65] François Piponnier, "From Hearth to Table: Late Medieval Cooking Equipment" in Flandrin and Montanari, eds., *Food*, pp. 342–346.

[66] Laurioux, *Manger au moyen âge*, pp. 191–194.

Seating was not the only indicator of rank at the medieval table: people were served different foods, cruder or more refined, as was appropriate according to whom they were. There was some precedent for this in ancient dietetic practice. It was a commonplace in Rome that people engaged in hard physical labor needed to eat heavier, coarser foods (pork instead of lamb, for example) and had digestions that could tolerate harsher seasonings (garlic instead of pepper). The distinction we find in the Middle Ages is subtly different. At issue was not the degree of physical activity one engaged in – after all, both peasants and aristocratic warriors needed great strength and expended considerable force in their daily work (hunting was the noble occupation *par excellence* in times of peace). What mattered was one's constitution, which was now understood to be wholly inherited from one's ancestors, a matter of blood that ran various shades of blue or red. Aristocrats needed to eat refined foods (generally those on the airy side of the spectrum), and the lower orders required earthy ones, lest they sicken and die. This was true in spite of physical activity or lack of it, although those factors continued to be second-order considerations in fine-tuning the dietary regime of individuals, as were the seasons of the year.[67]

Of course, peasants and princes rarely sat down at the same table, so the differentiation in the dishes that were placed up and down the length of the horseshoe table dealt in much finer distinctions. The general rule of thumb was that the choicest and most expensive dishes were reserved for people at the head table, whereas less prestigious and cheaper items were set before those who sat lower down. People seated at the head table were routinely offered larger quantities of food and more choices in each course.[68] One consequence of the long, narrow form of the table was that the less important guests at large banquets were seated yards and yards away from the host and the other top people. In practice, one was confined to eating the items that the servants placed within an arm's reach – two or at most three items per course. Thus, while those seated at the head table feasted on tender loins of venison, racks of lamb, and the breasts of plump, young pheasants, those farther down, "below the salt," made due with shoulders, shins, and boney wings. The less favored members of the company might also get dishes composed of less prestigious foodstuffs (pork instead of

[67] Capatti and Montanari, *Italian Cuisine*, pp. 65–67. See the discussion of foods that were appropriate for people of various social backgrounds in Allen J. Greico, "Food and Social Classes in Late Medieval and Renaissance Italy" in Flandrin and Montanari, eds., *Food*, pp. 307–312; and Laurioux, *Manger au moyen âge*, pp. 132–135.

[68] See the examples drawn from the household of Humbert II of Viennois in the middle of the fourteenth century discussed in Laurioux, *Manger au moyen âge*, pp. 185–190.

game, for example) and sauces prepared with a higher ratio of bread crumb and vinegar to spice. The pattern created by the placement of tureens and platters on the table traced the lines of rank established by the seating plan.

By modern standards, the equipment set at each place was sparse: diners were provided with a bowl and spoon for the *potage* and a trencher for holding solid foods and blobs of the thick, somewhat sandy-textured sauces that were typically served with the roast. In very grand houses, the plates and spoons used at the head table were often made of silver or gold gilt; however, people seated lower down were provided with equipment made of cheaper metal, such as pewter, or wood. Trenchers were made from a special kind of coarse brown bread baked in huge loaves for this purpose. Cut hours or even days in advance (with a special knife called a *tranchoir* in French), the stale slices were stiff and relatively impervious to sauces, cooking juices, and grease. High-ranking diners might receive up to three bread trenchers to use during a multi-course meal.[69] Knives were sometimes provided at each place, but it was also common for men and women to bring their own knives with them to the table. Forks, which had been introduced to Italy from Byzantium in the thirteenth century, were not in general use even in the most refined circles until the sixteenth century. Diners used their knives to slice and spear meat and other foods presented on platters and to transfer these items to their trenchers. These pieces were then lifted to the mouth with the fingers.[70]

The custom of seating diners along the outside rim of the table had the additional effect of inhibiting general conversation. This was especially true when the party was large and the tables were set up in a horseshoe. Neighbors spoke, of course, but often they were invited to focus their attention away from each other and away from the food, too. In monastic establishments, households of the secular clergy, and institutions linked with the religious life such as schools, hospitals, and orphanages, diners typically ate without speaking while passages from the scriptures or the works of the fathers of the church were read aloud. Festive meals given by the laity were usually accompanied by music or other forms of entertainment. In these cases, the setup of the banquet tables became an asset, with the center of the horseshoe providing a performance space for musicians, dancers, actors, acrobats, jugglers, and other entertainers high and low. The climax of the performance was usually timed to coincide with the entremets, and the delicacies served in that course were often conceived and decorated as part of the spectacle. For example, the dinner celebrating the installation

---

[69]   Barbara Ketchum Wheaton, *Savoring the Past: The French Kitchen and Table from 1300–1789* (New York: Simon and Schuster, 1983), p. 3.
[70]   Ibid., p. 5.

of Archbishop Wareham as the chancellor of Oxford University featured a sugar model of the eight towers of the university, plus figures of dons, and the text of four Latin verses appropriate to the occasion.[71] Even when there was no such unifying theme, the entremets typically included some dishes that were meant to impress or amuse: roasted swans with gilded beaks and feet, sewn back into their feathers and posed as if they were alive; rabbits baked in crusts with ears and fur reconstructed in pastry; and giant pies that concealed live song birds that flew out when the top crust was lifted, to the wonder and delight of the company.[72]

---

[71]   Mintz, *Sweetness and Power*, p. 91.

[72]   The swan in plumage was a perennial favorite, as was the presentation of "four and twenty blackbirds baked in a pie" (underneath the compartment where the birds were kept was a second crust that concealed the filling that was served after the birds flew the coop). The rabbit pâté was more unusual; see Redon, Sabban, and Serventi, *The Medieval Kitchen*, pp. 143–144; and Taillevent, *Le Viandier, d'après l'edition de 1468*, preface by Mary and Philip Hyman (Paris: Editions Manucius, 2001), p. 88.

CHAPTER 2

Opulence and Misery in the Renaissance

CONTINUITIES

In its fundamentals, the cooking of the Renaissance was a continuation of the late medieval style.[1] The structure of the menu remained intact. Roasted meat and fish continued to be paired with acidic and spicy sauces. Thanks to bigger supplies and falling prices, spices and sugar were used in ever greater quantities and were within the reach of a larger group of households. Confectionary, a branch of cooking that made extensive use of both sugar and spice, flourished as never before. Many recipe collections dating from the 1500s focus on sweetmeats, candies, preserves, and condiments, often to the exclusion of other kinds of foods.[2] The love of color, display, and fanciful presentations flourished in the courts of Italy, the châteaux of the Loire, and the guildhalls of London, Antwerp, and Amsterdam. The first book about cooking to roll off a printing press (a mere twenty years after Gutenberg invented moveable type) integrated the recipes of Martino of Como with a learned discussion of Hippocratic dietetics by the humanist scholar Bartolomeo Sacchi, known as Platina. *De honesta voluptate et valitudine* (*On Right Pleasure and Good Health*) was published in Latin circa 1473–1475. It was quickly translated into Italian (1487) and French (1505), a testimony

---

[1]   On the continuity of late medieval and Renaissance cooking, see Jean-François Revel, *Culture and Cuisine: A Journey Through the History of Food*, translated from the French by Helen R. Lane (New York: Doubleday, 1982), pp. 117–145. On the particular conservatism of sixteenth-century French cooking, see Wheaton, *Savoring the Past*, p. 43.

[2]   Philip Hyman and Mary Hyman, "Printing the Kitchen: French Cookbooks, 1480–1800" in Flandrin and Montanari, eds., *Food*, pp. 394–402. On sweetmeats, preserves, and condiments in sixteenth-century Italy and Elizabethan England, see the recipes collected and discussed by Elizabeth David in "Relishes of the Renaissance" and "Banketting Stuffe" in *Is There a Nutmeg in the House? Essays on Practical Cooking with More than 150 Recipes*, compiled by Jill Norman (New York: Viking, 2000), pp. 95–105 and 233–238.

to the persistence of the late medieval style and the internationalism of elite cooking.[3]

One of the evergreen myths of culinary history is the story of how the foundations of *haute cuisine* were laid by the Italian cooks who came to France in the suite of Catherine de' Medici when she married the future Henry II in 1533. As we shall see in Chapter 6, this tale originated in the eighteenth century, and its purpose was to discredit fancy cooking as dangerous to morals as well as health. It is true that Catherine enjoyed eating and that she spared no expense as the hostess of spectacular banquets. These fêtes integrated the service of elaborate menus with drama and ballet, a form of dance that had originated in Italy during the previous century. Without question, these entertainments were more refined than anything previously seen at the French court. However, the food itself was prepared in the familiar sweet and aromatic style that had long prevailed in both Italy and France.[4] It was only late in Catherine's life, during the reign of her son, Henry III, that signs of innovation appeared in the royal kitchen. In the 1580s, some courtiers began to use forks along with knives and spoons, and the *bouche du roi* (the office that prepared the king's meals) began to serve iced sherbets, a delicacy with Persian and Turkish roots that may have been introduced to France via Italy.[5]

The vigor of culinary tradition in the sixteenth century is apparent when one considers the assimilation of foods originating in the Americas. Dozens of edible plants and animals were introduced to Europe in the decades following Columbus's voyages. Some of these were readily accepted as food – turkeys, beans, chili peppers, for example – while others, such as potatoes and tomatoes, were not. Although a number of different factors were involved in the reception of New World foods, it is interesting to note that the items that were rapidly adopted all fit into niches that were clearly defined in the medieval culinary system.

For example, large fowl, both domestic and wild, were highly prized in the medieval kitchen. Capons, geese, swans, cranes, herons, and even peacocks were the pièce de résistance of many feasts and were thought to be especially appropriate for the tables of the nobility. The turkey had significant advantages over all of these – it was larger than the capon,

[3] Platine [Bartolomeo Sacchi], *Le Platine en françois: de honesta voluptate et vale-tudine*, following the edition of 1505, preface by Silvano Serventi and Jean-Louis Flandrin, transcription by Mathilde Ribot (Paris: Editions Manucius, 2003), pp. i–xii.

[4] Wheaton, *Savoring the Past*, pp. 43–55.

[5] Elizabeth David, *The Harvest of the Cold Months: The Social History of Ice and Ices* (New York: Viking, 1995), pp. 43–49.

meatier than the goose, and moister than other game birds. Accordingly, its rise to the pinnacle of European gastronomy was swift. In 1534, Marguerite, queen of Navarre, arranged for a farm near Alençon to raise turkeys for her table. Fifteen years later, sixty-six turkeys constituted the roast course at a banquet given for Catherine de' Medici. A menu for a slightly later feast that took place in Liège specified three different turkey dishes – boiled with a garnish of oysters, roasted and served cold, and in pastry (one wonders if the pattern of the feathers was recreated with crust). Turkeys were listed along with swans and cranes in the sumptuary laws that went into effect in England in 1541, and other English sources from around the same time mention the technique of fattening them on a diet of dried peas and serving them for Christmas.[6]

The plant kingdom provides some other instructive examples. *Phaseolus vulgaris* and other varieties of New World beans established themselves as favorites of European gardeners and cooks. First described in 1542 by the botanists Tragus and Fuchs, haricot beans were already labeled as "French" in 1572, a name that would stick despite their American origin. Many of the early recipes for American beans were similar to the traditional preparations for their Old World counterpart, the fava. Boiled, greased with bacon fat or olive oil, and puréed, they became important ingredients in *potages* of many sorts.[7] The reception of the chili pepper was even earlier, although its route to European tables was circuitous. Columbus probably brought samples of chilies back on his first voyage. Spanish and Portuguese ships took them to the East Indies in the following decades, and it was from Asia that they were introduced to Europe as a new kind of spice. Classified as hot and dry, chilies were used to correct cold, wet foods in the manner of black pepper and garlic and were welcomed everywhere as supplements to these traditional ingredients, appearing in Italy in 1526, in Germany by 1543, and in Hungary (in the form of paprika) by 1569.[8] Although maize seems to have arrived in Europe somewhat later than these other foods, becoming established in southern France, Iberia, and northern Italy by the

---

6   Davidson, *Oxford Companion to Food*, pp. 809–810. See also A. W. Schorger, *The Wild Turkey, Its History and Domestication* (Norman: University of Oklahoma Press, 1966).

7   Alfred W. Crosby, Jr., *The Columbian Exchange: Biological and Cultural Consequences of 1492*, 30th anniversary edition (Westport, CT, and London: Praeger, 2003), pp. 177–178. See also Laurence Kaplan, "Beans, Peas, and Lentils" in Kiple and Ornelas, eds., *Cambridge World History of Food*, pp. 271–281.

8   For details about the migration of chili around the world and associated bibliography, see Davidson, *Oxford Companion to Food*, p. 169–170; and Jean Andrews, "Chili Peppers" in Kiple and Ornelas, eds., *Cambridge World History of Food*, pp. 281–288.

SILIQVASTRVM
MAIVS ET MINVS.

Calechutischer Pfeffa

3. Chili peppers, "*Siliquastrum Maius et minus,*" woodcut from Leonhardt Fuchs, *De historia stirpium commentarii insignes,* 1542 (courtesy of the Newberry Library, Chicago).

middle of the seventeenth century, it made its mark in dishes that had long been prepared with other "inferior" grains. Examples include the polenta of Venice and Lombardy, formerly made with chestnut flour or barley, and the *las pous* (cornmeal porridge) and *armottes* (porridge cakes fried in goose fat) of southwestern France, which were originally made with millet. One traditional Gascon recipe still in use in the twentieth century calls for cold cornmeal porridge cut into shapes and sprinkled with orange flour water and sugar – a combination of ingredients that testifies to the medieval roots of the dish.[9]

[9] Paula Wolfert, *The Cooking of South-West France* (New York: Harper & Row, 1988), p. 138–140; and Davidson, *Oxford Companion to Food,* p. 616. Wolfert

4. Maize, *"Turcicum frumentum,"* woodcut from Leonhardt Fuchs, *De historia stirpium commentarii insignes*, 1542 (courtesy of the Newberry Library, Chicago).

The consequences of fitting into an existing culinary niche are neatly illustrated by the receptions of the sweet potato (*Ipomoea batatas*) and the common potato (*Solanum tuberosum*). Columbus encountered sweet potatoes in Haiti during his first voyage, and the plant became established in Spain prior to 1516 and in parts of Italy and southern France shortly thereafter.[10] Its need for warm temperatures meant that it never became a common garden plant north of the Mediterranean zone. However, by

says that corn was already being cultivated in the Basque region of France in the sixteenth century, rather earlier than some other estimates of its arrival.

10   Redcliffe N. Salaman, *The History and Social Influence of the Potato*, with a chapter on industrial uses by W. G. Burton (Cambridge: Cambridge University Press, 1949, reprinted 1970), pp. 71 and 130–131.

the end of the sixteenth century, sweet potatoes were regularly marketed as luxury imports in northern cities, where they commanded handsome sums.[11] The flavor of the sweet potato was often compared to the chestnut, and, like the chestnut, it had an affinity for sugar and spice. Cut into small pieces and candied, sweet potatoes were served as comfits or other types of sugary preserves. Boiled and then sliced or mashed and mixed with sugar, cinnamon, nutmeg, and mace, they were used as fillings for pies and pastries, often in combination with other deluxe ingredients, such as beef marrow, candied lemon, and eringo (the root of the sea holly, which was fashionable on Renaissance tables due to its high concentration of sugars).[12] Like many other roots, the sweet potato acquired a reputation as an aphrodisiac and booster of male fertility, considerations that outweighed its flatulent qualities and the fact that, like the common potato, its fingerling tubers suggested the twisted limbs of lepers to the contemporary imagination.

The common potato, in contrast, was mostly ignored as a culinary ingredient in European cooking until the eighteenth century. Whereas the sweet potato was compared favorably to the chestnut, the common potato was thought to be an inferior kind of truffle that lacked the aroma and flavor of the familiar European variety.[13] Olivier de Serres described it in 1600 as having arrived recently in France by way of Switzerland and Dauphiné and said that it was light brown in color (unlike the local variety of truffle, which was dark brown to black). Its principal value in Serres's opinion was that when buried in sand and protected from rats, it kept well over the winter.[14] In the few cases in which potatoes are mentioned in seventeenth-century documents, they were usually described as roasted in the embers of the fire – the classic preparation for black truffles. Serres's contemporary, the botanist Charles de l'Ecluse (Clusius), reported that he had heard that in some parts of Italy potatoes (called *taratouffi*) were cooked like turnips and carrots in stews of mutton.[15] If this report was correct, it was the exception that proved the rule. The practice of treating the bland but adaptable common potato as a vegetable side dish would have to wait almost two centuries before gaining wide acceptance.

---

[11]   Ibid., pp. 434–445. Salaman points out that both sweet-tasting and merely starchy varieties of *Ipomoea batatas* were cultivated by the natives of the Americas, but that Europeans were interested only in the sweet ones. See pp. 131–132.

[12]   Ibid., pp. 432 and 443–444.

[13]   Ibid., pp. 108–109 and 112–113.

[14]   Ibid., pp. 86–87; see also Olivier de Serres, *Le Théâtre d'agriculture et mesnage des champs,* introduction by Pierre Lieutaghi (Paris: Actes Sud, 2001), p. 872.

[15]   Salaman, *The History and Social Influence of the Potato,* p. 90.

In short, the new foods introduced to Europe in the Age of Discovery gave cooks a wider repertoire of ingredients with which to work, but they did not inspire innovation that broke with modes of preparation and seasoning that were long established. This was also true concerning the many vegetables and fruits of Old World origin that became increasingly fashionable on elite tables.

VEGETABLE RENAISSANCE

We have already noted the marginal role of vegetables in medieval cooking and the relatively small selection of cultivars that were generally available north of the Mediterranean zone. The kitchen garden maintained on the Île-de-la-Cité by the author of *Le Ménagier de Paris* (a fourteenth-century manuscript about household management that included recipes and culinary lore) grew cabbages, carrots, chard, cress, fava beans, fennel, leeks, lettuce, onions, parsley, parsnips, peas, spinach, squash (Old World *courges*), and turnips.[16] This list of fifteen plants, supplemented by herbs and wild greens, was a fair representation of the raw materials available to cooks north of the Alps at that date. Most of these vegetables had been cultivated since ancient times, although the carrots, chard, spinach, and probably some of the varieties of cabbage were recent introductions. For example, the carrot of familiar reddish orange hue (a native of Afghanistan) appeared in the eastern Mediterranean circa the eighth to tenth centuries, the initial period of Arabic-Islamic expansion. Carrots were established in Andalusia by the early twelfth century; in France, the Netherlands, and Germany in the fourteenth century; and after 1400 or so in England – a rather leisurely rate of diffusion.[17]

Interestingly, the pace of arrival in northern Europe of vegetables long acclimated in formerly Muslim areas of the Mediterranean seems to have accelerated in the late fifteenth and sixteenth centuries. The artichoke, probably a sport of the cardoon that developed in North Africa, arrived in Florence from Naples in 1466; it continued its northerly course, appearing in Venice around 1480, Avignon in 1532, and Paris shortly after

---

[16] *Le Ménagier de Paris*, pp. 118–124. See also Scully and Scully, *Early French Cookery*, pp. 254–258. Although the Scullys say that asparagus, cucumbers, celery, and eggplants were "relatively well-known in late-medieval kitchens," they seem to have been confined to Italy, Spain, and Provence prior to the late fifteenth century.

[17] Davidson, *Oxford Companion to Food*, pp. 140–141.

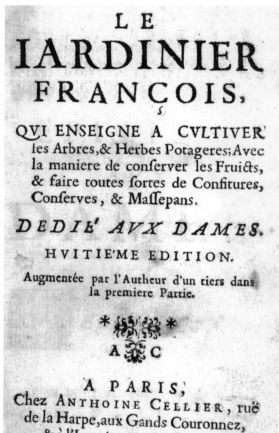

LE
IARDINIER
FRANCOIS,

QVI ENSEIGNE A CVLTIVER
les Arbres,& Herbes Potageres;Avec
la maniere de conferver les Fruicts,
& faire toutes fortes de Confitures,
Conferves, & Maffepans.

DEDIE' AVX DAMES.

HVITIE'ME EDITION.

Augmentée par l'Autheur d'un tiers dans
la premiere Partie.

* A * C

A PARIS,
Chez ANTHOINE CELLIER, ruë
de la Harpe,aux Gands Couronnez,
& à l'Imprimerie des Roziers.

M. DC. LXVI.
AVEC PRIVILEGE DV ROY.

5. Title page from the eighth edition of Nicolas de Bonnefons, *Le Jardinier françois*, 1666 (courtesy of the Newberry Library, Chicago).

that. Cauliflower was another plant bred by Arab gardeners that spread throughout Europe via the Italian peninsula. Eggplant, which had arrived in Andalusia around the same time as the carrot, if not earlier, seems to have moved north somewhat later.[18]

In the 1590s, Olivier de Serres described more than thirty plants that were highly desirable in the kitchen garden, twice the number discussed in

[18]   Ibid., pp. 36–37, 39–40, and 147. Watson, *Agricultural Innovation in the Early Islamic World,* pp. 83–84, outlines a number of possible reasons for slow rates of diffusion for crops introduced by the Arabs.

6. Frontispiece from *Le Jardinier françois* (courtesy of the Newberry Library, Chicago).

Le Ménagier de Paris: artichoke, asparagus, beetroot, cabbage, cardoon, carrot, cauliflower, chard, turnip-rooted chervil, chicory, cucumber, endive, fava beans, garlic, horseradish, leek, lettuce, melon, onion, parsley, parsnip, peas, pumpkin, radish, rampion, salsify, scallion, shallot, spinach, squash, and turnip (several varieties with different cultural and culinary applications).[19] Serres's list included thirteen of the plants grown by the *Ménagier* (all except cress and fennel). Of the remaining cultivars, only one, pumpkin, was clearly of New World origin, although Serres's assortment of squashes probably included both New and Old World varieties. The rest were either

---

19 Serres, *Le Théâtre d'agriculture*, pp. 788–849.

established local types or imports he obtained from Italian correspondents. One of the Italian items was a beetroot with a swollen shape, from which Serres succeeded in extracting sticky juice that he described as resembling sugar syrup (the identical composition of cane and beet sugar would not be demonstrated until the nineteenth century).[20]

The trend toward more variety in the kitchen garden continued in the seventeenth century. In 1651, Nicolas de Bonnefons recommended forty-two kinds of vegetables, a further increase of 30 percent. He, too, procured seed for the rarer varieties from Italian sources (and offered, for a price, to do the same for his curious readers). In addition to the items on Serres's list, he included broccoli, celery, cress, fennel, haricots (New World beans of several types, as opposed to favas, which he also grew), Jerusalem artichokes, kohlrabi, lentils, Spanish salsify (*Scorzonera hispanica*, which he grew in addition to the common salsify, *Tragopogon porrifolius*, cultivated by Serres), and stonecrop. In his section on cabbages, which ran to several pages, Bonnefons recommended planting about a dozen different types, all of which had distinct culinary uses.[21] Forty years later, Jean-Baptiste de La Quintinie, the horticulturalist who supervised the kitchen garden at Versailles, published a list of recommendations that was similar to Bonnefons's, although some of the earthier roots, such as Jerusalem artichokes and horseradish, had dropped off and cultivated mushrooms (*champignons*) had been added.[22] Except for the haricots, Jerusalem artichokes, pumpkins, and probably some of the squashes, the seventeenth-century additions to the kitchen garden were Old World natives.

This vast expansion of the selection of seasonal vegetables available gave cooks the means to increase the variety of foods they presented at the table. But equally important was a change in attitude toward the culinary potential of vegetables, which came to be seen as worthy of sophisticated treatment, on par with meats and fish.

In the medieval kitchen, vegetables were usually prepared very simply – to the point at which formal recipes often did not seem worth recording. Taillevent, an iconic figure in the history of French cooking and *chef de cuisine* to the kings of France in the fourteenth century, saw no need to include recipes for vegetables in his collection because, as he wrote, "any woman

[20]   Ibid., p. 824.
[21]   Nicolas de Bonnefons, *Le Jardinier françois qui enseigne à cultiver les Arbres & Herbes potagères avec le manière de conserver les Fruits & faire toutes sortes de Confitures, Conserves & Massepains*, dedicated to mistresses of households, with comments by François-Xavier Bogard (Paris: Ramsay, 2001), pp. 55–60.
[22]   See Jean-Baptiste de La Quintinie, *Instruction pour les jardins fruitiers et potagers avec un Traité de la culture des orangers, suivi de quelques Réflexions sur l'agriculture* (Paris: Actes Sud, 1999), pp. 831–834.

knows how to cook them."[23] He made only one exception to this rule, a recipe for stewed cress, which he justified on the grounds that it was an effective (and apparently novel) remedy for gallstones.[24] This dish was a *porée*, a type of *potage* in which the ingredients were boiled and then chopped or mashed and finally mixed with oil or lard and spices or other seasonings. Although leafy green vegetables and herbs were the most typical ingredients for *porées* (spinach and chard were especially popular), the technique was easily adapted for many other vegetables, too. Recipes survive for *porées* made of leeks, fennel, squash, fava beans (dried and fresh), peas, and lentils. Cooks were repeatedly advised to cook the *porée* in a manner that deepened its color. For example, leeks were often cooked in almond milk, to reinforce the ivory hue of the vegetable; spinach and chard were to be boiled only briefly, to preserve their brilliant green. A so-called black purée (*porée noir*) also called for spinach. In this recipe the leaves were sautéed with bits of salt pork to create a brown crust on the bottom of the pan; when liquid was added, the sediment dissolved, endowing the finished dish with its characteristic dark color.[25]

The other favored technique for vegetable cookery was frying. Occasionally tender specimens such as mushrooms were simply cleaned and dropped right into the hot fat,[26] but the majority of recipes called for the vegetables to be boiled until tender, drained, sautéed, and then seasoned with spices, herbs, and often a little verjuice, vinegar, or citrus juice. Sometimes the blanched vegetables were dusted with flour or bread crumbs or dipped in batter before frying to make fritters – a technique that the author of *Le Ménagier de Paris* recommended for turnips picked after the first frost.[27] Fried vegetable dishes often figured among the dishes presented in the entremets, especially on days of abstinence. Fast days also were occasions when meat or fish pies were replaced with pastries with vegetable fillings, such as the parsnip pie and mushroom tarts described by *Le Ménagier*.[28]

Finally, vegetables were served as salads in the *entrée de table*. Often raw vegetables were simply dressed in vinegar, oil, and seasonings, but they could also be boiled or roasted and allowed to cool slightly before being moistened – a technique still familiar today.[29]

23 Quoted in Scully and Scully, *Early French Cookery*, p. 255.
24 Ibid., pp. 255 and 259.
25 Redon, Sabban, and Serventi, *The Medieval Kitchen*, pp. 66–79; and Scully and Scully, *Early French Cookery*, pp. 256–257.
26 See Redon, Sabban, and Serventi, *The Medieval Kitchen*, p. 76, for sautéed mushrooms with spices.
27 Scully and Scully, *Early French Cookery*, pp. 257–260.
28 Ibid., pp. 96 and 257.
29 Ibid., p. 262.

This repertoire of *porées*, fried vegetables, pies, and salads was small and not particularly imaginative. Probably the association of vegetables with fasting discouraged the development of more sophisticated vegetable cookery in the Latin West, especially in comparison with contemporary Arabic-Islamic cooking, which featured a rich variety of dishes that used vegetables as principal ingredients.

It is interesting to note that the sixteenth century, when vegetables finally began to claim more serious attention, was a period in which the practice of fasting became far less severe. Initially this liberalization took the form of dispensations for those willing to pay, but with the Reformation and the Council of Trent (which reformed Catholic teaching and practice), the rules changed for everyone. Although the ecclesiastical calendar still imposed a pattern of meatless days on Catholic households (and, in a minor way, on Lutherans and Anglicans, too), their number decreased sharply. Furthermore, animal foods such as eggs, butter, and cheese that had been forbidden during Lent were now approved for consumption even by devout Catholics on all but a handful of occasions. Vegetables and fish no longer carried such a heavy burden of association with self-denial and penitence. Although it is impossible to establish a causal link between the decline of fasting and the rise of more innovative vegetable cookery, the two phenomena coincided. As we shall see in the following chapter, both vegetable and fish recipes were prominent among the dishes cooked in the "delicate style" of La Varenne and Nicolas de Bonnefons – the cutting edge of the culinary revolution of the seventeenth century.

Scholars have speculated that one of the factors behind the newfound interest in vegetables was the interest of the humanists in recreating the cuisine of ancient Rome. An intact manuscript of Apicius was discovered in a German monastery in 1455 and brought back to Italy by Enoch of Ascoli. This text was often cited by Platina and his friends in the Roman Academy in their discussions of what it would mean to live "in the ancient style."[30] Interestingly, truffles, porcini, and other mushrooms – all of which were prominently featured in Apicius's recipe collection – did have something of a comeback in the Renaissance, and this revival may be the specific result of Apicius's influence. However, the cuisine Platina described in *De honesta voluptate* was conceived in the "modern" (that is, late medieval) style of Maestro Martino and leaned heavily on the sweet and aromatic flavor palette.[31]

The revival of ancient texts on natural history, agronomy, and medicine certainly encouraged a reawakening of scientific interest in edible plants.

[30] Capatti and Montanari, *Italian Cuisine*, p. 98.
[31] Ibid., p. 99.

Scholars quarreled about such things as whether the Romans knew the artichoke or whether the "thistle" they consumed was really the common cardoon. (Throughout the sixteenth century, cooks usually treated these two cultivars as interchangeable, as in Bartolomeo Scappi's recipe, discussed later.)[32] As wave after wave of strange flora arrived from the New World, botanists struggled to fit the unfamiliar species into the plant families they inherited from Pliny and Theophrastus, and the doctors, like their Arabic-Islamic predecessors, strove to identify the composition and therapeutic applications of new vegetables, herbs, and fruits. For example, the first scientific description of the tomato appeared in 1544 in a work by Pietro Andrea Mattioli that was conceived as an update of the *Materia medica* of Dioscorides.[33] To facilitate these projects, botanical gardens were established at the medical faculties of Padua and Pisa in the 1540s for the purpose of creating comprehensive and systematic collections of specimens of all the known plant species of the world (Montpellier followed suit in 1598, Oxford in 1621, and Paris in 1640). Exchanges among these botanical gardens and other centers of medical science, such as the Flamenco hospital in Seville, where many American plants were first acclimated to Europe, helped to spread specimens throughout Europe. An elaborate network of private scholars stretching from Palermo to Antwerp, Frankfurt, and Stockholm also facilitated the diffusion of unusual cultivars, some of which were native to the New World and others to the Old. Somewhere along the line, specimens came into the possession of ordinary growers and nurserymen, who made them available to a wider clientele. One historian has speculated that the workers who tended the plants in botanical gardens and the plots of gentlemen scientists surely helped themselves to seeds and cuttings, thus establishing stocks outside the scholarly network of scientific exchange.[34]

The surge of interest in vegetable cookery in the 1500s operated within the familiar framework of dietary correctives and the preference for spicy, complex tastes. However, some sixteenth-century recipes also displayed a

32 Françoise Sabban and Silvano Serventi, *La Gastronomie à la Renaissance: 100 recettes de France et d'Italie* (Paris: Editions Stock, 1997), pp. 185–186.

33 Paula Findlen, "Courting Nature" in *Cultures of Natural History*, edited by N. Jardine, J. A. Secord, and E. C. Spary (Cambridge and New York: Cambridge University Press, 1996), pp. 63–64; Harold J. Cook, "Physicians and Natural History" in Jardine, Secord, and Spary, eds., *Cultures of Natural History*, pp. 92–97; Janet Long, "Tomatoes" in Kiple and Ornelas, eds., *Cambridge World History of Food*, p. 356.

34 Andrew Cunningham, "The Culture of Gardens" in Jardine, Secord, and Spary, eds., *Cultures of Natural History*, pp. 47–55. On the confluence of botanizing and business in the Muslim world, see Watson, *Agricultural Innovation in the Early Islamic World*, pp. 117–119.

new sensitivity to the texture and form of the principal ingredients, which were no longer simply boiled, mashed, and seasoned. These characteristics are illustrated by three of the recipes published by Bartolomeo Scappi, private chef to Pope Pius V and author of the *Opera*, a six-volume cookbook published in 1570 that circulated widely in France as well as in the Italian peninsula.[35]

Scappi's recipe for spinach with raisins is unusual in that it dispensed with the preliminary blanching of the spinach, calling instead for young, tender leaves (meticulously washed and dried) to be sautéed in oil with a sprinkle of salt. As the spinach began to wilt, one added the raisins and then some pepper, cinnamon, bitter orange juice, and verjuice.[36] Brought to a boil with the cooking juices from the spinach, the seasonings formed a little sauce that nicely balanced the composition of the principal ingredient while retaining the green color and fresh taste.

In Scappi's *minestra* (*potage*) of asparagus, the spears were to be kept whole throughout the cooking process. The washed, trimmed asparagus was poached directly in meat bouillon, without any preliminary blanching in water, along with slivers of ham, a little pepper, cinnamon, saffron, and verjuice or gooseberries (either of which would have added some sourness to the dish). Some finely chopped green herbs were sprinkled over the asparagus and their bouillon when they were presented at the table.[37] Against the saffron yellow of the sauce, the whole asparagus, lightly cooked and therefore bright green, made a striking visual display.

It is interesting to compare Scappi's recipe with another dish of asparagus with saffron that appeared in the late-fourteenth-century *Libro della cucina*. The earlier recipe calls for the asparagus to be cooked twice – first boiled and then, "when it is cooked," sautéed with oil, onions, salt, saffron, and spices.[38] This technique results in asparagus that is meltingly tender rather than slightly resistant to the tooth, and golden rather than green in hue. Although delicious, the identity of the asparagus is blurred by its fusion with the other ingredients, in good medieval fashion. Although Scappi's asparagus swims in saffron-flavored bouillon, it is clearly asparagus, thanks to the absence of blanching and the short cooking time.

A third example of Scappi's vegetable cookery is his recipe for stuffed artichoke bottoms. The trimmed bottoms, previously blanched, were filled with a mixture of chopped veal, ham, fresh cheese, salt, pepper, herbs, garlic,

[35]   On Scappi's career and influence, see Capatti and Montanari, *Italian Cuisine*, pp. 11–16 and 18–20.
[36]   Sabban and Serventi, *La Gastronomie à la Renaissance*, pp. 189–190.
[37]   Ibid., pp. 187–188.
[38]   See Redon, Sabban, and Serventi, *The Medieval Kitchen*, p. 75.

ginger, and cinnamon. The stuffed artichokes were placed in a dish, surrounded by some chicken bouillon, and baked until the stuffing browned and the vegetables were tender. They were served with a sauce of melted lard and vinegar scented with rosewater.[39] Thoroughly medieval in terms of their seasonings, the stuffed artichokes were an impressive dish capable of competing with the roast for the attention of sophisticated eaters. Like the asparagus with saffron, the artichoke recipe was conceived as a dish for meat days (although Scappi gave instructions on how to make an alternative version for days of abstinence, so as to give his readers maximum flexibility). Vegetables had arrived as principal ingredients to be treated with imagination and respect on all the days of the year.

DIVERGENT DIETS OF RICH AND POOR

The new wealth of vegetables was unevenly distributed on the tables of the rich and the poor. The imported novelties and improved strains of familiar plants that filled the kitchen gardens of Serres, Bonnefons, and their peers made no appreciable impact on the diets of the peasantry or the urban working classes until the eighteenth century at the earliest. Although no cottage was without its tiny vegetable patch and urban tradesmen often maintained small plots on the margins of towns, the variety of cultivars grown in such places was small and heavily weighted toward traditional items. Leeks and garlic (favorites for their strong flavors and hot and dry qualities), peas and beans (filling to eat and easy to preserve by drying), and turnips and cabbages (forgiving of frost and suitable for storage) would have predominated, along with a few herbs, greens, and perhaps a fruit tree or two. Subsistence gardeners typically lacked access to plentiful supplies of manure (a valuable commodity in the ancien régime), and their yields would have been correspondingly low. The ideal expressed by Serres and Bonnefons – namely that the kitchen garden should supply an ever-changing selection of fresh seasonal produce every month of the year – would have been impossible to achieve under these circumstances. While the role of vegetables in the elite diet became much more significant in the late sixteenth and seventeenth centuries, patterns of consumption by the rural and urban poor do not appear to have budged much from the late medieval norm.

This divergence between elite and popular practices in France is especially interesting in light of a more general reorientation of the European diet that took place at about the same time. Whereas the medieval diet had been relatively varied for all parts of the population, with a surprisingly high

---

[39] Sabban and Serventi, *La Gastronomie à la Renaissance*, pp. 185–187.

proportion derived from meat and other animal products, fats, and wine, consumption of all these items by the poor and middling classes dropped sharply after 1550 or so. Cereals, always the cheapest source of calories, came to dominate the popular diet at the expense of other foodstuffs, and in many places the quality of the bread declined, too. To give one example: at the end of the fifteenth century, farm workers in the Languedoc were eating white bread with their meat, as well as liberal rations of olive oil and red wine. Three generations later, meat rations had fallen drastically, wine and oil consumption had also dropped, and white bread had been largely replaced by dark loaves in which barley and rye predominated.[40] At a time when culinary choices were rapidly multiplying for the well-to-do, the popular diet became much less varied, nutritious, and plentiful. Famine, which had been relatively rare in the preceding centuries, returned with a vengeance, in part because of overdependence on cereals by the majority of the population.

The comparative bounty of the late medieval diet was a consequence of the sharp decline in population dating from the arrival of the plague in the 1340s. After the initial outbreaks in Italy and France in 1346–1348, the plague never completely disappeared, with severe reoccurrences in 1353–1355, 1377–1378, 1385–1386, and 1403 and 1419. Although mortality rates varied greatly from place to place – remote country districts were affected far less than crowded towns, cities, and monastic communities – they were devastating everywhere. In Normandy, the population in 1390 was only about 43 percent of what it had been around 1300, while in France as a whole, the population fell by something between 33 and 50 percent.[41] Similar drops in the number of inhabitants occurred in most other countries of Europe.

Although the initial impact of the plague on the food supply was disastrous – in many places so many people died that there were not enough laborers to tend the land or to transport food from the countryside to town markets – the long-term effect was to increase the quantity, quality, and variety of foods available to the average person. Much of the land brought under the plough in the previous period returned to forest and meadow, providing habitat for animals used for food. Manpower was scarce, and rural and urban workers of all sorts used the situation to their advantage. Peasants negotiated with their lords for better terms – effectively ending serfdom in

[40]   Emmanuel Le Roy Ladurie, *The Peasants of Languedoc,* translated with an introduction by John Day (Urbana, Chicago, and London: University of Illinois Press, 1974), pp. 42–44.

[41]   Georges Duby, *France in the Middle Ages, 987–1460,* translated by Juliet Vale (Oxford: Blackwell, 1991), p. 269.

many parts of France and Western Europe. Wages rose for laborers, servants, and urban artisans. Employers complained that a single day laborer demanded more than six servants had earned just a few years earlier. Much of this surplus income was spent on more and better food, with meat at the top of the list. Indeed, the historian Fernand Braudel went so far as to dub the period from 1350 to 1550 the era of "carnivorous Europe."[42]

Fresh pork and a huge variety of salted, smoked, and otherwise cured pork products were more plentiful than ever. So was beef, which was a cheap by-product of the growing market for leather goods (the hides of the animals were more valuable than their meat).[43] One historian has calculated that in Italian cities even people earning the lowest wages – boys who swept streets and women who cleaned or took in laundry – could afford to buy three pounds of boneless beef a week, a record that would not be matched again in some districts until after World War II. Servants in well-to-do households ate beef five times a week (the other days were fast days), and in charity hospitals patients were served a pound of beef per person on an average of three times per week.[44] The combined demand for hides and beef became strong enough by 1500 or so to entice stock raisers in such remote places as Denmark, Hungary, Tyrol and the Swiss mountains, Moldavia, and Galicia to drive thousands of head of cattle hundreds of miles to markets in the cities of Germany, northern Italy, Burgundy, and the Low Countries.[45] In the same period, the Paris market attracted cattle raised in Burgundy, Normandy, and the Limousin, areas that are still prime suppliers of stock for the French capital today. The long-distance cattle drive was a normal event in the Europe of the late Middle Ages and the early Renaissance.

By 1550, however, the economy began to shift gears. Although population levels took more than a century and a half to recover from the plagues of the fourteenth century, they had done so by the early 1500s. Wages stagnated and then fell in relation to the cost of living. Grain prices rose sharply and continued to climb, even though woodland and pastures were reconverted to fields in many places. Bread became so expensive that little was left to spend on other foods. Meat prices rose, too: between 1480 and 1585, they went up by a factor of four, while wages only tripled.[46] Except for miniscule amounts of pork, meat disappeared from the regular diet of the poor, who became ever more dependent on bread and other cereal foods. Butchers went out of business, as even better-off customers cut back.

42 Braudel, *The Structures of Everyday Life*, pp. 190–194.
43 Capatti and Montanari, *Italian Cuisine*, pp. 74–75.
44 Rebora, *Culture of the Fork*, pp. 43–51.
45 Braudel, *The Structures of Everyday Life*, pp. 192–193.
46 Le Roy Ladurie, *The Peasants of Languedoc*, pp. 42–44.

Braudel cited an example of a small French town that supported eighteen butchers in 1550, ten in 1556, six in 1641, two in 1660, and one in 1763.[47]

Faced with this situation, stock raisers with easy access to urban markets increasingly focused on value-added products, such as sausages and ham, or items such as veal, lamb, and poultry that commanded higher profit margins.[48] Elite consumers were prepared to pay for such luxuries, even if they bought them less frequently or in slightly smaller amounts than in the past. By the seventeenth century, meat cookery featured many dishes that made attractive use of modest quantities and cheaper cuts: ragouts, fricassees, *civets*, and other braised dishes had become fashionable. So had beef, the former working-class staple, which La Varenne and Bonnefons used in many different forms. According to Bonnefons, beef brisket was "the best cut of all" ("*le meilleure, la plus honneste à servir sur table*"), despite the fact that it needed long, gentle simmering to bring out its superb flavor. Small pieces from the round could be made into a *civet* with wine, bouillon, onions, orange peel, and bay leaf, and a large piece could be larded and braised with the same ingredients used in the *civet*, a preparation known as *boeuf à la mode*. Tongue was good braised in bouillon and served with a sauce of wine, vinegar, pepper, and cloves; heart, spleen, lungs, and tripe were excellent cooked *en ragout* with a sauce thickened at the end with egg yolks and verjuice.[49]

Stimulated by higher prices, regions that still had abundant pasture, such as Lower Normandy, began to specialize in dairy products and in beef raised for the table and slaughtered young. Such animals yielded tender meat that had culinary potential that was very different from the flesh of old farm oxen or milk cows. Indeed, Bonnefons claimed that *vache*, the meat of a cow, even a young and plump one, was never as good as *boeuf*, the meat of a steer fattened for the market.[50] Formerly, veal was for the master and beef was for the servants, but, by 1650, this was no longer true. The telling distinction had now become the one between those who ate quantities of meat – any meat – on a regular basis and those who did not.

Although this pattern held true for Europe in general (with a lesser degree of decline in meat consumption in Hungary, Poland, and England than elsewhere),[51] the situation in France was mediated, at least in terms

[47] Braudel, *The Structures of Everyday Life*, p. 196. Braudel notes that although the population of the town declined in this period, it did not do so by a ratio of 18 to 1.

[48] Rebora, *Culture of the Fork*, pp. 45–46, 53–54, and 80–85.

[49] Bonnefons, *Les Délices de la campagne*, pp. 263–275.

[50] Ibid., pp. 289–290. Normandy was also one of Bonnefons's favorite sources for butter.

[51] Braudel, *The Structures of Everyday Life*, p. 197.

of contemporary perceptions, by the Wars of Religion, which lasted from 1562 to 1594. The wars caused plenty of hunger on their own, as foraging armies commandeered supplies, forced people from their homes, and laid siege to towns. Paris, a bastion of fanatical Catholic opinion, refused to submit to the Protestant heir to the throne, Henry of Navarre (Henry IV of France, who reigned 1589–1610) for more than four years. By the time Henry – now a convert to Catholicism – entered the city in 1594, Parisians had been reduced to eating rats and other kinds of vermin. In many parts of the countryside the usual cycles of agrarian life had been interrupted by the hostilities, creating shortages of all sorts and great suffering among rural people and in the town markets they usually supplied.

Thus the effects of the war aggravated and masked the effects of the impersonal demographic and economic forces at work in the same period. From the perspective of 1600, Frenchmen could not measure or even identify the impact of the latter. When they reflected on the old days of abundance, "when we ate meat every day ... [and] gulped down wine as if it were water,"[52] it seemed natural to attribute the difference to civil strife and to hope for the return of prosperity with peace. Although Henry IV may never have said that he wanted the people of France to dine every Sunday on stewed chicken (*poule-au-pot*), the idea that he did was powerful because it evoked an image of well-being dimly remembered by his oldest subjects and now inscribed in village traditions as part of a lost golden age.

The history of cuisine always privileges the story of elite practices: the upper classes leave most of the documents that allow us to reconstruct dishes and menus and the ways in which these were served. In some societies the food enjoyed by the rich and the poor is similar, varying in quantity more than quality or kind. This was not the case in seventeenth-century France, where *poule-au-pot* was utterly beyond the reach of the vast majority of the king's subjects. Indeed, the gap between the cuisine of the rich and the sustenance of the poor has rarely been more starkly defined than in the period when the "delicate" cooking of elite Parisian households came to be recognized as definitively French.

---

[52] Ibid., pp. 195 and 197.

PART II

Toward a New Culinary Aesthetic

CHAPTER 3

Foundations of Change, 1600–1650

FEEDING BOURBON PARIS

Paris had long been the largest city in France and one of the most populous in Europe. In the 1560s, before the Wars of Religion, there were at least 280,000 Parisians, perhaps as many as 300,000. These figures would have made the French capital slightly smaller than Naples, the biggest city in sixteenth-century Europe, but twice as large as Venice, three times the size of Rome, and more than nine times the size of Marseilles.[1] The location of Paris in the Seine valley and close to the watersheds of the Marne and Loire gave it a natural advantage in trade since Roman times. Since the twelfth century it had been a great center of learning, its university drawing students from all of Latin Christendom. Even earlier it had become a seat of the kings of France. For centuries, this role played a relatively minor part in its development – royal government was too decentralized and too weak to overshadow the commercial and intellectual character of the city. In any case, the later Capetian and Valois kings preferred to hold court in the châteaux of the Loire valley. Paris's destiny as a royal capital would come into focus only with the first king of the Bourbon dynasty, Henry IV.

The Bourbons were a branch of the French royal family descended from a younger son of Louis IX (St. Louis). Henry's mother, Jeanne d'Albret, was in her own right queen of Navarre, a small territory in the Pyrenees on the border between France and Spain. Her court was an early center of Calvinism, and from the 1570s Henry was the most important leader of the

[1]   See Fernand Braudel, *The Mediterranean and the Mediterranean World in the Age of Philip II*, 2 vols., translated by Siân Reynolds (Berkeley: University of California Press, 1995), p. 345; Emmanuel Le Roy Ladurie, *The Ancien Régime: A History of France, 1610–1774*, translated by Mark Greengrass (Oxford: Blackwell, 1998), p. 97; and Roland Mousnier, *Paris au XVIIeme siècle* (Paris: CDU, 1961), fasicule 1. Colin Jones estimates the figure for 1560 was rather higher, 300,000 people; see Colin Jones, *Paris: Biography of a City* (New York: Viking, 2004), p. 132.

Protestant party in France's religious wars. In 1589, when the last Valois ruler, Henry III, was murdered by a Catholic religious fanatic, Henry of Navarre had the best dynastic claim to the throne. However, it would take some five years to defeat the rival claimants from the ultramontane Catholic house of Guise and their Spanish allies on the battlefield. Even then, the city of Paris, which had been a center of radical Catholic resistance, refused to recognize his authority until he publicly renounced Calvinism and was received into the Catholic Church. Paris, he reportedly said, was "worth a Mass."

When Henry finally entered Paris to the general acclaim of the populace on March 22, 1594, he found a city close to ruins. Years of siege warfare and its associated hardships had reduced the population by perhaps a third, to something around 200,000. Everywhere houses were in poor repair, streets were choked with trash and offal, markets were badly stocked, and many of the fountains that delivered water to residential neighborhoods had ceased to function. Henry immediately set out to address these problems with characteristic energy and determination. He pressured the wealthy merchants of the city – many of whom had sided with his political opponents – to tax themselves to pay for repairs to the fountains, streets, and bridges. Within a few years, significant progress had been made, and the quality of life in the capital improved.

Over the next half-century, Henry and his successors continued to change the face of the city both through direct commissions and by creating conditions in which private investors could undertake major projects. Henry personally supervised the completion of the Pont Neuf, begun in a previous reign, and the construction of the Rue Dauphine, which led south from the river into a rapidly developing area of the Left Bank.[2] He also greatly expanded the complex of the Louvre by building the galleries that connected it to the palace of the Tuileries, then on the western edge of the city. The crown made possible the development of two magnificent residential squares, the Place Dauphine, on the western tip of the Île-de-la-Cité, and the Place Royale (now the Place de Vosges), which rose on the site of the former royal palace of the Tournelles in the Marais.[3] After Henry's death in 1610, his widow, Marie de' Medici, and his son, Louis XIII, continued to build (notably the Luxembourg Palace and Gardens) and to encourage development by entrepreneurs. The formerly uninhabited Île-des-Vaches was reborn as the Île-St.-Louis, site of a fashionable residential quarter that attracted commercial families on the way up, financiers, judges, and

---

[2] Jones, *Paris*, pp. 136–141.
[3] Orest Ranum, *Paris in the Age of Absolutism: An Essay*, revised and expanded edition (University Park: Pennsylvania State University Press, 2002), pp. 81–92.

other royal officials. The sale by the crown of property in the Faubourg St. Germain facilitated the development of an even more exclusive neighborhood. Finally, proximity to the Louvre-Tuileries complex and the town residence commissioned in 1624 by Cardinal Richelieu (today the Palais Royal) made the Rue St. Honoré the neighborhood of choice for government ministers and high-ranking office holders, a class that grew by leaps and bounds under the first two Bourbon kings.[4]

By the time Louis XIV succeeded to the throne in 1643, the core of Paris had been transformed. The medieval city had been oriented along an axis stretching from the marketplace of Les Halles north of the river via Notre Dame to the university and schools on the Left Bank. Within fifty years of Henry IV's entry into the city, this axis was surrounded by a ring of new construction that stretched up to – and in some places, beyond – the defensive walls. The old axis reflected the commercial, religious, and scholarly character of the medieval city; the new buildings and neighborhoods that circumscribed it bore the stamp of royal sponsorship. Paris had long been the single most important town of the French kingdom, less a seat of government than the city no king could do without. In the early seventeenth century, Paris became the true capital of a powerful monarchical state, a fact reflected in its urban development.

One consequence of this was a sharp increase in the city's population. By the 1630s, the number of Parisians had doubled from the level of 1594, to 430,000, and fifty years later the city would have a million inhabitants – an enormous figure for an early modern city (only London was as populous).[5] Many elements contributed to this growth. The spectacular building boom created thousands of jobs for laborers and skilled artisans, as did the growth of the luxury trades. These positions were filled by emigrants from all the provinces of the realm, in addition to a smattering of foreigners. The regular presence of the court encouraged families of the traditional nobility to take up residence in their town houses, which were often new or recently refurbished. The number of officials serving the crown in Paris doubled in the reigns of Henry IV and Louis XIII, the largest administrative expansion in the history of the monarchy.[6] Many of the members of this "nobility of the robe" ("*noblesse de robe*," named for the gowns worn by judges and magistrates, as opposed to the swords worn by the military nobility, the "*noblesse d'épée*") were descendents of mercantile families of Parisian

---

4   Ibid., pp. 105–127.
5   Ranum, *Paris in the Age of Absolutism*, p. 239; and Le Roy Ladurie, *Ancien Régime*, p. 97. From this point on, Paris was matched – and eventually outstripped – for size only by London; see Jones, *Paris*, pp. 132–133.
6   Ranum, *Paris in the Age of Absolutism*, p. 122.

origin, but others were well-to-do provincials who came to the capital to make their fortunes. Below the robe nobility in status, but not necessarily in wealth, was the rich class of bankers, financiers, wholesale merchants, and manufacturers. These elite households, like those of the nobility, stimulated the demand for many types of goods and services provided by local artisans and professional men and also created openings for servants of many ranks and levels of skill. Growth at the lowest end of the economic scale was also marked and probably surged in the difficult years after 1630, as destitute peasants came in search of jobs as servants or casual laborers or – if all else failed – aid from the many charitable institutions active in the city.

The residents of the city consumed an enormous amount of food. One report, commissioned in 1637 to estimate the resources Paris would need to withstand a siege by the armies of Spain, calculated that each week the city consumed an average of 86,400 bushels of wheat (almost 4,500,000 bushels a year), 900 head of cattle (at least 40,000 a year, allowing for Lent), and 8,000 head of sheep (358,000 a year). Other foodstuffs mentioned in the report included 4,200 veal calves a year (mostly consumed between Easter and Pentecost), 25,000 pigs, 1,456,000 dry or salted codfish, 18,200 salted mackerel, 23,600 white herrings, 360,000 red herrings, 108,350 salmon, and 240,000 *muids* of wine (about 72,000,000 gallons).[7] These figures probably did not include foodstuffs grown on land owned by Parisians outside the walls and brought into town for their own use nor the produce of the many kitchen gardens, cow pastures, hen houses, and vineyards that lay within the confines of the city itself.

The agricultural hinterland that fed Bourbon Paris was huge. As the historian Steven Kaplan has described, contemporaries spoke of three provisioning "crowns," or circular zones of production that provided the capital with its supplies. By the early eighteenth century, the primary crown stretched almost a hundred miles in diameter, from Chartres in the southwest to Compèigne in the northeast, and encompassed the rich plains of the Brie, the Beauce, and the fringes of the Norman Vexin. Within this zone, the Paris market came to completely dominate production, to the point at which the locals sometimes protested that there was nothing left for them to eat. Grain was the principal crop, but the area also produced significant amounts of vegetables and fruit, eggs, poultry, butcher's meat, and dairy products. The Paris basin was also a major wine-growing area in the medieval and early modern periods, and much of the ordinary wine drunk in the city came from within the primary provisioning crown. Paris also drew on the second crown, which was double the size of the first and extended from

---

7   Ibid., pp. 240–242. The term *"muid"* was used to indicate both measures by weight and measures by liquid volume.

Blois, on the frontier of Touraine, to Chalons in Champagne and Amiens in Picardy and northwest to the English Channel.[8] This area supplied grain to the capital, especially when harvests were mediocre or poor closer to the city, but its most conspicuous contributions to the Paris market were specialty products, such as the wine of Champagne, butter and seafood from Normandy, and fruit from the Orléanais. The third crown had no precise boundaries, stretching as far as necessary to meet demand left unsatisfied closer to home. Burgundy, Flanders, Lorraine, Alsace, the Bourbonais, the Poitou, and the Auverne all sent foodstuffs to Paris.[9] Bulky items, such as casks of wine and bushels of grain, and barrels of oysters were shipped by water wherever possible in order to keep the cost of transport low. Grain also traveled overland by cart, as did hard cheeses, cured meats, and the sturdier sorts of fruits and vegetables. Fragile items that were expensive by weight, such as ocean fish, eggs, ripened cheeses, and soft spring and summer fruits were carried by porters on foot or horseback. Meat was usually driven on the hoof to the wholesale market at Poissy, north of the city, where the animals were purchased by members of the butcher's guild.[10]

The principal landlords in the primary provisioning crown were themselves Parisians. As in all agrarian societies, land was seen as the most stable and prestigious of investments, and since medieval times Parisians of all social groups had been eager to acquire farms, vineyards, and country houses beyond the city walls as their means allowed. Well-to-do artisans and middling merchants sank their capital into small parcels, while the rich bought large tracts of arable land. Often these holdings included residences of some kind, ranging from cottages to châteaux. These offered a pleasant and healthy change from the dirt and crowding typical of city life, especially in the warm months from June through September. The summer exodus of the propertied classes from the city, so marked a characteristic of Parisian life in our own day, was already an established pattern. Children were often sent out from Paris shortly after birth to be raised by relatives or family retainers in the more salubrious atmosphere of the countryside. Older members of the family often retired to the country house, where they took on the task of supervising the peasants who cultivated the farms and vineyards.[11] Proprietors who qualified as members of the noble estate or as *bourgeois de Paris* were allowed to import foodstuffs and wine produced on

---

8   Steven Laurence Kaplan, *Provisioning Paris: Merchants and Millers in the Grain and Flour Trade during the Eighteenth Century* (Ithaca, NY, and London: Cornell University Press, 1984), pp. 88–89; see also the map on pp. 90–91.

9   Ibid.

10   Ranum, *Paris in the Age of Absolutism*, p. 240.

11   Ibid., p. 272.

their estates into the city tax-free, a significant benefit to the household's economy.[12]

This pattern, which bound many propertied Parisians to country life, was long established at the beginning of the seventeenth century. However, the scale of investment shifted dramatically in the reigns of the first two Bourbons. With the rapid growth of the city's population, property in the old suburbs just outside the walls lost its rural character. Houses and farm buildings were subdivided or otherwise converted into tenement housing. Meadows, fields, pastures, and vineyards filled up with new structures that provided shelter for the poorest class of Parisians, while the landlords bought up farms and houses farther from the urban sprawl, where they acquired or built new residences for themselves.[13] Estates that encompassed fiefs and thus transmitted feudal rights to their owners were especially prized by upwardly mobile families, many of whom took their names from such properties.

This geographical expansion of the area in which the urban elite invested was accompanied by an increase in the amount of capital they tied up in land. In the three decades from 1620 to 1650, the rate of rural investment by rich Parisians climbed so sharply that it pushed the prices for farms and vineyards to a peak that would not be equaled again until sometime after 1720. Many families doubled or tripled their holdings. By 1650, Parisians, led by the office-holding class, appear to have owned as much as 70 percent of the arable land in the basin formed by the Seine, the Oise, and the Marne (the remainder belonged to the Church, long-established noble families, and the crown). Wealthy Parisians became "the principal suppliers and profit-takers on most of the foodstuffs, chiefly grain and wine, imported into the capital."[14] This situation made for some interesting tensions where food prices were concerned. As landowners, the elite benefited from high prices, especially for grain. However, as part-time residents of the city and owners of property there, they also had an interest in maintaining the peace, which was always threatened when bread became too dear for the hungry poor.[15] Such gentlemen farmers with access to urban markets were the primary audience for the work of Olivier de Serres and other writers who addressed horticulture and animal husbandry as an aspect of efficient estate management.

The great marketplace of the city was at Les Halles, in the heart of the Right Bank. It operated as a wholesale market in the morning and shifted to

---

12   Bonnefons, *Le Jardinier français*, 2001, p. 7.
•13   Ranum, *Paris in the Age of Absolutism*, pp. 271–272.
14   Ibid., p. 272.
15   Ibid.

Par un excez de friandise,
Et si lon donne du ragoust,
Et lon y vend, pour plaire au goust,
Toute sorte de marchandise.

Chascun y trauaille à son tour,
Chacun met la main à la paste,
L'on fait des pastes à la haste,
Et l'autre les met dans le four.

Pour de l'argent on donne à tous
Des macarrons, des darioles,
Des gasteaux diuers des rissoles,
Du biscuit, et de petits chous.

Cette boutique à des delices,
Qui charment en mille façons
Les filles les petits garçons,
Les seruantes et les Nourrices.

A Paris, Chez Abr. Bosse Graveur et Imprimeur du Roy pour la Taille douce, demeurant en l'Isle du Palais, sur le Quay qui regarde la Megisserie, à l'Esfhart aux Pouls.

7. *The Pastry Shop (The Trades, Plate 7)*, 1632–1635, by Abraham Bosse (Marie Antoinette Evans Fund, Museum of Fine Arts, Boston; photograph © 2008 Museum of Fine Arts, Boston).

retail in the afternoon. However, there were also many specialty markets and food shops throughout the city. For example, poultry and meat stalls were concentrated along the Quai de la Mégisserie.[16] Purveyors of fine olive oil, preserved and candied fruit, spices, and other luxury groceries clustered near the church of St. Germaine-en-Auxerrois, just in front of the Louvre.[17] Serious buyers from all over town flocked to the wine market across the Seine, near the present Place Maubert.[18] There were also many neighborhood market streets that offered a little of everything to a local clientele. Some of these were of ancient origin and many, such as Rue de Buci and the Rue de Mouffetard, continue to do brisk business in the twenty-first century.[19]

Paris had long enjoyed the services of several guilds of culinary professionals who supplied consumers with many kinds of ready-to-eat food.

[16] Wheaton, *Savoring the Past*, pp. 71–72.
[17] Ibid., p. 78
[18] Kaplan, *Provisioning Paris*, p. 109.
[19] Wheaton, *Savoring the Past*, p. 71.

Bakers sold bread of several varieties (of which the whitest were of course the most expensive), pastry cooks offered meat pies and sweet items, *rôtisseurs* prepared cooked poultry and joints of meat, and *charcutiers* supplied cured pork and other meats in the form of ham, sausage, rillets (finely chopped meat – pork or game for preference – mixed with fat, spices, and other heady flavorings and baked in a casserole or pot), and pâté (similar to rillets, but, as the name suggests, baked in a pastry crust). There was a separate guild for sauce makers (who also produced aspics, *potages*, and other dishes cooked in liquid) and another one for purveyors of lemonade and refreshing drinks. Members of the caterers' guild, the *traiteurs*, could provide entire menus to be served on short notice in their own premises, in a rented room or hall, or in the customer's place of residence. In theory, all of these activities were separate and distinct, also, from the specializations of the guilds that dealt primarily in foodstuffs rather than items that were ready to eat, such as the butchers, poulterers, grocers, fruitiers, and spice merchants or *épiciers*. In practice, of course, there was overlap – as when a *charcutier* wrapped one of his savory concoctions in a crust, creating a de facto pie, or a poultry merchant sold a grilled or fricasseed chicken. Disputes of this sort were arbitrated by the Paris lieutenant of police, who also held the guilds responsible for quality control and the enforcement of maximum and minimum prices.[20] The city authorities also generally backed up efforts by the guilds to keep freelancers out of the trades in which they held legal monopoly, although, in a city the size Paris had attained, there was a never-ending battle between properly articled members of the artisan elite and undocumented newcomers.

All of this was fairly typical of arrangements for provisioning early modern cities. What had long set Paris apart from, say, London or Vienna or Milan was the variety and lavishness of the ready-to-eat provisions that could be had. In the sixteenth century, the Venetian ambassador, not exactly a stranger to luxury, wrote in wonder that one could, in less than an hour of ordering, sit down to a sumptuous dinner for ten, twenty, or a hundred people.[21] Such catered meals were a boon to travelers visiting Paris, because they provided an alternative to the family-style meals at fixed prices offered by *tables d'hôte*. But they also provided flexibility to well-established Parisian households in need of occasional outside support.

---

[20] René de Lespinasse, *Histoire générale de Paris: Les Métiers et corporations de la ville de Paris* (Paris: Imprimerie Nationale, 1886), pp. 188–195; and Daniel Roche, *The People of Paris: An Essay in Popular Culture in the 18th Century*, translated by Marie Evans in association with Gwynne Lewis (Leamington Spa, Hamburg, and New York: Berg, 1987), pp. 249–250.

[21] Wheaton, *Savoring the Past*, p. 76.

Households prosperous enough to employ servants bought roasted joints of meat or poultry, pastry, and sauced dishes to supplement recipes made at home. Celebrations such as weddings or baptisms could strain the capacity of even large and well-staffed kitchens, enlarging the niche for the *traiteurs* and other outside specialists. Some of the furnished quarters available through caterers were pretty posh. From the 1620s, apartments in the former *hôtel particulier* of Marguerite de Valois were available for private parties through members of the catering guild – the cachet of royal associations must have been appealing to the upwardly mobile. Even the *bouche du roi*, the court agency that provided the king's meals, was known to recruit additional personnel to cook for major fêtes, and it became common for members of the Paris guilds to assist in preparing meals for the court on such occasions.[22]

Purveyors of ready-to-eat foods were also much patronized by Parisians of the poorer sort. In addition to the trades listed above, some of which sold inexpensive items, there was a lively market in the city for what Daniel Roche has called "second-hand food," the leftovers from wealthy households that were peddled by the servants.[23] Working-class women, even those with husbands to support the family, often labored for wages and had little time to cook. Cheap lodgings usually had only rudimentary cooking facilities. In the period 1695–1715, only 8 percent of Parisian wage earners and only 12 percent of servants occupied a home that had a separate kitchen. Indeed 57 percent of all dwellings in the city during this period consisted of a single room, which typically housed entire families. The percentage of one-room dwellings increased during the eighteenth century to 63 percent around 1780.[24] Food was prepared in an open fireplace that was also the only source of heat and the principal source of light and was therefore the focus of all of the residents' indoor activities. Wood was costly, and many families had to ration the size of fires and the frequency with which they were lit.[25] Sébastien Mercier, writing in the 1780s, left a vivid description of such a place: "A whole family occupies a single room, with four bare walls, wretched beds without curtains, and kitchen utensils rolling around with the chamber pots."[26] No wonder that small pies, bowls of soup, and other inexpensive take-out items were popular supplements to the bread that was the main sustenance of the poor.

---

[22] Ibid.

[23] Daniel Roche, *A History of Everyday Things: The Birth of Consumption in France, 1600–1800*, translated by Brian Pearce (Cambridge: Cambridge University Press, 2000), p. 234.

[24] Roche, *The People of Paris*, p. 111.

[25] Ibid., pp. 119–120.

[26] Quoted in Roche, *The People of Paris*, p. 97.

CAPTURING THE VARIETY OF NATURE

In the early 1650s, after a century in which no full-scale works on cooking were published in France, two books appeared that revealed a fundamental transformation in culinary practices and the ideas on which they drew: *Le Cuisinier françois* by La Varenne, published in 1651, and *Les Délices de la campagne* by Nicolas de Bonnefons, which appeared in 1654.

Le Cuisinier françois has always been the more celebrated of the two volumes. La Varenne was the nom de plume adopted by a man named François Pierre, who described himself as an *écuyer de cuisine* in the household of the marquis d'Uxelles, a Burgundian nobleman of ancient lineage and a lieutenant general in the royal army. The usual term to describe the servant who oversaw the kitchens of a great household was *officier de la bouche* or – for those whose duties included in addition supervision of all domestic arrangements – *maître d'hôtel*. *Ecuyer* was originally a chivalric title roughly equivalent to the English "squire"; it became attached to positions within the French royal household whose well-born incumbents were charged with responsibility for the king's table. At the end of the fourteenth century, the great chef Taillevent, a commoner by birth, had been raised to the status of *écuyer* as a mark of particular favor. Taillevent's tomb shows him dressed in knightly garb with a heraldic shield decorated with three stew pots.[27] By calling himself an *écuyer*, La Varenne, servant of a mere marquis, associated himself with an illustrious predecessor. Furthermore, by publishing his book under the nom de plume La Varenne he linked himself to another famous example of an ennobled cook. Guillaume Fouquet started his career as a cook in the service of the sister of Henry IV, the duchesse de Bar. Fouquet later moved to the royal household itself, where, in addition to whatever culinary duties he may have assumed, he functioned as a go-between between Henry and his many mistresses. He must have pleased his royal master, because he was rewarded with a number of sinecures and ennobled as the marquis de La Varenne. "He earned more through carrying the *poulets* [love letters] of the king my brother than he did larding them in the kitchen," the duchess punned.[28]

François Pierre was probably born around 1615 – an eighteenth-century source says he died in Dijon in 1678 at "aged more than sixty years."[29] He

[27]　See Scully and Scully, *Early French Cookery*, p. 10.

[28]　[François Pierre] La Varenne, *Le Cuisinier françois*, edited by Jean-Louis Flandrin and Philip and Mary Hyman (Paris: Montalba, 1981), pp. 67–68.

[29]　Philippe Papillon wrote in *Bibliothèque des auteurs de Bourgogne* (Dijon: P. Marteret, 1742), tome 2, pp. 342–343: "*Varenne, (Pierre), vint s'établir à Dijon ou il mourut en 1678 agé de plus de 60 ans. Il a fait le livre intitulé: Le Cuisinier*

seems to have entered the service of the marquis as a young man in the 1630s. In the letter of dedication that prefaced *Le Cuisinier françois* he wrote that it was during the ten full years that he cooked for d'Uxelles in Paris and on campaign with the army that he "found the secret of preparing foods delicately."[30] He did not claim to have invented this style of cooking, although he gained lasting fame by becoming the first to describe it in detail. Aimed at an audience of culinary professionals, *Le Cuisinier françois* found a wide public in the kitchens of the ancien régime, ultimately going through sixty-one editions, the last of which appeared in 1754. An English translation appeared in London in 1653, only two years after the first Paris edition.[31] In the nineteenth century, when French gastronomes went in search of the ancestors of the *haute cuisine*, they quickly identified La Varenne's *Cuisinier* as *the* seminal work of the canon, a status it retains today.

The second important cookbook of the 1650s was *Les Délices de la campagne* by Nicolas de Bonnefons. Bonnefons was a man on the way up in Parisian society, an aspirant to noble status who held the office of *valet de chambre* in the royal household. The *valets de chambre* were responsible for organizing the daily routine of the king. Formerly, these responsibilities had been the prerogative of noblemen of ancient lineage, but, by the reign of Louis XIV, the position of *valet de chambre* had become a venal office that placed incumbents and their descendents on a low rung of the ladder that eventually led to hereditary nobility. Several members of the Bonnefons family served as *valets de chambre* in the long reign of Louis XIV. Nicolas seems to have been attached to the household of Cardinal Mazarin before joining the royal household in 1650.[32] His official duties appear to have left ample time for a second career as an author and purveyor of nursery stock and seeds. Bonnefons wrote *Les Délices de la campagne* as a companion piece to a book on gardening he published three years earlier, in 1651, entitled *Le Jardinier français*.[33] Whereas La Varenne wrote for

François 9e edition, Lyon, Antoine Offray, in-12°. Il y eu depuis une multitude innombrable d'éditions de ce livre." Quoted in François Pierre La Varenne, *The French Cook*, translated into English in 1653 by I. D. G., with an introduction by Philip and Mary Hyman (Lewes: Southover Press, 2001), p. xii.

30   Ibid., p. 4.
31   Parisian printers brought out eight editions of the *Cuisinier* within a decade, which also saw publication of six foreign editions. During the 1660s, the book entered the catalogues of provincial printers in Lyon, Troyes, and Rouen, who produced cheap and widely circulated editions for another ninety years. La Varenne, *Le Cuisinier françois*, 1981, pp. 64–65.
32   Mathieu Da Vinha, *Les Valets de Chambre de Louis XIV* (Paris: Perrin, 2004), p. 364.
33   Nicolas de Bonnefons, *Le Jardinier français que enseigne à cultiver les arbres & herbes potagères avec la manière de conserver les fruits et faire toutes sortes de*

culinary professionals, Bonnefons addressed the masters and mistresses of rich bourgeois households who, like Bonnefons himself, aspired to a noble way of life and wished to organize their *ménages* in a manner that would support their claims to gentility.[34] Such people were situated at – or just beneath – the low end of Paris high society, while La Varenne's master, the marquis d'Uxelles, would have been near the top. It was in this milieu, ranging from aspiring bourgeois to noblemen of ancient lineage, that delicate cooking emerged as a distinct culinary style in the decades before 1650.

The new cuisine involved capturing and enhancing the unique flavor, aroma, and texture of a principal ingredient, what Bonnefons called "*le goût naturel*" (the natural taste) or "*le vrai goût*" (the true taste).[35] Whereas ancient and medieval cooking aimed for multi-layered complexity, delicate cooking strove for transparency: the goal was to convey the diversity of nature on a dinner plate. "A cabbage soup should taste entirely of cabbage, a leek soup of leeks, a turnip soup of turnips, and thus for the others," Bonnefons wrote, "Food should taste like what it is."[36]

The artistry of delicate cuisine lay in the cook's ability to match ingredients and seasonings in a manner that created a harmony of distinct but complimentary flavors. This was even true in cases in which a dish was specifically designed to be beneficial to health. Take the example of La Varenne's recipe for *potage de santé* (health soup), a capon broth that could be made with chicory (which soothed the stomach) or parsley root (a diuretic) or cardoon (a restorative pick-me-up), as the seasons and ailments indicated.[37] This recipe worked from a culinary point of view because each of the variations paired the capon broth with a single vegetable whose taste would have been clearly identifiable: the chicory slightly bitter, the cardoon

confitures, conserves & massepains (Paris: Pierre Des Hayes, 1651) was issued in eight subsequent editions between 1651 and 1662 and an additional ten by 1701. See the introduction to the modern edition by François-Xavier Bogard, p. 5. John Evelyn, the diarist, gardener, and future secretary of the Royal Society "transplanted" *Le Jardinier français* into English as *The French Gardener* (London: Benjamin Tooke, 1658); this translation also went through several editions.

34 Some culinary historians have traditionally pegged Bonnefons as an originator of the *cuisine bourgeois*, by which they mean a kind of cooking that privileged economy, as opposed to the lavish *haute cuisine* they see as descended from the work of La Varenne. As will become clear, this view is an anachronism that reads nineteenth-century practices back into the seventeenth century.

35 Bonnefons, *Les Délices de la campagne*, pp. 214 and 238.

36 Ibid., p. 217.

37 La Varenne, *The French Cook*, p. 21. The 1653 English translation of the *Cuisinier* was based on the second French edition of 1652, expanded and corrected by the author. The variations calling for chicory or cardoon or parsley do not appear in the first French edition of 1651.

bitter *and* sweet, the parsley fragrant and herbaceous. In his own discussion of *potage de santé*, Bonnefons stressed the importance of omitting all extraneous "hashes, mushrooms, and spices"[38] – that is to say, all those complex seasonings that a medieval cook would have included for both medicinal and aesthetic reasons. Simplicity was one of the keys to making a soup that was both restorative and delicious.

The other key attribute of good cooking, Bonnefons thought, was understanding the fundamental properties of one's ingredients, by which he meant not only their flavor and digestibility, but also how they responded to cooking techniques and temperatures and to pairing with other foods and seasonings. Too often, he wrote, cooks treated their ingredients with indifference, preparing them according to the same method regardless of their taste, texture, and digestibility. All sorts of meats, vegetables, and fish were boiled in bouillon from a stockpot that was a common receptacle for hashed-up odds and ends. Specimens that were young and old, tender and tough were accorded the same rough treatment, which robbed them of their individual character. Once cooked – or overcooked – they were doused with spice mixes and highly acidic sauces that finished the job of camouflaging *le vrai goût*. From the soup to the entremets, everything tasted the same, killing the appetite.[39]

Certainly there was some truth in these charges. One of the consequences of the multi-course, hierarchically differentiated menus that prevailed in the late Middle Ages and the Renaissance was that the kitchen staff in large private households operated on a scale approaching that of a modern restaurant, a situation that encouraged the use of common, pre-made elements in many different dishes. In addition to the muddy-flavored "bouillon from the common pot" that was a particular dislike of Bonnefons's, there was the indiscriminant use of the same spices on foods of all sorts. Pre-made spice mixtures were kitchen staples. A typical recipe for "fine spices for all foods" contained black pepper, cinnamon, ginger, saffron, and cloves.[40] Such blends were often sprinkled on dishes just before they were served, a practice that probably increased in popularity as spice prices decreased in the sixteenth and early seventeenth centuries. The culinary effect of this practice would have been "a bit like curry powder in the inferior sort of Indian cookery today," observed the sociologist Stephen Mennell, "That is to say, the dishes became rather undifferentiated and broadly 'tasted the same.'"[41]

38 Bonnefons, *Les Délices de la campagne*, p. 217.
39 Ibid., pp. 214–215.
40 Redon, Sabban, and Serventi, *The Medieval Kitchen*, p. 221.
41 Stephen Mennell, *All Manners of Food: Eating and Taste in England and France from the Middle Ages to the Present*, 2nd ed. (Urbana and Chicago: University of Illinois Press, 1996), pp. 53–54.

Delicate cooking, in contrast, stimulated and delighted the senses by capturing the unique qualities with which foods were endowed by nature. Bonnefons wrote, "There is nothing that pleases man more than variety, and the French above all have a particular inclination for it; this is why you try to do as much as you can to diversify [your dishes] and to distinguish them by their taste and their form."[42] A skillful modern cook achieved variety not through fanciful invention, exotic seasonings, or complex combinations – paths that had been well trodden by his medieval predecessors – but by subtly highlighting the elemental properties of raw materials. Meals were composed of specimens of nature's marvelous diversity, whose character was to be preserved rather than transformed by cooking. In this respect, the delicate style of cooking was much like the Dutch still life paintings that were so popular at the time. The beauty of such pictures seems to lie in the color and form of the natural objects represented; only upon reflection do we recognize the elegance of the composition, the fine brushwork, and the optical perfection of the illusion as signs of the artist's mastery of his craft.[43]

By the 1650s, proponents of delicate cooking had evolved a series of techniques and novel recipes – including a new class of silky sauces that were emulsified with butter, cream, or egg yolk or thickened with roux – that were intended to highlight the *goût naturel* of carefully chosen principal ingredients. However, before we turn to a detailed examination of these recipes and techniques, we must address the intellectual and material contexts in which delicate cooking developed.

THE REVOLUTION IN MEDICINE

Since ancient times, Hippocratic medicine had been a significant influence on the development of cooking. The structure of the medieval menu was built around a progression of courses thought to favor good digestion, and foods and seasonings were instrumental in efforts to preserve or restore the balance of the four humors of which the body was believed to be composed. In addition, many spices, herbs, and other foods were used as drugs to attack the symptoms of ailments ranging from stomachache to fever. The partnership between medicine and cuisine had been durable, surviving the fall of Rome, assimilating Celtic and Germanic preferences, absorbing ideas and new foodstuffs from the Arabic-Islamic world, and even adopting ingredients that originated in the Americas. But then, in the century before

---

42 Bonnefons, *Les Délices de la campagne*, p. 217
43 I owe this insight to a conversation with the late Richard Wolheim, philosopher, art historian, and connoisseur, which took place in May 2003.

the publication of *Le Cuisinier françois* and *Les Délices de la campagne*, the traditional system of medical knowledge began to unravel.

As Nancy Siraisi has argued, the transformation of medical theory developed, ironically, out of the efforts of early-sixteenth-century humanists to improve the knowledge of Greek medicine by seeking out and editing original texts by Galen (c. 129–200 or 216 AD, the most prolific medical writer of antiquity) and other Hippocratic physicians.[44] A complete edition of Galen's works in Greek was printed in Venice in 1525, and numerous other ancient texts in both Greek and Latin appeared in the first half of the century. However, "fuller knowledge of the writings of the ancients facilitated criticism as well as admiration."[45]

One of the most important critics was Andreas Vesalius (1514–1564), a Flemming who became professor of medicine at the University of Padua in 1537. Although medieval physicians had occasionally carried out dissections of the human body, it remained a controversial procedure, generally condemned by church authorities. Vesalius, however, was a convinced empiricist who believed that the direct observation of nature was vital to scientific knowledge. For an anatomist, this meant that the truth "had to be learned from dead bodies not dead languages."[46] His zeal led him to rob at least one wayside gibbet of its hanged corpse and to make deals with local authorities for the cadavers of executed criminals. His great work, *De humani corporis favbrica* (*On the Fabric of the Human Body*), published in 1542 with magnificent illustrations inspired by Leonardo Da Vinci, contradicted Galen on several points and raised damning questions about the general soundness of his methods, which focused on drawing analogies between the anatomies of animals and the human body.[47]

Vesalius's commitment to direct observation inspired many followers, who not only continued to correct errors in the traditional picture of the body, but to discover structures and organs that had been hitherto unknown.[48] This heroic period in anatomy culminated in 1628, when William Harvey (1578–1657), an English physician who had studied in Italy, demonstrated that the blood circulated through the body. Blood was not produced by the liver, as Galen taught, nor did it combine with air in the left ventricle of the heart or spread to all parts of the body due to the innate "pulsative faculty" of the arteries. Instead of being mysteriously used up

---

[44] Nancy Siraisi, *Medieval and Early Renaissance Medicine*, pp. 190–191.

[45] Ibid., p. 191.

[46] Porter, *Greatest Benefit to Mankind*, p. 178.

[47] Owsei Temkin, *Galenism: Rise and Decline of a Medical Philosophy* (Ithaca, NY, and London: Cornell University Press, 1973), pp. 138–140.

[48] Porter, *Greatest Benefit to Mankind*, pp. 178–183.

in the parts of the body to which it spread or accumulating in a particular organ or extremity (traditionally believed to be a principal cause of illness), blood returned to the heart through the veins, received air during its transit of the lungs, and repeated the circuit thanks to the pumping action of the heart.[49] Harvey's work laid the foundation for modern physiology; just as important, it destroyed the understanding of the body and the theory of the humors on which classical dietetics was based.

What were the effects of these developments on medicine on cooking? Some culinary historians have seen the decline of dietetics as the key to understanding the abrupt turn away from spicy, sweet cooking in the middle of the seventeenth century. They have noted that cookbooks gradually dropped references to seasonings as dietary correctives and that the use of spices in French (or, more precisely, Parisian) cooking began to fall sharply around the same time.[50] It is certainly true that one of the things that distinguished the delicate cooking of La Varenne and Bonnefons from their French predecessors and their Italian, English, Spanish, and Central European contemporaries is that few of their recipes for savory ingredients called for sugar or spices other than black pepper. Fewer than 5 percent of La Varenne's recipes called for sugar, traditionally regarded as a gentle corrective suitable to all constitutions, and fewer than 1 percent used ginger or cinnamon, which had been ubiquitous as warming agents in the fine cooking of the previous half-millennium.[51] Interestingly, the handful of recipes in the *Cuisinier* that do use sugar and spice make no reference to these as dietary correctives for principal ingredients in the time-honored Hippocratic manner. La Varenne appears to have included cloves in the stuffing for his entrée of turkey with raspberries because he liked the taste. Aromatic, sweet spices were integral to a few recipes for traditional favorites that Bonnefons published in *Les Délices* (such as *galimafrée*, a kind of mutton hash), but on the whole he treated them casually as optional ingredients that could be sprinkled over a dish before serving to someone "who likes spices."[52] Instead of being seen as essential ingredients in a dietary regime

---

49   Ibid., pp. 211–216.
50   See the editors' introduction to La Varenne, *Le Cuisinier françois*, 1981. As Fernand Braudel noted a generation ago, Germany, Scandinavia, and Eastern Europe remained prodigious consumers of spice for a century after the French made the transition to the delicate style; *The Structures of Everyday Life*, pp. 223–224.
51   La Varenne, *The French Cook*, pp. viii–ix. Bruno Laurioux has pointed out that French cooks in the late medieval period and the Renaissance were more sparing in their use of sugar than their Italian and English contemporaries. Even so, they used it more much more frequently than La Varenne and Bonnefons. See Laurioux, "Medieval Cooking," p. 299.
52   Bonnefons, *Les Délices de la campagne*, p. 34.

meant to reestablish or preserve health, sugar and aromatic spices were now used or not as a matter of personal taste.

On the strength of such evidence, Jean-Louis Flandrin proposed the hypothesis that "the relaxation of the links between cooking and dietetics in a sense liberated the gourmet instincts. No longer did culinary refinement aim at maintaining health. Now it could be directed at flattering the tastes of gourmets."[53] Once those gourmet instincts were freed from mistaken ideas about diet and health imposed by outmoded medical theory, this reasoning suggests, spicy food was decisively rejected in favor of the mild seasonings and silky, rich sauces that have characterized French cuisine since La Varenne.

There are a number of objections that can be raised against this argument, starting with the obvious fact that gourmet instincts do not necessarily reject spicy complexity, as the rich traditions of the ancient Mediterranean world and the modern cuisines of Mexico, India, and the Middle East demonstrate. There is nothing natural about the preference for *"le goût naturel."* Indeed, the love of transparency, of tasting the variety of nature at every meal that has came to characterize French cooking in the seventeenth century is less universal than the taste for spicy complexity that preceded it and continues to dominate the culinary aesthetics of most of the planet.

Furthermore, there is the issue of timing. Although elements of the Hippocratic theories of the body, health, and disease were subject to growing criticism starting in the first half of the sixteenth century, Harvey's decisive discovery dated from just twenty-three years before the appearance of the *Cuisinier françois.* And as we know from La Varenne's own testimony, the delicate style of cooking predated publication of his book by at least a decade, if not more. Greek medicine still had plenty of defenders in the mid-to-late seventeenth century. In particular, the medical faculty of the University of Paris was a bastion of Galenist orthodoxy for decades after Harvey's demonstration. The authority of Hippocratic teaching was one of the issues that fired the famous quarrel between the ancients and moderns that dominated Parisian intellectual life in the half-century starting in the 1680s.[54] Although the logical implications of discoveries in anatomy gradually undermined the medical theory and practices inherited from antiquity, this did not happen as quickly as modern readers might suppose.

One of the reasons for this was that even members of the progressive camp were uncertain as to the clinical implications of new findings in

---

53 Jean-Louis Flandrin, "Introduction: The Early Modern Period" in Flandrin and Montanari, eds., *Food,* p. 364.
54 Temkin, *Galenism,* pp. 158–177.

anatomy. If Harvey's demonstration implied that defluxion could not be the mechanism that triggered illness, the revised picture of the body that emerged from his work did not immediately lead to an alternative account of what did. Although a general theory of health and disease that drew on the mechanistic views of the body articulated by Descartes, Gassendi, Borelli, and Newton would emerge by 1700 (eventually providing the framework for a new theory of dietetics, as we shall see in Chapter 6), seventeenth-century physicians practiced without the benefit of a unifying medical philosophy. Faced with the necessity of doing something to alleviate the symptoms of their patients, they continued to prescribe many traditional treatments in the belief that these were efficacious for reasons that had yet to be properly understood.[55] Harvey himself defended bleeding patients on the grounds that "daily experience satisfies us that bloodletting has a most salutary effect on many diseases."[56] Muddling through while searching for the confluence of evidence and logical coherence was the order of the day.

Under these circumstances, it would have been surprising if physicians had *not* continued to prescribe "proven" treatments involving diet and the use of foodstuffs to combat disease. As Erwin Ackerknecht has pointed out, clinical practice continued to make much use of traditional dietary advice throughout the seventeenth century.[57] For example, sufferers from gout were put on regimes that stressed exercise and moderate consumption of meat and wine, a prescription unchanged from Roman times.[58] Scientists and physicians continued to speak of foods being hot, cold, dry, or moist, usually in reference to an obvious physical characteristic, and to attribute therapeutic or at least palliative powers to them as a result. The language of the humors persisted, and so did treatments originally devised to restore equilibrium among them. John Evelyn's treatise on salads, published in 1699, gave detailed instructions on how to choose ingredients in order to

---

[55]   Porter, *Greatest Benefit to Mankind*, p. 229.

[56]   Quoted in Audrey D. Davis, "Some Implications of the Circulation Theory for Disease Theory and Treatment in the Seventeenth Century" in *The Journal of the History of Medicine and Allied Sciences*, vol. 26 (1971), pp. 28–29. Interestingly, Harvey's conservative approach to treatment did not reassure many of his more conservative patients, who by his own account deserted him in droves in favor of physicians with more orthodox reputations; see Roy Porter and G. S. Rousseau, *Gout: The Patrician Malady* (New Haven, CT, and London: Yale University Press, 1998), p. 43.

[57]   Erwin H. Ackerknecht, "The End of the Greek Diet" in *The Bulletin of the History of Medicine*, vol. 45 (1971), pp. 243–244.

[58]   John D. Comrie, editor, *Selected Works of Thomas Sydenham MD with a Short Biography and Explanatory Notes* (London: John Bayle Sons & Danielson, 1922), p. 72; quoted in Porter and Rousseau, *Gout*, p. 45.

ward off ailments and to strengthen certain organs of the body. Fennel countered biliousness and the flatulence that went with it, moist spinach relieved constipation caused by too much beef and other drying meats, endive cleared obstructions of the liver, tarragon strengthened the heart, and lettuce fed the brain, the coldest part of the body – just to give a few examples.[59] Advice of this sort was not wasted on cooks. As we have seen, La Varenne adapted his recipe for *potage de santé* to fortify the body against a range of ills.

This ongoing interest in the therapeutic qualities of foods was bolstered by the most iconoclastic element in early modern medicine, the iatrochemistry of Paracelsus (Phillip von Hohenheim, 1493–1542) and his followers. Whereas Vesalius, Harvey, and their peers saw themselves as advancing medicine as a learned profession, Paracelsus declared that he was disgusted by the pretensions of university-trained physicians and appalled by the ineffectiveness of their treatments. "When I saw that nothing resulted from [doctors'] practice but killing and laming, I determined to abandon such a miserable art and seek truth elsewhere," he wrote.[60] The book of nature, he believed, was a surer guide to the art of healing than the opinions of ancient authorities. He learned about alchemy – indeed, as professor of medicine at the University of Basel, he refused to wear the traditional professorial robe for his lectures, appearing instead in the alchemist's leather apron. One of his reasons for rejecting the authority of Galen and other ancient authors was his desire to create a new and specifically Christian approach to nature and to healing. Inspired by the belief that a benevolent God had given humble people the means to cure ailments and fortify themselves against disease, he spent several years wandering the countryside collecting information about folk medicine and herbal remedies.[61]

Out of this wild combination of spiritualism, alchemy, folk medicine, and acute observation of the natural world came an entirely novel vision of health, disease, and the process of healing. Paracelsus argued that the fundamental life processes of the body were chemical in nature, that the primary role in governing health and disease was played by particular organs of the body (as opposed to the balance of the bodily constitution as a whole), and that disease was caused by invasion from the outside (instead of

---

59 John Evelyn, *Acetaria: A Discourse of Sallets* (Brooklyn, NY: Brooklyn Botanic Garden, 1937), pp. 16, 17, 35, 39, 43–44, 45, and 72.

60 Quoted in Porter, *Greatest Benefit to Mankind*, p. 202

61 On the life, work, and intellectual and social context of Paracelsus, see Walter Pagel, *Paracelsus: An Introduction to Philosophical Medicine in the Era of the Renaissance* (Basel: S. Kaerger, 1958); and Allen G. Debus, *Man and Nature in the Renaissance* (Cambridge and New York: Cambridge University Press, 1978) and *The Chemical Philosophy: Paracelsian Science and Medicine in the Sixteenth and Seventeenth Centuries*, 2 vols. (New York: Science History Publications, 1977).

disequilibrium of the humors).[62] Over the course of a century, physicians and scientists inspired by Paracelsus dedicated themselves to working out the details of this chemical theory of health and disease, and they established chemistry as a fundamental part of medical science. It is revealing that the first chemical laboratory in a medical school was established at the Dutch University of Leiden by Sylvius (François de la Boë, 1614–1672), a refugee French Huguenot and leading Paracelsian. It was also Sylvius who first demonstrated that digestion was not just the result of the application of heat, as taught by the Hippocratic physicians, but a chemical process that began with the exposure of food to saliva in the mouth and culminated with the action of the pancreatic juices in the intestines.[63]

Although Paracelsus's name was closely associated with the therapeutic use of metals and minerals (several of his remedies used mercury as an ingredient), he and his followers were also interested in the medicinal potential of chemical substances contained in common herbs, plants, and other foods. The idea was that some of these chemical substances, once absorbed through the digestive process, combated disease or strengthened organs of the body. Guy de la Brosse (c. 1586–1641), one of several Paracelsians among the French royal physicians, persuaded Louis XIII to establish the Jardin des Plantes as a facility for chemical research and the instruction of students in the preparation of herbal remedies and the art of distillation.[64] A few years later, Cardinal Richelieu bestowed special permission on another Paracelsian, Théophrast Renaudot (1584–1653), to set up an independent laboratory for analyzing therapeutic substances, including herbs, vegetables, and other foodstuffs.[65]

---

[62] Porter, *Greatest Benefit to Mankind*, pp. 203–204.

[63] Allen G. Debus, *The French Paracelsians* (Cambridge and New York: Cambridge University Press, 1993), pp. 137–139; and Debus, *The Chemical Philosophy*, pp. 529–530.

[64] Debus, *The French Paracelsians*, pp. 80–84. French royal physicians operated professionally under the protection of the crown and were, therefore, not subject to the jurisdiction of the medical faculty of the university, which was dominated by conservative Galenists. Several men who attained the standing of royal physicians in the seventeenth century were strongly influenced by Paracelsian ideas. In addition to de la Brosse they included Théophrast Renaudot and Joseph Duchesne (see following note), Theodore Turquet de Mayerne (1573–1665), and Jean Ribet de la Rivière (c. 1571–1605).

[65] Debus, *The French Paracelsians*, pp. 84–101; and Kathleen Wellman, "Nature and Culture in the *Discourses of the Virtuosi of France*" in *Experiencing Nature: Proceedings of a Conference in Honor of Allen G. Debus*, edited by Paul H. Therman and Karen Hunger Parshall (Dordrecht, Boston, and London: Kluwer, 1997), pp. 193–210.

One of the foods subjected to chemical analysis by Paracelsians at an early date was black pepper. In 1606, Joseph Duchesne (c. 1544–1609) published the following assessment:

> The great piquant or piercing quality of pepper, which one perceives in the taste and burning sensation it leaves on the tongue stems from what chemists call an aronic salt, which is subtle and penetrating and therefore cuts into, attenuates, and dissolves the tartars and viscidities of the stomach and other parts, and this is why the ancients found it to be good for the treatment of quartian fevers and various other maladies.[66]

In other words, Duchesne thought that although the ancients were wrong about the reasons, they were right in believing that pepper was beneficial to digestion and that it could be used to counter a number of diseases. It is a lovely example of how traditional remedies could be retooled and reconciled with new discoveries in medical science. In light of Duchesne's analysis, it is interesting to note that black pepper – alone of the spices favored in ancient and medieval cuisine – persevered as a seasoning in the new, delicate cooking of La Varenne and Bonnefons.[67]

A NEW STANDARD OF LUXURY

Given the continuity of medical practice in the seventeenth century and the ongoing interest in the therapeutic qualities of foods, it is implausible to attribute to medicine the primary responsibility for the rejection of spicy cuisine and the rise of delicate cooking. This leads us to consideration of a second hypothesis, sketched half a century ago by Fernand Braudel. He noted that imports of spices to Europe, especially to areas north of the Mediterranean, rose sharply in the first half of the seventeenth century. Between 1605 and 1641, the Dutch East India Company established a virtual monopoly on the spice trade, eliminating the Portuguese, who had dominated since the voyage of Vasco da Gama in the 1490s, and minimizing competition from English, Danish, and French rivals. Under Dutch management, the volume of spices imported into Europe increased dramatically: for example, about 20,000 quintals of pepper reached Europe in 1600 or about 20 grams for each of 100 million inhabitants; eighty years later,

---

[66]　Quoted in Jean-Louis Flandrin, "From Dietetics to Gastronomy: The Liberation of the Gourmet" in Flandrin and Montanari, eds., *Food*, pp. 426–427.

[67]　Editors' introduction to La Varenne, *Le Cuisinier françois*, 2001, n.p.

this amount had doubled to an estimated 50,000 quintals.[68] At the same time, prices began to fall, in effect creating a new and much larger market among the middling classes and in the countries of Eastern Europe and the Baltic, where spices had historically been in short supply. Spices, which still counted as luxuries in the 1590s, became items of ordinary consumption. Once "they were no longer a symbol of wealth and luxury, they were used less and their prestige declined" Braudel wrote, "Or so a cookery book of 1651 (by François Pierre de La Varenne) would suggest."[69]

Braudel went on to point out that spices had to compete for attention with new luxuries – tobacco from America; coffee, tea, and chocolate from the colonial trade; and distilled alcohol in the form of brandy, rum, and gin (products developed and distributed by the Dutch) – which commanded cachet as novelties and loyalty as addictive substances.[70] Sugar was not new or strictly addictive, but thanks to the establishment of plantations in the West Indies, the supplies reaching Europe continued to increase. This fueled the craving for caffeinated colonial beverages, which were drunk heavily sweetened, and the pastries and confections that were often eaten with them.[71]

Braudel also observed that, around the same time, the European diet at the upper levels of society was becoming increasingly diversified, thanks to the introduction of new vegetables.[72] In fact, this statement applies much more to France than to the Mediterranean (where a large selection of vegetables had long been available) or to England, the Germanies, or Eastern Europe, which continued to consume more meat and where vegetables never attained a very high profile. Interestingly, these northern countries continued to import ever-larger quantities of spices in the first half of the seventeenth century, even as consumption in France declined (spice use in Italy and Iberia seems to have held constant during this period). French – or at least Parisian – cuisine in the first half of the seventeenth century was unique in not one but two respects: the decline of spices and the rise of vegetables.

As we noted in the previous chapter, the diffusion in France of cultivars from the Mediterranean and the New World (with the exceptions of maize and, eventually, potatoes) tended to appeal to the rich, who could afford

---

[68] Braudel, *The Structures of Everyday Life*, p. 222. On the rise of Dutch commerce, see Jonathan I. Israel, *Dutch Primacy in World Trade, 1585–1740* (Oxford: Clarendon Press, 1989), particularly pp. 68–69, 102–104, 171–175, 248–255, 334–336, and 392 on Dutch efforts to monopolize the flow of spices from East Asia.

[69] Ibid., pp. 222–223.

[70] Ibid., pp. 222 and 243–247.

[71] Mintz, *Sweetness and Power*, pp. 108–112.

[72] Ibid., p. 223.

foods that generated a low ratio of calories to price. This was the very class of consumers whose kitchens had previously been distinguished through the lavish use of imported spices. The delicate style of cooking embodied a form of luxury that depended on being able to pick and choose ingredients and to structure menus around the best seasonal products of the moment. The success of many of the recipes we find in La Varenne, Bonnefons, and their successors depended on the quality and culinary potential of specific ingredients – asparagus stalks that were thick or thin, apples of a particular variety, chickens of a certain age and weight, pigeon chicks that were still covered with down, butter that was salted or fresh, cheese that had aged for years or only a few days – just to give a few examples. Compared with the complexity of medieval cuisine, modern cooking in the delicate style was straightforward, even simple. But it was also a highly refined form of conspicuous consumption.

Perfectly ripe vegetables and fruits were prized by the early Bourbon elite because they were short-lived and fragile. Supplies of such foods fluctuated through the year, which increased their exclusivity and built seasonal variety into the menu. (Thanks to their long shelf life, spices could be available any day of the year, imparting to cooking that monotony of which Bonnefons complained.) And in the northern climate of Paris, fine produce was always expensive, whether it was grown in one's own kitchen garden or purchased in the market from a growing network of well-capitalized specialty farmers who provided not only vegetables and fruits but also other perishable items, such as eggs, dairy products, and fattened poultry – a group that included genteel landowners and their more prosperous tenants.[73]

Horticultural guides stressed the substantial costs of establishing and maintaining a kitchen garden, as well as the need for meticulous planning. Protective brick walls and graveled paths had to be built, and, in places with poor drainage, raised beds, too. Other costs included amendments for the soil (mostly in the form of well-rotted manure, but also minerals and plant-based fertilizers); seeds, cuttings, and nursery stock for a greatly expanded list of cultivars; and wages for gardeners and laborers who were kept busy twelve months of the year.[74] If one wanted to grow heat-loving cultivars

[73] On the connection between landed interests and the Paris market, see Jonathan Dewald, *Aristocratic Experience and the Origins of Modern Culture: France, 1570–1715* (Berkeley and Los Angeles: University of California Press, 1993), pp. 149–151. Raising such high-value items for sale could generate significant income for farmers who had access to city markets as well as the necessary capital to invest in nursery stock, livestock, and equipment. Olivier de Serres, a Protestant capitalist *par excellence*, had already made this point at the turn of the century.

[74] Bonnefons, *Le Jardinier français*, 2001, pp. 6–7 and 9.

such as melons and cucumbers or engage in the lucrative trade of raising *primeurs* (vegetables harvested out of season as immature specimens) or forcing asparagus or sweet peas during the winter months, the investment required was even greater, encompassing special equipment (such as glass bells to protect tender plants) and enormous quantities of fresh manure (horse or donkey for preference), the decomposition of which fueled the hotbeds that provoked early germination in cold climates.[75]

The profusion of cultivars available to the well-to-do gardener in the region of Paris by mid-century created unprecedented opportunities to extend the season by planting varieties that ripened in succession. Both Bonnefons and La Quintinie demonstrated that it was possible to have a choice of fresh produce throughout the year, including the difficult months of January and February.[76] Although special gardening techniques, such as the use of hot beds, accounted for some of this bounty, the real key to diverse harvests throughout the year was the selection of cultivars that ripened in different weather conditions. For example, the forty-seven varieties of pear that La Quintinie recommended included types that produced fruit every week from July to February: nine ripened in the summer, ten in the autumn, and twenty-eight in the winter, a schedule that could be fine-tuned by growing some specimens as standards and others as espaliers. Each seasonal grouping included dessert pears as well as varieties suited for cooking and preserving.[77]

In *Le Jardinier français*, Bonnefons discussed how members of the cabbage family could be sequenced to provide harvests all year long. The tight-headed varieties that had long been familiar in northern France, such as the *blonds, Flandres, costes*, and *blanc d'Aubervillers*, were vegetables of the cold months. Indeed, the *blonds* benefited from exposure to frost, which sweetened and tenderized the leaves, making them better to eat.[78] However, the genus also included a large number of varieties that came to France from Italy, such as the *Romains, Verone, choux de Gênes, frisés*, and *pancaliers*, that were essentially spring and summer vegetables outside of their Mediterranean homeland. These "Italian" cabbages, as Bonnefons called them to distinguish them from the cold weather French varieties, could be ready to eat as early as May, if the first batches of seeds were sown in a hotbed and transplanted as soon as the danger of frost was past. With sequential sowings, the harvest of these varieties could continue

---

[75]   Ibid.
[76]   See the work and harvesting schedules outlined by La Quintinie, *Instruction pour les jardins fruitiers et potagers*, pp. 848–907.
[77]   Ibid., pp. 381–382.
[78]   Bonnefons, *Le Jardinier français*, 2001, pp. 58–59.

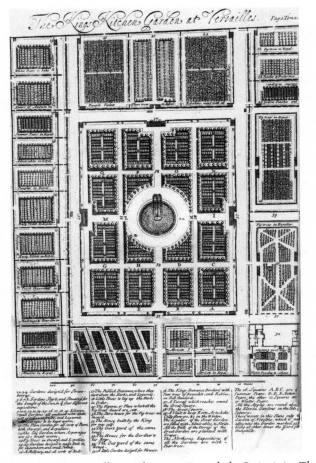

8. The *potager du roi* at Versailles as shown in Jean de la Quintinie, *The Compleat Gardener*, translated by John Evelyn, 1693 (courtesy of the Newberry Library, Chicago).

into the fall. March and April were the months when neither French nor Italian cabbages were to be had fresh (although properly stored specimens of the former might last for months), but the gap could be filled by related cultivars, two of which were recent arrivals from Italy. Cauliflower and kohlrabi shared a very long season that started in the fall, whereas broccoli, the first of the cruciferous vegetables to ripen in the spring, appeared around the time of the equinox.[79]

---

[79] Ibid., pp. 56–58. As noted earlier, cauliflower probably arrived in France from Crete via Italy; broccoli, descended from the flowers of bolting cabbage shoots, probably originated in Italy, although this is the subject of some dispute.

Whereas farmyards were usually located at a distance from the main house, it became fashionable to integrate kitchen gardens (or *potagers*, as they were called in French) into the formal plan of the gardens. Indeed, the location of the kitchen garden was frequently determined by the circuit of morning and afternoon walks taken by the family and their guests. The new *potager du roi* at Versailles was located – over La Quintinie's objections – on a site with poorly drained soil of only moderate fertility that happened to lie along one of the king's favorite paths.[80] Although set off from the purely ornamental gardens by its brick wall, the *potager* was to be contiguous with them, merging utility and beauty in a single space. To this end, the layout of the *potager* echoed the formal geometry of the parterres. Vegetables were planted in neat rows forming squares, rectangles, triangles, and diamond shapes and could be arranged to show off the complimentary foliage and growth habits of different cultivars. The center or the corners of such beds were frequently punctuated by small fruit trees that were sharply pruned to prevent casting too much shade on the plants that grew at their feet.[81] The juxtaposition of vegetables with fruit trees, herbs, and other flowering plants such as roses also linked the *potager* to the parterres, where the display of flowers was newly fashionable.[82] According to La Quintinie, the appearance of a well-tended kitchen garden improved as the trees and shrubs established themselves over the course of many seasons, gradually achieving a charm he linked to that of a good housewife, "a natural, unaffected cleanness, without any studied adornments."[83]

La Quintinie gave detailed instructions on how to pack various items of produce for transport to the proprietor's town house or the city markets. Firm fruits, such as apples and winter pears, and most vegetables were no problem – they only needed to be wrapped in paper and placed in a basket, in which they could travel by horse or cart, impervious to even the jarring and jolting that came with bad roads. Fragile spring and summer fruits, however, required extra protection: it was imperative to wrap apricots individually in cotton wool; strawberries were packed in special baskets lined with leaves and topped with wet linen; figs, bunches of grapes, peaches,

80   La Quintinie, *Instruction pour les jardins fruitiers et potagers*, pp. 85, 132, and 167–169.

81   Bonnefons, *Le Jardinier français*, 2001, p. 6.

82   On the introduction of flowers to European gardens see Andrew Cunningham, "The Culture of Gardens," p. 47.

83   Jean-Baptiste de La Quintinie, *The Compleat Gardener or Directions for Cultivating and Right Ordering of Fruit-Gardens and Kitchen-Gardens with Diverse Reflections on Several Parts of Husbandry*, in six books to which is added his *Treatise of Orange-Trees, with the Raising of Melons*, omitted in the French editions. Translated by John Evelyn, Esq. (London: Matthew Gillyflower, 1699), pp. 60–61.

and mellow summer and autumn pears had to be wrapped in vine leaves and laid (figs on their sides, peaches and pears blossom end up) on a bed of moss in a basket or sieve. Properly packed fruits were best carried in a specially designed basket that was square with storied compartments that could accommodate one sieve of fruit each without touching or weighing down the others. La Quintinie recommended securing the filled carrier basket with a padlock to which there were two keys – one for the sender and the other for the recipient – underscoring the value of the perishable foods inside.[84] Similar baskets were used to transport fresh butter and delicate cheeses, the latter often wrapped in the leaves of herbs for extra protection and perfume.

Cuisine based on "the delicacies of the country" thus came to be at home in the urban kitchens of the elite Parisians who owned property in the hinterlands of the city. La Varenne gave recipes for some 150 dishes that featured vegetables as principal ingredients, including entrées and entremets that were suitable for every season of the year.[85] In *Les Délices de la campagne*, Bonnefons published more than a hundred recipes for different vegetables plus dozens more for fruit, the latter mostly intended for a sweet desert course.[86] The section that dealt with vegetable and fruit recipes was the longest in the book, running to sixty-seven pages, as compared to forty-nine for bread and pastry, forty-six for wine and other beverages, twenty-one for eggs, nineteen for dairy products, forty-five for fowl, fifty-seven for meat, and fifty for fish. Other recipes for vegetables and fruits had already appeared in part III of *Le Jardinier français*.[87] Such dishes greatly diversified the menus of households that were able to afford them, relieving the alternating pattern of meat and fish days with an array of flavors that truly mirrored the variety of nature. Interestingly, vegetable cookery was also the single most innovative category in the delicate cooking of the 1650s. Many of the silky sauces emulsified with cream, butter, and egg yolks that became emblematic of the new cuisine first appeared in the chapters on vegetables.

In the course of the eighteenth century, cuisine based on fresh farm and garden products would become indelibly (if misleadingly) linked to the ideal of the simple and virtuous rural life as imagined by Rousseau. In reality, the modern French style of delicate cooking was expensive and exclusive, as its appeal was wholly dependent on access to an abundance of raw materials

---

84   La Quintinie, *Instruction pour les jardins fructiers et potagers*, pp. 93–94.
85   La Varenne, *Le Cuisinier françois*, 2001, pp. 86–89, 90–123, 144–146, 230–231, and 240–241.
86   Bonnefons, *Les Délices de la campagne*, pp. 99–166.
87   Bonnefons, *Le Jardinier français*, 2001, pp. 91–129.

that were seasonal, perishable, and most readily available to the gentlemen farmers who produced them.

DINING WITHOUT CEREMONY

Finally, we must consider the social milieu that fostered the delicate style of cooking. During the first half of the seventeenth century, the Parisian grand monde[88] (that is to say, high society) underwent a number of important transitions. Its membership changed, and so did the manners and daily habits associated with a noble style of life. The freewheeling nobles of the Valois era, prone to wayward loyalties and personal violence, were succeeded by gentlemen with polished manners, settled habits, and personal ambitions that were hitched to the stars of the Bourbon dynasty. It was this new aristocracy of civilized tastes who employed La Varenne and inspired the upwardly mobile aspirations of Bonnefons's bourgeois readers. What was the impact of this elite and their way of life on food?

There has been a strong tendency to see the seventeenth-century aristocracy and its cultural achievements – including early modern French cuisine – as the creations of court society. The celebrated sociologist Norbert Elias argued that the French preoccupation with personal refinement was the result of a long-term process – the civilizing process – by which the rebellious instincts of the traditional nobility were tamed by participation in the hierarchical patterns of life at the royal court. The standards of taste that emerged in this context were eventually internalized not only by the genteel classes but also by members of the bourgeoisie, who became wholly assimilated to courtly norms. Via the civilizing process, the cultural hegemony of the court reached into the middle ranks of society, a pattern that Elias believed set France apart from Germany (where the middle class concept of "*Kultur*" was hostile to the Frenchified manners of the nobility).[89]

---

[88]   On the meaning and usage of "grand monde" see Benedetta Craveri, *The Age of Conversation*, translated by Teresa Waugh (New York: New York Review Books, 2005), p. 396; and Emmanuel Bury, "Le monde de 'l'honnête homme': aspects de la notion de 'monde' dans esthétique du savoir-vivre" and Marc Fumeroli, "Premier témoin du parisianisme: le 'monde' et la 'mode' chez les moralists du XVIIe siècle" in *La Notion du "monde" au XVIIe siècle*, vol. 22 (Autumn 1994) of *Littératures classiques*, pp. 191–202 and 165–190.

[89]   Elias published a version of this work in 1939; an expanded edition appeared in 1968. He was especially concerned with explaining the difference between the French concept of "*civilisation*" and the German concept of "*Kultur*." This distinction is the subject of the first two chapters of Norbert Elias, *The Civilizing Process: The History of Manners and State Formation and Civilization*, translated by Edmund Jephcot (Oxford and Cambridge, MA: Blackwell, 1994).

More recently, Stephen Mennell has drawn on these ideas to try to explain the divergent paths taken by French and English cooking in the modern period. Inspired and nurtured by standards of aristocratic refinement, fine cooking in the style of La Varenne flourished in France. Deprived of a courtly base in the mid-1600s by the Civil War and Interregnum, English cooking developed in the kitchens of the country gentry and the middle classes, whose primary concerns were practicality and economy.[90]

In light of these ideas about the influence of the court on manners and cuisine, it is interesting to note that the cooking at the Louvre and at Versailles in the reigns of Louis XIII and Louis XIV was quite conservative. This was partly due to matters of personal taste. Louis XIII always began his meals with a dish of dried fruit (Corinth raisins for preference) – an entrée with a long pedigree that violated one of the cardinal rules of the emerging delicate style, namely that sweet foods served in the early courses of the meal killed the appetite and dulled the palate.[91] Louis XIV was one of those people to whom Bonnefons referred who liked spices and wanted them sprinkled on whatever he ate. The duke de Saint-Simon noted in his diary that everything served to the king was "heavily spiced, at least twice as

Elias's view of the hegemonic power of court society in French culture heavily influenced the more general analysis of French manners and taste offered by Pierre Bordieu in *Distinction: A Social Critique of the Judgement of Taste*, translated by Richard Nice (Cambridge, MA: Harvard University Press, 1984). On Bordieu's view, which gives Elias's thesis a leftist twist, aristocratic elites spawn criteria for what constitutes refined manners or consumption only to abandon these as they become appropriated by middle and lower class imitators in favor of new benchmarks of distinction, reinforcing class boundaries. Elias's picture of the hegemonic power of the court in seventeenth-century France has been attacked by the historians Emmanuel Le Roy Ladurie in *Saint-Simon and the Court of Louis XIV*, with the collaboration of Jean-François Fitou, translated by Arthur Goldhammer (Chicago and London: The University of Chicago Press, 2001), especially pp. 18–19 and 349–352; and Daniel Gordon, *Citizens without Sovereignty: Equality and Sociability in French Thought, 1616–1789* (Princeton, NJ: Princeton University Press, 1994), especially pp. 3–4 and 88–94. As long ago as the 1950s, the great literary critic Erich Auerbach made the case for the cultural originality of Parisian society in the early 1600s and its fluid relationship with the court after 1660 in the essay "La Cour et la Ville" in *Scenes from the Drama of European Literature: Six Essays* (New York: Meridian, 1959).

[90] Mennell, *All Manners of Food*, especially chapter 4, "From Renaissance to Revolution: Court and Country Food," pp. 62–101, and chapter 5, "From Renaissance to Revolution: France and England – Some Possible Explanations," pp. 108–127. See also the following discussion of French and English cooking in Chapter 5.

[91] Françoise Sabban and Silvano Serventi, *La Gastronomie au Grand Siècle: 100 recettes de France et d'Italie* (Paris: Editions Stock, 1998), p. 94.

9. *The Banquet of the Chevaliers de Saint-Esprit*, 1633, by Abraham Bosse (Rosenwald Collection National Gallery of Art, Washington; image © Board of Trustees, National Gallery of Art, Washington).

much as was usual for any ordinary dish."[92] The royal kitchen laid in stocks of spices, which were entrusted for safekeeping to the chef who headed the specialized group within the kitchen staff that was responsible for making the *potages*; he doled them out to the other cooks as needed.[93] Louis's table manners were as archaic as his palate. Although the fork came into use at the French court in the 1580s, the Sun King shunned it, preferring to eat solid foods with a knife and his fingers.[94]

Other factors were the scale of the royal household and the sense of tradition that informed the sensibilities of the officers of the *bouche du*

---

[92] Louis de Rouvroy, duke de Saint-Simon, *Mémoires de duc de Saint-Simon*, 7 vols., edited by G. Truc (Paris: Gallimard, 1947–1966), vol. 6, pp. 879–881; quoted in Wheaton, *Savoring the Past*, p. 136.

[93] Jousselin, *Au couvert du roi, XVIIe-XVIIIe siècles*, p. 77.

[94] Saint-Simon, *Mémoires*, p. 51. Louis's sister-in-law, the duchess d'Orléans, recounted an occasion when the king forbade his grandson, the duke of Burgundy (who was second in line for the throne), to use a fork when they dined together; Braudel, *The Structures of Everyday Life*, pp. 206.

roi, who were responsible for planning and serving the king's meals. For hundreds of years one of the markers of elite status, and royal status in particular, was the display and consumption of very large quantities of food, especially game and other meats. The table kept by Louis XIV continued this practice, even as it was becoming obsolete elsewhere. At a date when the average menu in a private household, even a rich and aristocratic one, consisted of two courses prepared in the kitchen (*potage* and roast) and a dessert course from the *office* (a kind of pantry removed from the sticky heat of the kitchen where sugary confections were made), the king's dinner and supper menus normally consisted of five courses featuring various kinds of game and butcher's meat (or fish and seafood on fast days) followed by dessert, making a total of six courses. A typical menu from 1683 for dinner served *au grand couvert* (that is, when the king ate alone as members of the court watched) consisted of the following:

POTAGES
Grand potage of two mature capons
Grand potage of four partridges with cabbage
Petit potage of six pigeons
Petit potage of cockscombs
Hors d'oeuvre of chopped capon
Hors d'oeuvre of partridge

ENTRÉES
Quarter of veal weighing twenty pounds
Pie of twelve pigeons
Fricassee of six chickens
Two hashed partridges
Hors d'oeuvre of three partridges *au jus*
Hors d'oeuvre of two grilled young turkeys
Hors d'oeuvre of three fattened chickens with truffles
Six pies with fillings of braised meats

BOILED MEATS
Ten-pound piece of beef
Short ribs of mutton
Capon
Piece of veal
Three chickens

ROASTS
Two fattened capons

Nine chickens
Nine pigeons
Two *hétourdeaux*
Six partridges
Four pies

ENTREMETS
Dish of six partridges
Dish of two woodcocks
Dish of three teals[95]

The absence of vegetable dishes from the categories of *potages*, entrées, entremets, and hors d'oeuvres was a clear indication of the conservative orientation of the royal kitchen (salads probably accompanied the roasts, in the traditional manner). Even on days of abstinence, vegetables did not appear on the king's table in the numbers one might expect. Only one of the seventeen dishes included in a fast day supper served in 1683 used vegetables as principal ingredients. It was a *potage* of new peas and asparagus and could have been easily overlooked amid the other dishes made of carp, turtle, sole, pike, trout, perch, eel, salmon, and one hundred each of oysters and crawfish. During Lent and especially on Good Friday, vegetables played a much bigger role, in conformity with Church rules about fasting that applied to everyone.[96] But this annual appearance of vegetables on the royal table confirmed that the *bouche du roi* continued to treat them as penitential foods long after practices had changed in Paris society. At the turn of the eighteenth century, as in the days of Taillevent, vegetables were of marginal importance on the royal table.

Vegetable dishes probably played a somewhat larger role in the menus for the private suppers the king enjoyed with his mistresses and, later, with his second wife, Mme. de Maintenon, whose personal staff took charge of their preparation. We know that Louis liked asparagus and sweet peas and that La Quintinie was under orders to deliver these items (along with figs, another royal favorite) regardless of the season.[97] In his book, published posthumously, La Quintinie expressed some mixed feelings about the feats of gardening prowess that made it possible to force asparagus week after week from November until April. Relief came around Easter, when the first

---

[95] Jousselin, *Au couvert du roi, XVIIe–XVIIIe siècles*, p. 72. Hétourdeaux were young male or female chickens that had not yet been neutered; poultry was (and is) often neutered in order to encourage the birds to fatten up at an accelerated rate.

[96] Ibid., p. 75.

[97] La Quintinie, *Instruction pour les jardins fruitiers et potagers*, pp. 11–51.

natural spears pushed up in the *potager* and when "Nature advertises me that it is time to put an end to the violences I have done her, and that she is willing, in her turn, to serve us some dishes prepared by her own skill."[98]

The home of culinary innovation in the delicate style was not the court, but the Parisian grand monde – the same world that fostered the plays of Corneille and Molière, the novels of Mme. de Lafayette, the letters of Mme. de Sévigné, and the painting of Poussin and Champaigne. After 1660, the court made itself the great patron of the arts and the prism through which the rest of Europe perceived the achievements of French culture; however, the dynamic center of that culture lay in the city, where the elite classes were engaged in working out a new vision of what it meant to lead a noble way of life.[99]

The transformation of aristocratic self-understanding in the early seventeenth century was driven by a number of factors. Decades of religious and civil war had decimated the ranks of the nobility of ancient lineage, extinguishing some families and leaving others under weak leadership.[100] Increasingly the descendents of such families found that landed income was dwarfed by the salaries, pensions, and other benefits enjoyed by those engaged in some branch of royal service as expanded by Henry IV and his successors. One could either rot in the ancestral château in the provinces or come to Paris to make a career as a judge, a magistrate, or a regular officer of the king's army, an institution that increasingly called for commanders who were well educated in mathematics, science, and foreign languages.[101] Families of the military aristocracy were just as likely as nobles of bourgeois descent to send their sons to the colleges run by the Jesuits and their great competitors, the Oratorians, in preparation for such careers. To give one striking example, the king's cousin, the prince de Condé (1621–1686), who could have claimed the most prestigious military command as a birthright, was carefully educated so as to be fit for these responsibilities – something that would not have happened in a previous generation.[102] His education included not only the subjects that were now prerequisites for a military command but poetry too, for which he developed a sensitive appreciation. The very fact that an aristocratic warrior such as Condé took

---

[98]　Quoted from John Evelyn's translation, La Quintinie, *The Compleat Gardener*, p. 170.

[99]　This idea was articulated with respect to literature and the theater by Auerbach, "La Cour et la Ville," especially pp. 138–139; and has been developed more broadly by Ranum in *Paris in the Age of Absolutism*, especially pp. 129–164 and 195–228.

[100]　Ranum, *Paris in the Age of Absolutism*, p. 196.

[101]　Dewald, *Aristocratic Experience and the Origins of Modern Culture*, pp. 20–21, 53–58, and 81–82.

[102]　Ibid., p. 83.

an interest in the arts showed that mores among the elite were starting to change.

Meanwhile, members of the robe nobility planned for the ongoing advancement of their families by buying offices and military commissions for sons and arranging prestigious marriages for well-endowed daughters.[103] Already by the second quarter of the seventeenth century, marriages between the two branches of the nobility had become commonplace, exciting none of the scandal provoked by much rarer unions between persons of noble and bourgeois status.[104] One example that stands for many is the family tree of Mme. de Sévigné (1626–1696). Her father, the chevalier de Rabutin-Chantal, was the son of an ancient and distinguished Burgundian family who had sought his fortune in the capital; her mother, a Coulanges, was from a family of Parisian financiers and magistrates whose *noblesse* was as recent as their wealth was great.[105] By the end of the century very few of the families of ancient lineage who made their fortunes at court lacked relatives whose ancestors had not yet been ennobled in 1600.

So the middle decades of the seventeenth century were a period of unusual fluidity in the composition of the elite. Although everyone was aware of gradations of prestige within the nobility, these were for the most part bridged by similar educations and careers and entwined family trees. Rank mattered, of course, but increasingly so did distinction achieved through personal refinement.

Virtually everyone in seventeenth-century society took it for granted that a person's fundamental identity was acquired at birth from parents and more remote ancestors. However, they also came to believe that this identity could be burnished and that one's character could be elevated through the acquisition of knowledge, the love of beauty, and the cultivation of virtue.[106] One of the favorite books of the day, the French translation of Castiglioni's *Book of the Courtier*, argued that true nobility lay at the intersection of birth and refinement.[107] The Jesuits and the Oratorians, intent on the spiritual and intellectual development of their pupils, conveyed much the same message in confessional terms. People of good birth now spoke of the importance of becoming *"honnête,"* that is, men and women

---

[103] Ibid., p. 60.

[104] On attitudes toward rank and marriage, see Le Roy Ladurie, *Saint-Simon and the Court of Louis XIV*, pp. 4–5 and 178–190.

[105] Marie de Rabutin-Chantal, marquise de Sévigne, *Selected Letters*, translated and with an introduction by Leonard Tancock (London: Penguin, 1982), p. 8.

[106] Ranum, *Paris in the Age of Absolutism*, pp. 197–215. See also the discussion in Auerbach, "La Cour et la Ville," pp. 162–179.

[107] Gordon, *Citizens without Sovereignty*, pp. 119 and 121.

of superior cultivation, "which meant convivial, genteel, well-bred, and morally decent all at once."[108]

This view was most forcefully presented by Pierre Corneille (1606–1684), the son of a robe family, who, in his great tragedies of the 1630s and 1640s, rewrote the book on what it meant to be truly noble. Traditional aristocratic values were all about extroverted action and self-assertion. Physical courage, passion, and the pursuit of glory and honor were the qualities of old-fashioned noblemen. Corneille's heroes had these traits in abundance, but they were matched by others that betrayed a new capacity for inner reflection and self-control – eloquence, love, and devotion to duty. It was a vision of nobility that captured the imaginations of genuine aristocrats as well as arrivistes. At the premier of *Le Cid* in 1636, Condé is said to have been moved to tears.[109]

Two new social institutions emerged from this new aristocratic milieu of civilized virtues. One was the salon, an intimate gathering (typically hosted by a woman) that was devoted to the discussion of literature, philosophy, science, and the arts.[110] Inspired by accounts of similar gatherings

---

[108] Ibid., p. 74. No English equivalent captures all the nuances of *"honnête homme,"* but "gentleman" is the closest. The linguistic confusion is multiplied by the fact that the French *"gentilhomme"* referred to someone who possessed the quality of *"gentillesse"* (genteelness), that is, a pedigree from a long line of unimpeachably noble ancestors. *Gentillesse* was a narrower category than *noblesse*, which included persons whose parents or grandparents were ennobled commoners. This usage was exactly the opposite in English, in which "nobleman" suggested the son of a peer and "gentleman" was the more inclusive category in which good manners made up for the absence of aristocratic ancestors. The qualities that made a man (or woman) *honnête* were widely discussed in seventeenth-century French literature, starting with *L'honnête homme, ou l'art de plaire à la cour* by Nicolas Faret, which first appeared in 1630. Although there was a link in the mind of some between *honnêteté* in women and chastity, the well-born courtesan and salon hostess Ninon de L'Enclos (1620–1705) claimed that she, too, was *honnête* by virtue of her civility and capacity for lasting friendship, an opinion that was widely shared within the grand monde. See Craveri, *The Age of Conversation*, pp. 219–221, 228–230, and 390.

[109] Ranum, *Paris in the Age of Absolutism*, pp. 204–209.

[110] The most accessible general introduction to the Parisian salon available in English is Craveri, *The Age of Conversation*. However, see also Carolyn C. Lougee, *"Le Paradis des Femmes": Women, Salons, and Social Stratification in 17th-Century France* (Princeton, NJ: Princeton University Press, 1976); and Elizabeth C. Goldman, *Exclusive Conversations: The Art of Interaction in 17th-Century France* (Philadelphia: University of Pennsylvania Press, 1988); for the salon in the eighteenth century, see Dena Goodman, *The Republic of Letters: A Cultural History of the French Enlightenment* (Ithaca, NY, and London: Cornell University Press, 1994). Peter Burke, *The Art of Conversation* (Ithaca, NY, and New York: Cornell University Press, 1993), pp. 102–108 discusses the French salon in a broad European

in the humanistic literature of the Italian Renaissance, the salon became a fixture of Paris society in the 1620s, thanks to the widely imitated example of Catherine de Vivonne, marquise de Rambouillet (1588–1665). From 1613 or so until her death in 1665, Mme. de Rambouillet hosted weekly gatherings in her *hôtel particulier* across from the Louvre in which men and women mingled freely in a setting that was both refined and relaxed (the term "salon" originally referred to the beautiful blue room, adjacent to the marquise's bedroom, where the meetings took place).[111] The presence of women was a critical element in the chemistry of the salon. They were expected to participate as equals in the conversation instead of merely deferring to the opinions of men, and the rules that came to govern polite speech in the salon were meant in part to enforce this parity.[112] The hierarchy of rank was also discarded in the salon, whose guests typically included people of different degrees of nobility and even writers and artists of bourgeois origin.[113] In court society, conversation was constrained by precedence. Addressing a superior without being spoken to first or disagreeing with a higher-ranking member of the court were considered unpardonably rude breeches of etiquette. In the salon, however, conversation was meant to allow the spontaneous expression of one's personality and the free exploration of ideas rather than ritual enactment of hierarchical roles.[114] One learned to participate in the give-and-take of argument, to explain ideas lucidly, to engage the interests of others, to be witty without being cruel. Mutual respect, reciprocity, and conviviality were the core values of salon society. The ability to sustain conversation according to these standards of *politesse* was viewed as both evidence of personal refinement and a means of honing it in a lifetime of sociable interaction.

The salon has been the subject of much study by historians and literary scholars, who have found in it a source of the development of the French language and literature, a school of polite manners, a means of empowerment

---

context. In French see Antoine Lilti, *Le Monde des salons: Sociabilité et mondanité à Paris au XVIIIe siècle* (Paris: Broché, 2005); Marguerite Glotz and Madeleine Marie, *Salons du XVIIIe siècle* (Paris: Nouvelle Editions Latines, 1949); Roger Picard, *Les Salons littéraires et la société française, 1610–1789* (Paris: Brentano, 1943); and Georges Mongrédien, *La Vie de société aux XVIIe et XVIIIe siècles* (Paris: Hachette, 1950).

[111] Craveri, *The Age of Conversation*, pp. 27–44. The standard reference on Mme. de Rambouillet is Nicole Aronson, *Mme de Rambouillet ou la magicienne de la Chambre bleue* (Paris: Fayard, 1988).

[112] Gordon, *Citizens without Sovereignty*, p. 109.

[113] Ibid., p. 39.

[114] On competing models of the rules of polite speech at the French court and Paris high society, see the discussion in Gordon, *Citizens without Sovereignty*, pp. 86–127.

for women in aristocratic society, and a font of scientific and philosophical ideas that shaped the Enlightenment and the French Revolution. Its sister institution, the dinner or supper party, has been largely overlooked.[115] Whereas traditional banquets, like conversation at court, revolved around hierarchical principles, the dinner party, like the salon, was a venue that fostered conviviality and candid discussion among a mixed company of equals. The dinner party provided powerful reinforcement for the humane values of salon culture, and its dynamics altered the priorities and practices of elite Parisian kitchens.

The key feature of the Parisian dinner party was that it abandoned the hierarchical seating plan in favor of an arrangement that placed people in close proximity to one another *around* a table of moderate size. Men and women usually sat next to one another in alternating chairs. Bonnefons gave an early description of how to set the table for such a meal, which had no "high" or "low" end in the medieval sense. Parties of twelve could be accommodated at either a round or a square table. The plates were to be spaced a chair's width apart, so diners would have sat almost shoulder to shoulder.[116] It was an arrangement that created a sense of intimacy among the guests. And it encouraged them to talk within the group – behavior not promoted by the traditional seating plan, which spread people out along the outer edge of the table.

The contrast between the two kinds of seating arrangements is nicely illustrated by a pair of engravings dating from the 1630s or 1640s by Abraham Bosse (1606–1672), a prolific printmaker and one of the original members of the Académie royale who specialized in genre scenes. His *Benediction at the Table* shows a family group seated in the traditional fashion: The father is in the center, facing the viewers, with his hand raised as he says grace. The mother is to his left and his daughters and their governess are to the left of her (two on the same side of the table as the parents, two on the corners of the narrow end, and the governess facing the sisters). The five sons are all paced to the father's right – the two eldest sitting next to him facing out, two younger ones seated facing their brothers, and the baby, still

[115] An exception is Lilti, *Le Monde des salons*, whose brief discussion compliments my own. Salon hostesses often invited their regular guests, the *habitués*, and distinguished visitors to dine or sup after the conclusion of the salon proper. To my knowledge, no hard evidence has emerged to link the introduction in France of dinner-party style service with salons. However, both institutions shared roots in the Italian humanism of the sixteenth century, and Mme. de Rambouillet was the daughter of a Roman princess who spent her early life in humanist circles – a suggestive confluence of facts. In any case, the dinner party, with its emphasis on promoting conversation, was an extension of the salon spirit during mealtimes.

[116] Bonnefons, *Les Délices de la campagne*, pp. 373–374.

10. *The Benediction at the Table* by Abraham Bosse (Marie Antoinette Evans Fund, Museum of Fine Arts, Boston; photograph © 2008 Museum of Fine Arts, Boston).

in skirts and too young to join the family meal, standing at the narrow end attended by a servant. The mood is solemn; everyone is in his or her proper place. Contrast this with Bosse's depiction of the return of the prodigal son, a story from the Old Testament that turns on the jealousy of the elder son, whose rightful place by his father's side was usurped by the young black sheep of the family. For this scene, in which rank was subordinated to joyous celebration, Bosse arranged the family around a small table, in the manner of a dinner party.

The practice of seating diners in intimate groups around round or square tables had some precedent in humanist circles in sixteenth-century Italy. Giovan Battista Rossetti, who was employed as a maître d'hôtel at the courts of Ferarra and Urbino, described such arrangements as "banqueting in the German style."[117] Because of the compact shape of the table, the dishes for each course were presented on oversized platters – one per table – that were divided into deep partitions, each filled with a different recipe. (In French such platters would come to be known as *"tourtières à l'italienne."*)[118] After

[117] Sabban and Serventi, *La Gastronomie à la Renaissance*, pp. 61–62; and Alberto Capatti and Massimo Montanari, *La Cuisine italienne: histoire d'une culture* (Paris: Seuil, 2002), p. 184.

[118] Sabban and Serventi, *La Gastronomie à la Renaissance*, pp. 61–62 and Maestro Martino, *The Art of Cooking: The First Modern Cookery Book/Composed by the Eminent Maestro Martino of Como*, edited with an introduction by Luigi Ballerini, translated and annotated by Jeremy Parzen, and with fifty modern recipes by Stefania Marzini (Berkeley and Los Angeles: University of California Press, 2005), pp. 4–5. On *tourtières à l'italienne*, see Bonnefons, *Les Délices de la campagne*, p. 381; Vincent La Chapelle, *The Modern Cook*, 3 vols., 3rd ed. (London: T. Osborne, 1744); vol. 1, p. 26 described how to turn an ordinary deep platter into a *tourtière*

11. *The Feast for the Prodigal Son* (*L'Enfant prodique*, set of 6 plates, plate 6) by Abraham Bosse (Elizabeth Day McCormick Collection, Museum of Fine Arts, Boston; photograph © 2008 Museum of Fine Arts, Boston).

helping themselves and each other, the guests ate and talked, uninterrupted by servants, until the next course arrived.

By the middle decades of the seventeenth century, similar practices had become established in fashionable Parisian households. Old-fashioned trestle tables of long and narrow shape went out of style and were replaced by round, square, oval, rectangular, or even triangle shapes that accommodated the circular seating plan. Manuals for maîtres d'hôtel began to include descriptions and, by the 1690s, lavish illustrations of how to lay the places on tables of different shapes with china, crystal glassware, and silver plates.[119] These dining tables were placed in the salon or even in

à l'italienne by baking a cross of pastry dough in the center and filling each angle with a different soup or bisque.

119   On Pierre de Lune's 1662 book, *Le Nouveau et parfait maistre d'hostel*, see Sabban and Serventi, *La Gastronomie au Grand Siècle*, p. 95. See also the examples described by L. S. R., *L'Art de bien traiter (1674)* in *L'Art de la cuisine française au XVIIe siècle*, edited by Gilles and Laurence Laurendon (Paris: Editions Payot & Rivages, 1995), pp. 193–204; by N. Audiger (including illustrations) in *La Maison réglée et l'art de diriger la maison d'un grand seigneur tant à la ville qu'à*

the principal bedroom, the usual place for the lady of the house to receive intimate friends. This flexible use of space may help to explain the great popularity of oval tables that collapsed into compact circles when the leaves were removed – a design that supplanted other shapes by the end of the century.[120] The first documented case of a purpose-built dining room in the region of Paris was at Vaux-le-Vicomte, the country house of Nicolas Fouquet, the king's finance minister, which was completed in 1659. The dining room was located just above the well-equipped kitchens that occupied the ground floor of the château, an arrangement that would be widely copied in future decades. (Fouquet is famous in the history of gastronomy for two additional reasons: his patronage of La Quintinie brought him to the attention of Louis XIV, who subsequently appointed him to design the *potager du roi* at Versailles; Fouquet was also an early employer of Vatel, the celebrated maître d'hôtel, who later worked for the prince de Condé and who reportedly committed suicide to redeem his honor when the fish ordered for a fast day banquet in honor of the king failed to arrive.)[121]

The circular placement of the guests around the perimeter of the table stressed the formal equality of everyone who sat down. This lack of hierarchical principle was also reflected in the menu, which made no attempt to distribute choicer foods to some members of the party. Indeed, the compact shape of the tables designed for small groups meant that all the serving dishes would have been within easy reach of each person or her immediate neighbor to the right or left. (Despite the occasional appearance of *tourtières à l'italienne*, Parisians preferred separate serving dishes for each recipe; these were placed on the tabletop in a geometrical pattern, a style of presentation that came to be known as *service à la française*.)[122] At tables set for twelve or more, equally appetizing and varied choices were offered on the two halves of the table – for example, crawfish bisque, *hachis* of pheasant, and artichokes for one and shellfish soup, ragout of partridge, and

la campagne in Laurendon and Laurendon, eds., *L'Art de la cuisine française au XVIIe siècle*, pp. 464–472; and the magnificent pull-out engravings bound between pp. 88 and 89 of François Massialot, *Le Cuisinier roïal et bourgeois qui apprend à ordonner toute sorte de repas & la meilleure manière des ragoûts les plus à la mode & les plus exquis*, corrected and augmented, with illustrations, 3rd ed. (Paris: Charles Sercy, 1698).

[120] On oval tables, see Audiger, *La maison reglée*, pp. 464–472; and the engravings in Massialot, *Le Cuisinier roïal et bourgeois*, referred to previously.

[121] Dominique Michel, *Vatel et la naissance de la gastronomie* (Paris: Fayard, 1999), pp. 13–32 and 43–48. The death of Vatel is the subject of two letters by Mme. de Sévigné dated April 24 and 26, 1671.

[122] Jean-Louis Flandrin, *Chronique de Platine: pour une gastronomie historique* (Paris: Editions Odile Jacob, 1992), pp. 291–299.

asparagus for the other. Alternatively, separate platters of the same foods could be placed on the two ends of the table.[123]

Another attribute of this style of service was that it required less intervention by waiters and footmen. Once the food was on the table, the guests mostly attended to themselves and each other, thanks to the compact table arrangement. As servants were no longer required to fetch servings of food from distant ends of the table, they became less visible, gradually retreating from the traditional position behind the chairs of the ladies and gentlemen they served to the perimeter of the room. By the turn of the eighteenth century, the service of wine had also been simplified, with carafes placed on a special stand within reach of the host or directly on the table – an arrangement that made it possible to dispense with servants altogether between courses.[124] At dinner parties, the guests ate and talked in an atmosphere that was not only more convivial but also more private than had hitherto been the case.

The style of service associated with the dinner party came into general use for family meals as well as occasions at which guests were present. Traditional banquet service came to be associated with institutional settings (including the dining halls of schools and colleges), with ceremonial occasions (such as weddings or the banquets given by guilds and municipal authorities), and, of course, with the royal court, where tradition continued to reign.[125] In Paris high society and the bourgeois circles that aspired to noble status, the trend was toward dining without ceremony.

The success of the dinner party changed the dimensions of the cook's job in a couple of significant ways. Once the ceremonial aspects of meals diminished, so, too, did the emphasis on creating spectacular visual effects with food. Dishes that had been popular for centuries because of their decorative character – such as peacocks and swans in their plumage, molded creams in gaudy colors, and pies filled with blackbirds or other living creatures – became rare and eventually disappeared from menus and cookbooks. La Varenne and Bonnefons included a few recipes for dishes that traded on trompe l'oeil effects, such as vegetable purée molded in the shape of sausages, an old Lenten favorite. It was much more their style, however, to

[123] Bonnefons, *Les Délices de la campagne*, pp. 373–374.
[124] Roy Strong, *Feast: A History of Grand Eating* (New York: Harcourt, 2002), p. 263. See also Béatrix Saule, "Tables à Versailles 1682–1789" in *Versailles et les tables royals en Europe XVIIème-XIXème siècle* (Musée National des Châteaux de Versailles et de Trianon, 1993–1994), pp. 58–60.
[125] Saule, "Tables à Versailles 1682–1789," pp. 58–60. Interestingly, by the end of the century, members of the royal family chose to be served informally, dinner-party style, when they retreated from Versailles to Marly, St. Cloud, or the other small châteaux they used as refuges from the rigors of court life.

present foods without attempting to disguise or even decorate them very much – for example, a piece of poached cod topped with butter and chopped parsley, or some asparagus spears napped with a band of ivory-colored sauce. Garnishes and sauces such as these were chosen because their flavors were considered to be complimentary to the principal ingredients, with visual interest being a second-order consideration.

The love of display and the playful inventiveness that were so important in the medieval kitchen seem to have been perpetuated in modern France mostly through confectionary and pastry making, in which fanciful shapes, jewel-like colors, and glittery decorations are integral to the foods' appeal. These branches of cuisine developed quickly in the late seventeenth and eighteenth centuries, and the skills and equipment associated with them became highly specialized. In the eighteenth century, bakers of petits fours (dainty pastries that were usually elaborately decorated) emerged as a separate category in the baking trade. In large households, similar treats as well as other pastries, confections, and desserts were prepared in the office, whose dedicated staff was distinct from the kitchen's hierarchy of chef, sous-chefs, and unskilled help.[126] In the growing market for French cookbooks in the 1650s and 1660s, it became common for separate volumes to be devoted to pastry and sweets, reflecting this division between the kitchen and the office.[127] The division of labor between the *confiseur-pâtissier* and the *chef de cuisine* may have accelerated the decline of decoration in cooking. In any case, the visual interest on dinner tables was typically provided by the silver plate and porcelain (itself a luxurious novelty) on which the food was served, rather than the food itself.

The second important change that coincided with the rise of the dinner party was the decline of the number of dishes the kitchen was expected to prepare relative to the size of the group being served. The traditional rule of thumb for menu planning had been to count on one dish per person per course (for example, forty-eight dishes, twelve per course, for a four-course menu for a dozen people). This took into account both the need to provide appropriate dishes for guests of different standing and the layout of the long, narrow table, which called for platters and tureens to be placed in an undulating ribbon that stretched from the high table to the far ends of the flanking ones. Each guest was expected to serve himself and his dining partner from the dishes that were within an arm's reach, which meant that the actual choice of foods available was small. Compact dining tables and the informal, circular seating plan changed the geometry of the tabletop:

---

[126]   See Wheaton, *Savoring the Past*, pp. 106–107 on the design and equipment of the *office*.
[127]   Hyman and Hyman, "Printing the Kitchen," p. 401.

fewer dishes were needed to cover the table with an abundant spread, but all or most of them were accessible to each guest or her neighbor. From the diner's point of view, the variety within the menu went up, even as the total number of dishes offered went down. For example, Bonnefons's menu for twelve people called for only eight dishes per course, a decline of one-third from the traditional standard.[128]

Medieval menus had been structured around the progression from entrées to *potages*, roasts, entremets, and dessert, followed by sweet wines and candied spices, a pattern that was thought to favor good digestion. Prior to 1650, this order had changed in elite Parisian households so that both dinner and supper opened with the soup course.[129] The entrées moved to the second position, despite their name, followed by the roast and then the entremets. These four courses were followed by the dessert, which was increasingly dedicated to sweet items only, as opposed to the mélange of sweet and savory dishes familiar on medieval and Renaissance tables.

Although four-course meals continued to be common after 1650 – ballooning up to eight courses for celebrations of big events – there was a trend toward menus of two courses prepared in the kitchen plus a dessert course from the office. One finds traces of both the two- and four-course schemes in *Le Cuisinier françois* and *Les Délices de la campagne* (not to mention the eight-course extravaganza described at the end of the latter). Although La Varenne had separate chapters for *potages* and entrées, his chapters on roasts (for meat and fish, respectively), refers to the *rôt* as "second," that is, the second course of the meal. Interestingly, the English translation of 1653 describes the chapter on entrées for meat days as "Potage of Entrées (or first courses) which can be made in the Armies or in the Field" – a title that is suggestive on a number of fronts. It indicated dishes that did not require a large staff or *batterie de cuisine* to execute, the sort of thing that La Varenne might have prepared when his master, the marquis, was on campaign with his regiment.[130] It also suggested an ambiguity

---

128   Bonnefons, *Les Délices de la campagne*, pp. 381–384. The quantities prepared in each recipe must have gone up in order to allow everyone to have at least a small portion. The importance of this point had already been pointed out by Rossetti with regard to German-style service; see Sabban and Serventi, *La Gastronomie à la Renaissance*, pp. 61–62.

129   Sabban and Serventi, *La Gastronomie à la Renaissance*, pp. 61–62. The reasons for this switch remain unclear, but it is interesting to note that the German-style banquets described by Rossetti also began with soup.

130   La Varenne, *The French Cook*, pp. 12 and 39. In the French edition, the heading for this section reads "*Table des entrées qui se peuvent faire dans les armies ou dans la campagne.*" See La Varenne, *Le Cuisinier françois*, 2001, p. 27. By the time La Varenne wrote this, fine cuisine seems to have appeared in the military camps of the

between which kinds of dishes cooked in sauce counted as *potages* and which ones, by virtue of their thicker sauces, crossed over into the category of entrées. It became common to offer in the first course a large tureen of soup, which would be accompanied by platters of entrées and small plates of hors d'oeuvres. In a similar fashion, the roast would be surrounded by side dishes that were sometimes referred to as entremets, although they did not always correspond to recipes that would have counted as such in an earlier generation.[131] This trend toward two-course menus in which entrées and entremets were reduced to side dishes would accelerate after 1660, as we shall see. The number of dishes per course continued to decline, and, on most occasions, so did the number of courses prepared in the kitchen.

As the quantity of dishes went down, the attention to detail and the use of exacting techniques went up. The practice of using bouillon from a common pot to prepare all the recipes made on a single day became less necessary. With fewer dishes to cook, it was feasible to poach a chicken in some stock made just for this purpose from the neck and feet with only the herbs one wanted to produce a particular effect. The cook could experiment with recipes that needed to be concocted at the last minute, such as the sauces emulsified with butter and egg yolks that La Varenne liked to pair with vegetables and fish. And more thought could be put into pairing ingredients from the array of seasonal foods available and to the cooking techniques that would yield the most luscious results. We find all of these developments, and more, in the French kitchen of the 1650s.

French army, as officers took their chefs and silver plate along on campaign. Jean Hérauld, sieur de Gourville, wrote of a visit to a commander in 1654, "I certainly [was] surprised in the evening, when supper was served to see that it was done with the same elegance [*propreté*] and delicacy that he would have had at Paris. Up until then no one had taken his silver dishes to the army, or thought to serve entremets or fruit. But this bad example soon spoiled others, and this carried so far that today there are no generals, colonels, or *maîtres de camp* who lack silver dishes, and they believe themselves obliged to do like the others, insofar as they can." Quoted in Dewald, *Aristocratic Experience and the Origins of Modern Culture*, p. 58.

131 Sabban and Serventi, *La Gastronomie au Grand Siècle*, pp. 94–95; and Jean-Louis Flandrin, *L'Ordre des mets* (Paris: Editions Odile Jacob, 2002), pp. 119–120.

CHAPTER 4

The French Kitchen in the 1650s

INNOVATIONS AND OLD FAVORITES

Between the covers of *Le Cuisinier françois* readers found recipes that carried out the program of delicate cooking on several fronts. There were recipes for dishes with familiar names – such as *poivrade* sauce for roasted meat, teals in hippocras, and pies of meat and fish – that were adapted in light of a culinary sensibility that preferred straightforward flavors to complex ones scented with aromatic spices. Other dishes used ingredients that had been unfamiliar or inaccessible to previous generations. In addition to the large selection of vegetables previously mentioned, La Varenne published recipes for more than forty kinds of fish and seafood, the majority of which were saltwater varieties (older cookbooks had relied heavily on a few freshwater species, so the presence of so many ocean fish suggests how much more sophisticated the Paris market had become). The recipes carefully adjust cooking methods, seasonings, and sauces to compliment the character and quality of the principle ingredient – both pike and perch are prepared with sauces thickened with butter and egg yolks, but the details of how these are concocted are unique. La Varenne explained how to make ragouts thickened with roux, a paste of flour sautéed in fat that was itself a recent invention, and silky sauces emulsified with butter (either white or brown) or a combination of butter and egg yolks, precursors of modern *beurre blanc, beurre noir,* and members of the hollandaise family. He also recommended sauces that were nothing but cream reduced until it was thick enough to coat vegetables.

Bonnefons's books continued in this vein, with a few differences in emphasis. His recipes for traditional favorites tended to be a bit spicier and sweeter than the versions recommended by La Varenne, and he had a freer hand with decorations and fancy presentations. Although he used roux to thicken ragouts, he was partial to simple butter liaisons in well-reduced sauces for meat and fish. He liked to use egg yolks to endow some of his cream sauces with extra richness but published no recipe for the kind of

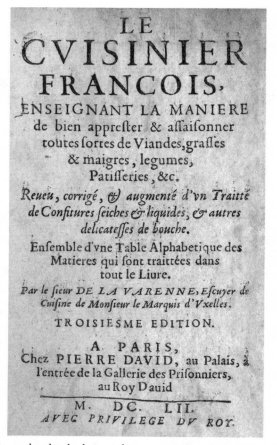

LE
CVISINIER
FRANCOIS,
ENSEIGNANT LA MANIERE
de bien apprefter & affaifonner
toutes fortes de Viandes, graffes
& maigres, legumes,
Patifferies, &c.

*Reueu, corrigé, & augmenté d'vn Traitté
de Confitures feiches & liquides, & autres
delicateffes de bouche.*

Enfemble d'vne Table Alphabetique des
Matieres qui font traittées dans
tout le Liure.

*Par le fieur DE LA VARENNE, Efcuyer de
Cuifine de Monfieur le Marquis d'Vxelles.*

TROISIESME EDITION.

A PARIS,
Chez PIERRE DAVID, au Palais, à
l'entrée de la Gallerie des Prifonniers,
au Roy Dauid

M. DC. LII.
AVEC PRIVILEGE DV ROY.

12. Title page from the third edition of François Pierre de la Varenne, *Le Cuisinier françois,* 1652 (courtesy of the University of Chicago Library, Special Collections Research Center).

butter and egg yolk emulsified sauces of the hollandaise type that formed the basis of La Varenne's reputation as a founder of the *haute cuisine.* If the cooking described in *Les Délices de la campagne* was less sophisticated than what the reader found in the *Cuisinier,* Bonnefons made up for this by supplying his readers with exhaustive information about ingredients and how to use them to the best culinary advantage (a subject on which La Varenne made scattered remarks, usually at the beginning of recipes). This aspect of Bonnefons's work is especially useful in grasping the link between the development of the delicate style and the availability of a large variety of superior products of the farm and garden. In addition, his recipes were unusually explicit, which was probably a function of writing for an

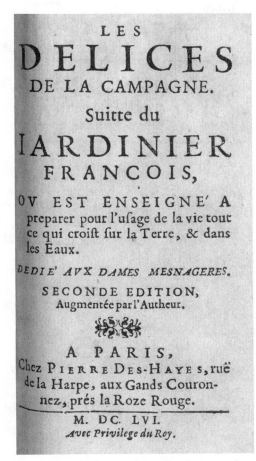

13. Title page from the second edition of Nicolas de Bonnefons, *Les Délices de la campagne*, 1656 (courtesy of the University of Chicago Library, Special Collections Research Center).

audience of amateurs rather than culinary professionals. La Varenne, like most culinary writers before and since, assumed that his readers already knew how to cook and generally required information only about the details of particular recipes or techniques that were unusual. Bonnefons made no such assumptions, spelling out basic techniques and procedures step-by-step, a characteristic that offers a unique window into the French kitchen of the 1650s.

The likenesses and differences between the styles of La Varenne and Bonnefons are neatly illustrated in their recipes for pigeon bisque. At this date, "bisque" meant a kind of *potage* that achieved a thickened texture by simmering in a basin with croutons; it was considered an elegant dish that

14. Frontispiece from *Les Délices de la campagne* showing a gardener and the artisans who transform his harvests into food and drink (courtesy of the University of Chicago Library, Special Collections Research Center).

was often served on festive occasions.[1] La Varenne's recipe was a succinct paragraph of 88 words, increased to 123 words in the second edition of 1652, thanks to more explicit instructions on how to truss the pigeons for poaching.[2] Here is the English translation of 1653, based on the second

---

[1] Other seventeenth-century recipes for pigeon bisque were published by Pierre de Lune and the anonymous writer known as L. S. R.; these have been reprinted recently in Laurendon and Laurendon, eds., *L'Art de la cuisine française au XVIIe siècle*. See also Barbara Wheaton's discussion of the version published in 1660 in *Le Cuisinier méthodique* and her remarks on the technique of simmering the crouton in the soup until the liquid is reduced and thickened in *Savoring the Past*, p. 128.

[2] See La Varenne, *Le Cuisinier françois*, 1981, pp. 9–10 and La Varenne, *Le Cuisinier françois*, 2001, p. 21.

French edition (a relatively verbose 137 words, thanks to the difference between French and English verbs):

> Take young pigeons, cleanse them well and truss them up, which you shall do in making a hole with a knife below the stomach and thrusting the legs through it. Whiten them, that is, put them into a pot with hot water or with pot broth, and cover them well. Then put them in the pot with a small twig of fine herbs, and fill up your pot with the best of your broths, have a special care that it may not become black. Then dry your bread and stove it in the pigeon broth; then take up after it is well seasoned with salt, pepper, and cloves, garnished with the young pigeons, cock's combs, sweetbreads of veal, mushrooms, mutton juice, and pistachios. Serve it up and garnish the brims of the dish with slices of lemon.[3]

Bonnefons took six pages to describe everything a novice – or a modern reader – would need to know in order to achieve good results.[4] He explained how to choose which pigeons to use (the youngest available, still covered with down, if possible) and how to poach them in plain bouillon, reserving the heads for decoration. Next came preparation of a ragout of *béatilles* – the garnish of cockscombs, sweetbreads, and mushrooms mentioned by La Varenne. It was important, Bonnefons wrote, to poach each of the ingredients for the *béatilles* separately until they were barely tender (the sweetbreads and cockscombs had to be cooked over very low heat, lest they toughen up and become "fit only for feeding to the dogs"). Meanwhile, one roasted a leg of mutton on the spit until it was rare, removed it from the fire, pricked it with a knife, and pressed it to yield mutton juice. The most labor-intensive step was the preparation of a *Jacobine*, an elaborate buttered crouton layered with minced, cooked chicken and beef marrow seasoned with cinnamon, which Bonnefons called for instead of the plain bread crouton specified by La Varenne. When all these separate elements were ready, one degreased the pigeon bouillon and corrected the seasoning by adding some of the mutton juice (which also deepened the color as well as the flavor), a little salt, and a few drops of lemon juice ("just enough to heighten the flavor without making it acid"). An hour or so before serving, one poured the bouillon into a large basin, placed the *Jacobine* in the middle, and simmered them slowly together until the liquid was partly absorbed and the crouton began to disintegrate, producing the slightly sandy texture characteristic of a bisque, with crusty bits around the edges. For the final

---

[3]   La Varenne, *The French Cook*, p. 21.
[4]   Bonnefons, *Les Délices de la campagne*, pp. 248–253.

assembly, the pigeon carcasses were arranged on top of the *Jacobine*, heads resting on the rim of the basin, spices were sprinkled over, the *béatilles* were added, and the dish was garnished with lemon slices, pistachio nuts, and pomegranate seeds. Bonnefons advised very small servings – pigeon bisque was a dish "to be tasted, not one to fill up on."[5] La Varenne's version would have been considerably lighter, thanks to the substitution of the plain crouton for the *Jacobine*.

These recipes for pigeon bisque published in the 1650s appear to have been adaptations of a dish that had been a favorite for generations. The presence of mutton juice in a dish of delicate poultry, the *béatilles* (a combination that became popular during the Renaissance), and the cinnamon in Bonnefons's version suggest roots in the cooking of the fifteenth and sixteenth centuries, as does the use of almond milk in La Varenne's recipes for *potage à la Jacobine* and *potage à la Jacobine au fromage*. Indeed, the latter bears a more than passing resemblance to the *"souppe Jacobine de chappons"* described in "Du fait cuisine," a manuscript by Master Chiquart, cook to the duke of Savoy, which was written in the 1420s.[6] Clearly cooks and eaters in mid-seventeenth-century Paris remained attached to old favorites, even as the cutting edge of the cuisine embraced *le goût naturel*.[7] This was true for individual recipes, such as pigeon bisque and *potage à la Jacobine*; for basic preparations, such as the liaison of bread crumbs that they used to thicken some of their sauces and techniques such as blanching meats before roasting them; and for whole categories of foods, such as the array of fritters, wafers, and other small pastries that had already been familiar in the fourteenth century. Similar recipes continued to appear in later editions of *Le Cuisinier françois* and in the works of other French culinary writers until the early eighteenth century. Tastes changed, but not all at once.

5   Ibid., p. 253.

6   La Varenne gave two recipes for *potage à la Jacobine*, one of which adds cheese to the poultry-topped crouton; see *Le Cuisinier françois*, 2001, pp. 9–10 and 21, and *The French Cook*, pp. 25 and 33–34. According to the Scullys, the *Jacobine* took its name from the Dominican convent in the Rue St. Jacques in Paris, whose aristocratic members were known for luxurious living. They suggest a modern adaptation of the *Jacobine*, with cheese, based on *Du Fait cuisine*; see Scully and Scully, *Early French Cookery*, pp. 105–107. Like so many of the international dishes of the late medieval and Renaissance kitchen, pigeon bisque and *potage à la Jacobine* were also popular in Italy, where they may have originated. Marcella Hazan's recipe for *sopa coada*, squab soup, is a modern descendent in which the crouton is layered with braised, boned squab meat and grated cheese, a *Jacobine* in all but name. See Marcella Hazan, *Marcella's Italian Kitchen* (New York: Alfred A. Knopf, 1986), pp. 68–69.

7   Barbara Wheaton, *Savoring the Past*, pp. 116–117.

Interestingly, La Varenne's versions of many dishes that bore traditional names or featured old-fashioned ingredients were subtly altered to make them more consistent with the delicate style. For example, his recipes for the classic sauces meant to be served with roasted meat were less spicy and acidic than their medieval forbears. Neither his *poivrade* (recommended for beef and many game birds) nor his green sauce (suggested for lamb and pork) contained ginger or the mixture of ginger, cinnamon, and cloves that figured in recipes for these sauces dating from the medieval kitchen.[8] Although both La Varenne and Bonnefons liked some acidity in their sauces for meat and fish, they suggested caution, lest the taste become too sour – a sprinkle of bitter orange or lemon juice, a drop of vinegar or verjuice sufficed. Even when indulging in old-fashioned trompe l'oeil surprises, such as the lean dish of "counterfeit" *andouillets de veau* – a mixture of puréed pumpkin, mashed hardboiled egg yolk, and minced mushrooms formed into sausage shapes and fried – Bonnefons stuck to herbs for seasoning.[9]

Some of the recipes in the *Cuisinier* and *Les Délices* used flavor combinations that had been popular in the late Middle Ages and the Renaissance with techniques that were modern. For example, the entrée of turkey with raspberries published by La Varenne used cloves in the forcemeat with which the turkey is stuffed, while the sauce called for both the sweet raspberries and a little vinegar and lemon juice. One would have expected a bread crumb liaison for a sauce with such flavorings, but instead he specified a roux cooked until it was very brown. The result was a sort of sweet and tart velouté sauce – suave and silky, but packing a tangy punch.[10]

A CHOICE OF INGREDIENTS

Although dishes that evoked the flavors and techniques of the medieval kitchen were certainly present in the writings of La Varenne and Bonnefons, the tone of both works was set by the conviction that the cook should take his cues from the variety and quality of his raw materials. The first task of a good cook was to learn to evaluate the culinary potential of a principal

---

[8] La Varenne, *Le Cuisinier françois*, 2001, pp. 84–85, and *The French Cook*, p. 78. For comparison see the sauce recipes from Taillevent and the *Ménagier de Paris* in Scully and Scully, *Early French Cookery*, p. 127.

[9] Bonnefons, *Les Délices de la campagne*, p. 252.

[10] La Varenne, *Le Cuisinier françois*, 2001, p. 31, and *The French Cook*, p. 41. Already by the 1670s, the archaic elements in *Le Cuisinier françois* excited some criticism from other culinary writers, in particular L. S. R., the author of *L'Art de bien traiter*. He denounced the recipe for turkey with raspberries as an example of La Varenne's "Arab" tastes. See *L'Art de bien traiter*, p. 23.

ingredient. How would its flavor and texture respond to heat? Did it require a moist environment or a dry one? A long or a short cooking time? Did it compliment other ingredients at the cook's disposal? And so on.

As we have seen, Bonnefons thought that the process of acquiring such knowledge began in the garden and that the special strength of the gardener-cook was his knowledge of the plant varieties that grew there, ripening in succession with the seasons. A cook who understood the difference between a loose-leafed Italian cabbage and a tight-headed *blanc d'Aubervillers* would not waste time trying to stuff the latter, a project sure to end in culinary disaster, and would choose instead to use it, sliced and wilted in butter or bacon fat, as the basis for a hearty soup. Beyond this grasp of the general characteristics of each type of vegetable or fruit, however, cooks needed to develop the ability to judge the quality and ripeness of the raw materials that were available to the kitchen on any given day. According to the fluctuations in the weather and other variables, these could be young, somewhat under-developed specimens or fully mature ones or something in between. The first peas that ripened in May were not just smaller than the big, wrinkled ones harvested in August – they tasted sweeter and responded differently to heat. Getting equally good, if distinct, results with such a range of materials would require recipes and modes of preparation appropriate to the specific qualities of the ingredients at hand.

Exploring this connection between ingredients, seasonings, and cooking techniques was the unifying theme of *Les Délices de la campagne*, and Bonnefons pursued it with regard to not only vegetables and fruit, but other kinds of ingredients as well. For example, in selecting partridges, it was important to know that the masles was the tastiest breed, that the flavor peaked in young adults that had not yet mated, and that their age could be determined by examining the beaks to see if they were still flexible. Such prime specimens should be roasted with a little bacon, whereas older birds were better cooked *en potage*.[11] Discernment was just as important when purchasing foodstuffs in the market as in contemplating how to use your own garden or farm produce. Bonnefons explained that the best milk available in Paris came from the black cows – not the white or red ones – pastured in the vicinity of Medoun, and that excellent butter came from Rouen in Normandy.[12] Indeed, Bonnefons's concern about ingredients even prompted him to comment on the water used to make bread. The secret – and irreplaceable – ingredient of the famous loaves produced by the bakers of Gonesse, a village outside Paris, was the pure water from a local spring,

---

[11] Bonnefons, *Les Délices de la campagne*, pp. 257–260.
[12] Ibid., p. 189.

he wrote.[13] Water was such an important component of so many recipes that it was critical for a fastidious cook to secure a supply that was sweet with no off-flavors of any kind, whether this came from a spring, a river, or a cistern for storing rainwater.[14] In short, no cuisine was better than the ingredients of which it was made.

Bonnefons's focus on the primacy of ingredients led him to organize his material in a way that was unusual at the time. Most early French cookbooks, from *Le Viandier* to *Le Cuisinier françois* and beyond, were divided into two big sections, one for meat days and the other for fast days. Within these divisions, recipes were grouped according to the categories of the menu: *potages*, entrées, roasts, and entremets. Organizing recipes according to their place on the religious calendar and their function within the meal aided in the composition of menus, but it encouraged frequent repetitions in the text, as many dishes were suitable for both meat and fast days and could be served as either an entrée or entremets.[15] Bonnefons broke with the conventional organizational scheme by dividing all his material into books defined by groups of ingredients: book I, on bread and wine; book II, on vegetables, eggs, and dairy products; and book III, on fowl, meat, and fish. Within these sections, recipes were organized into chapters according to their primary ingredient. Thus all dishes featuring chicken or eggs or asparagus were printed together, whether they were soups, entrées, roasts, or entremets. Even conserves were included under the headings of their principal ingredient. This method of organization minimized repetition, and, more significantly, it gave Bonnefons a logical place to discuss the general characteristics of each ingredient; the varieties available in the region of Paris; how to judge the quality, maturity, and freshness of specimens; and the consequences of these differences in cooking. Thus informed, the reader would be in a position to make the best possible use of the raw materials at her disposal, varying the mode of preparation and seasoning as appropriate to their nature and condition. The composition of menus – including allowances for the ecclesiastical calendar – would follow from this primary focus on ingredients.

As one would expect of the author of *Le Jardinier français*, Bonnefons was full of advice about the best ways to use vegetables of various varieties, sizes, states of maturation, and freshness. His artichoke recipes are a good example. Very young, fresh artichokes needed a minimum of trimming, only brief parboiling, and were to be presented with delicate sauces, such

---

[13] Ibid., p. 5.

[14] Ibid., p. 5.

[15] See the introductory essay by Philip and Mary Hyman to Taillevent, *Le Viandier*, pp. 1–12.

as one of cream thickened with egg yolks. Later in the season, more fully mature and therefore tougher specimens required meticulous preparation in order to be equally good. He gave step-by-step instructions on how to remove the bracts and the fuzzy white choke and on how to trim the bottoms into pieces that would cook evenly. He noted that artichoke bottoms prepared in this manner tended to discolor, a fault that could be corrected by adding vine leaves to the water in which they were blanched. Although mature specimens prepared this way were tasty when fricasseed with cream, he suggested more robust alternatives that took advantage of the stronger flavor of full-grown artichokes – stuffing with savory meat or fish forcemeats or braising with bacon, herbs, and a touch of acid in the form of a little bitter orange juice or wine vinegar.[16]

La Varenne, too, showed deliberate care in matching ingredients to precise cooking methods and seasonings. The reticent tone so characteristic of *Le Cuisinier françois* was abandoned in many of the vegetable recipes, which spelled out the details of how to choose ingredients and the culinary techniques appropriate to preparing them. For example, when making asparagus *à la sauce blanche,* it was important to choose the thickest specimens available, either white or green, trimmed to equal lengths and blanched briefly in salted water. Letting the asparagus boil too long would ruin the dish – the best asparagus spears were *"les moins cuites,"* presumably still firm and even a little crunchy.[17] In contrast, a fricassee of asparagus *à la crème* could be successfully made with thinner asparagus. In one version, the spears were cut into three pieces each, blanched, drained, and simmered in cream; for a thicker sauce than one obtained by just reducing the cream, one could add an egg yolk. The other type of fricassee, for which La Varenne specified green asparagus only, was prepared according to a more direct method that omitted the blanching. The asparagus spears were scraped, cut into small dice, and sautéed in butter or bacon fat. Parsley, scallions, an herb bouquet, and fresh cream were added to the pan, and everything simmered together until the asparagus was done. To serve, a grating of nutmeg could be added, at the cook's discretion.[18] La Varenne also recommended this method of fricasseeing *à la crème* for green peas.[19] The result would have been very close to a recipe given by Bonnefons, which he specified for young, sweet peas only. Mature peas required a longer cooking time, and for these Bonnefons recommended braising with lettuce hearts, scallions, parsley, salt, and

16   Bonnefons, *Les Délices de la campagne,* pp. 133–137.
17   La Varenne, *Le Cuisinier françois,* 2001, pp. 117 and 238. This recipe is printed in two separate sections of the book.
18   Ibid., pp. 118 and 238.
19   Ibid., pp. 120–121.

pepper. The wilting lettuce provided moisture for the slow braising process without producing lots of liquid that would thin out the cream added at the end. Also, the lettuce's sweetness offset the mealy quality of mature peas, in which sugars had been converted into starch. Because La Varenne had a recipe that was virtually identical, the dish must have already been popular by 1650 or so; indeed, it has become a classic of French cuisine and is still known today by the name under which Bonnefons published it – *"petits pois à la française."*[20]

The desire to find ways of cooking the fruits of the kitchen garden that captured their natural or true taste also shaped Bonnefons's approach to other kinds of foodstuffs. Perhaps the best way to get a feel for how nuanced his appreciation of ingredients was – and the level of attention to this matter he encouraged his readers to take – is to examine his chapter about chickens, which took up 15 percent of the total length of *Les Délices de la campagne*. It began with a discussion of the various breeds then available in the Paris region, their diets, and their weight at the age of slaughter. The smallest birds, *poulets de grain*, were the most delicate – so much so that the normal procedure of scalding with hot water as a preliminary to plucking would spoil their flavor and texture. It was worth the extra trouble, he said, to scorch the tiny birds for a few minutes over a hot fire to loosen the feathers, although the handwork required to remove them would still be more laborious than in the usual scalding method. Once plucked clean, the *poulets* should be threaded horizontally on a spit and roasted over the fire. The only acceptable sauce for their delicate flesh was a sprinkle of bitter orange juice or verjuice – any other preparation would swamp their natural flavor.[21]

Slightly older grain-fed chickens were appropriate for a wider variety of cooking methods and seasonings. Like all chickens, they could be roasted – Bonnefons gave suggestions for how to spit, baste, and sauce hens and capons of all ages[22] – but he thought that the ones of middle age and weight were especially good when quartered; flattened with the side of a heavy knife; marinated in white wine or vinegar, lemon or orange peel, pepper, salt, and herbs such as tarragon, chervil, chives, or thyme; and then grilled. A variation called for rolling the marinated quarters in flour or dipping them in beignet batter prior to frying in lard or bacon fat, a kind of early modern Southern fried chicken. His recipe for chicken fricassee also began with the jointed pieces briefly marinated, then browned in butter;

[20]   Bonnefons, *Les Délices de la campagne*, pp. 147–153; and La Varenne, *Le Cuisinier françois*, 2001, p. 120.

[21]   Bonnefons, *Les Délices de la campagne*, pp. 218–219.

[22]   Ibid., pp. 228–229.

simmered in bouillon (made from the chicken trimmings without extra herbs or flavorings) and white wine; garnished with shallots, mushrooms, bacon lardons, and fines herbes; and finished with a liaison of egg yolks beaten with verjuice (cream was an optional enrichment). Vegetables should be chosen according to the season and whatever the cook/gardener judged to be excellent at the moment.[23]

The pièce de résistance of middleweight chicken cookery was, however, a delicate recipe for a whole bird poached in a casserole with fines herbs, butter, and plain bouillon. The recipe unfolds with Bonnefons's characteristic attention to detail, including instructions about how to eviscerate the bird and cut a slit in the skin near the vent to create a self-trussing closure. Bonnefons pointed out that only a small amount of bouillon should be used – presumably the chicken was only partly submerged, allowing the tender breast meat to steam gently while the thighs simmered in the liquid. At the end of the cooking period, these juices were turned into a sauce by adding a liaison of one or two egg yolks beaten with a little verjuice. The finished dish was garnished with choice spring vegetables such as asparagus tips, peas, lettuces, and chicory, lightly cooked.[24] Bonnefons went on to explain that a heartier version of casserole-poached chicken could be produced with an older, tougher bird, whose more developed flesh could stand up to longer simmering and the flavor of more robust, late-season vegetables – leeks and parsley root for preference – that would cook along with the bird. He recommended stuffing these mature birds with a mixture of minced veal, beef suet, parsley, chives, tarragon, and chervil that was bound with egg. (A dense stuffing of this type would have been incompatible with a smaller, tender chicken, whose flesh would have fallen apart before the stuffing cooked through.) Bonnefons also pointed out that rice could be added toward the end of the cooking period, in which case the egg yolk liaison would presumably have been omitted.[25] This is a nice example of how a cook who understood ingredients could modify a standard technique to maximize the flavor and texture of the foodstuffs at hand.

This concern about matching cooking techniques and seasonings to principal ingredients was evident throughout *Les Délices de la campagne*. For example, a recipe for veal fricassee that followed the basic pattern described above for chicken called for bay leaf in place of the fines herbes,

---

[23] Ibid., pp. 225–228.

[24] Ibid., pp. 219–221.

[25] Ibid., pp. 221–222. This version also called for the veal stuffing, a versatile mixture that appeared in many of Bonnefons's recipes, including the cucumber boats and stuffed cabbage in the vegetable chapters – see pp. 123–125 and 129–130.

whereas a third fricassee of wild rabbits substituted garlic.[26] Clearly the goal was to create a range of dishes using a common method that made quite different impressions on the palate, each memorable for the pairing of meat and herb flavors. Other combinations he particularly recommended included fava beans with savory, turnips with leek or mustard, peas with thyme or marjoram, eggs with sorrel, goose with sage, duck with turnips, pigeons with sweet peas, boned veal breast with capers, and beef braised à la mode with orange peel and bay[27] – all combinations that have endured in modern French cooking.

Despite this clear, one might say, programmatic preference for juxtaposing principal ingredients with one or two well-matched seasonings, Bonnefons was partial to parsley, chives, and scallion, and he used them profusely, both alone and in combination. All three were so mild that they could be used to inject a note of savor into even the most delicate dishes of fish, eggs, and very young, tender veal, lamb, or chicken without upstaging the main ingredient or obscuring its distinctive characteristics. Parsley, "our French spice," was valuable for its color as well as its fresh taste, and Bonnefons readily admitted that he put it in almost everything. The whole leaves, which recalled the greenery of the kitchen garden, were his favorite decoration for plates.[28]

RAGOUTS, FRICASSEES, AND SILKY SAUCES

Many of the recipes that featured such pairings of herbs and principal ingredients were fricassees or ragouts, terms that were used more or less interchangeably in the seventeenth century for dishes cooked in a sauce that incorporated the juices of the principal ingredient, supplemented by other liquids such as bouillon, wine, or cream.[29] Whereas bisques were thickened by simmering bread croutons in bouillon, fricassees and ragouts typically used a liaison of beaten egg yolks (as in Bonnefons's chicken recipes, discussed previously) or a roux of flour browned in butter or other fat ("roux" means "russet" and suggests that early examples were cooked to a deep nut brown, a darker hue than is common in French cooking today).

---

[26] Ibid., pp. 265–266 and 317.

[27] Ibid., pp. 108–109, 147–155, 172, 237–238, 239–240, 254–255, and 288–289.

[28] Ibid., p. 110.

[29] On the whole, mid-seventeenth-century ragouts tended to use roux and fricassees used egg yolks, but the distinction as such was not drawn until the publication of the first edition of François Massialot's *Le Cuisinier roïal et bourgeois* in 1691.

These liaisons created smooth-textured, silky sauces variously described as satiny (for the egg yolks) or velvety (for the roux). The absence of graininess was a novel change from the classic medieval sauces, which relied on liaisons of bread crumbs, pounded almonds, or the disintegrating starch of croutons simmered in bouillon (as we saw previously in the recipes for pigeon bisque). The fats in the egg yolks and roux – not to mention the cream and additional butter that were used as enrichments in many cases – also produced a certain mouth-filling voluptuousness (what food writers today would call "a good mouth feel") that was very different from the bracing acidity of many traditional sauces.

By the 1650s, ragouts and fricassees had come to dominate the entrée course (now served after the *potages* or along with them, prior to the roast), but they also appeared as entremets. A large proportion of the vegetable recipes published in *Le Cuisinier françois* and *Les Délices de la campagne* qualified as fricassees or ragouts in terms of their mode of preparation, but the technique was easily adapted to poultry and meat, too. Whether the principal ingredient was asparagus or crawfish, artichokes or squabs, fava beans or veal, or truffles or beef, the ragouts and fricassees described by Bonnefons and La Varenne were exemplars of the delicate style.

Sauces rich in fats tend to magnify the flavor of the ingredients with which they are served, and this made them an invaluable aid in capturing *le goût naturel*. Cloaked in silky sauces, peas tasted like peas and asparagus like asparagus. This was even true in cases in which the sauce was prepared separately from the principal ingredient – as in La Varenne's *sauce blanche*, a kind of proto-hollandaise that he recommended for both vegetables and fish. From the medieval point of view, sauce, like all forms of seasoning, was a dietary corrective that played a critical role in the composition of a dish by modifying the essential qualities of the principal ingredient. The aesthetic preference for complex, densely layered tastes, in which spicy, acidic (or sweet-sour) sauces fused with principal ingredients, mirrored this understanding of cooking as the art of transforming raw material into wholesome, digestible, invigorating food. The role of the new silky sauces was very nearly the opposite: to accent the natural characteristics of principal ingredients, not to transform them chemically, nutritionally, or aesthetically.

We do not know who invented ragouts or fricassees, but there is reason to think that they could only have become significant elements in French cooking in the early decades of the seventeenth century, when a new item of equipment, the raised stove, became common in the kitchens of well-to-do households. In medieval and Renaissance Europe, cooking took place before the hearth. Food was roasted on the spit or under the ashes, grilled over the coals, boiled in a cauldron, or, in the homes of the very rich, baked in the oven after the bread was removed.[30] None of these techniques allowed precise control over the temperature at which foods cooked or the evenness with which the heat was distributed. Pots could be hung higher or lower over the fire, and the fire itself could be configured to burn somewhat hotter or cooler, but, as anyone who has ever cooked over a campfire knows, such strategies only permit crude adjustments. Smoke and heat would have made it difficult to monitor the simmering pots very closely, let alone to stir them constantly, as even a quick peek inside usually involved bending at the waist or crouching down. In order to produce consistent results in such conditions, recipes themselves had to be somewhat forgiving – no split-second timing, no delicate mixtures that could be ruined by heat that was too high or unevenly distributed. The grainy-textured, condiment-like sauces of the medieval kitchen were well adapted to these conditions. Ingredients were typically pounded in a mortar, boiled, thickened with bread crumbs or pounded almonds, and sieved one or more times until the desired texture was achieved. The critical steps in producing the right consistency were carried out apart from the cooking process itself; indeed, some sauces were concocted out of raw ingredients and pounded together, in the manner of a modern pesto. Medieval cooks did use eggs to fortify and impart a slightly viscous texture to soups, a technique that still survives in regional and home cooking. Significantly, this operation is typically executed after the soup is removed from the fire. The yolks are beaten in a tureen in order to break them up, a ladle of soup is whisked in by dribbles, and then the gradual addition of the rest of the hot soup cooks the yolks without coagulating them.[31] In contrast, warm emulsified sauces and sauces thickened with roux must be cooked over evenly distributed low or medium heat in conditions that allow the cook to monitor the process closely, stirring or skimming for extended periods of time. This level of control would have been very difficult to achieve when cooking in a traditional fireplace.

The raised stove (known in French as a *potager*, the same word used for "kitchen garden") was a rectangular structure of bricks, often faced in tiles,

---

30 For a description of the medieval *batterie de cuisine*, see Scully and Scully, *Early French Cookery*, pp. 38–39. Compare this with the list provided in 1674 by L. S. R. in *L'Art be bien traiter*, p. 54; obviously the standard stock of pots, pans, and utensils had become much more specialized by the second half of the seventeenth century.

31 See Taillevent, *Le Viandier*, pp. 116–119, and, for a modern example, the recipe for *aïgo bouïdo* (garlic soup) in Julia Child, Louisette Bertholle, and Simone Beck, *Mastering the Art of French Cooking* (New York: Alfred A. Knopf, 1983), vol. 1, updated, pp. 46–47.

built waist-high and sufficiently long to accommodate four to six *réchauds* or burners of different sizes heated by coals or charcoal in the fireproof compartment beneath the cooking surface. This design made it possible to use the stove standing up, with pots positioned at a convenient height for constant stirring and observation. A saucepan could easily be removed from the burner for a minute or two, lowering the temperature and thus avoiding culinary disaster. Ashes were removed from a receptacle beneath the stove.[32] The first documented appearance of the raised stove dates to the 1570s, when at least one was in use in the papal kitchens in Rome. The stove spread rapidly in the following decades, and, by the 1650s, La Varenne and Bonnefons took it for granted that their readers' kitchens were supplied with one. A detailed description of a well-planned kitchen published in Paris in 1674 recommended installing not one but two separate *potagers* with a total of at least eight to ten *réchauds* between them. Along with two hearths for traditional roasting, grilling, and boiling and a pastry oven, these facilities would make it possible to prepare meals for a large household "without pain or confusion."[33]

As its French name suggests, the original application of the raised stove was to simmer *potages* at a height that facilitated skimming, stirring, retrieval of solid elements, and degreasing, well away from the excessive heat and smoke of the hearth. However, its diffusion corresponded to the proliferation of other kinds of dishes that required regular attention from the cook, including those that needed very low or carefully modulated heat. These included fricassees and ragouts; omelets, custards, and other egg dishes; poached or sautéed fish and seafood; as well as a huge variety of preparations made with melted sugar – jams and marmalades, sweet fillings, candies, and spun sugar confections. Warm emulsified sauces, which have to be stirred constantly in order to achieve the proper suspension and which must be heated evenly and gently, and sauces thickened with roux, which burns easily over high heat and must be stirred as it darkens from pale gold to deep brown, are among the quintessential culinary inventions of the *potager*-equipped kitchen.

---

[32] Jean-Robert Pitte, *French Gastronomy, the History and Geography of a Passion,* translated by Jody Gladding (New York: Columbia University Press, 2002), pp. 96–97. See also Wheaton, *Savoring the Past,* p. 101; and Jean-François Revel, *Culture and Cuisine,* p. 190.

[33] L. S. R., *L'Art de bien traiter,* pp. 53–55. Big kitchens were usually equipped, in addition, with portable charcoal stoves – designed rather like a modern chafing dish – that were typically set up near windows to vent the potentially suffocating fumes they produced.

SAUCES THICKENED WITH ROUX

The majority of the ragouts described by La Varenne used roux, a paste of flour sautéed in fat. By the middle of the seventeenth century, a couple of different techniques for making roux had already evolved. The simplest method – and the one La Varenne specified most often – was to sprinkle flour over pieces of meat or vegetables as they sautéed in hot fat (typically lard or bacon fat) until a paste was formed. Moistened with bouillon, wine, and the liquids rendered by the principal ingredient, the lightly browned flour formed a sauce as the food simmered, with the characteristic velvety texture developing after twenty minutes or so. Sautéing flour removes its raw cereal odor. As we now know – and La Varenne could not – it also improves the suspension of starch and fat in the liquids (minimizing the amount of stirring needed to create a lump-free sauce) and activates the starch-digesting enzymes present in the flour (maximizing its thickening power). As the sauce simmers, the starch granules dissolve and disperse, resulting in a very smooth texture that becomes even more refined with prolonged cooking.[34] Except for a final correction of the seasoning just before serving, all the care and attention goes into the early stages of preparation. And because sauces thickened with roux may be cooled and reheated without any loss of flavor or texture, they may be prepared in advance, a factor that led one writer to describe roux-based sauces as "convenience foods at the highest level."[35]

Sometimes La Varenne recommended adding some additional roux to a ragout partway through the cooking process, presumably to create some additional thickening power for large quantities of sauce. For example, the recipe for shanks or knuckles of veal *à l'epigramme* began by sautéing the pieces of flowered meat in lard. After adding salt, pepper, cloves, a bundle of herbs, and some bouillon, one was to "flour them [the veal pieces] with some paste and smother them with the pot lid, simmer them leisurely thus covered for three hours, after which uncover them and reduce the sauce until it achieves a better consistency."[36] Roux could also be introduced to a ragout in which no flour at all had been used up to that point. An example is the *estoufade* of partridges with truffles and mushrooms, in which the flour

---

[34]   Harold McGee, *On Food and Cooking: The Science and Lore of the Kitchen* (New York: Simon and Schuster, 1997), pp. 344–345.

[35]   Robert Sokolov, *The Saucier's Apprentice* (New York: Alfred A. Knopf, 1976), quoted in McGee, *On Food and Cooking*, p. 332.

[36]   La Varenne, *Le Cuisinier françois*, 2001, p. 32.

liaison is beaten into the reduced cooking juices as necessary to achieve the desired texture.[37] Many of Bonnefons's ragout recipes also use roux in this manner.

Such cases called for roux that was prepared separately from the rest of the recipe. It was a staple ingredient in the larder of a well-organized kitchen, and La Varenne gave detailed instructions on how to make and store it in a section of his book devoted to kitchen fundamentals.[38] His recipe called for flour sautéed in lard (carefully strained of the mammocks or bits of lean pork that floated free as the lard melted) until it was well browned, an operation that required care, lest it stick to the pan and burn. Chopped onion was added to the browned flour and sautéed until it became soft, a technique that lowered the temperature in the pan, forestalling the scorching that might otherwise occur, while adding sweetness and fragrance as the caramelizing vegetables released their juices into the hot fat and flour paste. At this point, mushrooms, bouillon, and a little vinegar were stirred into the flour-lard-onion mixture and brought to a boil, a step that developed and blended the flavors of the ingredients. Finally, the mixture was strained, removing bits of vegetables, and allowed to cool. The finished roux could then be stored in a covered pot for future use.[39] Because sautéing a truly russet roux – the color of peanut butter on the way to chocolate – requires about fifteen to thirty minutes or more, depending on the intensity of the heat source and the thickness of the pan, preparing it ahead in large quantities would have made sense. La Varenne recommended warming the portion needed for a particular recipe over hot ashes before adding to hot cooking liquids.[40] Interestingly, the closest descendents of La Varenne's russet, vegetable-scented roux are found today not in France, but in the Cajun and Creole cooking of southern Louisiana, in which many of the techniques and preferences of the early modern French kitchen are preserved.[41]

In the 1650s, roux appears to have been used primarily in sauces that cooked along with principal ingredients. One exception was *sauce*

---

[37] Ibid., p. 51.

[38] See La Varenne, *The French Cook*, pp. 105–108.

[39] La Varenne, *Le Cuisinier françois*, 2001, pp. 125–126.

[40] Ibid., p. 126.

[41] Louisiana cooks usually leave the minced vegetables (typically a combination of onion, celery, and bell pepper) in the roux used to thicken gumbos and sauces. For a discussion of Louisiana roux, see Marcelle Bienvenu, Carl A. Brasseaux, and Ryan Brasseaux, *Stir the Pot: The History of Cajun Cooking* (New York: Hippocrene, 2005), pp. 131–133; and Peter S. Feibleman, *American Cooking: Creole and Acadian* (New York: Time-Life Books, 1971), pp. 32–34; Leon Soniat, Jr., *La Bouche Creole* (Gretna, LA: Pelican, 2006), pp. 18–19; and Paul Prudhomme, *Chef Prudhomme's Louisiana Kitchen* (New York: William Morrow, 1984), pp. 26–29.

tournée, a favorite of Bonnefons, who liked to pair it with noble fish such as turbot, brill, trout, salmon, and sturgeon. It was made by combining blonde roux with fish bouillon. After much stirring and simmering, it was enriched just before serving with egg yolks, cream, and extra butter to make a deluxe, ivory-colored cloak for fine seafood.[42] These ingredients and techniques anticipate those used in the *sauce allemande* described by Antonin Carême and Georges Escoffier in the nineteenth century, one of the principal variants of the class of *velouté sauces*.[43] (Sometime between the Franco-Prussian War of 1870–1871 and World War I, *sauce allemande* was rechristened *sauce parisienne*, by which name it still appears.) Thus *sauce tournée* counts as the progenitor of that vast class of roux-thickened sauces (*béchamel, Mornay, suprème, espagnole, Bordelaise, Madeira, Perigueux*, to mention a few) without which classic French cooking would be unthinkable.

EMULSIFIED SAUCES

The Parisian kitchen of the 1650s was also the nursery (if not the birthplace) of the other major branch of classic French sauces, those thickened by emulsification. Emulsified sauces achieve their texture through the suspension of tiny droplets of one liquid in another with which it cannot freely mix, for example, oil in water. As anyone who has ever made a vinaigrette salad dressing knows, such combinations have a natural tendency to separate, with the oil and water coalescing into pools. Emulsifying agents – including some of the proteins, salts, and derivatives of fatty acids present in milk solids and egg yolks – stabilize suspension of the droplets by bonding with both the water and oil molecules, creating a slightly viscous texture. This is why beating an egg into vinaigrette – as in a Caesar salad – turns it into a single creamy mass. Cream, which is nothing more than a naturally occurring emulsion of butterfat in water, can be made into a sauce thick enough to coat principal ingredients by simply reducing it over heat. Thanks to the emulsifying properties of the milk solids it contains, butter can transform a spoonful of acidic liquid such as white wine or lemon juice into a creamy *beurre blanc*, and, when beaten into the reduced cooking juices of a roast, it forms a glossy, lightly thickened *jus*, the luscious French alternative to

---

[42]   Bonnefons, *Les Délices de la campagne*, pp. 337, 347–352, and 357.
[43]   Compare Bonnefons's description of *sauce tournée* with the recipe for *sauce allemande maigre* in Jennifer Harvey Lang, editor, *Larousse Gastronomique* (New York: Crown, 1988), p. 11.

Anglo-American gravy.[44] Modern hollandaise sauce, béarnaise sauce, and their numerous variants – all descendents of La Varenne's *sauce blanche* – achieve their denser but silky texture from the formidable emulsifying power of the egg yolks (thanks to the presence of phospholipids, a family of emulsifying agents to which lecithin belongs, a single large egg yolk can bind up to four ounces of butter in a warm hollandaise-type sauce and much higher amounts of oil in cold sauces such as mayonnaise).[45]

Of all the emulsified sauces, those using cream are the easiest to execute successfully: one simply boils the cream over moderate heat until the liquid is sufficiently evaporated. Perhaps for this reason, cream sauces were favorites of Bonnefons and appeared frequently in *Les Délices de la campagne*. His recipe for *petits pois à la française* (described previously) outlined his method. Tender young peas were simmered in a casserole with butter, salt, chives, and a little parsley until they were almost done. Then the cream was added and the liquids reduced as the peas finished cooking, yielding a lightly thickened sauce.[46] This technique was adapted to many other vegetables, including carrots, *mousserons* and other mushrooms, cauliflower, lettuce, artichokes, asparagus, and fava beans. The seasonings in these creamed dishes varied to suit the principal ingredient – savory was recommended in the fricassee of fava beans, for instance – but they were always subtle, consisting of a few herbs, salt, and pepper, and occasionally a drop of lemon juice or vinegar to cut the richness. In the case of Spanish salsify, Bonnefons suggested adding an egg yolk to the reduced cream (presumably over very low heat to avoid coagulation), which would have resulted in a thicker consistency, silkier texture, and even richer taste. This was deluxe treatment for the vegetable he called "the most excellent of roots."[47] Similar cream sauces – usually without the enriching egg yolk – also appeared in La Varenne's work.[48]

Butter sauces were somewhat more difficult to make than those emulsified with cream, but nevertheless they played a prominent role in the

---

[44]   See Harold McGee's excellent discussion of the chemistry of emulsified sauces in *The Curious Cook: More Kitchen Science and Lore* (New York: Hungry Minds, 1990), pp. 90–93 and 100–104.

[45]   Ibid., pp. 107 and 118–121.

[46]   Bonnefons, *Les Délices de la campagne*, p. 147.

[47]   Ibid., p. 104. Egg yolks have a greater emulsifying power and thus are capable of forming denser sauces than either cream or butter because they contain higher concentrations of proteins and fatty acids such as lecithin, cholesterol, monoglycerides, and diglycerides; McGee, *The Curious Cook*, p. 91.

[48]   For examples see La Varenne, *Le Cuisinier françois*, 2001, pp. 118, 120, 233, 238, and 239.

cooking of Bonnefons and La Varenne. Both writers were especially fond of using butter sauces in recipes for fish and seafood, a culinary category that was changing almost as fast as vegetable cookery. After centuries of being associated with days of abstinence, fish had started to appear side-by-side with meat dishes on festive occasions. In the description of an eight-course dinner party for thirty people with which Bonnefons concluded *Les Délices de la campagne*, fish dishes composed the entire fifth course and were served following two different courses of roasted meats; *potages* and ragouts of seafood may well have composed part of the offerings for the earlier courses of the meal, too.[49] Whereas medieval seafood dishes usually called for lean versions of the same sauces served with meat, the fish cookery of La Varenne and Bonnefons featured buttery sauces that eschewed strong seasonings and aimed to let the character of the principal ingredient shine through.

For example, of the eighty-seven recipes for fish or seafood entrées given by La Varenne, only a handful called for sauces that were sweet or pungent updates of medieval classics (for example, lamprey with *sauce douce*, chub with *sauce Robert*, carp or eel with green sauce, and dried, salted, or smoked fish such as herrings or pilchards with mustard). Another category of recipes used bread crumb liaisons of the sort that had been popular for centuries but omitted the spices that traditionally went with them and added butter instead, producing a texture that was both slightly sandy *and* creamy at the same time. However, much the largest group of recipes, almost half of the total, called for butter glazes or mildly flavored sauces thickened with egg yolks or a butter liaison.[50]

La Varenne's butter sauces fell into two categories. The first combined melted butter with flavorings to create a thin glaze for the principal ingredient. The simplest of these, specified in the recipe for poached salt cod *"de terre neuve,"* was nothing more than fresh, sweet butter combined with parsley and spread over the warm poached fish – a dish almost naïve in its

49 Bonnefons, *Les Délices de la campagne*, pp. 374–377.
50 Some of the recipes in this chapter called for no sauce of any kind (fish pies and tourtes, for example), whereas others used just a few drops of citrus juice or vinegar (typically fried or grilled fish). A small number of recipes simply directed the cook to use whatever sauce he thought best, whereas another group specified sauces made of the cooking juices, but left the choice of liaison up to the chef. It is interesting to note that the chapter on entrées appropriate for fast days outside of Lent was rounded out by two recipes for frogs and four for *macreuse* (barnacle goose), bringing the total number of recipes in this section to ninety-three. Geese and frogs had been classified as seafood by the Catholic Church and therefore could be served on menus that were, technically, meatless. La Varenne, *Le Cuisinier françois*, 2001, pp. 177–209.

conception. The 1653 English translation dubbed this recipe "green fish" after the parsley garnish, as there was not much else to the preparation.[51] However, the majority of cases in which La Varenne used thin butter glazes called for a *sauce rousse*. To make it, one heated butter in a pan until the milk solids toasted to a deep russet brown (the color gave the sauce its name). This step could be tricky to execute, thanks to the low burning temperature of butter. A dash of verjuice or vinegar was added to the browned butter, and the sauce was finished with chopped parsley and, in some cases, capers. In other words, La Varenne's *sauce rousse* was a version of the *beurre noir* or black butter that is still commonly served with skate in bistros all over France. Interestingly, skate is one of the fish La Varenne paired with *sauce rousse*, and he also used it in recipes for fresh herring and cod, sardines, salmon, and marinated tuna.[52] Bonnefons also thought that *sauce rousse* provided the best possible finish for skate. His recipe was similar to La Varenne's.[53]

The second type of butter sauce described by La Varenne used the same ingredients as *sauce rousse* – butter, acidic liquid, and herbs – to a very different effect. Whereas *sauce rousse* was a thin glaze, these sauces were creamy, although they contained no cream, only butter and a reduction of the wine or court bouillon in which the fish was previously poached. La Varenne described them as "strongly reduced and well thickened" (*fort courte et bien liée*).[54] Although he did not give an explanation of the technique he used to achieve these results, it is obvious that he is describing an emulsified butter sauce similar in its composition and chemistry to a modern *beurre blanc*, which is made by beating up to half a pound of cold butter into a tablespoon or two of concentrated wine, vinegar, court bouillon, or lemon juice (an acidic pH helps to prevent the curdling of egg and milk proteins and balances the richness of the sauce).[55] Conventional opinion

---

[51] Ibid., p. 199; and La Varenne, *The French Cook*, pp. 156–157.

[52] La Varenne, *Le Cuisinier françois*, 2001, pp. 197, 198, 200, 202, and 203. Edouard de Pomiane points out that acrolein, a compound that is created by heating butter to a high temperature, neutralizes ammonia, a fact that helps to explain the affinity for *beurre noir* with skate, a tough fish that is traditionally aged for a day or two before being eaten. *Cooking with Pomiane*, introduction by Elizabeth David (New York: Modern Library, 2001), pp. 74–75.

[53] Bonnefons, *Les Délices de la campagne*, p. 356. For delicate freshwater fish, such as perch, he recommended a glaze made by melting butter on the *réchaud* without browning it and seasoning it with drops of verjuice and a little nutmeg; see pp. 335–336.

[54] La Varenne, *Le Cuisinier françois*, 2001, p. 178; see also the similar recipes for other fish on pp. 233, 236–237, and 272.

[55] McGee, *On Food and Cooking*, pp. 355–361, and *The Curious Cook*, pp. 89–94.

holds that *beurre blanc* originated in the Loire valley (the towns of Nantes and Anjou both claim to be its birthplace), and that it arrived in Paris with migrants from this region around the turn of the twentieth century, so it is interesting to note that the basic technique of making such a sauce was already established in Parisian practice at a much earlier date.[56] The proteins and fatty acids present in the milk solids coat the globules of butterfat, suspending them in the water and creating a dense, creamy mass that is quite stable as long as it is kept warm.[57] La Varenne understood the necessity of keeping the sauce within a rather narrow temperature range. In his recipe for monkfish ragout, he cautioned the reader to keep the contents of the pan well below the simmer, thus preventing "your sauce from turning, that is, becoming oil."[58] He also pointed out that such sauces could not be reheated successfully and therefore needed to be made just before serving.[59] Despite these limitations, La Varenne used this type of sauce frequently as a subtle foil for pike, chub, barbel (a cousin of the North American catfish), and other freshwater fish, as well as for several species of delicate saltwater fish, including sole, dab, and plaice, and even for a ragout of oysters.

Bonnefons added a third kind of butter sauce – the buttered deglazing sauce – that was thinner than *beurre blanc* but thicker than a simple glaze. Pans in which foods were sautéed or the *lechefritte* (the pan that caught the drippings from meats roasted on the spit) were deglazed with bouillon, wine, or other liquid; the resulting juices were reduced over high heat, and then a piece of butter was swirled in, forming a light emulsion. This technique resulted in a glossy, thin-textured sauce dominated by the taste of its principal ingredient. Bonnefons used such deglazing sauces sparingly, recommending them in a recipe for roasted capon, in which the drippings were dissolved in the juice of two oranges and flavored with garlic, and in another for baby lamb, which called for water, drops of orange or lemon

[56] See the historical notes and the recipes in *Larousse Gastronomique*, p. 95; Richard Olney, *Simple French Food*, new introduction by Patricia Wells, foreword by James Beard (New York: Collier, 1992), pp. 119–122; and McGee, *The Curious Cook*, pp. 93–94.

[57] McGee, *The Curious Cook*, pp. 96–97. Butyrophilin, the major component of the protein membrane surrounding the fat globules in milk, begins to lose its normal shape and properties at 136 degrees, which explains why butter sauces heated to higher temperatures begin to separate. Below 85 degrees or so, the fat globules crystallize, producing a coarse, grainy texture; if reheated, the sauce would separate into pools of oil and water. If La Varenne's sauce had been thickened with roux, none of these problems would have been a concern.

[58] La Varenne, *Le Cuisinier françois*, 2001, pp. 182–183.

[59] Ibid., p. 188.

juice, salt, and an optional scallion.[60] The deglazed meat juices, further magnified by the butter liaison, underlined the flavor of the principal ingredient, making this type of sauce more robust than other emulsified sauces. In the following century, deglazing sauces emulsified with butter would become regular partners for roasted meats; however, in the 1650s, they represented the avant-garde edge of Bonnefons's aesthetic preference for preparations that highlighted the distinctive character of his raw materials.[61]

Sauces thickened with egg yolks are less common than butter or cream sauces in *Les Délices de la campagne* and *Le Cuisinier françois*. Bonnefons used yolks to enrich the cream sauces he served with certain vegetables, as we have seen in the case of Spanish salsify. However, he also used egg yolks as the principal liaison for sauces accompanying delicate ingredients poached *en casserole* and for fricassees of poultry, veal, turtle, snails, frog legs, tench, and other freshwater fish. All of these recipes followed the method initially described in the recipe for casserole-poached chicken discussed previously. Indeed, Bonnefons sometimes referred to this kind of sauce as a "*sauce des poulets*," even when specifying its use with other types of poultry, meat, or seafood. The principal ingredient, sometimes previously browned and sometimes not, was moistened with bouillon, wine, or a combination of both; seasoned; and allowed to simmer until it was tender. Shortly before serving, one or two egg yolks were beaten first with a little verjuice and then into the cooking liquids in the casserole, which would have reduced slightly and become infused with rich flavor. As the contents of the pan warmed over low heat, the yolks would thicken, creating a light cloak for the meat or seafood. Bonnefons recommended cream as an optional enrichment for such fricassees.[62] Similar techniques are still used today in such classic dishes as *blanquette de veau*, a delicate veal stew bound with egg yolks and cream, and innumerable versions of chicken fricassee. Liaisons of egg yolks beaten with verjuice were also popular with La Varenne.

However, La Varenne also developed – or at least published – a recipe for a thicker emulsified sauce – *la sauce blanche* – that combined egg yolks with acidic liquid and large quantities of butter. Among the vegetable recipes, it appears with deluxe ingredients such as asparagus, cauliflower, and artichoke hearts. Interestingly, in the chapter on seafood entrées, it is paired

---

60 Bonnefons, *Les Délices de la campagne*, pp. 229 and 290–293.

61 The growing interest in deglazing sauces as accompaniments to roasts is already visible in the 1670s in the work of L. S. R., the author who was so sharply critical of La Varenne's use of traditional spicy-sweet sauces.

62 Bonnefons, *Les Délices de la campagne*, pp. 225–227 (casserole-poached chicken and chicken fricassee); 265–266 (fricassee of veal); 341 (tench fricassee); and 342–346 (fricassees of turtle, snails, and frog legs).

not only with lobster, langoustines, and elaborate pâtés of eel and frog legs, but also with more ordinary ingredients, including sardines, cuttlefish, cod tripe, and barbel. The details of how to season *sauce blanche* varied from one principal ingredient to another. For example, for pike La Varenne specified chives, nutmeg, citrus peel, and an optional anchovy in a base consisting of a little of the acidic court bouillon in which the fish was poached (the court bouillon would have contained vinegar). Perch, however, needed a little more acidity, so he called for extra vinegar in addition to court bouillon made with white wine.[63]

The recipe for barbel is especially instructive, because it is a rare case in which La Varenne spelled out the details of his technique as well as the quantities needed to produce the desired results. Half a pound of butter and a dash of vinegar or an equivalent amount of court bouillon (in this case, a mixture of white wine simmered with a little butter, salt, pepper, scallions, parsley, and the capers used for poaching the fish) were combined in a saucepan and gently warmed. As the butter started to melt, one or two egg yolks, depending on their size, were beaten into the butter-vinegar mixture until a liaison was formed, taking care that the sauce did not separate.[64] This proportion of butter to egg yolks is similar to the one used in Escoffier's classic recipe for hollandaise sauce.[65] Although the technique by which La Varenne combined these ingredients was different from the one generally recommended today, the chemistry of emulsification is such that La Varenne's instructions do result in a properly thickened sauce (see the recipe for *sauce blanche* in the Appendix). Indeed, because the yolks are warmed gradually in the relatively large volume of liquid formed by the acid base and the melting butter, the chances of curdling are probably slightly less with La Varenne's technique than with the method that has since become conventional.[66]

---

[63]   La Varenne, *Le Cuisinier françois*, 2001, pp. 225–227.

[64]   Ibid., pp. 187–188.

[65]   Auguste Escoffier, *The Escoffier Cookbook: A Guide to the Fine Art of French Cuisine* (New York: Crown, 1969), pp. 22–23.

[66]   McGee points out the advantage of this technique in his instructions for what he calls "the ultimate simplification of your favorite hollandaise or béarnaise recipe. Throw all the ingredients into a saucepan (doing the reduction of the vinegar beforehand, if that's called for), turn on the heat, and start beating. Stop when the sauce reaches its desired consistency." See *The Curious Cook*, pp. 107–108. See also the interesting recipe in Child, Bertholle, and Beck, *Mastering the Art of French Cooking*, vol. 1, pp. 256–257 for *poulet sauté aux herbes de Provence*, which approximates La Varenne's method for *sauce blanche*: egg yolks, lemon juice, reduced white wine, and softened butter are beaten together over low heat until the mixture achieves a thick, creamy texture "like a hollandaise."

CUISINE "AU NATUREL"

Sauces thickened with roux or emulsified with egg yolk, butter, or cream (or all three) were fundamental to the emergence of the delicate style of cooking, and they mark the continuity of French cuisine from the 1650s down to the present day. La Varenne and, to a lesser extent, Bonnefons have been rightly celebrated as early practitioners of the *saucière's* art. Because of the attention received by ancestral forms of sauces that have since become classics, it is important to stress that the most radically modern recipes in *Le Cuisinier françois* and *Les Délices de la campagne* did not include any sauce other than natural cooking juices, let alone the elaborate stuffings, decorations, or architectural embellishments that subsequently became identified with the *haute cuisine*. Fine ingredients cooked and presented "au naturel" were the ultimate fulfillment of the idea that food should taste of what it was, and that the variety of the menu should spring from nature rather than the overheated imagination of the cook.

One of the pieces of advice Bonnefons repeated over and over again for the benefit of his readers was to learn restraint, to check the impulse to add extra elements to a recipe that ultimately detracted from the character of the principal ingredient. An example is his discussion of roast goose. Many people liked to stuff them with forcemeats of veal, chestnuts, capers, anchovies, or even a confit of oysters – a mistake in Bonnefons's opinion. If one wanted stuffing, it should be cooked separately in a terrine, and the goose's cavity should be seasoned with nothing but chives or an onion stuck with cloves, sage, salt, and pepper. Anything else detracted from the flavor of the goose, which was so delicious in itself. "Each food in its natural taste is always more agreeable" (*chaque viande dans son goût naturel est toujours plus agreeable*), he wrote.[67] Similar sentiments were repeated throughout the book with regard to other items of poultry (spring chickens, capons, ducks); tender slices of top-quality veal; joints of beef (which Bonnefons thought should be served rare, so that the pink juices formed all the sauce that was needed); and even butter (which should never be salted, except in cases of emergency).[68] The vegetable section included a recipe for the youngest, sweetest garden peas that was startling in its simplicity. To make *petits pois à l'anglaise*, one put quickly blanched, drained peas in a tureen with a sprinkle of salt and a piece of butter, put the cover on the dish, and shook it, cloaking each pea in a little melting butter.[69] Less was more.

---

[67] Bonnefons, *Les Délices de la campagne*, pp. 237–238.
[68] Ibid., pp. 189, 218–219, 272–273, and 286–287.
[69] Ibid., p. 153. Why Bonnefons named this recipe after the English remains a mystery. Elite English cooking at this date was still thoroughly medieval, full of spice,

Similar ideas were advocated by La Varenne. A surprisingly large proportion of his roasts and entrées of meat and fish were meant to be served dry (*sec*) without any sauce other than a few drops of bitter orange juice or the court bouillon or pan juices in which it cooked. Pheasant, quail, partridge, turkey, capon, pigeons, lamb, teal, rabbit, pork, and suckling pig were among the roasts he singled out for the minimalist treatment.[70] When working with fish and seafood, it was often the best specimens that were prepared with the greatest simplicity. The finest oysters were served raw on the half shell, whereas those that were not so fresh were roasted in their shells with butter, bread crumbs, and a little nutmeg. Barbel could be prepared in many attractive ways – stewed, roasted, poached, or served with deluxe *sauce blanche* – but, according to La Varenne, the smallest (and therefore the sweetest ones with the finest flesh) should be served with only their natural cooking juices, which were "all the seasoning [*ragoust*] that they required."[71]

The decision to serve foods without accompanying sauces made technique and timing especially important, because it would be impossible to compensate for any loss of juiciness and flavor caused by careless cooking. For example, when preparing suckling pig au naturel, the cook had to be prepared to baste the roast frequently or to take the additional step of rubbing it at the beginning with good olive oil, which resulted in a brown but soft skin.[72] La Varenne frequently warned about the dangers of ruining ingredients by overcooking them. This was a particular danger when preparing seafood, and he repeatedly reminded his readers that the fish should always be removed from the heat before the flesh separated from the bone. One of the little tricks he recommended was to sort fish to be cooked whole, such as trout, into batches by size – a step that would have made it easier to judge the cooking times. Poached in carefully made court bouillon until they were just done and full of their own juices, the trout could be presented very simply – garnished with parsley and wrapped in a napkin.[73]

This preference for simple presentations is noteworthy, especially in comparison with the elaborately decorated confections preferred by medieval and Renaissance cooks. La Varenne proposed roasts of lamb adorned

---

sweetness, and complexity. Perhaps the secret lay in the liberal use of butter, which the English preferred to olive oil for virtually all culinary applications.

[70] La Varenne, *Le Cuisinier françois*, 2001, pp. 67–84.

[71] Ibid., p. 187.

[72] Ibid., p. 75.

[73] La Varenne, *The French Cook*, p. 160.

only with a crust of bread crumbs and parsley and entrées of asparagus napped with an ivory sauce. When a festive occasion called for decorations he, like Bonnefons, often resorted to the garden, as in the recipe for wild goose garlanded with flowers "according to the season and commodity."[74] This was food that not only tasted, but also looked, like what it was.

[74]   Ibid., p. 78.

CHAPTER 5

Refined Consumption, 1660–1735

DELICATE COOKING BECOMES FRENCH

The second half of the seventeenth century saw something of a publishing boom in French cookbooks as writers and publishers saw opportunities to profit from the interest of readers eager to learn about ragouts, roux, emulsified sauces, and other elements of the delicate, modern style of cooking. Between 1651 and 1660, *Le Cuisinier françois* was printed in eight French editions, while *Les Délices de la campagne* was republished, augmented, and corrected by the author, in a second edition that appeared two years after the first. Stimulated by the success of these works, other authors jumped into the field. Ten new titles appeared by 1674, seven of which were general works that addressed all aspects of cooking (the other three, sometimes ascribed to La Varenne, were devoted to pastry, confectionary, and preserves).[1] The fact that one of these, *L'Ecole des ragousts*, was published in Lyon by the firm of Conier et Fleury shows that culinary innovations from Paris were beginning to penetrate the provinces. It was also in the 1660s that Lyonnais printers began to bring out editions of *Le Cuisinier françois* in cheaper formats that were meant to appeal to audiences of modest

---

[1] These were: *Le Patissier françois* (Paris: Jean Gaillard, 1653); Pierre de Lune, *La Cuisinier* (Paris: Pierre David, 1656); *La Maistre d'hostel* (Paris: Pierre David, 1659); *Le Confiturier françois* (Paris: Jean Gaillard, 1660); *Le Cuisinier méthodique* (Paris: Jean Gaillard, 1660); *L'Ecole parfaite des officiers de bouche* (Paris: Jean Ribou, 1662); Pierre de Lune, *Le Nouveau et Parfait Maistre d'hostel* (Paris: Charles de Sercy, 1662); [La Varenne], *Le Parfaict Confiturier* (Paris: Jean Ribou, 1667); *L'Ecole des ragousts* (Lyon: Jacques Conier e Martin Fleury, 1668); and L. S. R., *L'Art de bien traiter* (Paris: Jean Du Puis, 1674). See Hyman and Hyman, "Printing the Kitchen," p. 401. *L'Ecole des ragousts*, published in the provinces, was in fact a compilation of extracts from *Le Patissier françois*, *Le Cuisinier méthodique*, and *Le Confiturier françois*, all of which were originally printed by the Parisian firm of Jean Gaillard. See the editors' introduction to the 1981 edition of La Varenne, *Le Cuisinier françois*, pp. 54–55.

means – another sign of the diffusion of the new cuisine beyond the Parisian elite.[2] After 1674, the rate at which new titles appeared declined: a single new title, an anonymous *Traité de confiture*, appeared in the fifteen years down to 1689. However, the following decade brought two works of encyclopedic scope by François Massialot, *Le Cuisinier roïal et bourgeois* (1691) and *Nouvelle instruction pour les confitures* (1692). Both of these volumes went through many editions, regularly updated by the author, and dominated the French market through the 1730s.[3] By this time, delicate cooking that strove to capture *le goût naturel*, which was still something of a novelty in the days of La Varenne and Bonnefons, had become the foundation of a cuisine already recognized by contemporaries at home and abroad as characteristically French.

Although some of these new books were more innovative than others, all of them confirmed the break with culinary tradition that we have already observed in *Le Cuisinier françois* and *Les Délices de la campagne*. The number of dishes with obvious medieval pedigrees declined. By the 1690s, Massialot included only two such recipes (for *potage d'hypocras* and *gallimafrée de mouton*) in the six hundred pages of *Le Cuisinier roïal et bourgeois*. The proportion of recipes that called for spices other than pepper continued to drop. Cardamom, coriander, anise, cumin, and saffron virtually disappeared from the repertoire. Cinnamon became associated with sweets and pastry, ginger with charcuterie. Only nutmeg and cloves continued to turn up regularly in recipes for savory foods. Both appeared as seasonings for pâtés, whereas nutmeg also became associated with cream sauces and cloves became a common ingredient in bouillon and other braising liquids.[4]

As medieval elements continued to retreat, ingredients and techniques associated with the delicate style advanced. Bread crumb liaisons, which were still common in the early 1650s, had become rare forty years later, while ragouts, fricassees, and sauces thickened with egg yolks, butter, cream, or roux continued to proliferate. As suggested by the title of the omnibus volume *L'Ecole des ragousts*, sophisticated eaters increasingly judged the quality of a meal less on the quantity of roasted meat offered and more on the variety and finesse of the sauced dishes presented with them. These included a wide variety of vegetables, frequently fricasseed in cream, in the manner of Bonnefons, or served with *sauce blanche* or *beurre blanc* or *beurre noir* made according to recipes similar to those published by La

---

2   Ibid., p. 55.
3   Hyman and Hyman, "Printing the Kitchen," p. 401.
4   Flandrin, "Dietary Choices and Culinary technique, 1500–1800" in Flandrin and Montanari, eds., *Food*, pp. 408–409.

Varenne.[5] The interest in dishes cooked au naturel also continued. One welcome addition was a recipe published by L. S. R. for crawfish boiled in water seasoned with onion, fines herbes, salt, verjuice, and vinegar and served in a rosy pyramid decorated with parsley and flowers.[6]

During this period, it became common for French travelers in other parts of Europe to express surprise – and disdain – when they encountered flavors in the local cooking that were legacies from the medieval kitchen. From Spain to Poland, Venice to Brussels, foods that were highly seasoned, sugared, or served with spicy, acidic sauces were denounced as inedible and indigestible by Frenchmen and women hungry for subtle ragouts and butter sauces. For example, the marquis de Coulanges, who visited Germany in 1657, wrote home about the German predilection for what he considered to be weird combinations of meat with fruit and spices (such as chicken with cloves and gosling stuffed with prunes and apples).[7] Gaspard d'Hauteville, who lived in Poland for a while in the 1650s and 1660s, remarked on the exotic character of the food, which was full of saffron, sugar, pepper, cinnamon, nutmeg, olives, capers, and raisins.[8] Interestingly, chicken spiced with saffron was sometimes described in French cooking literature as prepared "in the Polish style."[9] On a trip to Flanders Jouvin de Rochefort expressed "astonishment and annoyance" at being served sugared salad, a dish he also encountered in Ireland. And in Spain in 1691 the Countess d'Aulnoy found the meals she was offered in Madrid and Toledo either disgusting ("meats reeking of perfume") or inedible ("full of saffron, garlic, onion, peppers, and spices"). Even the Italians, whose profuse use of vegetables anticipated seventeenth-century French practice, retained a fondness for spices and sweet-sour tastes that made their cooking seem odd in comparison to the delicate style. Provencal cooking was also seriously out of step with Parisian trends. As early as 1630 a northern visitor wrote, "Food is prepared in the Italian style, with abundant spices and extravagant, strongly flavored sauces, and, as in Italy, [they also make] numerous

---

5   Except for Jerusalem artichokes, which seem to have fallen out of favor, and radishes, increasingly served raw, as they still are today, all the vegetables for which Bonnefons and La Varenne gave recipes are represented in the cookery literature of the later seventeenth century. A new addition (in Massialot's work of 1691) was bulb fennel (Bonnefons used fennel leaves and stalks as herbal seasonings for other ingredients, but recorded no recipes for the plant as a vegetable).

6   L. S. R., *L'Art de bien traiter* in *L'Art de la cuisine française au XVIIe siècle*, p. 165.

7   Flandrin, "Dietary Choices and Culinary Technique, 1500–1800," pp. 410–411.

8   Ibid.

9   La Chapelle, *The Modern Cook*, vol. 1, p. 302.

sweet sauces with Corinthian grapes, raisins, prunes, apples, pears, and sugar."[10]

Such witnesses, most of whom never set foot inside a kitchen, appear to have been unaware that the dishes they found so foreign to their own habits and tastes were similar to ones enjoyed by their ancestors in the environs of Paris before *le goût naturel* became the touchstone of culinary excellence. The same cannot be said of L. S. R., the anonymous author of *L'Art de bien traiter* (1674), who was eager to purge French cooking of the last vestiges of the old medieval style. He went so far as to criticize some of the recipes published by La Varenne that mingled savory and sweet tastes or combined modern elements, such as silky roux-based sauces, with spicy flavorings. Dishes such as La Varenne's frog legs with saffron or his turkey with raspberries had no place in the modern French kitchen, L. S. R. wrote, and "would be more willingly tolerated among the Arabs ... than in a refined atmosphere such as ours, where propriety, delicacy, and good taste [reign]."[11]

COOKING FOR *LA COUR ET LA VILLE*

Innovative cooking in the second half of the seventeenth century continued to be intimately linked to the dinner party. The trend toward streamlined menus, already apparent in the 1650s, accelerated as the calendar moved toward 1700. L. S. R. condemned the "prodigious abundance" of the previous generation and recommended a maximum of five dishes in each of four courses to serve twelve people, a mere twenty dishes for the entire menu (as opposed to a total of thirty-two recommended by Bonnefons for a group of the same size).[12] L. S. R. pointed out that reduction of the menu allowed one to focus on ingredients that were at their seasonal peak even at times of the year when the selection was rather limited and helped cooks to create an ensemble of dishes that complimented each other while still offering sufficient choice to the guests.[13] By the 1690s, Massialot and Nicolas Audiger (who wrote an important guide for maîtres d'hôtel in addition to winning lasting fame as the man who introduced out-of-season sweet peas to the

---

[10]   Flandrin, "Dietary Choices and Culinary Technique, 1500–1800," pp. 410–411. See also the account of Philippe Gillet, *Par mets et par vins: Voyages et gastronomie en Europe 16e-18e siècles* (Paris: Payot, 1985), pp. 159–167.

[11]   L. S. R., *L'Art de bien traiter*, p. 23. See also the discussion of L. S. R.'s criticisms of La Varenne in Wheaton, *Savoring the Past*, pp. 150–151.

[12]   Ibid., pp. 39–40.

[13]   Ibid.

court of Louis XIV) were recommending even smaller menus to be served in a meal of only two courses, *potage* and roast. For example, a representative menu for twelve by Massialot called for nine recipes per course – a principal dish (*plat*) of soup or roast plus four medium-sized side dishes (now called "entrées") and four small side dishes (known as "hors d'oeuvres," thanks to their placement "outside" the arrangement of the *plat* and entrées that filled the center of the table). The same recipe, such as Massialot's *pigeons au basilic*, could serve as either an entrée or an hors d'oeuvre, depending on the amount served and the arrangement on the tabletop.[14] The menus recommended by Audiger were smaller still – only seven dishes per course (a soup or a roast each accompanied by four entrées and two hors d'oeuvres) for a dinner for twelve people and only three dishes (soup or roast plus two entrées) for dinner for six.[15] Thus, Massialot's two-course menu for twelve called for a total of eighteen dishes, whereas Audiger's menu required only fourteen.

Even as the intimacy of the dinner party pushed cooks to seek perfection in the details of each dish, the need of high society to provide an elegant but informal format for entertaining large numbers of people encouraged the development of another kind of meal, the *ambigu* or *collation* (at a *collation*, all the food was cold, whereas an *ambigu* might include hot dishes, too).[16] Served late in the day, between the usual hours for dinner and supper, the *ambigu* involved the simultaneous presentation of all the courses, including the dessert. Although an *ambigu* could be served to guests seated at the table, in the style of a dinner party, it was typically presented as a buffet. The guests nibbled at whatever pleased them from the array of savory and sweet offerings, which were often presented in bite-sized portions. The buffet tables could be set up in the main salon of the house, on a terrace,

---

14 Massialot, *Le Cuisinier roïal et bourgeois*, pp. 12 and 367. Flandrin, *L'Ordre des mets*, pp. 120–122, claims that the term "hors d'oeuvre" came into use with the first edition of Massialot in 1691. Prior to the nineteenth century, the term routinely meant a side dish served on a small plate (an *"assiette"*). Only in the 1800s did "hors d'oeuvre" come to refer to appetizers served prior to the main body of the meal for the purpose of whetting the appetite; see Wheaton, *Savoring the Past*, p. 139.

15 Audiger, *La Maison reglée*, p. 466. Perhaps sensing that the menu for six might look a little Spartan to some readers, he added that one could serve salads with the roast in addition to the two entrées for a more bountiful spread.

16 L. S. R., *L'Art de bien traiter*, pp. 170–181 and 205–216, as well as the remarks by Laurendon and Laurendon, eds., *L'Art de la cuisine française au xviie siècle*, pp. 569–570. The *collation*, or cold repast, seems to have originated as a festive meal served out of doors as part of celebrations that might incorporate other activities such as masquerades and dancing. Such fêtes were popular at the Valois court in the era of Catherine de' Medici.

in the garden, or even, as L. S. R. pointed out, in a grotto surrounded by fountains. Thus the service of the meal could be integrated into musical performances, dance, or other entertainments without resorting to the rigid hierarchy associated with the traditional banquet form and the performance space in the center of the horseshoe-shaped table.

Whereas decorations were kept to a minimum on dinner tables (for want of space), buffet tables invited fancy displays of candelabra and plates, sugar sculptures, porcelain figurines, flowers, and pyramids of fruit reaching several feet in height. La Quintinie lamented the popularity of the latter. The demand for fruit that looked pretty and stacked well without oozing juice on the tablecloth pushed gardeners to devote lots of space to varieties that had dry, woody flesh, thus privileging appearance over flavor. The fruit was often picked when it was still green, for better durability.[17] It was possible to make pyramids with fruits ripe enough to eat, including small items such as cherries, by stacking these in a series of tiered metal or porcelain dishes that supported the weight of the arrangement. But these creations tended to be unstable and liable to collapse during the festivities. To avoid mishaps, the cooking literature of the day advised gluing the fruit together with caramel syrup or freezing it with water in a cone-shaped metal mold, methods that removed any question of actually serving it as part of the meal.[18] How much better it would be, La Quintinie wrote in his posthumous book, "to send out a pretty basket filled with the choice eating fruits of the season, all fair and goodly, and all perfectly ripe."[19] He observed that such fruit was always consumed with great enjoyment, while the pyramid, the product of much labor and expense, was left untouched, a sad memorial to the triumph of ostentation over good taste.

The *ambigu* provided a festive and informal format for feeding large numbers of people at receptions in private houses. However, the *ambigu's* affinity for outdoor settings, fanciful decorations, and musical entertainments also made this sort of menu ideal for the fêtes for which Versailles became famous during the early years of Louis XIV's personal reign. Starting in the early 1660s, Louis transformed the modest hunting lodge dating from his father's reign into a palace set in splendid gardens. For twenty years, until it became the seat of government, Versailles served as the

---

[17] La Quintinie, *Instruction pour les jardins fruitiers et potagers*, pp. 275–276 and 335–336.

[18] For details on the different methods of making fruit pyramids, see François Massialot, *Nouvelle instruction pour les confitures* (Paris: Charles de Sercy, 1962), pp. 247–248, 298–300, and 437.

[19] Quotation follows John Evelyn's contemporary translation of La Quintinie, *The Compleat Gardener*, p. 69.

king's retreat from the pressures of the capital, a country house where he could pursue sports, dancing, masquerades, and love affairs in the company of a few chosen companions. He also used the château and its grounds as the setting for magnificent parties that unfolded over periods of several days and revolved around themes from literature or mythology. For example, in 1664, six hundred guests participated in the fête of the Enchanted Isle, a three-day extravaganza modeled after a story by Ludovico Ariosto. There were parades, costumes, concerts, ballets, masques, and theater pieces by Molière. As evening fell on the first night, a *collation* was served under the light of hundreds of torches and candles that illuminated the splendid scene as bright as day. The food was presented by dozens of waiters costumed as the four seasons, each bearing a basket or platter with foods associated with the appropriate time of the year. Because this was the court, the seating followed the traditional pattern for banquets. The king sat in the center of a huge crescent-shaped table, flanked by his mother, wife, brother, and sister-in-law, with the other members of the party in declining order of precedence (the royal mistress Louise de La Vallière not excepted). For all the gaiety of the occasion, hierarchy still reigned. The marks of social deference embodied in the seating plan would have been legible to contemporaries of François I or Louis XII.

The principle of hierarchy was embodied in a different way in the meals that the king took alone in public – *au grand couvert,* when he dined or supped in one of the grand salons in the presence of the whole court, or *au petit couvert,* which was served in the antechamber of his bedroom with a correspondingly smaller group of onlookers. These forms of service were relatively new in French court practice, having been established by ordinances of Henry III dating from 1575 and 1585. Before ascending the French throne previously occupied by two of his brothers, Henry had briefly served as the elected king of Poland and had traveled to several Italian and central European courts. He was apparently much impressed by the elaborate ceremonies and etiquette he encountered on his travels, which inspired his efforts to institute similar refinements at the Valois court.[20] The ancient conventions of banquet service symbolized the king's standing as the first gentleman of the realm. He was the feudal lord to whom the others had sworn oaths of loyalty, so it was appropriate that he be seated in the position of honor and served with the choicest meat and drink. However, the other diners were gentlemen, too, which was why they were bidden to sit down and eat with the king. The fine gradations of rank that determined the seating pattern connected the lowest knight to the prince himself; all were

---

[20] Jousselin, *Au couvert du roi,* pp. 7–11. See pp. 33–48 for precise descriptions of service *au grand* and *au petit couvert.*

part of a single fellowship. The symbolism of the *grand* and *petit couverts* was quite different. Dining alone while the courtiers watched stressed the gulf that separated the sovereign prince from his subjects, even the grandest of them who were also his blood relations. The *grand* and *petit couverts* were ceremonial expressions of absolutism, rather than feudal notions of mutual fellowship.[21]

Interestingly, Louis XIV appears to have instinctively grasped the significance of dining alone in public, which he did much more consistently than any of his predecessors or successors, despite the obvious inconveniences the ceremony entailed. Among these was the impossibility of eating a hot meal on a cold day. Until the 1730s, when Louis XV built a new kitchen directly below his private apartments, the king's meals were prepared about a quarter of a mile from the rooms where they were usually served. By the 1690s, the *bouche du roi* had acquired a battery of equipment for warming up the king's food, but it is unlikely that this assortment of chafing dishes had enough firepower to get the dishes really hot.[22] Such were the sacrifices that the king made for majesty. Only in his old age did Louis XIV forsake the ritual of dining in public on a regular basis. That he sometimes tweaked the details of the ordinances of Henry III by occasionally inviting his brother or, later, his son to sit at his table *au petit couvert* or by bestowing on a number of duchesses and other court ladies the right to sit on stools instead of standing as they watched him dine just underlined the idea behind the ceremony, namely, that the king's status was exalted above all other men's and was inherent in his person (not in the office of kingship), and that, therefore, his will was all.

Over the years, the role of Versailles in Louis's life changed. After he moved there permanently in the 1680s, ministers of state, ambitious aristocrats, and men who hoped to rise through service in the royal household were compelled to become resident courtiers for at least part of the year. Life at the château, formerly full of *joie de vivre*, hardened into a dull routine structured around an endless round of ceremonies that occupied the entire day, from the king's *levé* in the morning to his *couché* at night. As Louis aged, he became increasingly pious, a development encouraged by Mme. de Maintenon, his straight-laced second wife, and his Jesuit confessor, who stressed that the king – a former adulterer and the father of several illegitimate children – had many sins for which to atone. The mood at court became correspondingly somber, and fêtes became few. The younger

---

21 On other dimensions of nascent absolutism in Valois and early Bourbon court ritual, see the classic account of Ernst Kantorowicz, *The King's Two Bodies* (Princeton, NJ, and New York: Princeton University Press, 1997), reprint edition.

22 Jousselin, *Au couvert du roi*, p. 29.

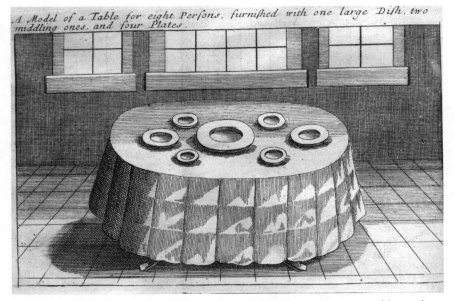

15. How to arrange serving dishes with geometrical precision on a table set for a dinner party of eight as shown in François Massialot, *The Court and Country Cook*, 1702 (courtesy of the University of Chicago Library, Special Collections Research Center).

generation, led by Louis's nephew, Philippe, duke de Chartres (1674–1723, who succeeded his father as the duke d'Orléans and served as regent of France during the minority of Louis XV), came to view Versailles as a kind of gilded prison from which they escaped as frequently as possible. Country houses in the vicinity of Versailles were one refuge. (The king himself retreated with increasing frequency to the small château at Marly, where etiquette and routine were relaxed.) Paris, the home of the salon, the dinner party, and the *ambigu* without a hierarchical seating plan, offered a cosmopolitan alternative.

It was within this circle of grandees who divided their time between Versailles and private houses in Paris and the surrounding countryside that François Massialot (1660–1733) made his reputation. Massialot was a provincial, born in Limoges.[23] When he arrived in Paris and how he learned to cook remain matters of conjecture. Domestic service was the most common type of employment for provincial boys new to the capital, and a long climb from scullion to head chef in a private household would have been the easiest way for a youth to acquire culinary skills. It is also possible

[23]   Michel, *Vatel et la naissance de la gastronomie*, p. 189.

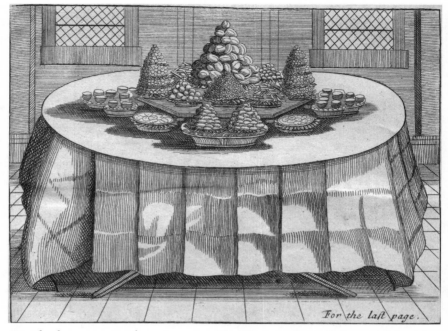

16. The dessert course, featuring pyramids of fruit, as shown in François Massialot, *The Court and Country Cook*, 1702 (courtesy of the University of Chicago Library, Special Collections Research Center).

that Massialot trained as a cook in the kitchens of the royal household or as an apprentice in one of the guilds that controlled the food trades in Paris. Interestingly, the regulations of the *traiteurs'* guild allowed the personnel of the royal kitchens to move laterally into trade in the city without having to serve the normal apprenticeship, and probably there was mobility in the other direction, from capital to court, as well.[24] By the time Massialot published the first edition of *Le Cuisinier roïal et bourgeois*, at the age of thirty or thirty-one, he had left behind whatever masters he once had. No patron is acknowledged anywhere in the book, which lacks the customary letter of dedication to an employer. Whereas La Varenne was proud to identify himself as *écuyer de la cuisine* in the household of the marquis d'Uxelles, Massialot portrayed himself as something altogether different – a chef for hire, a successful culinary entrepreneur.

Whether Massialot operated as a proper, guild-certified *traiteur* or as a freelancer who worked under court protection, by 1690 he was providing the food for dinner and supper parties given by members of the high nobility in Paris and at their estates in the surrounding countryside. *Le Cuisinier roïal*

[24]   Wheaton, *Savoring the Past*, p. 73.

et bourgeois opens with a list of menus for occasions such as a supper given by the marquis de Langlois in honor of the duke de Chartres on March 28, 1690, dinner and supper on Easter Day for the duke d'Orléans (Chartres's father and the king's brother), and, in May, a *grand repas* commissioned by the marquis de Seignelay, the elder son of Colbert, on the occasion of a visit of the dauphin and other members of the court to Seignelay's château at Sceaux. Other clients included the marquis d'Arci, Cardinal d'Estrees, and the duke d'Aumont, who ordered Christmas dinner for forty-two people.[25] Interestingly, the only client mentioned by name who was not an important nobleman was a M. de Livri, who was described as *"premier maître-d'hôtel du roi"*[26] – a professional contact, one wonders, perhaps a former boss? It was an illustrious list of customers and one that vouched to Massialot's readers for the fashionable cachet of his cooking.

As a successful culinary entrepreneur, Massialot faced some special problems. Like a chef in a large private household, he was responsible for training his staff and supervising them so as to produce the results he desired. However, he and his team often cooked in kitchens that were not their own, and they worked in cooperation with the full-time staff of the person who employed them to produce their special menus. For example, Massialot noted that the grand dinner he prepared at Sceaux for the marquis de Seignelay required two days' work on the part of thirty-six people, half of whom were chefs and the other half assistants.[27] Many members of this group would have surely been employed in the household of the marquis. They were not necessarily familiar with all the techniques that Massialot's menu called for, but their labor would have been indispensable to produce the following menu for an unspecified (but obviously very numerous) party of guests: a first course consisting of five different *potages*, four large entrées and twelve medium-sized ones, and thirty-six hors d'oeuvres; a second course of six types of roasts garnished with ten small salads, plus four entrées, twelve entremets, twenty-two hors d'oeuvres, and ten additional salads; the dessert course was extra.[28] Massialot noted that producing this menu required a *batterie de cuisine* consisting of sixty small handheld saucepans, twenty round casseroles (ten large and ten small), twenty marmites (ten large and ten small), and thirty spits. The first day of cooking was devoted to roasting chickens and partridges that would be used the next day in the stuffings (*farces*) required for some of the dishes and to making several kinds of bouillon, to be used on its own and as an ingredient

---

25   Massialot, *Le Cuisinier roïal et bourgeois*, p. 1.
26   Ibid.
27   Ibid., pp. 24–25.
28   Ibid.

in "the *jus de boeuf, jus de veau, petit-jus, coulis* and *essence de jambon* you will make separately to flavor the *potages*, entrées, and entremets."[29] The ragouts alone required a very large quantity of chopped scallion and parsley and many bundles of herbs, too; preparing these would have kept an assistant busy for many hours of the two-day cooking marathon.[30] Even with the convenience of *bouillon, jus*, coulis, *essence*, and *farces* made a day ahead, the cooks must have had to hustle on the day of the meal.

Massialot's account of this menu and the effort it required suggests that by 1690, elite clients expected that the food they ordered for big events would meet the standards of refinement and attention to detail that had hitherto been associated with intimate dinners and supper parties. Achieving impeccable results on a consistent basis would have required excellent planning and organization, impeccable timing, and the ability to communicate clearly with many people, including those previously unfamiliar with Massialot's recipes. It is likely that Massialot's sous-chefs and assistants were organized into groups according to specialized skills (as in a modern restaurant staff), the better to prepare sauces, garnishes, and other elements that would be brought together in the finished dishes.

Massialot's writing shows that he had a keen sense of how to explain techniques to the uninitiated and how to break down recipes into a series of manageable steps – rare talents among the authors of cookbooks and ones that were surely informed by his experiences in the catering trade. He also rethought the art of writing a recipe, employing a precise vocabulary designed to make instructions transparent to the reader. Finally, he greatly expanded the role of basic preparations in French cuisine, turning them into the building blocks of whole families of recipes and greatly extending the creative range of cooks.

Basic preparations are mixtures made in advance that cooks combine with principal ingredients to concoct an infinite array of dishes. La Varenne and Bonnefons discussed a few such preparations: simple bouillons for meat and fast days, pastry dough for pies and pâtés, roux, and a few old-fashioned items such as almond milk and spice mixtures. By the 1690s, however, many new sorts of basic mixtures had come into use – marinades, forcemeats and stuffings, glazes, *restaurants* (bouillons consisting only of rendered meat juices with no water added), herb bundles, and, above all, the whole range of concentrated flavorings known variously as *jus, essence,* or coulis.[31] The credit for inventing these preparations surely belongs to many different

---

29 Ibid.
30 Ibid.
31 Ibid., pp. 209–215 and 284–285.

cooks, many of whom are unknown to history. But Massialot was the first to assemble an extensive catalogue of basic mixtures, to standardize the techniques by which they were made, and to lay down systematic principles for their use. Coupled with the precise culinary vocabulary Massialot was the first to define, basic preparations provided the means by which fine dishes in the delicate style rose to new heights of sophistication and at the same time became easier to reproduce.

CUISINE AS A SYSTEMATIC ART

The book in which Massialot achieved this breakthrough, *Le Cuisinier roïal et bourgeois,* was divided into two sections. The first discussed menus for each month, beginning with an example of one of Massialot's tours de force for a well-known client and continuing with remarks about other dishes that could be made with ingredients that were readily available at that time of year.[32] He argued that because his menus – even the most sumptuous ones – were seasonal and because they used ordinary ingredients that were easy to find in the countryside around Paris, they could be adapted to the means of bourgeois households. Such foods as chickens, pigeons, butcher's meat, local vegetables, fruits, and herbs "can be made into the richest and most succulent of dishes," he wrote.[33] These items do, in fact, dominate the menus for even the most festive of Massialot's meals. The road to gourmandise in his cuisine was not paved with *primeurs* or other rare ingredients, but with careful attention to technique and the details of preparation.

The second part of the book, the cookbook proper, was an early example of a culinary encyclopedia, organized alphabetically from A to Z. There were four types of entries: for ingredients (pigeon or crawfish, for example), for components of the menu (soups, roasts, and so on), for basic preparations that were elements in many recipes (including, among others, coulis, *farce, jus,* liaison, and marinade), and for families of dishes united by similar modes of preparation (such as bisques, fricassees, and ragouts). Readers who wanted to know more about a particular topic or to find recipes that used a particular ingredient or basic mixture could find the information by consulting the surprisingly thorough index at the end of the volume. This organizational scheme made the book practical to use for reference as well as for planning menus and parceling out tasks within the kitchen, factors that

---

[32]   Ibid., pp. 1–85.
[33]   Ibid., preface, n.p.

must have contributed to its enduring popularity over a period of almost half a century.[34]

In the web of cross-references, the articles about basic mixtures and modes of preparation played an especially important role, one that revealed the inner logic of Massialot's approach. Whereas *Le Cuisinier françois* and *Les Délices de la campagne* were conceived as collections of recipes organized according to menu plan or ingredient,[35] *Le Cuisinier roïal et bourgeois* approached cooking as a systematic art that branched out from a handful of key recipes and techniques that together constituted the foundations of the cuisine. Out of these building blocks, it was possible to construct an infinite variety of dishes limited only by the seasonality of ingredients and the well-honed judgment of the chef. Massialot went so far as to say in his preface that his readers were free to borrow the fundamentals from his book, but to employ them differently as means and imagination allowed. This process of improvisation would yield good results, he wrote, as long as "the cook is guided by impeccable cleanliness [*une grande propreté*], good taste [*un bon goût*], and verve [*esprit*]."[36]

The idea that cooking is a systematic art that builds families of dishes on the basis of master recipes and techniques would have a great future in the history of French cuisine – witness the work of Carême and Escoffier in the nineteenth century. Massialot was the first writer to express this view and to embody it in his culinary style. In his hands, it became a tool for creative innovation and also for organizing the practical work of cooking in kitchens large and small. Some examples treating basic mixtures and techniques of preparation will serve to illustrate how this systematic impulse functioned in Massialot's cooking.

French recipes for sauces and ragouts dating from the turn of the eighteenth century made much use of concentrated flavorings known variously as *jus, essence,* or *coulis.* The most elemental of these basic mixtures was *jus,* which consisted of the natural, clear juices extracted from fowl, meat, or fish. Massialot gave three different methods for making *jus* that were appropriate to different ingredients. The first of these, for partridge, was

---

[34]   Regularly updated, it appeared in several editions, the last of which came out in 1734, a year after Massialot's death. Between 1712 and 1730, the book was enlarged from one volume to three and acquired a new title, *Le Nouveau Cuisinier royal et bourgeois.* See Hyman and Hyman, "Printing the Kitchen," p. 398.

[35]   The other important cookbooks of the day, *Le Cuisinier,* by Pierre de Lune, and *L'Art de bien traiter,* by L. S. R., both used a variation of the menu format, which made for lots of repetition. Combined with the lack of indexes, this made the books cumbersome to use.

[36]   Massialot, *Le Cuisinier roïal et bourgeois,* preface, n.p.

the model to be used with other feathered game and with domestic ducks and capons. The bird was roasted on a spit, carved, and then pounded in a mortar to extract the juices, which were strained and degreased before using. Presumably, this roast-and-pound method coaxed extra juices out of the bony parts of the carcass, much as a modern Rouen-style duck press does today. It produced *jus* flavored by the smokiness of the fire and the caramelized taste of browned meat.[37]

Massialot recommended another technique for working with mutton, beef, and veal, which he described in the master recipe for *jus de veau*. This called for heating slices of veal *rouelle* (a cut containing the small end of the shoulder blade and the end of the upper arm) in an earthenware pot sealed airtight with dough of flour and water over very low heat for a minimum of two hours. No seasonings were used, so the small quantity of juice yielded by the meat (which sweated without browning) carried the delicate and unadulterated taste of the veal itself. When degreased and strained, it had a pleasant, light, limpid texture, slightly thickened by the gelatinous material in the meat.[38] Liquids produced in this manner, as the result of prolonged exposure to very gentle heat, were thought to be fortifying and especially easy to digest. Exactly the same method employing the sealed pot was used in Massialot's recipe for *potage sans l'eau*, a restorative (that is, "*restaurant*" in the original sense) recommended for aged, infirm, or those in need of a soothing, nourishing tonic.[39]

Making *jus* from fish required yet another technique. Tench, carp, or a mixture of the two were browned slowly in butter and then sprinkled with flour, which was also allowed to brown. At this point, the fish were moistened with a little court bouillon seasoned with a bouquet of herbs, salt, and citron peel studded with cloves. The whole contents of the pan were then strained through a cloth while the cook pressed firmly to extract all the juices. *Jus de poisson* was actually a delicate form of fish broth to which the flour liaison imparted a little body and a buttery hue.[40]

---

[37]   Ibid., pp. 284–285 and 364–365.

[38]   Ibid.

[39]   Ibid., p. 386. The recipe for *potage sans l'eau* called for beef and mutton in addition to the *rouelle* of veal, as well as a capon; four pigeons; two partridges; slices of onion, parsley root, and parsnip; fines herbes; and a little salt. These ingredients cooked in a sealed pot that had been set inside a second, larger one filled with simmering water for five to six hours before the liquid was strained and degreased. Massialot noted that the poultry meat could be used to make forcemeats for use in other recipes. He also included recipes for some *restaurants* that were simpler, quicker, and cheaper to make, such as *eau de veau*, *eau de poulets*, and *eau de chapon*; see pp. 155–156.

[40]   Ibid., p. 285.

Massialot treated *jus* of all kinds as a kitchen staple. It was frequently made in advance of being needed and stored for brief periods in covered jars. Adding a spoonful or two of *jus* was a handy means of precisely intensifying the flavor of a soup, ragout, or sauce without altering its consistency or texture. *Jus* was also an ingredient in another type of basic mixture that served as a flavor enhancer – the family of liquid purées known as coulis or *essence*.

A coulis was distinct from a *jus* in that it had a slightly sandy texture caused by the presence of very finely puréed meat, poultry, fish, vegetables, or almonds, in addition to bread crusts and other solid ingredients such as aromatic herbs or even pounded crustacean shells (included for their color, as in crawfish coulis, for example).[41] However varied the ingredients might be, the technique of making a coulis was pretty standard. The solid ingredients were combined, moistened with a small amount of liquid (usually *jus* or *jus* combined with bouillon), and then rubbed through a fine sieve to create the characteristic puréed texture. When a coulis was added to sauced dishes, it changed the consistency as well as the taste, and sometimes the color, too, so it created quite a different effect than a *jus* derived from the same principal ingredient. Having a range of both kinds of basic mixtures at his disposal enabled a skilled cook to create exactly the nuance he wished to impart to a particular dish. Massialot recommended keeping batches of different kinds of *jus* and coulis on hand, carefully sealed up in individual casseroles, to be used on short notice "for diversifying ragouts."[42]

The imaginative use of basic mixtures such as coulis and *jus* allowed the cook to create many different culinary effects. Massialot frequently used them to underscore the flavor of a principal ingredient – for example, by enriching the *sauce espagnole* to be served with roasted partridge with a coulis containing *jus de perdrix* and the mashed liver of the bird.[43] Some types, however, especially those flavored with ham, mushrooms, or anchovy, added a complimentary but distinct taste to recipes made with other principal ingredients; examples included a dish of braised artichoke hearts with a coulis-enriched *sauce jambon* and a crawfish salad topped off with *jus de champignons*.[44] In addition, coulis could also be used to create a light liaison for a sauce. For instance, Massialot's recipe for *poularde aux olives* paired the roasted bird with a ragout of anchovies, green olives, and capers in a champagne sauce that was thickened by adding a few spoonfuls

---

[41]   Ibid., pp. 210 and 278.
[42]   Ibid., p. 8.
[43]   Ibid., pp. 364–365.
[44]   Ibid., pp. 23 (artichokes with *sauce jambon*) and 242 (crawfish salad, *jus de champignons*).

of coulis at the end.[45] Even foods for Good Friday, the strictest fast day of the ecclesiastical year, when a certain austerity was appropriate, could be enlivened with a savory and colorful coulis of carrots, parsley root, parsnips, and onions.[46]

Although time and meticulous care were required to make basic mixtures such as *jus* and coulis, their presence in the kitchen ultimately served to streamline the preparation of interesting and varied meals. Concentrated flavorings, herb bundles, seasoning mixtures, pastry doughs, roux, *beurre manié* (butter worked with flour, which was used in tiny quantities to adjust the consistency of sauces), marinades, and many forms of bouillon were typically made in advance, even a day or more ahead, during the downtime between peaks of kitchen activity.[47] In households employing more than one servant in the kitchen, responsibility for preparing these items was delegated to junior members of the staff. This was an assignment that built basic skills, such as modulating the position of the saucepan on the *potager* burner so that a flour and butter roux cooked thoroughly without burning or browning too much; degreasing bouillon and other liquids; pounding ingredients through a fine sieve until the proper texture was achieved; and so on. It also taught beginners about the significant differences in taste, color, and texture that could be created by using alternative techniques. For example, the herbs and aromatic vegetables used to flavor a sauce could be chopped with a knife, yielding small, individual particles that retain their juices and crispness, or pounded in a mortar, creating a semi-liquid paste.

Because basic mixtures of many kinds could be derived from a small number of master recipes utilizing a handful of key techniques, assistants with a minimum of training (who were often illiterate and unable to read recipes for themselves) were capable of assembling the building blocks of a sophisticated meal. The chef needed only to tell his assistants that dinner would require a recipe of such-and-such a bouillon or coulis, or roux cooked to a particular shade of brown or gold, or so many bunches of chopped or pounded herbs in order to move quickly when the time came to assemble the finished dishes. Useful as this was in large households, advance preparation of basic mixtures would have been a decisive factor in the ability of smaller kitchens to turn out sophisticated food. With a pantry full of different kinds of coulis, *jus*, roux, and other staples, even a lone cook could produce many of Massialot's recipes with a minimum of last-minute fuss.

An example of such a recipe is *poularde aux olives*, a chicken paired with a richly flavored ragout prepared while the barded bird roasted on

---

[45]   Ibid., pp. 338–339

[46]   Ibid., pp. 213–214.

[47]   Ibid., pp. 24–25.

the spit. To make the ragout, the cook started with a roux of flour sautéed in pork fat to which an anchovy and some chopped parsley, scallions, and capers were added at the end of the browning period. Two spoonfuls of *jus* (prepared in advance from a chicken or capon) and a glass of champagne were stirred into the roux and brought to a boil, forming a *sauce velouté*. Olives *ecrasées* (lightly cured green olives) and an herb bouquet were added to the sauce, which simmered, developing a suave texture, until the chicken was done. While the bird rested, several spoonfuls of chicken coulis were stirred into the sauce to enrich the flavor and adjust the consistency; seasonings were corrected, and the sauce was degreased and poured into a deep, warm platter. The chicken was carved into serving pieces and transferred to the platter, each piece pressed down into the sauce, and allowed to steep for a few minutes before being served, piping hot.[48] The preparation time for this recipe would have been governed, of course, by the size of the chicken and the temperature at which it roasted; the ragout, however, could be made in half an hour, most of which was unsupervised simmering time. The recipe would be easy to execute for anyone who had mastered the basic preparation of roux, *jus*, and coulis as explained in Massialot's directions.

The entries devoted to modes of preparation helped readers to see the kinship among whole families of recipes. Clusters of articles, linked by cross-references, defined fundamental culinary techniques and the families of recipes derived from them. Readers learned that ragouts were always thickened with roux, whereas fricassees used egg yolks, cream, or both.[49] The entry for "marinade" described both a bath of acidic liquid in which foods were steeped and the process of preparing fried dishes with principal ingredients that had been previously soaked in such a liquid.[50] A *mironton*, Massialot's readers learned, was a dish consisting of thin pieces of meat or fish layered in a casserole with a rich stuffing and cooked over very gentle heat.[51] Massialot also devoted entries to techniques such as braising, roasting, cooking foods *en casserole* or as a *civet, daube, estoufade, hachis,* or *poupeton.*

Together with recipes for basic mixtures, entries that explained modes of preparation were the building blocks of Massialot's cuisine. A cook who familiarized herself with these essentials was poised to execute sophisticated recipes that combined several different elements, such as bisque. The fundamental difference between a bisque and an ordinary soup in the seventeenth-century kitchen was that soup consisted of a bouillon (with or

48 Ibid., pp. 338–339.
49 Ibid., pp. 141–144 and 436–437.
50 Ibid., pp. 299–301.
51 Ibid., pp. 305–310.

without meat, vegetables, or other solid ingredients) poured over a piece of bread at the moment of serving, whereas in a bisque the bread (or other starchy element, such as the elaborate *Jacobine* crouton described by Bonnefons) was simmered in the bouillon until most of the liquid was absorbed, a crust began to form on the bottom of the dish, and starch molecules dispersed into the sauce, creating a lightly thickened texture. Before serving, the bisque was topped with a principal ingredient such as crawfish or small birds (quail, young chickens, or, of course, pigeons) that had been poached in a previous operation. In keeping with its festive reputation, the bisque was sauced with a ragout and decorated with a garnish chosen to compliment the principal ingredient.

Thus the process of making a bisque – any bisque – always involved five distinct operations, a pattern held no matter what was chosen as the principal ingredient, the ragout, or the garnish or what kind of bouillon or starchy crouton was used.[52] While bisques might appear in a hundred different variations, the concept "bisque" was absolutely constant. It was as if the *esprit de system* so characteristic of Cartesian thought suddenly found expression in cuisine.

Once a sophisticated dish such as a bisque was understood as the sum of its parts, it was possible not only to vary it by altering one or more of these elements, but also to facilitate its preparation by breaking the work into a series of manageable tasks that could be performed sequentially by a single cook or cooperatively by members of a kitchen staff. For example, Massialot's master recipe called for bouillon and *jus*, which could be made ahead, leaving time later to prepare a decorative topping (such as poached cockscombs) that required last-minute attention. The ragout's ingredients could be sautéed, moistened, simmered, and sauced in the hour or so it took to poach the pigeons prior to uniting them with the croutons and bouillon. Massialot provided all the information needed to execute these steps – none of which was difficult in itself – either in the master recipe or in a cross-referenced entry. By internalizing the method of making a bisque as illustrated in the master recipe, the reader would have gained the understanding and fundamental techniques to create other combinations of her own.

Of course, as a matter of practical tradecraft, master cooks learned to juggle the elements of their culinary repertoires and developed a feel for how these might be changed up and recombined in imaginative ways. Apprentices in catering establishments and assistants in large households

---

[52]   Massialot, *Le Cuisinier roïal et bourgeois*, pp. 131–133. Interestingly, the recipes for pigeon bisque published by La Varenne and Bonnefons include all the steps specified by Massialot. However, neither writer explains the making of bisque as a systematic process that could be applied to many sets of ingredients.

would have picked up this know-how as they moved up the rungs of the culinary ladder to become skilled professionals. The luxury of this kind of training would have rarely been enjoyed by the kitchen staffs of smaller establishments, whether noble or bourgeois, which typically consisted of a cook and one or two helpers. This was the target audience for Massialot's book.

By *writing* master recipes in a manner that articulated the logic of his cuisine and specified the details of technique, Massialot took an unprecedented step toward demystifying the art of refined cooking and putting it within the grasp of a much wider circle. Whereas his predecessors had published recipes, Massialot's encyclopedia initiated the reader into a culinary system, which hitherto was the preserve only of those who had the experience of working in a large kitchen. The cross-referenced articles on techniques, basic mixtures, and ingredients set against the background of model menus created a three-dimensional picture of how one would actually go about planning and preparing a sophisticated meal. Although Massialot was proud of his recipes, he was prouder still of the comprehensiveness of his account of *how* to cook, as this was the key to his readers achieving excellent results.[53] By placing the secrets of the catering trade in a systematic context, Massialot gave cooks in modest kitchens the means of attaining the level of refinement that had formerly been available only to grand households. In this sense, the title of *Le Cuisinier roïal et bourgeois* (*The Royal and Bourgeois Cook*) was exactly right. This "how-to" element of the book, although implicit in its very structure, became even more clearly articulated in later editions with the addition of new articles and the elaboration of old ones. For example, when a new entry for "ragout" appeared in the 1712 edition, it was the longest in the book.[54]

Massialot's approach to writing about how to cook anticipated by fifty years the monumental effort to diffuse the know-how of skilled craftsmen of all sorts in the *Encyclopédie* of Diderot and D'Alembert. Although the *Encyclopédie* is best known today as the centerpiece of the French Enlightenment and a font of radical ideas about politics and society, it was conceived as a practical work of reference that aimed to change the way its readership thought about matters of philosophy and taste. One of the ways it aimed to achieve this was to make accessible to the general reading public a wealth of technical information that had hitherto been the preserve of guilds and other closed groups within society. Diderot, whose father was a master cutler, understood very well how much discrete details – say, the proper temperature at which to forge the blade of a steel scalpel or to emulsify an

---

[53]   Ibid., preface, n.p.
[54]   Wheaton, *Savoring the Past,* p. 155.

egg-yolk and butter liaison – made enormous differences in the finished product, and he also saw the degree to which such information needed to be placed within a comprehensive framework in order to be rendered truly useful to the non-specialist. The *Encyclopédie* aimed to do both by means of alphabetically arranged articles cross-referenced to each other, to a systematic tree of knowledge printed in the first volume, and to magnificent engravings that illustrated tools, techniques, and processes. The production, distribution, and preparation of food was one of the subjects to which the editors devoted considerable attention. As a result, the *Encyclopédie* is one of the most informative sources we have on cooking and the food trades in the middle of the eighteenth century, and one to which we will return in the following chapter.

FRENCH COOKING IN ENGLAND IN THE AGE OF MASSIALOT

By reducing cooking to a system characterized by key techniques and recipes, a precise culinary vocabulary, and general principles for combining ingredients and basic mixtures to form an infinite variety of dishes, Massialot hoped to make sophisticated food accessible to cooks who were trained outside the circle of grand Parisian households or the catering trade. His success in this endeavor left a lasting mark on French cuisine. His books on cooking and confectionary (regularly updated and issued in new editions) dominated the market for culinary literature. By the 1730s, the method he advocated of building recipes around basic mixtures had became so deeply embedded in culinary practice that it provoked a reaction among progressive chefs, the founders of the so-called *nouvelle cuisine* (see the following chapter). His influence was also felt outside of France. By turning cooking into a systematic art and organizing it from A to Z, Massialot made it easier for outsiders, including foreigners, to learn the fundamentals of French cuisine, a factor that contributed to its diffusion in Europe. Late Stuart and early Georgian England offers an especially interesting example of this phenomenon.

By the time Massialot's book appeared in English in 1702, under the title *The Court and Country Cook*,[55] elite cooking in France and England

---

[55] This volume included updated versions of both *Le Cuisinier roïal et bourgeois* and *Nouvelle instruction pour les confitures, les liquers, et les fruits.* Is was published anonymously as *The Court and Country Cook: Giving New and Plain Directions How to Order All Manner of Entertainments, Together with New Instructions for Confectioners*, faithfully translated out of French into English by J. K. (London: A. and J. Churchill and M. Gillyflower, 1702).

had a long shared history fueled by trade, social and political contacts among elites, and, prior to the 1520s, the dietary restrictions imposed by a common religion. The Reformation freed most Englishmen from mandatory fasting for much of the year, which seems to have led to immediate and permanent decreases in the per capita consumption of olive oil and fish. But in other respects, post-Reformation English cooking remained true to the techniques and flavors of the medieval style. For example, one of the best-selling English cookery books of the seventeenth century, *A True Gentlewoman's Delight*, which was printed in twenty-one editions beginning in 1653, included such traditional dishes as a Florentine pastry of kidneys, capon, and rabbit that was seasoned with cloves, mace, nutmeg, sugar, cream, currents, eggs, and rosewater.[56]

Sixteen fifty-three was also the year of publication for an English translation of La Varenne's *Le Cuisinier françois*. At that date, English food was considerably sweeter and spicier than the delicate French style. Whereas fewer than 5 percent of the recipes in *Le Cuisinier françois* used sugar, fewer than 1 percent specified cinnamon or ginger, and none used mace, half of the savory recipes published in John Murrel's *New Book of Cookery* (1615) called for sugar, 31 percent for cinnamon, 27 percent for ginger, and more than 15 percent for mace. In 1654 Joseph Cooper specified cinnamon in 40 percent of the savory recipes in his popular *The Art of Cookery*, while about a third of his dishes called for sugar or ginger or both, and another 14 percent used mace.[57] Aromatic, sweet-and-savory recipes were also prominent in *The Accomplished Cook*, by Robert May, a work that was first published in 1660 and continued to be reprinted for thirty years. As a teenager in the first decade of the century, May had done an apprenticeship in France.[58] Many of the recipes he wrote up fifty years later were souvenirs of that moment, when French and English tastes were still united in their love of spicy complexity. By 1660, however, May had come to see his style of cooking as distinctly English, in comparison with the newfangled cuisine that had emerged in France since his youth. The latter, he wrote, featured "Mushroomed Experiences" that privileged "Sauce rather than Diet"[59] – an interesting reference to the turn away from the use of spices as dietary correctives, which we have already mentioned in discussing the cooking of La Varenne and Bonnefons. Interestingly, May's criticism of contemporary

---

[56] Elizabeth David discusses this recipe and others in "A True Gentlewoman's Delight" in *Is There a Nutmeg in the House?*, pp. 112–113.

[57] See the editors' introduction to La Varenne, *The French Cook*, pp. viii–ix.

[58] Colin Spencer, *British Food: An Extraordinary Thousand Years of History* (New York: Columbia University Press, 2002), pp. 141–143.

[59] Quoted in Mennell, *All Manners of Food*, p. 92.

French cuisine did not prevent him from plagiarizing La Varenne's entire chapter on egg dishes, as Elizabeth David has pointed out.[60]

Perhaps in valorizing traditional spicy cooking as English while also appropriating some elements of the modern French style, May was spreading his bets about the tastes of his readers. *The Accomplished Cook* appeared just as Charles II returned to the throne lost by his father during the Civil War. The new king, the queen mother, and many Royalist gentlemen had waited out the hostilities and the Interregnum in exile on the Continent: Paris and Holland had been the refuges of choice. Stuart ties to France were strong (the queen mother, Henrietta Maria, was the youngest child of Henry IV), and the tone of Restoration high society was resolutely Francophile. English aristocrats in the 1660s were the first and extremely receptive target audience for the "new clarets" produced for export by Bordeaux winegrowers and, as we shall see in Chapter 7, the same grandees were probably responsible for the invention of sparkling champagne. Sojourns in the vicinity of Paris awakened interest in the expanded kitchen gardens that flourished there. It was a revelation to see such a large variety of cultivars, including many items of Mediterranean provenance, thriving in an environment similar to that of the Home Counties. John Evelyn's fascination with the French kitchen garden led to his translations of works by Bonnefons and La Quintinie and to his own experiments, which informed *Acetaria*, his book on salads. Interestingly, his ideas about how these should be composed betrayed a pronounced taste for *le goût naturel*: the taste of each kind of vegetable and herb was to be easily discernable, complimenting the others like the notes of a song.[61] It is therefore not at all surprising that the English upper class also hungered for the kind of delicate cooking that many of them had come to know in France. Those who could afford it employed French cooks;[62] others made do with recipes and cookbooks in the French style.

---

[60] David, "A True Gentlewoman's Delight" in *Is There a Nutmeg in the House?*, pp. 113–114.

[61] Evelyn, *Acetaria*, p. 59.

[62] Mennell points out that in all probability few English aristocrats actually employed French chefs, although many may have aspired to do so; *All Manners of Food*, pp. 125–126. He is surely correct about this, as French-trained cooks (usually male) commanded up to ten times the annual wages of "plain cooks" (usually female); see the introductory essay by Jennifer Stead in Hannah Glasse, *First Catch Your Hare: The Art of Cookery Made Plain and Easy by a Lady (1747)*, a facsimile of the first edition, supplemented by the recipes that the author added up to the fifth edition and furnished with a preface, introductory essays by Jennifer Stead and Priscilla Bain, a glossary by Alan Davidson, notes, and an index (Totnes: Prospect Books, 2004), p. xxvii.

One can see this effort to adapt French sensibilities and techniques in the work of Patrick Lamb, who for fifty years served as a master cook to members of the royal family. *Royal Cookery: Or, the Compleat Court-Cook*, a summary of his career in the kitchen, included some dishes of medieval origin that were sill popular in England, such as *poivrade* sauce. Most of his recipes, however, echoed French cooking from La Varenne to Massialot and in some cases directly reproduced them, without attribution. For example, Lamb's readers learned to sauce blanched artichoke hearts with cream, egg yolks, chives, and parsley; to fricassee chicken with mushrooms and champagne (the sauce emulsified with two egg yolks); and to prepare partridge "the Spanish Way," with wine and coulis thickened with the bird's pounded liver – a dish differing from Massialot's *perdrix à l'espagnole* only in a few insignificant details.[63] All but one of the twelve recipes in the eight-page entry on "cullis" in the second edition of *Royal Cookery* were lifted from Massialot's *Court and Country Cook* (published in London fourteen years earlier) with only minor changes in wording.[64] Interestingly, the 1716 edition of Lamb's book (unlike the first edition that appeared in 1710) was organized as an alphabetical culinary dictionary, a further testimony to Massialot's influence and to the usefulness of the format he embraced.

The process by which French culinary techniques and recipes became naturalized in English kitchens was also documented by William Verral. Although Verral was English (he succeeded his father as the proprietor of the White Hart Inn in Lewes, Sussex), he learned to cook as an assistant to a M. de St.-Clouet, a Frenchman who directed the kitchens of the Duke of Newcastle. Verral's book, *A Compleat System of Cookery*, shows that he had mastered the fundamentals of French cuisine as they had evolved since the days of La Varenne. For example, his entremets of macaroni called for the cooked noodles to be tossed with a little meat or poultry coulis; seasoned with scallion, parsley, drops of lemon juice, and a speck of nutmeg; topped with parmesan cheese; and baked until golden. He explained that this method of making a gratin could be adapted to other ingredients, such as oysters or scallops (in which case a white sauce thickened with roux would replace the coulis).[65] Verral, like Massialot, emphasized that cooking was a

---

[63] Patrick Lamb, *Royal Cookery: Or, the Compleat Court-Cook. Containing the Choicest Receipts in All the Several Branches of Cookery, to Which Are Added Bills of Fare for Every Month of the Year*, 2nd ed. (London: A Nutt and J. Roper, 1716), pp. 3–4 and 141; and Spencer, *British Food*, pp. 163–165.

[64] Compare Lamb, *Royal Cookery*, pp. 55–63; and [Massialot], *The Court and Country Cook*, pp. 101–104.

[65] William Verral, *A Compleat System of Cookery in Which Is Set Forth a Variety of Genuine Receipts Collected from Several Years Experience under the Celebrated Mr. de St. Clouet, Sometime since Cook to His Grace the Duke of Newcastle*

systematic art that made the most of easily obtainable, seasonal materials. He devoted considerable effort to describing different techniques and to explaining the details of how to make basic preparations such as bouillon, "coulis of meat and fish, forcemeats, braising mixtures, and liaisons of egg yolks and *beurre manié.*"[66]

One of Verral's concerns was to defend French cooking against accusations that it was wildly extravagant. The foremost proponent of this view was Hannah Glasse, author of the very popular *Art of Cooking Made Plain and Easy*, published in 1747. Glasse devoted a chapter of her book to ranting about the cost of French sauces, and she boasted that she could make a substitute just as good for less than half a crown – a claim that was hardly substantiated by her bizarre recipe for gravy, which contained catsup, mace, cloves, and pepper. It was presumably her concern for economy that led her to print instructions for salvaging venison or hare that was musty or stinking by rubbing it with ginger – a procedure quite unthinkable in contemporary French cooking, with its emphasis on impeccable ingredients. Incidentally, her recipe suggests that by the 1740s the price of ginger had dropped so low in relation to the price of meat that such an expedient made financial if not culinary sense – a reversal of the norms in the ancient and medieval world.[67]

Verral was not intimidated by Glasse's charges. In the preface to his book, he described St. Clouet as an economical cook whose culinary knowledge and superior skills allowed him to concoct a feast out of "a couple of rabbits or chickens and six pigeons" – materials that would have formerly served only as garnishes for big joints of meat.[68] Certainly basic mixtures such as coulis and *jus* called for expensive ingredients; however, being concentrated, they went a long way and could be used to make cheaper foods (such as the aforesaid rabbits, chickens, and pigeons) into elegant fare. It was also possible to dispense with coulis and *jus* altogether and use inexpensive

---

(London: printed for the author, 1759), pp. 215–216. Verral's book was reprinted as *The Cook's Paradise or A Compleat System of Cookery* (London: Sylvan Press, 1948). For a discussion of this recipe, see Elizabeth David, *Spices, Salt and Aromatics in the English Kitchen: English Cooking, Ancient and Modern* (London: Penguin, 1970), vol. 1, pp. 101–103.

66 Wheaton, *Savoring the Past*, p. 166.

67 See Hannah Glasse, *First Catch Your Hare*, pp. i–ii, 8, and 53–54. Glasse's modern editors have pointed out that despite her invective about "French tricks," her attitude toward French cooking was conflicted: many of her recipes (especially for "made dishes," i.e., ragouts) were copied from French sources, a fact that she acknowledged and justified on the basis that the dishes were good. See the editors' introductory material, pp. xxv–xxvii.

68 Verral, *A Compleat System of Cookery*, p. xxx.

but meticulously prepared bouillon as the basis for all sauces.[69] Although French cooking was associated in England with rich aristocratic households, Verral argued that simple but refined French dishes were well within the reach of the local gentry, not to mention a middle-class publican like himself.

Verral describes an occasion on which he was invited into the house of a local gentleman to cook some of his French dishes for a special occasion. The biggest problem he encountered was not the lack of ingredients (which were plentiful), but the insufficient *batterie de cuisine*. The kitchen contained a single stewpot and a nasty sieve that was also used for sanding the stairs! Verral persevered and showed the household cook, a woman called Nanny, how to make a chicken fricassee. This dish made an excellent impression in the dining room – leading to praise for Nanny and the acquisition of some better cooking equipment to encourage her development as a French-style cook.[70]

The great divide between the French and English styles of cooking as they had evolved by the early eighteenth century was not so much a result of the prohibitive cost of ingredients, but rather the specialized skills, painstaking techniques, and, above all, the amount of time that French cooking required. Making a proper *coulis de jambon* took hours, but a ham gravy took minutes – and, unlike the coulis, the gravy required no picky degreasing or straining operations. As we shall see, these same factors posed something of a challenge in the diffusion of elite Parisian cuisine downward into the middle and lower ranks of the French bourgeoisie, where all the cooking and marketing duties were typically handled by a single female servant. In France, however, the desire to emulate aristocratic society in its pursuit of culinary perfection was strong, encouraging the bourgeoisie to create a streamlined version of the delicate style. Their efforts were supported by caterers, pastry makers, *restaurateurs* (sellers of prepared *restaurants* and bouillons), and other culinary professionals whose wares supplemented items produced in the home kitchen and provided shortcuts for the busy cook. These conditions did not apply in England. The very title of Hannah Glasse's book stressed the *ease* with which her recipes could be executed, a seductive promise to households in which servants were few and skills were general. As Stephen Mennell has pointed out, practicality would become one of the earmarks of the modern English culinary sensibility, a fact that reflected the middle-class orientation of the English culinary camp, which the great and powerful had deserted.[71] From the point of view

[69] Ibid.
[70] Ibid., preface, n.p.
[71] Mennell, *All Manners of Food*, pp. 120–121 and 126–127.

of such middling households, the refined results produced by Massialot's recipes simply did not justify the trouble they required.

One consequence of this privileging of practicality and ease over refinement and technical skill was that English cooking became quite conservative. This was true not only in method, but also in terms of taste. Although plainness would become synonymous with English food, the medieval love of sweet-and-savory mixtures, tart fruit sauces and jellies, and even pungency (in the form of preparations such as catsup and Worcestershire sauce, and, as of the 1740s, Indian curries and pickles, too) would live into our own day.[72] The priorities of the medieval kitchen also persisted in the prominence accorded to large joints of meat, which were typically served with pungent condiments, such as mustard or horseradish sauce, or sweet ones, such as applesauce or mint jelly. One area in which eighteenth-century English cooks led the world was in finding new ways to use sugar, a favorite medieval ingredient, although one that was scarce until Barbados and Jamaica started exporting large quantities after 1660. By the beginning of the nineteenth century, the English consumed an average of eighteen pounds of sugar per person per year, an increase of 2,500 percent in a hundred years, outstripping by far rates of contemporary consumption in France and elsewhere on the Continent.[73] This influx of relatively inexpensive sugar coincided with the rise of tea drinking in England, but it also inspired the proliferation of a vast range of puddings and desserts.[74] Often spiced as well as sweetened, such puddings became, along with roast beef, the iconic dishes of the English culinary tradition.

∽

The later editions of Massialot's book, those that appeared after 1712 in a multi-volume format as *Le Nouveau Cuisinier royal et bourgeois*, were characterized by increasingly elaborate dishes and longer menus. A third course was added, and there was a tendency to offer more side dishes in proportion to the principal recipes. For example, a menu printed in the 1734 edition called for thirteen dishes per course, of which six were hors

---

[72] Glasse was the first English cookery writer to publish recipes for Indian-inspired recipes such as curry and pilau; see *First Catch Your Hare*, pp. xxxi and 52. On the reception of Indian cooking in England, see Lizzie Collingham, *Curry: A Tale of Cooks and Conquerors* (Oxford: Oxford University Press, 2006).

[73] Mintz, *Sweetness and Power*, pp. 67 and 73.

[74] One of the promoters of puddings and other sweets was Hannah Glasse. Sweet puddings figure prominently in *The Art of Cooking Made Plain and Easy*, along with creams, cheesecakes, jellies, syllabubs, and cakes. Following on the great success of this work, she published a second book devoted entirely to sweets, *The Compleat Confectioner, or, the Whole Art of Confectionary* (London, 1760).

d'oeuvres.[75] The note of restraint that was evident in menu planning during the last quarter of the seventeenth century gave way to a desire to fill the table with as many tempting tidbits as possible. This tendency toward elaboration is also visible in many of the recipes dating from the Regency and the early years of Louis XV's personal reign. One basic mixture was piled on top of another, creating dishes that were complex beyond anything in Massialot's original culinary vision. Although recipes featuring everyday ingredients continued to appear, often unchanged from the 1691 edition, there was an increasing emphasis on luxurious foodstuffs and basic preparations that were wildly expensive to make. Ostentatious consumption was fashionable again, not in the form of *primeurs* (which, to tell the truth, never went out of style, despite Massialot's early indifference to them), but in dishes that juxtaposed one rich mixture with half a dozen others.

This tendency toward excess was perfectly captured in the recipe for *pigeons à la lune* published in *The Modern Cook* (1733) by Vincent La Chapelle, a Frenchman who directed the kitchens of the Earl of Chesterfield.[76] To make it, one began by braising pigeons that had been split in two with slices of veal, ham, and bacon. The cooked pigeons were arranged on an ovenproof platter and surrounded by a band of meat and poultry *farce* (basic mixture #1). The pigeons were then cloaked with a *salpicon* of sweetbreads, truffles, and mushrooms (basic mixture #2), and the *salpicon* was covered with heart-shaped pieces of puff pastry (basic mixture #3). The pigeons with their toppings were baked until the pastry puffed and browned; juices rendered by the pigeons and the *salpicon* were drained off. Next, the spaces between the pigeons were filled in with two different ragouts consisting of more sweetbreads, mushrooms, truffles, foie gras, cockscombs, and crawfish tails. Half of these ingredients were prepared with a creamy white sauce that contained a coulis of chicken (basic preparation #4) and a liaison of egg yolks and cream (basic preparation #5); the other half were cooked with poultry *jus* (basic preparation #6) and ham coulis (basic preparation #7) to make a brown sauce for a two-tone presentation.[77] The culinary historian Barbara Wheaton has compared this dish to the "intricately worked gold and enamel snuff boxes of the period, in the making of which an infinity of work was lavished on every surface, and the use of precious materials

---

[75] Wheaton, *Savoring the Past*, p. 155.

[76] More than a quarter of the recipes in the first edition of *The Modern Cook* were plagiarized from *Le Cuisinier roïal et bourgeois*; Philip and Mary Hyman, "La Chapelle and Massialot: An Eighteenth-Century Feud" in *Petits Propos Culinaires*, no. 2 (August 1979), pp. 44–54. As far as I can tell, however, *pigeons à la lune* was an original creation of La Chapelle.

[77] La Chapelle, *The Modern Cook*, vol. 2, pp. 252–253.

sometimes became an end in itself."[78] If there was ever such a thing as rococo cooking, this was it.

The lavish complexity embodied in dishes such as *pigeons à la lune* provoked a culinary backlash. In the 1650s, Bonnefons had proclaimed a style of cooking that mirrored the variety of the natural world by faithfully conveying the taste of fresh vegetables and other principal ingredients. In the mid-eighteenth century, this interest in tasting the diversity of nature's products would be wedded to a preference for simplicity, and this union was the impetus behind the next stage in the development of modern French cooking.

[78]   Wheaton, *Savoring the Past*, p. 171.

PART III

Cooking, Eating, and Drinking in the
Enlightenment, 1735–1789

CHAPTER 6

Simplicity and Authenticity

Toward the end of the 1730s, cuisine became the subject of intellectual controversy among the Parisian grand monde. Discussions of foodstuffs and modes of preparation that a century earlier had been the purview of culinary professionals suddenly erupted into the public sphere, which was itself a new phenomenon in the society of the ancien régime. The arguments about cooking that unfurled over the middle decades of the eighteenth century involved physicians and men of letters and Jesuits and their sometime opponents, grouped around the *Encyclopédie*. No less a figure than Rousseau took a vigorous stand on the issue of what should be eaten and how it should be prepared. His idealized view of nature and man's place within it fostered an interest in rustic recipes and ingredients, including many vegetarian items. Debates about cuisine intersected with arguments about health and disease, luxury and virtue, absolutism and equality. Whereas mid-seventeenth-century cooks embraced *le goût naturel* out of a love of variety, the philosophes and their readers tended to see simple cooking as an emblem of the good and virtuous life.

The ideal of simplicity was evoked in a number of different styles, ranging from Rousseauian rusticity to the sophisticated *"nouvelle cuisine"* that emerged in the years around 1740. The most popular of these was the so-called *cuisine bourgeoise,* a style that managed to be unpretentious and delicious at the same time. It was the subject of the best-selling cookbook of the century, *La Cuisinière bourgeoise,* by François Menon, which first appeared in 1746 and was reprinted in many subsequent editions.[1] In our own day, *"Faites simple"* (make it simple) has become a favorite slogan of many culinary authorities.[2] But the idea of simplicity as the definitive principle of good cooking (as compared to a contingent fact of the pursuit of variety) was a concept born in the age of Enlightenment.

---

[1]   Hyman and Hyman, "Printing the Kitchen," p. 398.
[2]   See the excellent discussion of this point in Richard Olney, *Simple French Food*, pp. 6–13.

NOUVELLE CUISINE, CIRCA 1740

The turn toward simplicity began, somewhat ironically, with the emergence of the *nouvelle cuisine*, a style that could be just as expensive, subtle, and exacting to execute as its twentieth-century namesake. In the 1730s, elite Parisian kitchens were still heavily influenced by the kind of cooking that Massialot had pioneered in the 1690s and that La Chapelle and other enterprising chefs had developed in France and abroad early in the reign of Louis XV. Technique and organization focused on stocking the kitchen with basic preparations, sauces, and garnishes that could be combined with principal ingredients and with each other to produce an infinite array of dishes. Although Massialot himself stressed the necessity of restraint and good taste in devising new recipes,[3] his modular approach made it easy for less sensitive cooks to repeat flavors within a menu (e.g., by putting ham coulis or a mushroom *farce* in several different dishes) or to commit acts of excess by piling up one mixture on top of another (as in the previously described recipe for *pigeons à la lune*, which called for no fewer than seven basic mixtures in a single and very rich entrée). The search for novel combinations (often represented by fanciful names) could easily overwhelm the character and quality of principal ingredients, and the omnipresence of basic preparations could cause everything to taste the same. Or so the proponents of the *nouvelle cuisine* would argue as the 1730s drew to a close.

The term *"nouvelle cuisine"* was coined in 1742 by François Menon (the same writer who did so much to codify and popularize *cuisine bourgeoise*).[4] He first used it in the third volume of the expanded edition of his *Nouvelle traité de la cuisine* to describe an approach to cooking that produced elegant results while avoiding the pointless elaboration of the older style. Menon was not the only culinary professional to engage in experiments of this kind in the late 1730s. In 1739, within a few months of the publication of the first volume of the *Nouvelle traité*, François Marin, who had served in the households of the duchess de Gesvres and the maréchal de Soubise, published a book that was conceived in a similar spirit, *Les Dons de Comus*.[5] Interestingly, it was Marin's book rather than the *Nouvelle Traité* that quickly became the subject of controversy.

In its original form, *Les Dons de Comus* was an aide-mémoire for maîtres d'hôtel that dealt primarily with menus and table service and

---

3   Massialot, *Le Cuisinier roïal et bourgeois*, preface, vol. 1, n.p.
4   Hyman and Hyman, "Printing the Kitchen," p. 398.
5   [François Marin], *Les Dons de Comus d'après l'édition de 1742*, 3 vols., preface by Silvano Serventi (Paris: Editions Manucius, 2001), editor's introduction, n.p.

contained only a handful of recipes (a two-volume edition with more recipes appeared in 1740, and a three-volume version with a new preface was published in 1742 under the title *Suite des Dons de Comus*).[6] What attracted the attention of a wider public was the *avertissement* that prefaced the main part of the text. Laced with references to Greek and Latin authors, the *avertissement* gave a brief history of cooking from classical times to the present and dared to argue that the cooking of contemporary France – as exemplified in the recipes that followed – compared favorably with the cuisine of the ancients: "The Romans were principally interested in pursuing profusion and rarity, and perhaps in this regard we are their inferiors; but we have brought the art and variety [of cooking] much farther than they."[7] Furthermore, the *avertissement* argued that contemporary cuisine in the style of Marin (described here as *"la cuisine moderne"*) was vastly superior to old-fashioned French cooking of the sort associated with Massialot (referred to as *"la cuisine ancienne"* to distinguish it from both Marin's culinary style and the classical cooking of the Romans and the Greeks). The *avertissement* continued: "Contemporary cuisine, established on the foundations of the old-fashioned kind [but] with much less ado, less apparatus [and] as much variety, is simpler, more hygienic [*propre*], and perhaps even more scientific [*encore plus scavant*]. Old-fashioned cooking was extremely complicated [*fort compliquée*] and extraordinarily detailed."[8] In a couple of pages, the *avertissement* set up Marin's work as a rival to the culinary style that had dominated French cooking for half a century. It also dragged *Les Dons de Comus,* a book that otherwise focused on issues of interest to culinary professionals, into the great quarrel between the ancients and the moderns, a perennial topic of debate among men of letters since the 1690s. Although the quarrel had originated in a debate about the authority of the classical cannon for modern writers, it had come to stand more generally for the war between progress and tradition in many aspects of eighteenth-century life and thought. In literature and the arts, in philosophy and politics, the defenders of tradition were pitted against men who thought that recent developments in science had allowed modern man to surpass the ancients in knowledge and taste.[9] Thanks to the *avertissement,*

---

[6]   See the editor's introduction in Stephen Mennell, ed., *Lettre d'un pâtissier anglois et autres contributions à une polémique gastronomique du XVIIIème siècle* (Exeter: University of Exeter Press, 1981), pp. xv–xvi.

[7]   *"Avertissement"* in Mennell, ed., *Lettre d'un pâtissier anglois,* p. 5.

[8]   Ibid., p. 6.

[9]   The literary quarrel between the ancients and moderns is treated in John Lough, *An Introduction to Seventeenth-Century France* (New York: McKay, 1961) and *An Introduction to Eighteenth-Century France* (London: Longmans, 1960). For the broader implications of the quarrel for other aspects of eighteenth-century life and

cooking joined the battleground on which this contest between progress and tradition was fought.

As several authorities have noted, this provocative introduction was certainly not the work of Marin's own hand. It has been traditionally ascribed to two Jesuit priests, Pierre Brumoy (1688–1742) and Guillaume-Hyacinthe Bougeant (1690–1743). How and why they got involved with Marin's project remains unknown. Although they were provincials by birth (Brumoy from Normandy and Bougeant from Brittany), both spent most of their careers in Paris. By 1722 Brumoy had established himself as a teacher of mathematics at the college of Louis-le-Grand, the most prestigious of the one hundred or so schools that the Jesuits operated in France prior to their expulsion in 1762.[10] He also became a regular contributor to the Society's monthly review, *Mémoires pour l'Histoire des Sciences et des Beaux-Arts* (also known as the *Journal de Trévoux*), an influential publication that strove to bring the fruits of contemporary scholarship (as seen through the prism of Catholic orthodoxy) to a wider reading public. Brumoy probably became acquainted with Bougeant through the journal, which the younger priest joined as a contributor in 1725. The Jesuits of Louis-le-Grand enjoyed the patronage of many members of the high aristocracy, including the duke du Maine, a legitimized son of Louis XIV, who underwrote the cost of the journal for many years. This circle of patrons overlapped with that of Marin's employers, and this may be how Brumoy and Bougeant came to write the *avertissement*.

Both men were broad-ranging humanists of the sort that the Society of Jesus excelled at producing. Bougeant wrote theological treatises, a catechism, a history of the Thirty Years' War, and three comedies that satirized the Jansenists (a neo-Augustinian movement within Catholicism that had been condemned as heretical by the pope but nevertheless found many followers among the robe nobility and the French episcopate). The plays met with some success on the Paris stage. However, in 1737 Bougeant fell afoul of the censors with a discourse about the capacity of animals for language – a topic that strayed dangerously close to the issue of whether animals had souls – and he was briefly exiled to a Jesuit college in the provinces as a result. Brumoy's interests were also quite diverse. In addition to

thought, see Peter Gay, *The Rise of Modern Paganism*, vol. 1 of *The Enlightenment: An Interpretation*, 2 vols. (New York: Norton, 1966), pp. 279–321.

10 On the role of Louis-le-Grand in Parisian intellectual and cultural life before and after the suppression of the Jesuits, see the author's introduction in R. R. Palmer, *The School of the French Revolution: A Documentary History of the College of Louis-le-Grand and Its Director, Jean-François Champagne, 1762–1814* (Princeton, NJ: Princeton University Press, 1975), pp. 9–40.

teaching mathematics, he wrote volumes on church history, poetry on sacred subjects, and a number of plays on edifying themes that were performed by the pupils of Louis-le-Grand.[11] His name as a scholar rested, however, on a three-volume work about theater in ancient Greece. First published in 1730, *Le Théâtre grec* was reprinted frequently and became widely recognized as the definitive work on the subject. An English translation prepared by Charlotte Lennox with the assistance of Dr. Samuel Johnson appeared in 1759, ensuring Brumoy's posthumous reputation even in the Anglophone world.

The ideas about cooking presented in the controversial *avertissement* for *Les Dons de Comus* were framed by an historical analogy: the culinary influence of ancient Greece on Rome was compared to that of modern Italy on France. Brumoy and Bougeant began by asserting that in the earliest times, the cooking of the Greeks must have resembled that of the natives of America, who, "limited to simple necessity, do not think of the superfluous and in whose homes one perceives no other art than the instinct of [fulfilling] natural needs or [using] the diversity of products offered by their environment."[12] According to the authors, the art of cuisine arose first in Asia, specifically in Assyria and Persia, where "the climate, without doubt, must have played no small role in making these peoples so voluptuous."[13] From Persia, fine cooking spread to Greece, where the Athenians quickly excelled in this, as in all the other arts.

In contrast, Sparta clung to the old diet – humble ingredients simply prepared, whose only seasoning was "exercise and appetite."[14] This austerity was illustrated by the story of a Spartan who, on buying a fish to cook for dinner, was asked by the merchant if he also wanted cheese, vinegar, and oil to make a sauce. The Spartan declined, saying that if he had sauce, there would be no need for the fish, too. A typical dish of the Spartan kitchen was a ragout of hare in which the sauce was made with the entrails and the blood of the animal – a recipe that eliminated waste and additional expense.[15]

Not surprisingly, it was fine Athenian cooking that captured the rest of the Greek world and eventually passed to Rome (via the Greek cities in Sicily and southern Italy) along with the other accomplishments of

[11] On the role of performance in Jesuit education and at Louis-le-Grand in particular, see Judith Rock, *Terpsichore at Louis-le-Grand: Baroque Dance on the Jesuit Stage in Paris* (Saint Louis, MO: The Institute of Jesuit Sources, 1996), pp. 1–41.

[12] "*Avertissement*" in Mennell, ed., *Lettre d'un pâtissier anglois*, p. 3.

[13] Ibid.

[14] Ibid.

[15] Ibid. Brumoy and Bougeant claimed that this sauce was similar to the *sauce noir* still made in eighteenth-century France, presumably an ancestor of the *civet* of hare we know today.

Hellenistic civilization: science, medicine, philosophy, and the arts. The unparalleled power and wealth of Rome provided the conditions for the creation of a cuisine that was unprecedented in "delicacy, magnificence, and profusion."[16] The meats and fish used by the cooks in rich Roman households came from all over the known world, as did the rare seasonings and spices used in their ragouts, and this profusion inspired cooks to ever greater artistry. Thus Greek genius for invention combined with Roman opulence to produce results that were both refined and sumptuous.[17]

Since the sixteenth century, according to the *avertissement*, French cooking had emerged as a superior form of cuisine, thanks to Italian influence, much as the Roman kitchen had benefited from the creativity of the Greeks: "it was from them [the Italians], without doubt, that we learned how to eat."[18] Interestingly, the *avertissement* said nothing about the actual recipes, ingredients, or techniques associated with this supposed reception of Italian culinary practices in Renaissance France. (As we have seen, elite cooking in both countries shared common roots and throughout the sixteenth century remained closely linked to medieval tradition.) Instead, the authors identified two aspects of Italian influence: the spread of polite manners in France (including, presumably, table manners, although the details of these are not discussed) and the increasing luxury of French cooking from generation to generation: "What was luxury for our fathers is common [today], it is not luxury for us," they wrote.[19] Indeed, Brumoy and Bougeant largely equated excellence in cuisine with the higher levels of delicacy and refinement that they associated with greater expenditure.

This claim about the increasing luxury of French cooking echoed an idea presented in one of the sources cited in the *avertissement*, J.-F. Melon's *Essai Politique sur le Commerce* (1734), which argued that everyday consumption by the present generation equaled or exceeded what was considered extraordinary for their fathers. Melon, whose work was inspired by Bernard Mandeville's *Fable of the Bees* (1714), thought that it was the materialistic aspect of human nature, especially its ambition and greed, that propelled luxury – and progress – forward across the generations. Thus the vices of man became, paradoxically, the font of increased production and employment that brought positive good to humanity.[20] One wonders if Brumoy and Bougeant actually meant to endorse the iconoclastic argument

---

[16]   Ibid., p. 4.
[17]   Ibid., pp. 4–5.
[18]   Ibid., p. 6.
[19]   Ibid.
[20]   Christopher J. Berry, *The Idea of Luxury: A Conceptual and Historical Investigation* (Cambridge: Cambridge University Press, 1994), pp. 135–137.

about vice generating virtue made by Melon and Mandeville or whether they accepted Melon's claim about increasing standards of luxury in daily life as straightforward reportage. In any case, the Jesuits endorsed the idea that the progress of luxury and civilization were linked and ultimately had beneficial effects. As we will see in the following discussion, Rousseau took direct aim at this position.

According to Brumoy and Beaugeant, contemporary French cuisine resembled Roman cuisine in its inspiration by foreign (that is, Italian and Greek) practices and also by the common willingness to spend large amounts on elegant meals and service. From one generation to the next, the bar of what counted as fine cooking rose higher and higher. Constant innovation in the kitchen was a mark of culinary superiority, according to this view. As new dishes and techniques developed in elite kitchens, older practices trickled down to households of lower status. Brumoy and Bougeant contended that the kind of cuisine made famous throughout Europe by the French chefs of Massialot's generation was appearing on the tables of craftsmen (*gens de métier*) in the 1730s. Meanwhile, the modern style (as exemplified by the dishes described by Marin) had found a following in refined households that prided themselves on serving excellent food.[21]

Part of what was appealing about contemporary cuisine, according to Brumoy and Bougeant, was its lightness and simplicity. Indeed, a sampling of Marin's recipes (as we shall see in the following) shows that he did not go in for the elaborate constructions of pastry-stuffing-garnish-sauce(s) that figured so prominently in the rococo style. His signature dishes depended on sauces whose character came from the reduced bouillon that was their principal component – an elixir that was prepared with painstaking care and used lots of expensive ingredients. According to the *avertissement,* the combination of meats, vegetables, and herbs in such a bouillon was so subtle that the individual ingredients blended into a harmonious whole, much like the effect created when the painter blended his colors.[22] Whereas old-fashioned French cooking achieved its effects by piling one fussy preparation on top of another, contemporary cuisine, the *avertissement* continued, "is a kind of chemistry. The science of the cook consists today of deconstructing foods, turning them into quintessences, of taking their nourishing and light juices and blending them together so that none dominates the others."[23] Such bouillons and *restaurants* (as particularly pure and concentrated bouillons were called) facilitated digestion by aiding the functions of the stomach by turning solid foods into a kind of artificial chyle (a milky liquid that

---

21   *"Avertissement"* in Mennell, ed., *Lettre d'un pâtissier anglois*, p. 6.
22   Ibid.
23   Ibid.

forms in the small intestine and aids in the absorption of nutrients). By eliminating some of the digestive complaints that gave rise to serious diseases, contemporary cooking contributed to health in addition to giving aesthetic pleasure.[24] Finally, the authors argued that the refinement of the sense of taste through the appreciation of fine food of the sort described by Marin also contributed to the development of taste as a form of judgment.[25] Good cooking was therefore a *moral* issue as well as an aesthetic and medical one.

These were provocative claims to make on behalf of the *nouvelle cuisine*: it possessed a distinguished pedigree and flattering historical antecedents; it was scientific and artistic, healthy to eat, and a mark of social distinction; and it conferred pleasure and contributed to moral development. The idea that innovation was integral to culinary excellence seemed to equate the new with the good – a move sure to offend not only traditional cooks but also those men of letters who saw it as an invitation to confuse aesthetic merit with the merely fashionable. Criticism came swiftly, in late 1739, in the form of a pamphlet modeled on the satires of Jonathan Swift that was entitled *Lettre d'un pâtissier anglois au nouveau cuisinier françois avec un extrait du Craftsman.*[26]

Authorship of the *Lettre*, which appeared anonymously, has been attributed to Roland Puchot, count des Alleurs (1693–1754), sometime soldier, diplomat, and man-about-town.[27] The intellectual pretensions of the *avertissement* presented an irresistible target for Des Alleurs's wit and

---

[24]   Ibid., p. 7. Brumoy and Bougeant cited the *Traité de digestion* by Philippe Hecquet (1661–1737), a prominent Parisian physician, as an authority on this point. It is interesting to note that Hecquet was the foremost French proponent of iatromechanical theories of medicine, which the Scottish physician George Cheyne used as the foundation of a new science of dietetics; see the discussion of Cheyne's ideas in the following. On Hecquet's ideas, career, and the relationship between his Jansenism and iatromechanism, see L. W. B. Brockliss, "The Medico-Religious Universe of an Early Eighteenth-Century Parisian Doctor: The Case of Philippe Hecquet" in *The Medical Revolution of the Seventeenth Century*, edited by Roger French and Andrew Wear (Cambridge: Cambridge University Press, 1989), pp. 191–221.

[25]   "*Avertissement*" in Mennell, ed., *Lettre d'un pâtissier anglois*, p. 7.

[26]   On the dating of the pamphlet see Mennell's introduction to *Lettre d'un pâtissier anglois*, pp. xxi. Although the quarrel between the ancients and moderns first broke out in France, it also engulfed British men of letters, notably Jonathan Swift, who made several contributions to the debate on the side of the ancients, including *A Tale of a Tub*; see Joseph M. Levine, *The Battle of the Books: History and Literature in the Augustan Age* (Ithaca, NY, and London: Cornell University Press, 1991), pp. 112–120. *The Craftsman*, also known as *Say's Weekly Journal*, was a popular London magazine.

[27]   Mennell, ed., *Lettre d'un pâtissier anglois*, p. xxi.

provided the inspiration for his only known contribution to the Republic of
Letters.

The choice of an English persona as the supposed author of the *Lettre* allowed Des Alleurs to poke fun at his countrymen's attachment to
systematic philosophy (apparent in some of the quasi-Cartesian notions
expounded by Brumoy and Bougeant), their love of sensuous pleasures of
all kinds, and their particular tendency to overestimate the significance of
food. His fictional *pâtissier* observed that the philosophical spirit had made
such progress in France that it was to be found not only in the academies, but
also among ladies, artisans, and now cooks, too.[28] Like all the other sciences,
the new French cooking was ruled by the laws of geometry, and the ultimate
objective of the *"cuisinier savant"* was to concoct a ragout suitable for the
"delicately voluptuous" that would consist only of "rational quintessences,
precisely purged of all earthiness."[29] The idea that judgment in a moral
and spiritual sense could be shaped by training the palate was also mocked.
Noting that the *avertissement* stressed special interest in the new cooking
taken by members of the nobility, the *pâtissier* proposed different diets for
young aristocrats intended for different careers:

> [F]or a young seigneur destined to live at court, rich dishes such
> as whipped cream and calf's feet; for one who wants to cut a figure
> in high society, the heads of linnets [a songbird], quintessence of
> June bugs, coulis of butterflies, and other light things; for a lawyer
> who wants to excel at chicanery in the courts and shine at the bar,
> mustard, verjuice . . . and other things a little acid and piquant. And
> so for the others.[30]

Finally, the fascination with culinary innovation for its own sake fundamentally changed the focus of dining in company, according to the *pâtissier*.
Twenty years ago, he claimed, all that was needed for a supper menu was
"an adequate variety of dishes, some simple ragouts, and excellent wines.
Scrupulous attention was paid to the choice, number, and decorum of the
guests."[31] Thanks to the new French cuisine, things had changed. Conversation and flirtation, once the raison d'être of the dinner party, took a back
seat to the food: novelties such as *"hors d'oeuvres alambiqués"* and *"entrées
quintessenciées"* assumed center stage.[32]

---

[28] Ibid., p. 15.
[29] Ibid., p. 13.
[30] Ibid., p. 14.
[31] Ibid., p. 15.
[32] Ibid.

The *pâtissier* regretted this loss of sociability, especially because he thought that the quest for innovative cooking embodied in the *nouvelle cuisine* yielded disappointing results. The emphasis on blending flavors in subtle quintessences undermined the flavor of principal ingredients. "The great art of the *nouvelle cuisine* is to give fish the taste of meat and meat the taste of a fish and to give to vegetables no taste at all."[33] To make matters worse, chefs in love with novelty utterly banned old-fashioned favorites from the table. It was a way of life, concluded the *pâtissier*, "far removed from the rustic simplicity of our fathers."[34] Indeed, the classical authors quoted in the *avertissement* – Cicero, Xenophon, Seneca, Plutarch, and others – would have deplored the frivolity and silliness (*niaiserie*) inherent in the *nouvelle cuisine*.[35]

The *pâtissier*'s critique of the ideas in the *avertissement* called forth a defense of the *nouvelle cuisine* by a third party, Ann-Gabriel Meusnier de Querlon (1702–1780). As the editor-in-chief of the *Gazette de France*, a weekly paper that published official court news, Meusnier occupied a prestigious position within literary and intellectual circles. His defense of the *nouvelle cuisine* consisted of two installments: a pamphlet that appeared in 1740, *Apologie des modernes, ou reponse du Cuisinier françois, auteur des Dons de Comus, à un pâtissier anglois,* and a preface to the expanded, three-volume edition of Marin's cookbook that was published two years later, in 1742.[36]

The *Apologie* argued for *nouvelle cuisine* in the context of the general superiority of modern science and culture vis-à-vis the forces of tradition. As great as the achievements of the ancient theatre were, it knew only two genres of drama, Meusnier pointed out, whereas we moderns have developed more than twenty, each illuminating an aspect of human experience.[37] Progress was not limited to belles lettres. Agriculture had never been more productive or varied in its crops, providing an unprecedented abundance of good things to eat. Equipped with spectacles and microscopes that enabled them to see a formerly hidden world and with the analytical power of superior forms of mathematics, scientists daily discovered remedies unknown to the ancients.[38] Inspired by Newton and Descartes, scientists were in the process of discovering the precise composition and workings of the body, and this research demonstrated that the choice and proper preparation of

[33]   Ibid., p. 16.
[34]   Ibid.
[35]   Ibid., p. 19.
[36]   Ibid., pp. xxii–xxiii.
[37]   Ibid., p. 29.
[38]   Ibid., pp. 28 and 35.

food was central to maintaining or restoring health.[39] Under these circumstances, Meusnier concluded, clinging blindly to traditional recipes and techniques was a form of obscurantism and resistance to the improvement of the human condition.

A NEW SCIENCE OF DIETETICS

The *Apologie* did not elaborate the supposed health benefits of the *nouvelle cuisine*, nor did it explain the science on which these were founded. These tasks were central to Meusnier's second piece, the introduction to *Suite des Dons de Comus.*

Meusnier began by affirming some traditional advice: moderation was the key to health and long life, and this was especially so where eating and drinking were concerned.[40] To the ancients, moderation meant not only temperance – that is, the restraint of greedy impulses that encouraged men to eat more than was necessary – but also choosing and preparing foods in a manner that promoted health. Meusnier noted that it was difficult to establish a system of rules for the healthy use of foodstuffs – it was a perennial issue that pitted cooks and physicians against each other.[41] Despite this caveat, he proceeded to wholeheartedly endorse the principles that had been recently articulated by the Newtonian physician George Cheyne (1671–1743).[42]

A Scot by birth and education, Cheyne moved to England in 1702 and thereafter divided his time between Bath and London, where he established a fashionable practice. His success rested on his assiduous attention to his patients, his ability to empathize with their complaints, his appeal to spiritual as well as physical discipline, and his reputation as one of the most influential medical authors of the day. As a young student, he had been introduced by his teacher, Archibald Pitcairne, to iatromechanism, a theory inspired by Newton that strove to unify "medicine, mathematics, and mechanics into a single system explaining all activities of the human body."[43] Cheyne's early writings on iatromechanism helped to establish

---

[39]   Ibid., p. 35.
[40]   [Marin], *Les Dons de Comus*, vol. 1, pp. ii–iii.
[41]   Ibid., pp. x–xi.
[42]   Ibid., pp. xxi–xiv.
[43]   Anita Guerrini, *Obesity and Depression in the Enlightenment: The Life and Times of George Cheyne* (Norman: University of Oklahoma Press, 2000), p. 36. According to Guerrini, Pitcairne, who taught in Leiden as well as in Scotland, wanted to replace "the learning of the ancients with his new Newtonian mathematical medicine as the basis for learned, elite practice." Iatromechanism, which drew on the ideas of

his credentials as a practitioner in touch with contemporary scientific developments. After about 1720, inspired by his own ill health, he turned to a new project, the development of dietary therapies that were consistent with the iatromechanical theory of the body. Other physicians who embraced a mechanistic view of the body also affirmed the general notion that a proper diet was a key element in maintaining good health (for example, Philippe Hecquet, whose treatise on digestion was cited by Brumoy and Bougeant), but they did not give a systematic explanation of why and how dietary therapies worked. Over a period of twenty years, Cheyne published a number of works in which he fundamentally recast the science of dietetics, which had been in disarray for a hundred years. Like his Hippocratic predecessors, he emphasized the *curative* as well as the prophylactic powers of diet, while framing his account in terms of mechanistic philosophy. Cheyne's ideas were influential in scientific circles on the Continent as well as in Britain (his books were quickly translated into French), and they form the core of Meusnier's argument on behalf of the healthiness of the *nouvelle cuisine*.

As Steven Shapin has pointed out, "the overall framework of Cheyne's iatromechanism is not radically different from that of other early eighteenth-century Newtonian physicians."[44] The human body was a machine that operated according to the same laws of physics and mechanics that governed the rest of the universe. Two kinds of matter composed this machine: the "solids," inherited from one's father, and the "juices," which came from one's mother. In a healthy human being, the solids were firm, elastic, and well-toned, and the juices (including blood, but also chyle and other secretions) were thin and free-flowing. Chronic ailments of all sorts – including gout, constipation, stomachache, kidney stones, heart trouble,

---

both Newton and Descartes, as well as the work of Lorenzo Bellini (1643–1704) and Giovanni Alfonso Borelli (1608–1679), replaced Galenism as the reigning theory of the London College of Physicians in the 1690s, "although therapies remained largely unchanged." The Royal Society endorsed the mechanical theory of the body even earlier, in the 1670s. See Guerrini, *Obesity and Depression in the Enlightenment*, pp. 30–42; and Theodore M. Brown, "The College of Physicians and the Acceptance of Iatro-Mechanism in England, 1665–1695" in *The Bulletin of the History of Medicine*, vol. 44 (1970), pp. 12–30. The chief alternatives to iatromechanics in contemporary medical theory and practice were empirically based neo-Hippocratism (which focused on case histories and bedside experience) and iatrochemistry, which descended from the Paracelsians. See Robert E. Schofield, *Mechanism and Materialism: British Natural Philosophy in an Age of Reason* (Princeton, NJ: Princeton University Press, 1970), pp. 23–24, 40, and 49–50.

[44] Steven Shapin, "Trusting George Cheyne: Scientific Expertise, Common Sense, and Moral Authority in Early Eighteenth-Century Dietetic Medicine" in *The Bulletin of the History of Medicine*, vol. 77 (2003), p. 274.

joint pain, muscle spasms, failing vision, and nervous complaints – were caused by obstructions in the tubes that conveyed the juices around the body. In some cases, this damage was rooted in inherited weaknesses in the tubes themselves. More commonly, however, problems were generated by juices that had become gluey, viscous, or thick or had formed encrustations on the tubes.[45]

Although Cheyne prescribed drugs, purges, and bleeding for his patients and believed that exercise was a necessary component to any healthy regime, he thought that long-term improvements were secured primarily through modifications to the diet that aimed to restore the free flow of fluids through the tubes. At the outset, he usually advised a patient to cut back on the consumption of meats and alcohol and to increase the intake of vegetables, grains, dairy products, and mineral water. If such moderation did not produce the desired results, he typically prescribed a series of "lowering" diets that gradually eliminated meats and fish, and then eggs, fruits, and vegetables, as necessary to the specific complaint. In extreme cases only milk (asses' milk for preference) and seeds such as oatmeal, rice, and sago were permitted. Patients were advised that it might be necessary to stick to these diets for months or years in order to affect a cure.[46]

The milk-and-seed diet was the most famous of Cheyne's dietary therapies, but he insisted that it was an extreme prescription for the most serious and intractable cases, not general counsel for the healthy. People who were free of illness or infirmities could eat a diet consisting of meat, dairy products, vegetable foods, and "good ripe wine."[47] The trick was to limit consumption and to choose foods that would maintain bodily juices in their ideal thin and free-flowing consistency. Although this general point was reiterated in many parts of his oeuvre, it received its fullest treatment in the *Essay on Health and Long Life* (1724). In addition to giving an iatrome-chanical explanation of the relationship between diet and health, this book also set forth some simple rules of thumb for deciding what and how much to eat.

Cheyne thought that most people above the class of manual laborers ate too much. Appetite was not a reliable guide to quantity at the table. Because of "the *luxurious* artfulness of *cookery* . . . the fondness of mothers and the cramming of nurses," man's natural ability to sense hunger and satiety has

---

45   Ibid., pp. 274–276, and George Cheyne, *An Essay on Regimen, Together with Five Discourses, Medical, Moral, and Philisophical* (London: for C. Rivington; Bath: J. Leake, 1740).

46   Ibid., pp. 284–292.

47   George Cheyne, *The English Malady or a Treatise on Nervous Diseases of All Kinds*, 2nd ed. (London: G. Strahan, 1734), p. 165.

been completely corrupted, he wrote.[48] He calculated that a daily ration of eight ounces of meat or fish, twelve ounces of bread or other vegetable foods, and a pint of wine was sufficient for most men of moderate activity. Cheyne gave the following advice about portion control: for the main meal of the day, a serving of meat should consist of two wings of a chicken of moderate size or one wing and both legs, or three ribs of an average neck of mutton or two slices of a leg or shoulder, fat and skin removed before serving.[49] Men of sedentary professions should eat less than these amounts, lest they become "hypochondriacal, melancholy, and vapourish," a condition that could be remedied only by abstinence and more exercise.[50]

Moderation meant not only limiting the absolute quantity of food consumed, but also eating a diet that avoided items composed of large, tube-clogging particles or "an abundance of sharp and acrimonious salts" that caused the juices to become corrosive.[51] To guide his readers – and their cooks – in the formulation of a healthy diet, Cheyne gave some additional rules: Fatty or oily foods (which were composed of large, gluey particles) were to be avoided in favor of lean or starchy ones. The flesh of young animals or of individuals that were small for their breed was finer in texture and therefore less clogging than the meat of older or larger specimens. Spring-ripening fruits and vegetables had less corrosive salt than cultivars that matured later in the season. Freshwater fish and shellfish were to be preferred to saltwater varieties. In general, foods that were white or light in color were healthier than dark or reddish ones because they were composed of finer particles and contained fewer salts (a view that Cheyne claimed was based on observations in Newton's *Optics*).[52] Thus, milk and eggs, light in color and fine in texture, were the animal foods most beneficial to health and could be eaten in quantity. Because chicken, turkey, pheasant, and rabbit were lighter than duck, goose, woodcock, and snipe, they could be consumed more frequently and in larger portions. Turnips, parsnips, and potatoes were better for humans than carrots, beets, and other ruddy vegetables. Fine, white-fleshed fish such as flounder, perch, and sole were healthier than salmon, sturgeon, herring, and mackerel. Beef, the favorite of Cheyne's fellow Britons, was so crammed with large particles and salts that he thought that it should be eaten very sparingly: mutton and veal were recommended instead.[53]

---

[48]   George Cheyne, *An Essay of Health and Long Life*, 10th ed. (London: G. Strahan, 1745), p. 39.
[49]   Ibid., p. 40.
[50]   Ibid., p. 34.
[51]   Ibid.
[52]   Ibid., pp. 20–26.
[53]   Ibid., p. 24.

The diet and environment of animals consumed for food also made a difference in the quality of nourishment they provided. Species that lived on a vegetable diet had finer and milder flesh than carnivores – a reason to avoid consuming many sorts of fish that were cannibalistic as well as carnivorous.[54] Cheyne thought that the common practice of fattening poultry and cattle on diets of corn and confining them in stalls or barns in order to encourage unnatural rates of weight gain rendered such animals unfit as sources of food:

> Perpetual foulness and cramming, gross food and nastiness, we know, will putrefy the juices and mortify the muscular substance of human creatures; and sure they can do no less in brute animals, and thus make even our food poison... The only way of having sound and healthful animal food is to leave them to their own natural liberty, in the free air, and their own proper element, with plenty of food and due cleanness, and a shelter from the injuries of the weather, when they have a mind to retire to it.[55]

The same logic also led Cheyne to condemn vegetables and fruits that were forced out of season in hot beds. Grown in filth – the fresh, rotting manure that raised the temperature of the soil – and deprived of their normal cycle of maturation, such plants were pure poison, no matter how fashionable they might be.[56] This was validation for the reservations that the great La Quintinie had felt about his wizardry with *primeurs* and looked forward to the celebration of natural foods initiated by Rousseau after mid-century.

Finally, Cheyne warned his readers not to eat spicy food. "High relish comes from abundance of salts," he wrote. Plants that absorbed and retained large amounts of solar heat (a condition that concentrated corrosive salts) produced a burning sensation on the tongue and a strong odor in the nose – sure signs that they should be avoided. People who ate such things as garlic or hot spices "swallow so much live coals, which will at last inflame the fluids [in the body] and burn up the solids."[57] Iatromechanical principles led Cheyne to a scientific rationale for the abandonment of spices in cooking some seventy-five years after La Varenne and Bonnefons made this move in the kitchen.

Cheyne's rules for selecting culinary ingredients were accurately paraphrased and attributed by Meusnier in his introduction to *Suite des Dons de*

---

[54] Ibid.
[55] Ibid., p. 28.
[56] Ibid.
[57] Ibid., pp. 26–27.

Comus.[58] Interestingly, the distribution of recipes in the three volumes that followed was mostly consistent with Cheyne's praise of certain ingredients and suspicion of others. In all, 270 pages were devoted to recipes for veal and lean, light-fleshed poultry, while recipes for duck, geese, beef, mutton, lamb, and goat (meats with high concentrations of salts, fats, and large particles) filled a total of only 157.[59] The chapter on pork, which Cheyne regarded as potentially dangerous to people of sedentary occupations, was only 54 pages long and was mostly devoted to ham and other items of charcuterie that were meant to be eaten in small quantities. The majority of Marin's recipes for fresh pork were for heads, tails, ears, and tongue and seem to have been throwbacks to modes of preparation that were popular in the seventeenth century rather than examples of the *nouvelle cuisine. Suite des Dons de Comus* included only 3 recipes for other cuts of the mature pig, plus 5 for *cochon de lait,* an immature, light-fleshed piglet that would have been less lethal than its adult parents according to Cheyne's rules.[60] In sharp contrast to previous French culinary writers, Marin largely ignored furred game – formerly the most prestigious of ingredients but dangerous according to the criteria of iatromechanical dietetics. Instead he scattered a few recipes for venison and wild boar in the chapters on butcher's meat, suggesting that they be prepared as variations on recipes for beef, mutton, or pork.[61]

Vegetarian foods received a lot of coverage. Dishes that used cereals or vegetables as principal ingredients filled more than a hundred pages of volume two, while volume three contained 84 pages of egg recipes suitable for all occasions.[62] Eggs, vegetables, and grains also figured prominently in the chapters on soups, *tourtes,* savory pastries, *crèmes,* and entremets and in the special section about *potages* for days of abstinence. This strong interest in vegetarian ingredients was consistent with Cheyne's belief that most people ate too much meat. However, Marin also devoted 177 pages to fish and other aquatic creatures[63] – more than one would expect given Cheyne's reservations about the role of seafood in the diet. Significantly, this material appeared toward the end of volume three, following a chapter on *potages* and bouillons for lean days. Although some of these recipes included ingredients that would make them unsuitable for days of strict abstinence, fish cookery

58   [Marin], *Les Dons de Comus,* vol. 1, pp. xii–xiv.
59   Ibid., vol. 1, pp. 137–301, and vol. 2, pp. 78–257.
60   Ibid., vol. 2, pp. 1–54.
61   For example, see the recipes for *saucisson de venaison* and *cochon sauvage* in ibid., vol. 2, pp. 23–24 and 52–53.
62   Ibid., vol. 2, pp. 371–474, and vol. 3, pp. 239–323. In addition, these foods were heavily represented in the chapters on *potages* and on fast day menus.
63   Ibid., vol. 3, pp. 365–542.

as a whole continued to be linked to fasting. Thus the religious obligations of the French cook and his Catholic audience counterbalanced the Scottish doctor's warnings about consuming a lot of fish.

Cheyne insisted that even wholesome ingredients could be ruined through the ignorance or perversity of cooks. Roasting and boiling were the only techniques that preserved the quintessential properties of raw foodstuffs: everything else involved an alteration for the worse. Frying added fatty particles that could cause obstructions. Ragouts and other "made dishes" typically included seasonings, rich sauces, and fancy garnishes that cancelled out the benefits of healthy foods such as poultry or vegetables and amplified the clogging and corrosive attributes of red meat and fish. Furthermore, sauced dishes and flavorful condiments tempted one to eat more than necessary, a habit that set the scene for a host of ailments. Although Cheyne constantly exhorted his patients to exercise self-control at the table, he also thought it was foolish to place temptation too obviously in their path. (His own weight peaked at 450 pounds and stabilized at around 300 after a decade of dietary therapy.) He singled out two types of cooking that were especially liable to provoke overeating: the spicy pickles and chutneys newly introduced to England from the East and "the French style of cooking" that was held in such high repute in elite social circles.[64] It is interesting to note that Vincent La Chapelle was employed by one of Cheyne's patients, Lord Chesterfield, and it would be fascinating to know whether the doctor had occasion to become personally acquainted with La Chapelle's luscious food.[65] Surely he would have rated *pigeons à la lune* as both a dietary nightmare and a wicked pleasure.

Although the *nouvelle cuisine* offered no solution to the problems of overeating (apart from the calls to moderation issued in *avertissement* and later in Meusnier's introduction), it aimed at creating dishes that were lighter and easier to digest than old-fashioned French cooking. The choice of principal ingredients played a role in this, as we have seen, but techniques of preparation and menus that were "simple and natural" were perhaps even more important. It is to these issues that we now turn.

CUISINE NOUVELLE, CUISINE BOURGEOISE

The cornerstone of the *nouvelle cuisine*, on which recipes of all sorts were built, was bouillon. Of course, bouillon had long been a prominent element

---

[64] Cheyne, *The English Malady*, p. 51.
[65] Guerrini, *Obesity and Depression in the Enlightenment*, pp. 8–21. On Chesterfield's employment of La Chapelle, see Barbara Wheaton, *Savoring the Past*, pp. 167–168.

in European cuisine, serving as a cooking medium and a base for *potages* and sauced dishes for hundreds of years. Since the days of La Varenne and Bonnefons, French cookery writers had universally held that the quality of the bouillon could make or break a recipe and that meticulous preparation with carefully chosen fresh ingredients was the key to fine results. The old habit of boiling up assorted odds and ends and using the liquid to prepare all the dishes made in the kitchen that day had been roundly denounced as slovenly and – just as bad – imparting a dull sameness to every dish in which it was used. Massialot developed the practice, previously advocated by Bonnefons, of preparing different kinds of bouillon tailored to the needs of a particular recipe, without extraneous herbs or flavorings. He also used concentrated meat stocks in the form of *jus* or coulis to fortify the flavor and to impart body to sauces. Reliance on bouillon in its many rarefied forms was one of the distinguishing marks of French cooking of the Massialot school.

The problem, from the point of view of iatromechanical dietetics, was that bouillon was a dangerous food. Composed primarily of beef, it contained high concentrations of large particles and corrosive salts. Cheyne conceded that weak meat broths were nourishing for healthy people, especially when they were thickened with purées of boiled vegetables. However, bouillons that were concentrated were, in his estimation, even more difficult to digest than the same weight of solid beef.[66] A typical French menu, which would have included bouillon-based soups and sauces in addition to dishes of meat or fish, would have been loaded with unwholesome substances. No wonder that Cheyne thought that a steady diet of French cooking was likely to cause serious illness.

Marin's aim was to make bouillons that improved the flavor and texture of soups and sauces but were also healthier to eat. *Les Dons de Comus* included several recipes that resulted from these efforts.[67] His preferred method was to combine a reduced quantity of beef with veal or chicken or both. This yielded bouillon that was full in flavor and body but *léger* (that is, light in color and not very salty).[68] He pointed out that the quality of all bouillons – even those that for reasons of economy were made with beef alone – could be substantially improved by meticulous skimming during the cooking process and subsequent straining and clarification, which removed all visible particles and fat. The result was liquid nourishment that was easy to digest, beautiful to look at (a limpid, clear golden color), and delicious to eat.[69]

---

[66]   Cheyne, *An Essay of Health and Long Life*, p. 42.
[67]   [Marin], *Les Dons de Comus*, vol. 1, pp. 1–9.
[68]   Ibid.
[69]   Ibid., pp. xiii–xix and 5–7.

Such bouillon could be used as a base for soups and sauces, and it was also an essential ingredient in consommé, quintessence, and *jus*. In Marin's parlance, all three of these were double-rich preparations, that is, they combined previously made bouillon with freshly extracted juices of additional meats and vegetables. Consommé started with a large volume of liquid that simmered and condensed over a period of many hours. Quintessence, cooked in a covered casserole, used much less liquid and derived more of its character from the fresh ingredients. The preparation of *jus* involved browning meats and vegetables over a lively flame and then simmering them with bouillon and seasonings for an hour or so.[70] All three techniques resulted in liquids that were golden to amber brown in color and somewhat gelatinous in texture. Mellow, unctuous, and purged of all impurities, they were added by the spoonful to dishes designed to serve many people.

Although Marin gave recipes for thickeners, including roux, egg yolk liaisons, and coulis (although he regarded the latter as a holdover from "*l'ancienne cuisine gauloise*," presumably because of its sandy texture), his preferred technique of making sauces was to reduce cooking liquids over high heat and enrich and thicken them with a spoonful of consommé, quintessence, or *jus*. According to dietetic theory, this was playing with fire, but the advocates of the *nouvelle cuisine* seemed to think that it constituted an acceptable compromise between the imperatives of good health and the desire for sophisticated food. "I am for the simplest method, and I believe that it the best for health," Marin declared.[71]

He used this technique to finish the sauces for ragouts and fricassees of all sorts as well as to concoct free-standing sauces to be served with roasted or poached meats and fish. For example, one made *sauce à l'ivoire*, which was meant to accompany roasted or grilled poultry or veal, by sautéing some sliced onion and tidbits of veal, ham, and salt pork; when these were brown, they were seasoned with fines herbs and garlic, moistened with a glass of champagne, and left to simmer until the solid ingredients had rendered all their flavorful juices, which were strained, degreased, reduced, and finally thickened with a little consommé.[72] As the culinary historian Barbara Wheaton has noted, such recipes produce results that are "fresh and refined" and bear a certain resemblance to the sauces created in our own day by contemporary practitioners of *nouvelle cuisine*.[73] She also notes that these sauces – like those of Paul Bocuse and other twentieth-century

[70] Ibid., pp. 6–9.
[71] From the two-volume edition of *Les Dons de Comus*, published in 1740, as quoted by Wheaton, *Savoring the Past*, p. 205.
[72] [Marin], *Les Dons de Comus*, vol. 1, pp. 39–40.
[73] Wheaton, *Savoring the Past*, p. 205.

chefs – were neither easy nor cheap to make, thanks to their dependence on concentrated bouillons. For example, Marin's recipe for consommé, which yields about a quart, calls for two pounds of beef, two pounds of veal, two partridges, a large chicken (*poularde*), a couple of slices of ham, onions, carrots, turnips, a parsnip, and a celery root plus seasonings and bouillon made previously from additional meats and vegetables.[74] Furthermore, making good sauces and the bouillons and essences that went into them required patience and attention to detail as well as finely honed judgment about quantities, seasonings, and levels of reduction, as Marin himself noted.[75]

That said, Marin's dishes affected a certain straightforward simplicity on the plate and on the palate – the painstaking techniques and many steps executed in the kitchen were meant to be invisible in the finished product. For example, preparing *filet de boeuf à la glace* was an all-day project that involved larding a whole filet of beef and braising it; when tender, the meat was chilled, carved, arranged on a platter, and enrobed in aspic made from top-quality bouillon, which itself was the product of hours of labor.[76] However, the dish appeared on the plate as a plain slice of cold meat whose only adornments were a thin glaze of jelly and a sprinkle of minced herbs and cracked pepper. No extraneous garnishes, no multicolored sauces, no pastry croutons. Anyone who was not a cook could be excused for assuming that *filet de boeuf à la glace* was actually easy to make.

This sort of recipe, which combined understated appearances with clean, complimentary flavors, appeared frequently in Marin's work and illustrates the qualities that made the *nouvelle cuisine* fresh and appetizing to sophisticated eaters who had become weary of fancy food. He observed that elaborate dishes tended to appeal to very particular tastes and that many of them were instantly forgotten. By embracing simplicity, the *nouvelle cuisine* allowed the natural goodness of the ingredients to show through and created food that was universally appealing. "The small number [of recipes] to which I have limited myself will without doubt always be in fashion unless nature itself undergoes a major change," he wrote.[77]

Although dishes such as *filet de boeuf à la glace* were not as uncomplicated as they seemed, many other recipes in Marin's repertoire really were simple to execute, with a minimum of expense, equipment, and technique. Two of the sample menus in the 1742 edition were composed of recipes he described, accurately, as "simple and natural."[78] Among the featured

74   Ibid. See also [Marin], *Les Dons de Comus*, vol. 1, p. 7.
75   For examples see [Marin], *Les Dons de Comus*, vol. 1, pp. 3, 7, 8–9, and 13.
76   Ibid., vol. 1, pp. 181–182.
77   Ibid., vol. 1, p. 424.
78   Ibid., vol. 1, pp. 419–426.

dishes were a *potage de santé* made with a light, poultry-based bouillon and root vegetables; boiled veal shank served with a sprinkle of coarse salt; grilled mutton chops; braised turkey wings; casserole-roasted chicken with onions; grilled pigeons (whimsically named *"à la crapaudine"* – froglike – for their flattened shape); poached eggs; crawfish tails dressed in olive oil; green salad; asparagus; cardoons; custard; and rice pudding. Marin pointed out that none of these dishes called for costly ingredients or specialized kitchen skills: "no *jus*, no coulis, no consommé, no reductions, no *restaurants*."[79] At most, one would serve on the side a *sauce ravigotte*, a mixture of pounded herbs (chervil, tarragon, cress, parsley, chives, shallots, garlic, and celery for preference) tossed in a mustard and anchovy vinaigrette.[80]

Uncontrived recipes of this sort played an important role in Marin's cuisine – they appear in all of the sections of his book and are paired seamlessly on menus with dishes that were more expensive and complicated to make. The measure of a dish's quality was not its cost or the amount of time and expertise required to produce it, but the harmoniousness of its flavors and the purity of its effect. In these respects, a grilled pigeon with *sauce ravigotte* was as excellent as *filet de boeuf à la glace*: the aesthetic of simplicity embraced them both.

Half a century earlier, Massialot had argued that good taste rather than expense was the key to creating fine food. He believed that by publishing precise descriptions of advanced techniques and recipes for basic mixtures he was equipping the upper level of bourgeois kitchens with the means to replicate the dishes he served to his aristocratic and princely clientele. Marin took up this theme, even as he rejected Massialot's cuisine as pretentious, out of date, and, ultimately, dull. Instead of wasting money and time trying to produce dishes that had been fashionable in the reign of Louis XIV, he wrote, households with smaller staffs and modest budgets should spent their money on good, fresh ingredients and cook them without fuss, in the manner of the *nouvelle cuisine*.[81]

Many recipes found in all three volumes of *Suite des Dons de Comus* were suitable for this purpose, as the "simple and natural" menus demonstrated. It was also feasible to adapt recipes written for expensive foodstuffs to cheaper ones. For example, one could vary the recipe for *griblettes de boeuf* (thick slices of beef coated with seasonings and bread crumbs and grilled) by using cooked brisket left over from making broth instead of

---

[79]   Ibid., vol. 1, p. 421.

[80]   Ibid., vol. 1, p. 76. If one minced the herbs and anchovy instead of pounding them before tossing them with the mustard vinaigrette, the result was *sauce rémoulade*; see vol. 1, pp. 72–73.

[81]   Ibid., vol. 3, pp. 543–544.

costly, quick-cooking raw filet.[82] Marin explained that although it was ideal to use several kinds of meat to make bouillon, one could still get good results from a single, cheap cut, provided that it was fresh and of good quality. (Marin stressed over and over again that buying ingredients that were over the hill was a false economy: better to choose a vegetable or cut of meat that was less expensive to start with than discounted goods that had been marked down because they were second-rate or on the verge of spoiling.)[83] More important than variety or the specific cut of meat when making bouillon was the determination of the cook to skim every bit of scum that rose to the surface of the simmering liquid and later to remove every drop of fat from the finished product.[84] Like Massialot before him, Marin thought that perseverance was the key to perfection, trumping special equipment, unusual skills, or expense. Economical broths could be turned into a variety of appetizing soups, depending on which vegetables were available at the right price on any particular day: onions, carrots, parsnips, turnips, celery root, cabbage, and mixed green herbs all offered interesting possibilities.[85]

In addition to directing his readers to recipes from previous chapters that could be easily adapted to their means, Marin also included some special dishes in his section on bourgeois cooking. Several of these used meats left over from making bouillon,[86] but others called for fresh ingredients that were inexpensive and easy to come by. Shoulder of veal was cut into cubes, moistened with a glass of white wine and some water, and braised with aromatic vegetables.[87] Pigeons could be fricasseed in the same manner, with artichokes or peas added according to the season, and chicken giblets were also tasty when prepared according to this method.[88] A whole chicken was savory and delicious when smothered in paper-thin slices of onion and slow-roasted in a covered casserole over the embers of the fire (a method that left the cook free to attend to other chores).[89] A slice of round steak could be

---

[82]   Ibid., vol. 3, pp. 573–574.

[83]   Ibid.

[84]   Ibid., vol. 3, pp. 544–545. In the same spirit, Marin even gave a recipe for an economical form of *jus* made with a small quantity of boned veal shoulder, salt pork, and onion; see vol. 3, pp. 547–548.

[85]   Ibid., vol. 3, pp. 556–561.

[86]   In addition to the *griblettes* made with boiled brisket, these recipes included a fricassee with mushrooms, a *mironton*, two versions of beef with parsley sauce (one hot, one cold), sliced beef with onion sauce, fritters, and a meat loaf (*hachis de boeuf en pot*); see ibid., vol. 3, pp. 567–576.

[87]   Ibid., vol. 3, p. 581.

[88]   Ibid., vol. 3, pp. 586–588.

[89]   Ibid., vol. 3, pp. 584–585.

pounded; filled with a stuffing of minced beef, salt pork, and herbs; rolled; and braised in a casserole with wedges of blanched cabbage; the degreased juices served as a sauce.[90] On fast days, Marin advised his readers to choose freshwater fish, which were always cheaper and usually fresher in the Paris market than *poissons de mer*. Carp, eel, or other varieties could be filleted; cut into pieces the thickness of a finger; marinated with lemon, onion, and herbs; and then floured and sautéed over lively heat. Alternatively, the fish could be stewed with red wine and onions or poached in a court bouillon composed of water and a little wine – one of the cheapest and nicest ways to cook them, according to Marin.[91] Typically these easy and economical dishes were served with sauces composed of the reduced, degreased cooking juices. Sometimes these were thickened with a butter liaison, but never with consommé, a mixture too expensive and demanding of time to be a staple in modest kitchens. Grilled, roasted, or fried foods were finished with a few drops of verjuice, lemon, or bitter orange juice – a practice reminiscent of La Varenne and Bonnefons.

By mid-century, the *nouvelle cuisine* was no longer new, but its culinary techniques and recipes continued to shape cooking until the end of the ancien régime. One of the people who was responsible for this was François Menon, who published a number of popular books, beginning with *Le Nouveau Traité de cuisine,* that advanced ideas similar to Marin's.[92] Throughout his voluminous oeuvre, Menon argued that cooking should strive for elegant understatement, achieved by the choice of good ingredients; harmonious combinations of clean, fresh flavors; uncluttered presentations; and fastidious (although not necessarily difficult) techniques. This was an imperative of health as well as of aesthetics.[93] Thanks in part

---

[90]   Ibid., vol. 3, pp. 583–584.

[91]   Ibid., vol. 3, pp. 595–597.

[92]   Although Menon's recipes were less innovative than those published by Marin, he made up for this in the sheer volume of his work and his enduring popularity with a wide and varied readership; in this respect, he was the Martha Stewart of the age. Between 1739 and 1761 Menon published nine separate titles, many of which were issued in multiple editions and with significant additions: *Le Nouveau Traité de cuisine* (1739 in two volumes, with a third volume subtitled *La Nouvelle Cuisine* appearing in 1742), *La Cuisinière bourgeoise* (1746 and many subsequent editions), *La Science du maître-d'hôtel cuisinier* (1749), *La Science du maître-d'hôtel confiseur* (1750), *Les Soupers de la Cour* (1755), *Cuisine et Office de santé* (1758), *Le Manuel des officiers de la bouche* (1759), *Almanach de cuisine* (1761), and *Almanach d'office* (1761). See Hyman and Hyman, "Printing the Kitchen," p. 401.

[93]   For example, see the *"Dissertation Préliminaire sur la Cuisine moderne"* that begins *La Science du maître-d'hôtel cuisinier* (Paris: Chez les libraires associés, 1749; reprint Paris, 1982), pp. iii–xxiv.

to Menon's influence, *"la cuisine bourgeoise"* would emerge as a distinct culinary trend, linked to thrift (or at least a rejection of obvious luxury). However, in its commitment to simplicity and the straightforwardness of its technique, *cuisine bourgeoise* was very much an offshoot of the *nouvelle cuisine*.

The idea behind Menon's hugely successful *La Cuisinière bourgeoise* was to cater to households in which the kitchen staff consisted of women rather than men. Because men always commanded more prestige and higher wages than women with similar skills, male chefs tended to be employed in the grandest of aristocratic households, where the servants numbered in the hundreds and the kitchen staff alone might account for twenty or more. In contrast, most noble households in eighteenth-century France employed a total of between six and twenty servants; the upper reaches of the mercantile class and the country gentry, between six and twelve; a professional household of modest but comfortable means, three or four; and a prosperous artisan, one or two.[94] The smaller the household, the more likely it was to have a female cook and the less likely she was to have any regular help from the other servants. Even in households with a staff of three or four, the cook was often solely responsible for the daily marketing, in addition to preparing breakfast and multi-course menus for dinner and supper.

Such one-woman kitchens were efficient out of necessity, economical with preparation time as well as ingredients. As in Marin's remarks on bourgeois cooking, Menon stressed recipes for modestly priced, readily available ingredients: more mutton than lamb and lots of chicken, pigeon, and freshwater fish.[95] Despite this concurrence about ingredients, the two authors took quite different approaches to devising recipes. Marin, ever the perfectionist, was interested in creating scaled-down versions of *nouvelle cuisine* dishes that were just as refined as the originals. This goal was frequently reached through the investment of a lot of the cook's time. Marin's economy version of beef bouillon used cheaper ingredients and fewer of them, but required the same attention to detail to produce broth that was full-flavored, perfectly reduced, skimmed, degreased, and clarified. It was the sort of recipe that could be easily managed in households of the upper bourgeoisie, where the cook could count on some assistance from the lower servants. In a one-woman kitchen, however, this level of perfection would

---

[94]   Olwen H. Hufton, *The Prospect Before Her: A History of Women in Western Europe, 1500–1800* (New York: Alfred A. Knopf, 1996), pp. 81–82.

[95]   [François Menon], *La Cuisinière bourgeoise*, new ed. (Paris: Guillyn, 1762), pp. 54–95, 154–157, 160–172, 182–193, 202–214, and 239–276.

17. *The Kitchen Maid*, circa 1735, by Jean-Baptiste-Siméon Chardin (Samuel H. Cress Collection, National Gallery of Art, Washington; image © Board of Trustees, National Gallery of Art, Washington).

have been much more difficult to attain on a consistent basis. Although many of Menon's recipes specify something called bouillon, this usually meant a rapidly prepared stock brewed up in an hour or less. His gazetteer of culinary terms included no entry for "consommé" or "*restaurant.*"[96] As a cooking medium and base for sauces, Menon's stock was much less suave than Marin's bouillon, but it sufficed well enough when the cook was pressed for time. Whereas Marin explained to his readers how to turn the boiled beef that was a by-product of bouillon making into delectable entrées and hors d'oeuvres, such as the *griblettes* discussed previously, Menon suggested presenting the meat on a deep platter with a little cooking liquid and coarse salt. *Bouilli de boeuf* was not an elegant dish or even a particularly

[96]   [Menon], *La Cuisinière bourgeoise*, pp. iii–xxiv.

savory one (Jean-Anthelme Brillat-Savarin, the famous gourmet, said that
he never ate *bouilli* because the meat, drained of its natural juices by boiling, tended to be dry and lacking in flavor),[97] but it had the incomparable
advantage of requiring no additional preparation time. *Bouilli* appeared
more often than any other dish in the menus recommended by *La Cuisinière
bourgeoise* for dinners and suppers throughout the year.[98] It was a clear
indication of Menon's orientation toward the one-woman kitchen.

Many of the sauces in *La Cuisinière bourgeoise* owed their character
to a base of minced vegetables and herbs that were sautéed, simmered
with liquid, and then puréed to form a light liaison, without the addition
of roux, egg yolks, or other thickening agents. Menon's variations on this
technique included his recipes for *sauce à la crème* (shallots, chives, parsley,
and garlic sautéed in butter and simmered with cream), *sauce provençale*
(mushrooms, shallots, parsley, chives, and two cloves of garlic sautéed in
olive oil and simmered with white wine), and *sauce piquante* (onion, carrot,
parsnip, thyme, bay leaf, basil, and two cloves of garlic simmered in broth
and seasoned with a spoonful of vinegar).[99] Unlike roux-thickened veloutés,
which developed their silky texture by long simmering over a slow fire, such
sauces were fast to make from scratch. They were also foolproof, in contrast
to emulsified sauces, which could curdle or separate if they were heated
too much or if the cook miscalculated the proportions of egg yolk or butter
to the other ingredients. Another intriguing example of an easy, quickly
made, risk-free sauce was the one Menon specified for *gigot à l'Anglaise*
(a whole poached leg of lamb, English style). A glass of the cooking liquid
was boiled with capers, anchovies, chives, shallots, and parsley and finished
with some finely minced hard-boiled egg yolk.[100] Alternatively, the lamb
could be served with a sauce thickened with a substance that Menon called
"*coulis bourgeois.*" It was made by browning a small quantity of veal and
root vegetables in fat and then deglazing the drippings; the rendered juices
were strained and thickened with flour, yielding a mixture that was closer
to a concentrated, Anglo-American-style gravy base than a true coulis,
whose sandy texture derived from the puréed principal ingredients. *Coulis
bourgeois* could be made ahead and was used a spoonful at a time to turn pan
juices into brown sauce – another economical shortcut for the hard-pressed
female cook.[101]

[97] J.-A. Brillat-Savarin, *Physiologie de Goût*, with an introduction by Jean-François
     Revel (Paris: Flammarion, 1982), p. 370.

[98] [Menon], *La Cuisinière bourgeoise*, pp. 1–18.

[99] Ibid., pp. 383 and 388–389.

[100] Ibid., pp. 58–59.

[101] Ibid., pp. 130–131.

THE ENLIGHTENMENT CRITIQUE OF ARTIFICE

The success of simple cooking neither eclipsed the ongoing presence of *la cuisine ancienne à la mode de Massialot* nor did it lay to rest the subjects of philosophical or scientific controversy that marked its reception circa 1740. Right down to 1789, we find variants of the *nouvelle cuisine* coexisting in the cooking literature and on Parisian tables with dishes conceived in the rococo spirit. For example, the anonymous *Traité historique et pratique de la cuisine* (1758) featured a ragout of songbirds that was presented in a case of forcemeat molded to look like a galley (a ship propelled by both oars and sail) with a "deck" made of veal scallops and a "mast" (an inedible skewer) festooned with "sails" of cockscombs, bacon, and foie gras.[102] The impulse toward decoration and artifice ran as deep in eighteenth-century culinary practice as the contrary desire for simplicity and naturalness. One sees the former even in the presentation of dishes that were otherwise uncomplicated, such as the salad of green beans described in the *Traité historique*. This was nothing more than beans, blanched and chilled, in an herb-flavored vinaigrette. It could be simply presented on a deep platter, of course, but, as the author pointed out, "some people like to make various heraldic designs with this salad, such as a knight's cross, a Maltese cross, a star, or some other design."[103] This was twenty years after Marin claimed that fancy food was utterly passé.

This duality of artifice and simplicity, the contrived and the authentic, also characterized the visual arts in the middle decades of the eighteenth century. The rococo had emerged at the end of the reign of Louis XIV and flourished under the Regent as a graceful and sensuous alternative to the stiff and ponderous baroque of Versailles. Whereas the baroque had used huge scale, rare and costly materials, and rigidly geometrical facades, floor plans, and vistas to create an atmosphere of overwhelming, intimidating grandeur, rococo architecture created intimate spaces that were often curved or asymmetrical in shape. These were lavishly adorned with gilded and painted stucco and plasterwork in the form of cupids, garlands, shells, and other such motifs. Spaces in between the plaster decorations were washed in pastel shades or, for preference, filled with canvases painted with pastoral scenes. Whether these showed nymphs and gods, shepherds and shepherdesses, or courtiers on a picnic could be difficult to discern and deliberately so. Official patronage of architects and painters who worked in the rococo style reached its apogee in the 1740s and 1750s, thanks in part to the influence of Mme. de Pompadour, the mistress of Louis XV.

---

102 Wheaton, *Savoring the Past*, p. 206.
103 Ibid., p. 270.

For twenty years she controlled commissions emanating from the royal household and was a tireless promoter of artists she admired, including the painter François Boucher (1703–1770), who made several portraits of her, in addition to supplying other paintings and decorative panels for her numerous dwellings.

Boucher's rise as the prince of rococo painting depended on his subtle palette and representation of light, his graceful compositions, and a certain theatricality in the representation of his subjects. All of these qualities are present in one of his best-known pictures (currently in the Louvre), which shows Diana, goddess of the hunt, resting with a nymph companion. Diana is seated with her left leg crossed over her right, toes pointed in a pose of exaggerated refinement that defies nature. The art historian Kenneth Clark observed that Boucher "created an image that Venus Naturalis would like to see in the mirror, a magic reflection in which she ceases to be natural without ceasing to be desirable."[104]

In the eyes of Boucher's admirers, the theatricality of *Diana* and similar paintings was fundamental to their charm. By mid-century, however, it had come to be seen by some as not only contrived but hypocritical and false – the very opposite of what art should be. This condemnation of theatricality was a central theme in contemporary writings on aesthetics, most notably in the work of Denis Diderot (1713–1784).[105] Diderot was a man of many talents – a philosopher, translator, editor of the *Encyclopédie*, novelist, theorist of drama, and one of the first people to write systematic criticism of art. His *bête noir* as a critic of both painting and the stage was any hint of phoniness or posturing in an artist's representation of his subject:

> Every personage who seems to tell you: "Look how well I cry, how well I become angry, how well I implore" is false and *mannered.*
>
> Every personage who departs from what is appropriate to his state or his character – an elegant magistrate, a woman who grieves

[104]   Kenneth Clark, *The Nude: A Study in Ideal Form* (Princeton, NJ: Princeton University Press, 1956), p. 150.

[105]   This argument is developed in compelling detail in Michael Fried, *Absorption and Theatricality: Painting and the Beholder in the Age of Diderot* (Berkeley and Los Angeles: University of California Press, 1980). Whereas most accounts of eighteenth-century French painting suggest that the painters of the 1750s and 1760s were preoccupied with creating works that would appeal to the middlebrow tastes of an emerging middle class, Fried argues that their fundamental concern was to free painting from the contrivance that was central to rococo art by establishing the fiction that the beholder does not exist – a radical solution to the problem of theatricality.

and artfully arranges her arms, a man who walks to show off his legs – is false and *mannered*.[106]

The opposite of a posing, mannered figure, according to Diderot, was one who was absorbed in activity or thought and whose expression, posture, and movements were therefore spontaneous and genuine. The master of such authentic representations in painting was Jean-Baptiste-Siméon Chardin (1699–1779), a contemporary of Boucher but his opposite in every respect. Chardin painted still-life pictures and genre scenes that caught the look and texture of daily experience among the bourgeoisie and the servant class. His typical subjects included young people engaged in amusements (building a house of cards, blowing a soap bubble, playing a game of knucklebones), mothers interacting with children (reciting a lesson, finishing a morning toilette, saying grace before a meal), and cooks going about their work (peeling vegetables, fetching stores from a barrel, resting on the landing of the stairs after returning from the market). From the time Chardin first started to exhibit his paintings, in the 1730s, audiences admired his art

for the truthfulness with which it depicted *"les petits details de la vie commune"* (the little details of ordinary life), a virtue in keeping with the "lesser" genres he practiced. Around the middle of the century, however, the reaction against the Rococo began to gather force; the persuasive representation of absorption emerged in the criticism of the time as a conscious and explicit desideratum; and concomitantly Chardin's genre paintings, including those of the 1730s and 1740s, were seen not only as satisfying such a desideratum but as exemplary, in that crucial respect, for the pictorial enterprise as such.[107]

In short, Chardin's art came to be admired not only for its verisimilitude but also for its authenticity, that is, the trueness of the subject to itself.

The sense of posing for an audience that was so condemned by Diderot and other critics of rococo art would have seemed second nature to contemporaries who were part of court society. At court, the world really was a stage in which spontaneity of movement and speech were checked by the role one was assigned to play. We have already examined the contrast between polite speech as practiced at court, with its emphasis on deference to one's superiors, and in the world of the Parisian salon and dinner

---

106 Ibid., pp. 99–100.
107 Fried, *Absorption and Theatricality*, p. 52.

party, where candor and reciprocity were prized (Chapter 3). In the age of Louis XIV, members of the elite switched back and forth between the two forms of *politesse* as if untroubled – or unaware – of the contradictory ideas these embodied. However, by 1750 or so, such smooth transitions were becoming more difficult to sustain. The posturing that was central to courtly standards of conduct came to be seen not as an affirmation of one's identity within the hierarchy, but as phoniness, a negation of the genuine self. Even the conventions of the salon and dinner party, which evolved to provide a liberating alternative to court etiquette, were now seen by some as just another set of theatrical poses. Jean-Jacques Rousseau (1712–1778) devoted much of his career to tracing the evils that flowed from the deeply ingrained artifice of polite society and to thinking through the means by which human beings could escape from it into a life of spontaneity and authenticity. The enthusiasm with which the French (and European) public embraced his works, beginning with *The Discourse on the Arts and Sciences* (1750) and culminating with his autobiography, the *Confessions* (published posthumously in two parts in 1782 and 1789), showed just how fundamental these issues were to the contemporary social imagination.[108]

It was in this context, in which many people were coming to view theatricality as false and corrupting, that discussions about simple cooking moved into a higher gear. Around 1740, the aesthetic preference for culinary simplicity had been justified in terms of health, moderation, and good taste. After mid-century, it came to be associated, in addition, with the rejection of artifice and the embrace of an authentic way of life.

A good place to pick up the thread of this discussion is in the *Encyclopédie* of Diderot and D'Alembert, the great multi-volume reference work that appeared between 1751 and 1772 and ultimately filled seventeen volumes of text and eleven volumes of plates.[109] Although it was not the

---

[108] Rousseau's suspicion of civilization and progress generated tensions between him and his fellow philosophes, while at the same time developing the Enlightenment's commitment to freedom as the fundamental right of human beings. See the assessment of Rousseau's relationship to the Enlightenment in Gay, *The Science of Freedom*, vol. 2 of *The Enlightenment*, pp. 529–552. See also Mark Hulliung, *The Autocritique of the Enlightenment: Rousseau and the Philosophes* (Cambridge, MA: Harvard University Press, 1998). On the appeal of Rousseau's ideas and his unique voice to eighteenth-century readers, see Robert Darnton, "Readers Respond to Rousseau" in *The Great Cat Massacre and Other Episodes in French Cultural History* (New York: Basic Books, 1984), pp. 215–256.

[109] For background on the creation and history of the *Encyclopédie*, see Arthur M. Wilson, *Diderot* (New York: Oxford University Press, 1972), pp. 73–83, 117–172, and 232–247; and Robert Darnton, "Philosophers Trim the Tree of Knowledge: The Epistemological Strategy of the *Encyclopédie*" in *The Great Cat Massacre and Other Episodes in French Cultural History*, pp. 191–213.

first work that attempted to summarize human knowledge in the form of an alphabetical dictionary, it was easily the most ambitious. In Diderot's words, the *Encyclopédie* aimed to change "the common way of thinking in matters of philosophy and taste."[110]

This goal was pursued from a number of different angles. The *Encyclopédie* reported on recent developments in all branches of science (indeed, one reason that Diderot and D'Alembert were chosen as editors was D'Alembert's reputation as a mathematician of distinction and Diderot's record as a translator of medical texts). Readers were also introduced to the progressive line in social and political thought. The entry on "Government" explained that "all *legitimate* sovereign power must emanate from the free consent of the people" – a radical idea in the age of absolute monarchy.[111] Adam Smith took the famous example of the division of labor featured in *The Wealth of Nations* (1776) from the article "Pin" (*Epingle*) that appeared in the *Encyclopédie* in 1755.[112] "Intolerance" and "Intolerant man" made a radical case for religious pluralism.[113] Readers were invited to see social, political, and religious experience through the lenses of science and reason rather than those of deference and piety. They were encouraged to draw inferences from the cross-references supplied at the end of articles – a technique that allowed the authors and editors to outwit censors alive to any hint of unorthodox religious opinion or ideas hostile to absolute monarchy.[114] For example, whereas it would be too aggressive to directly attack the privileges that the nobility and the Roman Catholic Church enjoyed in French society, a critical stance could be suggested by cross-referencing the article on "France" to "Taxes" and "Toleration."[115]

Another side of the mission to change the common way of thinking involved the dissemination of practical and technical knowledge of all sorts. In early modern Europe, detailed information about the mechanical arts and crafts tended to be passed along within professions or trade guilds. The written documentation that did exist tended to be fragmentary and fully intelligible only to men who had prior hands-on training in the trade. As we have seen, most of the culinary literature of the age was an example of this, with the *Délices de la campagne* of Bonnefons and the *Cuisinier roïal*

---

[110] *"Encyclopédie"* in *Encyclopédie, ou Dictionnaire raisonné des sciences, des arts et des métiers, par une société de gens de lettres*, edited by M. Diderot and, for the part on mathematics, M. d'Alembert, 28 vols. (Geneva [Paris and Neufchastel], 1772), vol. 5, p. 635.

[111] Quoted in Wilson, *Diderot*, p. 234.

[112] Ibid., pp. 235–236.

[113] *"Intolérance"* and *"Intolérant"* in *Encyclopédie*, vol. 3, pp. 843–844.

[114] Darnton, "Philosophers Trim the Tree of Knowledge," pp. 191–214.

[115] *"France"* in *Encyclopédie*, vol. 7, p. 282.

et bourgeois of Massialot as the outstanding exceptions. As early as 1675, Jean-Baptiste Colbert, Louis XIV's principal minister, had commissioned the Royal Academy of Sciences to publish explanations and illustrations of machinery and equipment used in the mechanical arts and crafts, but the project languished, with the first installment appearing only eighty-four years later, in 1761.[116] Meanwhile, the *Encyclopédie* had claimed the area as its own. Diderot thought that the tradition of keeping knowledge bottled up within professional communities retarded the march of human progress and that it was of critical importance to explain technical processes to the general public, who would then be free to adapt and perfect them.[117] While the Academy proceeded at a deliberate pace, the society of men of letters who contributed to the *Encyclopédie* forged ahead with their massive how-to book. "There does not exist a single pamphlet on the art of making shirts, stockings, shoes, bread; the *Encyclopédie* is the first and unique work describing these arts useful to men," wrote one contributor.[118]

All of these aspects of the *Encyclopédie* contributed to its usefulness as a source of information about food and culinary practice in the middle of the eighteenth century.[119] The imperative to report on scientific developments meant that there were numerous articles about medicine and dietetics, for example, on topics such as "Chylification" and "Taste (Physiology)."[120] Many animals and plants used for food were also described at length – for example, "Apple" (in which the fruit was cross-referenced to "Indigestion" and also to "Tisane," a soothing infusion), "Beef" (both the animal and the meat), and "Chocolate" (a superb article by Diderot that discussed the drink's history in Mexico and Spain, the method of preparing it, and its uses in stimulating the appetite, plus cross-references to substances used to season it – "Achiote," "Pepper," and "Vanilla" – and to the tree that produced it, "Cacao").[121] The article "Artichoke" gave details on how to cultivate

---

[116] Wilson, *Diderot,* pp. 360–364.

[117] Ibid., pp. 136–138.

[118] Ibid., p. 136.

[119] On the many dimensions of the treatment of food and cooking in the *Encyclopédie,* see Jean-Claude Bonnet, "The Culinary System of the *Encyclopédie*" in *Food and Drink in History: Selections from the Annales Economies, Sociétés, Civilisations,* edited by Robert Forster and Orest Ranum, translated by Elborg Forster and Patricia M. Ranum (Baltimore, MD, and London: Johns Hopkins University Press, 1979), pp. 139–165.

[120] *"Chylification"* and *"Goût (Physiologie)"* in *Encyclopédie,* vol. 3, pp. 405–408, and vol. 7, pp. 758–761.

[121] *"Pomme," "Boeuf,"* and *"Chocolate"* in *Encyclopédie,* vol. 2, pp. 291–294; vol. 13, pp. 2–3; and vol. 3, pp. 359–360.

the plant as well as an actual recipe for *artichauts à la poivrade*, a raw salad with a peppery dressing. Techniques of preparation were also defined, such as "Fricassee" and "Ragout," as were items of kitchen equipment, including *"Huguenotte"* (a kind of casserole), *"Marmite"* (an iron kettle), and many kinds of dishes, for example, "Omelet" and *"Ramoulade."*[122] In keeping with its mission to demystify the arts and crafts, the *Encyclopédie* also explained how such artisanal products as bread, wine, and cheese were made, descriptions that in many cases remain useful today.

Finally, there were articles that brought together practical information about food and cooking with analysis and commentary from the point of view of history, science, and moral philosophy. A critical mass of these, including "Cuisine," "Frugality," "Gourmandise," "Nourishment," and "Ragout," were the work of a single contributor, Louis, chevalier de Jaucourt (1704–1779).

Jaucourt was the son of an old family of the military nobility. Despite this tradition, he chose to make a career as a scientist, studying in Geneva, Cambridge, and Leiden, where he took a medical degree under the great clinician Herman Boerhaave. After returning to Paris, Jaucourt devoted himself to writing a six-volume book on anatomy, and, in 1751, he volunteered his services to Diderot and D'Alembert, eventually becoming the single most prolific contributor to the *Encyclopédie*, with more than 14,000 articles to his credit. Initially his assignments focused on physiology, pathology, chemistry, and botany, as befitted his scientific expertise. However, his unusual command of ancient and modern languages and his insatiable curiosity made him into a polymath who was knowledgeable about an unusually wide range of subjects. In the worlds of one modern critic, "it was the modest and unpretentious Jaucourt who was as responsible as anyone for making the *Encyclopédie* the great focal point and gathering place of factual information."[123]

In many respects, the account of cooking given by Jaucourt revisited the terrain already addressed by Brumoy and Bougeant in 1739 and Meusnier in 1742 – but drew different conclusions. Whereas these predecessors were anxious to reconcile contemporary medical advice and traditional appeals to moderation with fine cooking in the form of the *nouvelle cuisine*, Jaucourt took a much tougher line. According to him, the only benefit bestowed on humanity by cuisine – *nouvelle* or *ancienne* – was the discovery of

---

[122] "Artichaut," "Fricassée," "Ragoût," "Hugenotte," "Marmite," "Omelette," and "Ramoulade" in *Encyclopédie*, vol. 1, pp. 721–777; vol. 7, p. 306; vol. 13, p. 759; vol. 8, p. 333; vol. 10, p. 131; vol. 11, p. 467; and vol. 13, p. 785.
[123] Wilson, *Diderot*, pp. 201–202.

various means of preserving food by salting, smoking, drying, and pickling in acid.[124] Although the cooking of "abstemious or poor people is comprised only of the most common art of preparing dishes to satisfy life's needs," he wrote, fine cuisine was nothing but "the secret, reduced by scientific method, of eating beyond what is necessary."[125] Jaucourt continued:

> Dairy, honey, the fruits of the land, vegetables seasoned with salt, bread cooked in embers, these were the foods of the first peoples of the earth. They made use of these benefits of nature without any other refinement and were as a result only stronger, more robust, and less exposed to disease. Boiled, grilled, and roasted meats or fish cooked in water followed. They were taken in moderation: health did not suffer; temperance still reigned; and appetite alone regulated the timing and number of meals.
>
> But this temperance did not last long: the habit of always eating the same things and with practically the same preparation engendered disgust; disgust gave birth to curiosity; curiosity led to experiments; and experimentation brought about sensuality. Man tasted, tried, diversified, chose, and came to make an art of the most simple and natural action.[126]

Whereas Brumoy, Bougeant, and Meusnier saw the birth of cuisine as a mark of the progress of civilization, Jaucourt, like Rousseau, linked it to the fall of natural man into a life of luxury, corruption, and artifice. From Asia, cuisine spread to Greece (except Sparta, which wisely resisted it) and then to Rome, where it reached hitherto unimaginable extremes. Skilled Roman cooks

> sharpened the appetite of their masters through the number, the force, the diversity of dishes.... They imitated fish that were desired but unavailable, giving to other fish the same taste and even the same form of those that the climate or the season refused

---

[124] "*Cuisine*" in *Encyclopédie*, vol. 4, pp. 538–539.

[125] Ibid.

[126] Sean Takats, whose English translation I follow here, notes that the last sentence quoted is a close paraphrase of Meusnier's preface to the 1742 edition of *Suite des Dons de Comus*; see "Cuisine," translated by Sean Takats, *The Encyclopedia of Diderot and D'Alembert Collective Translation Project* at http://www.hti.umich.edu/d/did/

to gluttony. Using fish meat, Trimalcion's cook even in this manner fashioned different animals: wood-pigeons, turtle-doves, fat pullets, etc. Atheneus speaks of a half-roasted pig, prepared by a cook who had the dexterity to gut and stuff it without splitting it open.[127]

Cooks who excelled in this "tricky art" were rewarded with huge salaries – the equivalent of 864 pounds or 19,000 *livres* a year. One chef who pleased Anthony at a banquet given in honor of Cleopatra received a city in compensation.[128]

Jaucourt thus presented the rise of cuisine as characteristic of a world turned upside down, in which servants received princely rewards and man's natural inclination toward temperance was subverted by art in the service of gluttony and the irresistible passion for luxurious novelties. He also specifically linked fine cooking to the royal court – that vehicle for phoniness of all sorts – during the era of Valois decadence. Whereas Brumoy and Bougeant had attributed the rise of fine dining in France to the general (and beneficent) influence of Italian culture on French manners, Jaucourt singled out Catherine de' Medici (the sinister queen mother of the religious wars) as the culprit responsible for establishing culinary excess in a country that had hitherto resisted it:

> The Italians first inherited the remains of Roman *cuisine*. It is they who introduced the French to fine dining, whose excesses several of our kings tried to repress through edicts, but in the end it triumphed over the law during the reign of Henri II. So the ultramontane cooks came to establish themselves in France, and it is one of our least debts to this throng of corrupt Italians which served in the court of Catherine de' Medici.[129]

Jaucourt gave no evidence for this claim about Catherine's decisive influence on the history of French cooking. Interestingly, the idea that sophisticated cuisine was brought to France by "voluptuous Italians" in her suite appeared in another *Encyclopédie* article, "Seasoning" (*Assaisonnement*), which was published in volume 1.[130] This article was anonymous, so we cannot be sure if it was written by Jaucourt, Diderot (who contributed many short articles,

127 Ibid.
128 Ibid.
129 Ibid.
130 *"Assaisonnement"* in *Encyclopédie*, vol. 1, p. 765.

some of which were unsigned), or a third party. It seems, however, that these passages are the original source of the enduring myth – still repeated today – that Catherine's Florentine cooks were the true founders of *haute cuisine*.[131]

As a physician trained in Newtonian iatromechanics, Jaucourt shared the assumptions behind Cheyne's views of disease and health, and he endorsed many of the Scottish physician's recommendations about diet.[132] Dairy products, bread, fruits, vegetables, and grains – the natural "foods of the first peoples of the earth" – were universally wholesome, according to Jaucourt.[133] Wine, meat, and fish were generally fine, too, provided that they were consumed in moderation and in the absence of ailments such as gout, the symptoms of which they could aggravate. In general, Jaucourt thought that fresh foods were preferable to preserved ones, however valuable the latter might be in averting hunger in times of want. The salts and acids that prolonged the shelf life of smoked, cured, and pickled ingredients could trigger a wide variety of symptoms by irritating the solids and corrupting the juices of the body, and thus consumption ought to be limited, even for healthy people.[134] Fatty foods could cause cardiac problems and biliousness; fruits could promote gas, colic, and diarrhea. Even breads and other starchy foods, which were easily digested by most people most of the time, could trigger flatulence and bloating of the stomach.[135] Thus it was critically important for healthy people to learn to judge how much of different sorts of food they could tolerate and to keep consumption strictly within these limits.

Seasonings and condiments of all kinds were deeply problematic for two reasons. Because they tended to be loaded with corrosive salts, they ate away at the solid tubes of the body. Even ordinary table salt was a mild irritant whose corrosive effects increased the secretion of digestive juices.[136] In addition, Jaucourt thought that seasonings hastened the atrophy of taste buds, a process that inevitably occurred with age. The sense of taste was most acute in infants and young children and gradually diminished over time: stimulation of the taste buds day after day, year after year inevitably dulled their sensitivity. This was why mild flavors that were so pleasing to children, such as milk, seemed too bland to adults, who

[131]   Barbara Wheaton, *Savoring the Past*, pp. 43–48; and Revel, *Culture and Cuisine*, pp. 119–120.
[132]   "*Nourriture*" in *Encyclopédie*, vol. 11, p. 263.
[133]   "*Cuisine*" in *Encyclopédie*, vol. 4, pp. 537–538.
[134]   "*Nourriture*" in *Encyclopédie*, vol. 11, p. 263.
[135]   Ibid.
[136]   "*Cuisine*" in *Encyclopédie*, vol. 4, pp. 537–538.

preferred salty foods. However, the atrophy of the taste buds could be greatly accelerated by eating pungent, spicy dishes or foods that were served at very hot or cold temperatures. Prolonged indulgence in such dishes typically resulted in the loss of the ability to distinguish flavors and foods, a condition that in turn interfered with the ability of the esophagus and stomach to sense hunger and thirst.[137] Thus, according to Jaucourt, the combination of diet and physiology contributed to the tendency toward gluttony in adults, with all the dangers, moral and physical, that this vice entailed.

To illustrate this point, Jaucourt recounted a story about the Roman statesman Cicero in the article "Ragout" (a term that Jaucourt noted derived from a Latin phrase meaning "highly flavored"). Cicero was famous as a defender of old-fashioned Roman virtues, including temperance and frugality, and a critic of the luxurious and corrupt lifestyles of many of his contemporaries. While the likes of Anthony and Cleopatra feasted on rare delicacies concocted by their well-paid chefs, Cicero preferred menus that featured humble ingredients of local provenance. But moderation was foiled when Cicero's cook prepared a vegetable ragout that was so deliciously seasoned that Cicero ate much too much, triggering a bout of indigestion that incapacitated him for weeks.[138] Moral of the story: cuisine (as opposed to simple cooking) poisons the body and confounds man's natural capacity for judging what and how much to eat.[139]

Jaucourt thought that there was no solution to this problem. Although savages were still content to eat the unadorned fruits of the land, civilized human beings were not. The art of cuisine had stimulated the love of variety to the point at which man's natural capacity for judgment had atrophied. This inclination toward excess was tempered only occasionally by the admonitions of science and moral philosophy. Altering this state of affairs would involve changing man's habits as well as his ideas, reconciling the laws of nature with the demands of civilization. This sort of utopian project did not appeal to the practically minded Jaucourt. But it was to

---

[137] Ibid. and also *"Goût (Physiologie)"* in *Encyclopédie,* vol. 7, pp. 758–761.

[138] *"Ragoût"* in *Encyclopédie,* vol. 13, p. 759.

[139] This idea also appears, in slightly different words, in the articles *"Cuisine,"* vol. 4, pp. 537–538, and *"Gourmandise,"* vol. 7, p. 754 – all by Jaucourt – as well as the anonymous *"Assaisonnement"* (Seasoning), vol. 1, p. 765. Jaucourt's choice of this example is interesting in that Roman moral commentaries about cuisine, including the works of Cato, Pliny, and Cicero himself, focused on condemning the conspicuous consumption of luxurious and usually exotic foodstuffs (flamingoes' tongues, stuffed dormice, etc.) and on praising vegetable dishes, porridge, and other traditional fare associated with the simpler but virtuous days of the Roman Republic.

become an element in the radical reimagining of the human condition undertaken by his fellow encyclopedist, Jean-Jacques Rousseau.

Rousseau's concern with food and cooking stemmed from a couple of different sources. A lifelong hypochondriac as well as a periodic sufferer from depression, urinary complaints, and stomach, digestive, and liver problems, Rousseau had a personal stake in the dietary therapies devised by Cheyne and adapted by Jaucourt and other practitioners. Rousseau resorted to milk cures (baths as well as lowering diets) on at least two occasions.[140] By middle age, he had developed a preference for dairy products and other vegetarian foods, although we know that he enjoyed eating fowl and that other meats continued to be served at his table.[141] Cheyne and Jaucourt had already articulated the view that dairy products, vegetables, fruits, and cereals were the foods intended for man by nature but that humans had lost their taste for such simple fare as society became increasingly sophisticated and civilized. Rousseau not only affirmed these ideas but elaborated them with unprecedented vigor and passion: his critique of cuisine drew on his larger vision of how man, born free, had gradually become enslaved by social convention and artifice.[142] He argued that civilized man's passion for luxury had turned him away from natural foods to dishes of meat, often highly seasoned and elaborately sauced – and to other exotic delicacies.

[140]   Leo Damrosch, *Jean-Jacques Rousseau: Restless Genius* (Boston: Houghton Mifflin, 2005), pp. 117, 123–124, 140, and 382.

[141]   Ibid., pp. 369–370. Thérèse Levasseur, Rousseau's partner, was acknowledged by contemporaries as an excellent cook who produced delicious meals on a small budget. Visitors to the home she shared with Rousseau mentioned eating succulent *gigots* of mutton, *bouillis* of beef and veal, cold pork dishes, and pickled trout, although it is unclear whether Rousseau himself ate any of these things. For a discussion of Rousseau's vegetarianism, see Jean-Claude Bonnet, "*Le Système de la cuisine et du repas chez Rousseau*" in *Jean-Jacques Rousseau et la Médecine naturelle*, edited by Serge A. Thériault (St. Denis, Montréal, and Québec: Les Editions Univers, 1979), pp. 123–127.

[142]   Rousseau developed these themes in *The Discourse on the Arts and Sciences* (1750) and *The Discourse on the Origin of Inequality* (1755). His views about the role of luxury in driving this progressive enslavement forward owed a certain debt to Mandeville's diagnosis of the passions. See Edward Hundert, "Mandeville, Rousseau and the Political Economy of Fantasy" in *Luxury in the Eighteenth Century: Debates, Desires and Delectable Goods*, edited by Maxine Berg and Elizabeth Eger (New York: Palgrave Macmillan, 2003), pp. 28–40. On the more general debate about luxury in eighteenth-century France, see John Shovlin, *The Political Economy of Virtue: Luxury, Patriotism, and the Origins of the French Revolution* (Ithaca, NY, and London: Cornell University Press, 2006), especially pp. 13–48; and Sarah Maza, "Luxury, Morality, and Social Change: Why Was There No Middle-Class Consciousness in Prerevolutionary France?" in *The Journal of Modern History*, vol. 69, no. 2 (June 1997), pp. 199–229.

Driven by these acquired tastes, man violated the harmony of nature by slaughtering animals that did him no harm and forcing fruits and vegetables out of season. He vied with his neighbors in the sumptuousness of his table, turning the straightforward satisfaction of hunger into a means of displaying wealth, power, and a false sense of sophistication. Health and morals suffered as a consequence of this break with the natural order, which Rousseau assumed to be harmonious and beneficent. Embracing a simple and mostly meatless diet became for Rousseau part of the larger project of learning to live in accord with nature – a theme developed at length in *Émile*, his book about child rearing and education that was published in 1762.

Émile is narrated by the wise tutor to whom the protagonist is entrusted shortly after birth. The tutor's mission is to instill the child with a love of nature and a capacity for self-direction that will endure even after he returns to the convention-bound world of civilization, which, as a grown man, he must inevitably do. The process begins with the milk Emile receives from his mother's breast. Rousseau was an advocate of maternal breastfeeding and a critic of the common practice of employing wet nurses, and his hero, Emile, benefits from this best of all possible beginnings in life.[143] Rousseau acknowledged, however, that prolonged breastfeeding by a nurse was infinitely preferable to weaning a child too early on pap and other artificial foods. Infants who were nursed into their second year of life benefited from the superior nutritive properties of breast milk, growing larger, stronger, and hardier in the face of disease.[144]

Rousseau thought that most parents undermined some of the benefits their child received from breast milk by insisting that the wet nurse change her diet. Obsessed with the consumption of meat, parents typically paid supplements to the nurse's basic wage on the condition that she eat substantial rations of beef during the period of lactation. This was counterproductive, Rousseau argued. Heavy meat consumption increased the

---

[143] Jean-Jacques Rousseau, *Emile or On Education*, introduction, translation, and notes by Allan Bloom (New York: Basic Books, 1979), pp. 57–58. Wet nurses were often accused of neglecting their charges, but there were also medical arguments in favor of maternal breastfeeding. As early as 1708, the physician Philippe Hecquet argued in *De l'obligation aux femmes de nourir leurs enfans* that no two women gave identical milk and that a child would be necessarily best nourished by its mother, whose own risk of post-partum death would be decreased by the act of nursing. He also claimed that because wet nurses had typically given birth weeks or months earlier, their milk – which changed in consistency from week to week – was usually too rich for the delicate digestions of newborns. See Brockliss, "The Medico-Religious Universe of Philippe Hecquet," pp. 202–203.

[144] Rousseau, *Emile*, p. 57.

acrid salts in breast milk, making it bitter, and encouraged the development of colic and the presence of worms in the child's digestive tract.[145] He
pointed out that humans never consumed the milk of carnivores, whereas
dairy products made from the milk of herbivores such as cows, goats, and
sheep were delicious and highly prized. Vegetable juices were the source
of plentiful, sweet-tasting milk – a rule that held true in humans, too. The
extra money provided by affluent parents to their children's nurses would
be better spent on increasing their intake of the vegetarian foods that composed the bulk of the peasant diet.[146] Mothers from the noble and bourgeois
classes who chose to suckle their own children were urged to adopt a similar
regime.[147]

As a woman's diet changed with the seasons, the flavors in her milk
changed, too, exposing the infant palate to a succession of foods and providing the first lessons in taste. As nurslings grew old enough to eat solid
food, they naturally developed preferences for the vegetarian ingredients
from which breast milk was composed. They liked breads and cakes, eggs,
fruits, vegetables, butter, and mild, fresh cheeses. And they were largely
indifferent to meats and fish and had an active aversion to pungent, spicy
flavors, just as the physicians would have wished.[148] Thus breastfeeding
laid the foundation for a lifetime of healthy eating.

Because the flavors in breast milk were mild, sweet, and pure, they left
intact the innate ability of children to distinguish wholesome foods from
potentially dangerous ones, even when confronted with unfamiliar ingredients. The sense of taste functioned in the uncorrupted infant palate just
as it did in animals, as a detector of spoilage and the presence of substances
that were threats to health. Indeed, Rousseau thought that the aversion to
pungent or spicy flavors was a natural mechanism designed to preserve this
sensitivity. Strong seasonings, especially when combined with elaborate
preparations, could mask the presence of unwholesome elements lurking in
the food, even as they artificially stimulated the appetite. Even worse, prolonged exposure to highly seasoned or pungent foods gradually corrupted
the palate, rendering it unable to perform the fundamental task of distinguishing wholesome ingredients from those that were rotten, adulterated,
or otherwise unsuited for human consumption.[149]

---

[145] Ibid.
[146] Ibid.
[147] Ibid., p. 58.
[148] Ibid., p. 153.
[149] Ibid., pp. 151–152. A similar view about the debilitating effect of seasonings on the
sense of taste had already been developed by Jaucourt in *"Goût (Physiologie)"* in
the *Encyclopédie*, vol. 7, pp. 758–761.

In Rousseau's view, the development of the acquired taste for highly seasoned complexity went hand-in-hand with the great prestige that most societies accorded to a carnivorous diet. Eating quantities of meat was a common symbol of strength and dominance. Killing animals for food demonstrated man's power over nature, and a disproportionate share of the spoils set masters apart from subordinates. It marked man's fall from the state of innocence into which he was born. Eating meat coarsened character, hardened hearts, and encouraged cruelty to fellow humans as well as beasts. Rousseau wrote:

> All savages are cruel, and it is not their morals which cause them to be so. This cruelty comes from their food. They go to war as to the hunt and treat men like bears. Even in England butchers are not accepted as witnesses, and neither are surgeons. Great villains harden themselves to murder by drinking blood.[150]

One of the signs that carnivorous diets were unnatural was the nearly universal aversion to eating meat it its raw state. Unlike fruits, vegetables, and milk, which were delicious straight from the garden or the cow, meat had to be transformed – that is, disguised – by the art of cookery in order to make it palatable. Rousseau continued:

> The dead flesh is still repugnant to you; your entrails cannot take it. It has to be transformed by fire, to be boiled or roasted, and to be seasoned with drugs disguising it. You have to have butchers, cooks, and roasters, people to take away the horror of the murder and dress up dead bodies so that the sense of taste, fooled by these disguises, does not reject what is alien to it and savors with pleasure the cadavers whose sight even the eye would have difficulty bearing![151]

Whereas his predecessors (Brumoy, Bougeant, Meusnier, Cheyne, and Jaucourt) assumed that the rise of cuisine was linked to man's love of variety and his wish to make meals more interesting from day to day, Rousseau saw

---

[150]   Rousseau, *Emile*, p. 153.
[151]   Ibid., p. 155. This purple passage and others about the horrors of eating meat were loose paraphrases of Plutarch, one of Rousseau's favorite authors and a convinced vegetarian.

it in a much more ominous light: as a necessary adjunct to man's artificial and murderous taste for meat.[152]

Rousseau also disapproved of forms of agriculture that manipulated the conditions of the growing season to produce vegetables and fruits out of season. Such techniques were yet another manifestation of man's divorce from nature. They transformed ordinary seasonal produce into expensive luxuries, feeding our social pretensions through conspicuous consumption while they poisoned the body:

> It takes effort – and not taste – to disturb the order of nature, to wring from it involuntary produce which it gives reluctantly and with its curse. Such produce has neither quality nor savor; it can neither nourish the stomach nor delight the palate. Nothing is more insipid than early fruits and vegetables. It is only at great expense that the rich man of Paris succeeds, with his stoves and hothouses, in having bad vegetables and bad fruits on his table the whole year round. If I could have cherries when it is freezing and amber-colored melons in the heart of winter, what pleasure would I take in them when my palate needs neither moistening nor cooling? Would the heavy chestnut be very agreeable to me during the broiling dog days of summer? Would I prefer it – straight from the oven – to currants, strawberries, and other refreshing fruits that the earth offers me without so much trouble? To cover the mantel of one's fireplace in the month of January with forced vegetation, with pale and odorless flowers, is less to embellish winter than to spoil spring; it is also to take away the pleasure of going into the woods to seek the first violet, spy out the first bud, and shout in a fit of joy, "Mortals, you have not been abandoned; nature still lives."[153]

Rousseau's culinary prescription could be stated in simple terms: eat fruits, vegetables, breads, eggs, and dairy foods that are seasonal and local and

---

[152] Ibid., pp. 154–155. In these passages, Rousseau focused on the corrupting effects of meat eating on human morals. However, in other texts, he also stressed the imperative to avoid cruel treatment of animals because, like men, they were sentient beings – an argument that anticipated Jeremy Bentham's famous observation that "the question to be asked about animals was neither 'Can they *reason?*' nor 'Can they *talk?*' but 'Can they *suffer?*'" Quoted in Keith Thomas, *Man and the Natural World: Changing Attitudes in England, 1500–1800* (New York and Oxford: Oxford University Press, 1984), p. 176; see also his remarks on the development of vegetarianism in eighteenth-century Britain, pp. 287–300.

[153] Ibid., p. 346.

18. *Fruit, Jug, and a Glass,* circa 1755, by Jean-Baptiste-Siméon Chardin (Chester Dale Collection, National Gallery of Art, Washington; image © Board of Trustees, National Gallery of Art, Washington).

prepared in the simplest possible way. When not eaten raw, principal ingredients should be poached, boiled, or roasted with no seasonings other than a little salt and a pinch of fresh herbs from the garden. Sauces did not appear in Rousseau's anti-cuisine except for a knob of fresh butter added to hot vegetables at serving time or a trickle of cream on fruit or custard. "If I am given milk, eggs, salad, cheese, brown bread, and ordinary wine I am sufficiently entertained," he wrote.[154] There were no good reasons, physical or moral, to eat anything else.

It is interesting to note that some of Rousseau's fictional characters – the virtuous ones – share his taste for a meatless diet. An outstanding example is Julie, the heroine of *La Nouvelle Héloise*, published the same year as *Émile*. The reader is told that she "did not like meat, nor ragouts, nor salt, and had never tasted undiluted wine. Excellent vegetables, eggs, cream, fruits – those were her ordinary nourishment, and were it not for fish, which she liked very much [she lived on the shore of Lake Geneva] she would have been a true Pythagorean."[155]

154 Quoted in Wheaton, *Savoring the Past*, p. 224.
155 Quoted in Bonnet, "*Le Système de la cuisine et du repas chez Rousseau*," p. 126.

In *Émile,* the young protagonist is raised by his tutor on just such a diet, with the result that he arrives at adolescence with the sensitive and uncorrupted palate of a newly weaned child. Guided by taste buds that unfailingly distinguish the wholesome from the bad, Emile freely tries all sorts of foods that are unfamiliar or prepared in novel ways. This kind of universal taste is very different from the sensibilities of children taught to like only flavors that are featured in the traditional cooking of the society in which they were raised. A typical French child, Rousseau claimed, would "die of hunger in other countries if he is not everywhere attended by a French cook"; returned from his travels, "he will say one day that only in France do they know how to eat. That is, parenthetically, amusing praise!"[156]

Healthy and sturdy, Emile showed no sign of gluttony, except for a slight weakness for a certain kind of cake that the tutor used as a reward for tasks well done. Accustomed only to pure and wholesome foods, he had trouble understanding the concept of adulteration when it came up in the course of a chemistry experiment that used wine that had been doctored with lead.[157] In short, nothing in Emile's upbringing compromised his spontaneous preference for eating in a manner that accorded with the natural order of things. Having reached puberty with these sensibilities intact, Emile was likely to retain them for life: "Since one always yearns to return to this age, later it is difficult to destroy any childhood tastes that are preserved during it [adolescence]."[158]

The ultimate test comes when Emile and his tutor are invited to two dinner parties in a short period of time. The first one, at a château owned by a financier, is the very model of artifice and luxury. The menu is elaborate and sumptuous, consisting of many courses of rare delicacies imported from afar. The food is served on precious china dishes by an army of liveried lackeys to an assembly of guests whose conversation is as empty as their dress is fashionable. The second dinner party is a rustic meal at the home of a farmer in the neighborhood that features local ingredients cooked and presented in the simplest possible way.[159] The tutor asks Emile which of the dinners he preferred:

> Recall these two meals, and decide for yourself which you ate with the most pleasure. At which did you notice more joy? At which did one eat with greater appetite, drink more gaily, laugh more

[156] Rousseau, *Emile,* p. 152.
[157] Ibid., pp. 182–183.
[158] Ibid., p. 432.
[159] Ibid., pp. 190–191.

goodheartedly? Which went on longest without boredom and without needing to be renewed by other courses? Meanwhile, look at
the difference: This whole wheat bread you find so good comes
from wheat harvested by this peasant; his wine, black and coarse
but refreshing and healthy, is the product of his own vine; the
linen comes from his hemp, woven in the winter by his wife, his
daughters, and his servant girl. No hands other than those of his
family made the preparations for his table; the nearest mill and the
neighboring market are the limits of the universe for him. In what
way then did you really enjoy everything provided at that other
table by distant lands and the hands of men? If all that did not give
you a better meal, what have you gained from this abundance?[160]

Wedded to the standards of nature rather than the false conventions of
society, Emile preferred simplicity and authenticity, that is, "the good fruits,
good vegetables, good custard, and good people" at the farmer's rustic
table.[161] His gustatory education had been a success, leaving both his palate
and his moral sense uncorrupted.

ANTI-CUISINES: THE FOOD OF THE POOR AND EARLY
RESTAURANT COOKING

One of the ironies of Rousseau's work was that the ample country diet of
milk and cream, eggs, cheeses, fruits, salads, and pastries that he described
was utterly beyond the means of the peasantry with whom he associated
it. The decline in the popular diet that was already visible by 1600 had not
been reversed a century and a half later. In some respects, the situation
had become worse. The 1600s had been a period of one catastrophe after
another: wars, epidemics, and famines that caused starvation on a mass
scale. After 1700, warfare, although all too frequent, was conducted in
a manner that had less impact on the civilian population. Outbreaks of
bubonic plague ceased, and smallpox and other contagious diseases killed a
smaller proportion of the population. For reasons demographers still debate,
the population of France began to grow, as births began to exceed deaths by
a wider margin. To live, however, did not mean to flourish. The downside
of the upward demographic curve was an increase in the number of people
to be fed in relation to the same amount of arable land. The result was
that holdings were subdivided into smaller allotments and an ever larger

---

160 Ibid., p. 191.
161 Ibid., pp. 191–192.

number of people lived closer to the minimum required to sustain life. "If outright starvation vanished with the seventeenth century," observed the historian Olwen Hufton, "permanent undernourishment was the lot of the poor, and as *pauvre* merged into *indigent* or *nécessiteux*, both the quality and the quantity of food deteriorated."[162]

Hufton's findings make depressing reading. Because of demographic pressures on the land, between 50 and 90 percent of rural families (varying by region) were unable to raise sufficient food to meet their minimum needs. The gap was filled – precariously – by wages earned by some members of the family who became seasonal migratory laborers or by handicraft work undertaken at home. Much of this work was poorly paid; for example, women who made lace on a piecework basis earned as little as two *sous* a day, which was just enough to buy one pound of bread. Even when work was plentiful and brought a decent wage, it was difficult to make ends meet: "Wage earners in command of the elevated daily wage of 20 sous, whether in town or country, at the end of the ancien régime needed to spend 88 per cent of their income on providing themselves and their small families with a basic bread ration (with bread at 2 sous the pound)."[163] This worked out to a daily ration of about eight pounds of bread per day (two four-pound loaves) for a family of two adults and a couple of children – perhaps three pounds each for the grown-ups and a third of that for the young ones.

The poor ate so much bread because it was by a huge margin the cheapest source of calories. Its only rival was gruel, made of the same mixture of grains and consumed in many homes for breakfast, dinner, and supper. These cereal products provided "ninety-five percent and upwards" of the caloric intake of the poor.[164] Except in Paris, where the working class clamored for the white loaves of pure wheat flour associated with an elite diet, bread was made from a mixture of wheat with other, less costly grains: rye, barley, oats, buckwheat, maize, or chestnuts, according to the region. When times got hard, the amount of wheat used in proportion to these inferior grains dropped precipitously or disappeared altogether. In parts of central France, chestnuts provided almost all of the calories in the popular diet for several months of the year. Elsewhere, buckwheat or maize played the same role.[165] The balance of the popular diet was meager. Families who were fortunate enough to have a cow or some chickens typically limited their own consumption of milk, butter, cheese, and eggs so as to be able to

---

[162]   Olwen H. Hufton, *The Poor of Eighteenth-Century France, 1750–1789* (Oxford: Oxford University Press, 1974), p. 48.

[163]   Ibid., p. 46. Twenty *sous* equaled one *livre* of currency.

[164]   Ibid., pp. 44.

[165]   Ibid.

sell these items in town or city markets, generating cash to pay taxes and dues of various kinds or, when home-grown stocks of grain fell short, to buy flour or bread. Thus:

> The usual accompaniment [to bread] was vegetables made into soup: cabbages and turnips, onions, carrots, and greenery from the hedgerows. The soup was sometimes thickened with cereal, old boiled bread, or pearl barley, and sometimes seasoned with a little oil or a piece of fat pork in those regions where pigs were kept. If the family had a cow, the milk was used in the preparation of the soup. In fact, milk, an occasional egg, scraping of cheese, a little pork fat, fish on the Breton coast – fresh mackerel in summer, salt cod in winter – and the same salt cod on the Mediterranean littoral were the only protein food the poor ever saw and, fish apart, depended on the ability of the poor to keep an animal of some kind. Cider or wine, or water in the mountainous regions, accompanied some, if far from all of the meals.[166]

For purposes of comparison, it is useful to remember that Cheyne recommended that an adult of moderate physical activity should eat a daily ration of eight ounces of meat or fish, twelve ounces of bread and vegetables, and a pint of wine. People engaged in heavy labor were supposed to eat more of everything, but such a menu was clearly beyond the means of most working people. If Rousseau's picture of the farmhouse table groaning with egg and cheese dishes, custards, fruits, and cream looked like a rustic culinary utopia to his elite readership, it would have been even more so to the vast majority of the French people.

Interestingly, the potato, which had been introduced to France in the 1500s and which in the 1800s would become an inexpensive and nutritious supplement to the French (and European) diet, played only a minor role up to the eve of the Revolution.[167] As late as 1748, the *parlement* of Paris passed a law banning cultivation of the potato on the grounds that it was a source of leprosy (a theory that had been proposed a couple of hundred years before and that had a tenacious hold on the popular imagination). A few years later, the *Encyclopédie* attempted to set the record straight. An

---

[166] Ibid. Hufton points out that many workers who lived in towns had small gardens somewhere in the neighborhood where they grew a few common vegetables and perhaps kept a hen or a few rabbits, bringing their patterns of consumption closer to those of their rural cousins than otherwise would have been the case.

[167] Michel Morineau, "The Potato in the Eighteenth Century" in Forster and Ranum, eds., *Food and Drink in History*, p. 24.

article written by Jaucourt gave a careful botanical description of the plant, which was often confused with the sweet potato and the Jerusalem artichoke. He noted that the potato was very nourishing and provided the main food source of some groups of American natives. When roasted whole under the cinders, it had a taste he described as approaching that of a parsnip – not a bad recommendation. Interestingly, Jaucourt's article was followed by a second one by another contributor that treated potatoes, Jerusalem artichokes, sweet potatoes, and white and black truffles together as items of the diet. It observed that all of these tubers could be prepared in a variety of similar ways and were best eaten with butter. Although wholesome, they caused flatulence, like all starchy roots, and were, therefore, proper food for peasants and laborers.[168] The *Encyclopédie* punctured the myth that the potato caused disease and vindicated it as a nourishing food, although not one suited to delicate digestions or refined people. Unfortunately, this was a case in which the *Encyclopédie* failed to change the common way of thinking: the potato would continue to be a marginal food in France for another quarter of a century, at least.

In 1765, when these articles were published, potato cultivation was far from universal in France. Apart from a few isolated spots in the Massif Central, the plant was best established on the periphery of the kingdom: in Alsace, Lorraine, Dauphiné, the Franche-Comté; in the northeastern districts bordering on the Austrian Netherlands (now Belgium); and in the upper valleys of the Pyrenees.[169] This pattern probably reflected the diffusion of the potato from Spain and from the zone along the western edge of the Alps and the upper Rhine that connected Spanish possessions in Italy and the Low Countries in the sixteenth and seventeenth centuries. The spread of the tuber in Alsace and the southern Netherlands may also have been reinforced by proximity to early botanical gardens in Basel and Antwerp, where potatoes were cultivated by the 1560s.[170]

In these regions, the potato played a role similar to that of buckwheat and maize in other areas. In good years, it was consumed as a supplement to wheat and rye (with the balance of the harvest used as fodder). When the principal grain harvest failed, however, the potato became central to human sustenance.[171] However, this critical role in alleviating hunger did nothing to enhance the potato's reputation. In Lorraine and other districts where it became established, it was "associated with calamity . . . considered

---

[168] *"Pomme de terre (Botanique)"* and *"Pomme de terre (Diete)"* in *Encyclopédie*, vol. 13, p. 4.

[169] Morineau, "The Potato in the Eighteenth Century," pp. 20–21.

[170] Ibid., p. 33, note 3.

[171] Ibid., pp. 21–23.

a necessary evil, but an evil, all the same."[172] As one historian has observed: "This feeling that the potato represented at least a qualitative lowering of the standard of living was very real: it was a substitute, an ersatz for better food that was not available, and sometimes it was given up as soon as a plentiful supply of grain was restored."[173] Elsewhere in France, the potato seems to have been known prior to the 1770s as an occasional ingredient in the soups dispensed by charitable institutions to feed the indigent. For example, barley was often used to give bulk and body to vegetable soups; potatoes, however, were cheaper than barley, and, if boiled to the point of disintegration, they produced a similar, lightly thickened texture.[174] As in the regions where potatoes were an ordinary field crop, these uses of the potato as an ersatz ingredient simply reinforced the reluctance of most people to eat it except in circumstances of extreme want. A popular gardening manual, *L'Ecole du Potager*, described the potato as enjoying "the most evil reputation of all the vegetables according to general opinion."[175] Potatoes were not unknown in Paris, the guide continued, but they were found only on the tables of desperate people.[176]

In the 1770s and 1780s, the potato became the focus of a promotional campaign waged by Antoine Parmentier, the pharmacist of the Invalides. He had become acquainted with potatoes as a prisoner in Prussia during the Seven Years' War (1756–1763) and became convinced that the tuber was the key to resolving the subsistence crises that were a regular feature of French life. Potatoes kept well through the winter (as Olivier de Serres had

---

[172] Ibid., p. 24.

[173] Ibid.

[174] Beatrice Fink, "Saint-John de Crèvecoeur's Tale of a Tuber" in *Eighteenth-Century Life*, vol. 25, no. 2 (spring 2001), pp. 228–229 and note 17, p. 233. Fink points out that a collection of documents published in Dijon in 1772 under the title *La Cuisine des pauvres* included two works by a M. Mustel on the potential of the potato in relieving hunger that predate Parmentier's more famous efforts of the 1770s and 1780s, *Mémoire sur les pommes de terre et sur le pain économique* (1767), followed by a *Supplément*. The French were not alone in seeing the potato as a cheap alternative to more expensive ingredients in institutional cooking. When Benjamin Thompson, Count Rumford (the Anglo-American scientist and inventor) became responsible for administering the workhouses in the kingdom of Bavaria in 1784, he changed the daily fare of the inmates from barley gruel to even cheaper potato soup. However, he found it necessary to conceal the fact that potatoes rather than barley thickened the soup by having it prepared behind a screen, out of sight of the inmates. See Davidson, *Oxford Companion to Food*, p. 627.

[175] Quoted in P.-B.-J. Le Grand d'Aussy, *Histoire de la vie privée des français depuis l'origine de la nation jusqu'a nos jours (1782)*, 2 vols. (Paris: Sens Editions, 1999), vol. 1, p. 105.

[176] Ibid.

already discovered by 1600), and they were believed to yield three times the nutrient value as the same acreage planted in wheat.[177] Some of the varieties that had become available by the mid-eighteenth century were ready to harvest as early as June or July, a difficult period of the year, when stores of grain from the previous year were running out and the new crop was not yet ready. In a series of papers published between 1773 and 1781, Parmentier made the case for the potato's value.[178] He transformed a previously barren field in Neuilly, outside Paris, into an experimental potato patch, yielding enough food to feed a multitude. After the famine that hit northern France in 1785, his work attracted the patronage of the king and queen, to whom he presented a bouquet of potato flowers (Marie-Antoinette promoted the cause by wearing a potato flower in her hair and the king sported another in his buttonhole). But even with royal backing and the support of the scientific establishment, potatoes had trouble making a dent in French culinary tradition, high or low.

Part of the problem was that Parmentier focused on using potatoes as a substitute or extender for wheat flour in bread. Potato starch lacks gluten, the protein that gives fermented wheat dough its texture, shape, and absorptive qualities when baked. Although small amounts can be used in bread, too high a proportion results in an unpleasantly gluey texture. Early forms of potato bread had crumb that was too damp to soak up broth or sauce – one of bread's primary functions in any French meal and absolutely vital to the soup-based cooking of the poor.[179] Eventually Parmentier developed an improved formula that resulted in a somewhat drier, more absorbent crumb. It combined starch extracted from potatoes that had been grated, dried, and ground with the flesh of potatoes that had been roasted or boiled and mashed, a laborious method described in detail in *Manière de faire le pain de pommes de terre, sans mélange de farine* (1779).[180] But even these more palatable forms of potato bread failed to dislodge the overwhelming preference for white wheat bread.

The potato won a regular place on the French table only when cooks began to explore its vast potential as a vegetable rather than as a substitute

---

[177]　This ratio, high according to modern estimates, was calculated by the Scottish economist Adam Smith in *The Wealth of Nations*, published in 1776, in the midst of Parmentier's campaign. See "Potatoes, White" in Kiple and Ornelas, eds., *Cambridge World History of Food*, vol. 1, p. 192.

[178]　His findings on the nutritional value and uses of the potato and other tubers, including the Jerusalem artichoke, were summarized in the magisterial *Recherches sur les végétaux nourrissans* (Paris: Imprimerie Royale, 1781).

[179]　Wheaton, *Savoring the Past*, p. 83.

[180]　Antoine Augustin Parmentier, *Manière de faire le pain de pommes de terre, sans mélange de farine* (Paris: Imprimerie Royale, 1779), pp. 28–44.

for flour. There were a few moves in this direction during the last half-century of the ancien régime. Parmentier noted that the hospital of the *Charité* in Lyon and the convent of the *Soeurs grise* in the parish of St. Roch in Paris had developed a number of dishes that did not attempt to disguise the fact that potatoes were the principal ingredient. He mentions recipes in which potatoes were prepared by steaming, frying, baking, or browning in fat, as well as hashes, beignets, and *boulettes*, not to mention a cold potato salad. Another dish was a gratin of potatoes and salt cod, probably an ancestor of the dish known today as *morue à la Bénédictine* in honor of its monastic origins. Surely many of these recipes were intended for poor relief, although some of them sound sufficiently posh to have graced the nuns' own table – the potato and cod gratin, for example, as well as potato garnishes for legs of mutton, potato stuffings for turkeys and geese, and a potato-based liqueur.[181] Perhaps inspired by this creativity, Parmentier held a banquet in 1778 for the leading lights of Parisian science and politics (Benjamin Franklin was prominent among the guests, as was the chief of police, Lenoir) at which all the courses from soup to dessert featured potatoes. According to Le Grand d'Aussy, the first historian of French cuisine, whose work was published in 1782, the publicity surrounding this event sparked a flurry of interest in potatoes in some of Paris's finer kitchens. "But," he noted, "this moment of favor, so little deserved, passed promptly" due to the "pasty taste, the natural insipidity, and nasty quality of this food, which, like all unleavened starches, is flatulent and indigestible."[182]

We find no published recipes for potato entrées or entremets in the cookery literature until after 1800, when they suddenly became quite common. Perhaps in light of all the other changes that ordinary French people had to absorb in the decade of the Revolution, learning to cook and to eat potatoes seemed like a minor adjustment.[183] By the time the Empire succeeded the Republic, the potato had secured a regular niche in the *haute*

---

[181]   Parmentier, *Recherches sur les végétaux nourrissans*, p. 108.

[182]   Le Grand d'Aussy, *Histoire de la vie privée des français*, vol. 1, pp. 105–106; see also Wheaton, *Savoring the Past*, p. 84.

[183]   On the acceptance of the potato in France and other parts of Europe in the first decades of the nineteenth century, see Massimo Montanari, *The Culture of Food*, translated by Carl Ipsen (Oxford: Blackwell, 1994), pp. 136–140. Even in areas where it had been grown previously, the potato became a genuinely popular food only in the period of the French Revolution and Empire. According to Redcliffe Salaman, author of the definitive treatise on the social history of the potato, it was in the period between 1795 and 1814, when the price of wheat soared due to bad harvests and the commercial effects of the Napoleonic wars, that the English finally turned to potatoes as a staple and developed many ways to prepare them. See Salaman, *The History and Social Influence of the Potato*, pp. 537–542.

cuisine and *cuisine bourgeois*, a development documented in Grimod de la Reynière's 1808 guide for gourmets, the *Manuel des Amphitryons*.[184] The willing acceptance of the potato in the cooking of the rural and urban working classes is more difficult to pin down, for obvious reasons, but it, too, seems to have become an established fact during the quarter-century after 1789.

Ironically, one of the more likely places to find menus of the sort Rousseau advocated was not the countryside, but the chic urban environment of early Parisian restaurants. Restaurants, which first appeared in Paris in the 1760s, were initially a novel sort of eating establishment that combined the individualized service and refined décor associated with cafés with a menu of light dishes and mineral water that were believed to be good for digestion and health. Only later, on the eve of the Revolution and especially during the First Empire, did they turn into the palaces of gastronomic bliss with which Paris became so closely identified in the nineteenth and twentieth centuries.[185]

Le Grand d'Aussy described one early restaurant, owned by a M. Boulanger of the rue de Poulies (today the rue de Louvre), which he claimed was already in business by 1765.[186] Boulanger's trade seems to have been selling ready-made bouillons, consommés, and *restaurants* (those especially concentrated meat and poultry broths we have encountered in Massialot and Marin). These were available by the cup, for immediate consumption in Boulanger's shop, and in quantity as take-out items. (Given how time-consuming it was to make these kitchen staples from scratch, buying them already prepared in just the amount needed would have made a lot of sense for smaller households.) According to Le Grand d'Aussy, it was also possible to eat a light meal at Boulanger's. He mentioned two dishes that were available: eggs poached in bouillon (*oeufs frais*) and boiled chicken with a sprinkle of coarse salt (*volailles au gros sel*), a by-product of making many sorts of *restaurants*.[187] According to some authorities, Boulanger later got into legal trouble and was sued by a group of *traiteurs* who claimed that

---

[184]   Alexandre-Balthazar-Laurent Grimod de la Reynière, *Manuel des Amphitryons*, edited by Misette Godard (Paris: Editions A. M. Métailié, 1983), p. 186. Grimod's work also documents the reception of the tomato in elite Parisian cooking. Like the potato, the tomato was introduced to Europe in the sixteenth century but was slow to find a place in the culinary repertoire outside of southern Spain and a few parts of Italy. Grimod mentions a dish of sautéed chicken served with a sauce made of "*tomates conservées*"; see p. 110.

[185]   Rebecca L. Spang, *The Invention of the Restaurant: Paris and Modern Gastronomic Culture* (Cambridge, MA: Harvard University Press, 2000), pp. 25–33.

[186]   Le Grand d'Aussy, *Histoire de la vie privée des français*, vol. 1, p. 387.

[187]   Ibid.

he violated their monopoly of the retail trade in ragouts when he began to offer an expanded menu of such dishes as sheep's feet in white sauce.[188] In any case, the dishes he served on the premises were presented *"propre-ment"* (that is, neatly, cleanly, and attractively) to customers seated at small marble-topped tables, just like the ones found in cafés.[189]

In order to understand the novelty and cachet of such an early restaurant meal, one must remember that the available alternatives – dinner at an inn or *table d'hôte* – typically offered no choice of dishes. Meals at the *table d'hôte* were usually available only at fixed hours. Customers paid a set sum for a family-style meal. How much and precisely what one got to eat in these circumstances depended on appearing punctually and eating quickly, so as to reach for seconds before others were served. One was forced to rub shoulders with one's fellow diners, no matter how unattractive they might be. In contrast, cafés, which had become immensely popular in Paris by the middle of the century, served coffee and light refreshments, but no meals. However, they did pioneer the practices of serving individually priced portions of the drinks on offer, of keeping open-ended hours (enabling customers to get a drink at any time from morning to night), and of seating customers at small tables (so as to facilitate the reading, writing, and quiet conversation that normally occupied patrons who came in alone or to meet acquaintances).

Restaurant service incorporated all of these features and applied them not only to beverages, but to food, too. Many early restaurants also adopted the sort of elegant décor, dominated by mirrors and gilded moldings, that had become associated with cafés that catered to an upscale clientele.[190] The genteel atmosphere was congenial to female patrons of the elite classes, who generally shunned other sorts of public eating houses. Although some early establishments initially reserved separate salons for women, restaurants quickly joined the short list of public venues where men and women of polite society could mingle freely.[191] Typically, restaurant patrons spoke only to members of their own party (in contrast to *tables d'hôte*, taverns,

---

[188] Spang, *The Invention of the Restaurant*, pp. 9–11, 24, and 34, is skeptical of the story of the lawsuit and points out that many early restaurateurs avoided entanglement with the *traiteurs'* guild by purchasing privileges as court cooks, who worked outside guild regulations. I, myself, have not found a source for this part of the story earlier than the second quarter of the nineteenth century.

[189] Le Grand d'Aussy, *Histoire de la vie privée des français*, vol. 1, p. 387.

[190] Spang, *The Invention of the Restaurant*, p. 55. This type of décor was introduced by Francesco Pocopio Coltelli, the owner of the Café Procope, which opened for business in 1686 at an address near the fashionable quarter of St.-Germain-des-Prés; see Jean Leclant, "Coffee and Cafés in Paris, 1644–1693" in Forster and Ranum, eds., *Food and Drink in History*, p. 90.

[191] Spang, *The Invention of the Restaurant*, p. 80.

and inns, where general sociability was the rule), offering women protection from the attentions of strangers while encouraging conversation within the group. The ambience of the restaurant thus echoed the intimate informality of the dinner party, which had been a primary setting for mixed company for more than a century.

The combination of light, refined food, individualized service, and polite company was so attractive that before long numerous restaurants had popped up in the neighborhoods of the Louvre, the Palais Royal, the Faubourg St.-Germain, and other parts of town frequented by fashionable crowds.[192] To give a few examples, there was Minet, an establishment open for business in the rue de Poulies by March 1767; Vacossin, which opened in the rue de Grenelle no later than July of that year; and Roze de Chantoiseau, active in the rue St.-Honoré from 1768; not to mention Duclos (c. 1769), and Berger (c. 1772), whose proprietor was a wine merchant–turned-restaurateur.[193] This success was despite the fact that restaurant prices were high. In 1769, Roze de Chantoiseau advertised "fine and delicate meals for 3–6 *livres* per head."[194] This was a lot of money for a little food, given that bread sold at that date for two *sous* (one-tenth of a *livre*) per pound and that full dinners were widely available at *tables d'hôte* for less than a *livre*. Indeed, according to one contemporary observer, the sheer expense was one of the things that made eating in a restaurant chic.[195]

The high cost was also justified by the claim that restaurant food was just what the doctor ordered for people of delicate constitutions as well as for those who wished to maintain their health through a moderate diet. Boulanger is said to have displayed the Latin motto *"Venite ad me omnes qui stomacho laboratis, et ego restaurabo vos"* (Come to me, all you whose stomachs labor, and I will restore you), a paraphrase of Jesus' offer of comfort and repose to those who labor for their bread. Although mildly blasphemous, the saying was considered sufficiently amusing to be adapted by other restaurateurs in the publicity for their establishments.[196] One of them, M. Vacossin, ran an advertisement in which he vowed to serve: "only those dishes that contribute to the conservation or re-establishment of good health. . . . For those who have weak and delicate chests, and who rarely eat

---

[192]   Le Grand d'Aussy, *Histoire de la vie privée des français*, vol. 1, p. 387.
[193]   Spang, *The Invention of the Restaurant*, pp. 24 and 34.
[194]   Ibid., p. 22.
[195]   Le Grand d'Aussy, *Histoire de la vie privée des français*, vol. 1, p. 387.
[196]   According to Le Grand d'Aussy, this motto adorned the front of Boulanger's restaurant; *Histoire de la vie privée des français*. According to Spang, a slight variant was used by Vacossin in the rue de Grenelle. She also identifies the link to Matthew 11:28. See *The Invention of the Restaurant*, p. 28.

two large meals, it will be convenient to find some decent place where they can go both to enjoy the benefits of society and to take their *restaurants*."[197] Menus featured bouillons and *restaurants*, of course, served in tiny porcelain cups. Cheyne and like-minded physicians had warned that concentrated bouillons, although full of nutritious matter, were challenging to the digestion in proportion to their volume. Therefore they were to be consumed in miniscule quantities as substitutes for a normal lunch or supper, which was precisely the context in which restaurants presented them. Poached eggs and boiled fowl also fit within dietetic guidelines that focused on light, white foods. People with constitutions too fragile to tolerate meat broth or those who simply shared Rousseau's preference for dairy and other vegetarian dishes had an ample array from which to choose. For example, Vacossin's restaurant (which actually welcomed Rousseau himself as a guest on at least one occasion) offered many items that would have pleased Emile, not to mention his creator: porridge, rice pudding, semolina, eggs, fresh fruits, preserves, butter, and delicate cream cheeses. Such foods suited the needs of patrons who were following lowering diets, but these "foods of the countryside picnic"[198] appealed to many perfectly healthy clients, too.

A reputation for wholesomeness according to the iatromechanical theory of dietetics was one feature that united all of the typical items found on early restaurant menus. The aesthetic of apparent simplicity was another. As we have seen, *restaurants* and concentrated bouillons were complex products, requiring many ingredients and a big investment of time and labor. But when properly made, bouillon was sufficiently pure and transparent to reveal the flowered patterns inside the porcelain cups in which it was served. A few sips replaced a meal of many courses – what could be simpler than that? Other restaurant foods were also simple and appealing: A perfectly poached egg – a dish that was tricky to make, but satisfying in itself, with the still-liquid yolk forming a sauce for the firm white. Rice simmered in milk with cream and sugar. Or a fresh, barely coagulated cream cheese or a perfectly ripe peach.

Like the brown bread and local wine Rousseau extolled, restaurant foods were complete in themselves, in no need of embellishment. Presented without garnishes or sauces, there was nothing about their appearance to

---

[197] Spang, *The Invention of the Restaurant*, p. 35.
[198] Ibid., pp. 53–54. Rousseau mentioned his visit to Vacossin in the fourth chapter of his last book, unfinished at his death, *The Reveries of the Solitary Walker*, translated with a preface, notes, and an interpretative essay by Charles Butterworth (New York: Harper, 1982), pp. 53–54.

prompt reflection on the labor, knowledge, and skill of the artisans who made them. Although fabricated in the kitchen or the dairy, their simplicity made them appear as souvenirs of a golden age when man had not yet broken with the order of nature. As antidotes to the life of civilized artifice, such simple foods, of course, commanded enormous premiums in the gilded salons of Paris's first restaurants.

CHAPTER 7

The Revolution in Wine

Ever since France was Gaul, wine had been the drink of choice for all hours of the day for both sexes and all ages and classes of people. It was consumed – usually watered, but sometimes not – for breakfast, dinner, and supper, and for refreshment in between. If the poor could sometimes not afford even the cheapest grade of wine, they made due with *piquette*, the harsh, low-alcohol liquid that emerged from the final pressing of the grape skins and other detritus of the winemaking process. Only in marginal areas where vines did not flourish or grow at all did the people have recourse to cider, perry, or beer. Everyone drank water, but few trusted it – a justifiable doubt, especially in towns and cities, where sources were often contaminated with human, animal, and commercial waste. This picture, intact for centuries, changed – as did so many aspects of European life – in the seventeenth century, when the art of distilling and the introduction of caffeinated beverages from colonial lands transformed the menu of drinks that fueled *la vie quotidienne*.

NEW TASTES: BRANDY AND COLONIAL BEVERAGES

The technique of distillation had been known in Europe since the Middle Ages, when it was introduced by Muslim physicians who used it in the preparation of medicines. It continued to be largely the provenance of apothecaries and alchemists until the 1620s, when Dutch merchants began to organize the production of brandy (*brandewijn* or "burnt wine") along the Atlantic coast of France. The region from the mouth of the Loire south to Bordeaux had traditionally produced light white wines of no distinction. Their lack of character made them ideal raw material for distillation: two passes through the still turned them into agreeably smooth spirits (more robust wines needed several additional passes to remove tannins and other substances that created off-flavors in the finished brandy). The Dutch had been major customers in the French Atlantic market for centuries, and thus

211

benefited from a deep web of commercial connections. The region also had abundant forests, which provided fuel to fire the stills. The first of these was set up in 1624, with initial shipments leaving the port of La Rochelle the following year. Fifteen years later, brandy was added to the list of commodities that were taxed, which, as one historian noted was "a sure sign of its growing significance." By 1660, the area was the center of "a massive distilling industry" that supplied spirits not only for the Dutch market (including its merchant fleet of 10,000 ships), but also for re-export to northern France, England, Germany, the Baltic, Russia, and the far-flung Dutch maritime empire.[1] The demand for brandy became so great that winemakers in other parts of France also began to distil their lower-quality wines. Brandy became a common drink in Languedoc in the 1660s, and by the end of the century the region also exported some 10,000 hectoliters of spirits through the port of Sète.[2]

Brandy was popular because it was strong, registering up to eight times the concentration of alcohol as the same measure of wine. It was compact and therefore easy to transport. Unlike wine, it did not spoil. In fact, small amounts of brandy could be used to stabilize wine that might otherwise turn to vinegar and to impart body to thin vintages. Added to casks of drinking water, brandy kept them from going sour during long sea voyages, a significant breakthrough in that era of global maritime empires.[3] It was this property of distilled alcohol that helped to stimulate the initial Dutch interest in the brandy trade, even before it became obvious that a huge market awaited in Europe itself. In addition to offering the intoxicating effects of wine or beer in concentrated form, brandy also imparted an immediate warming sensation to everyone who drank it straight or as the principal ingredient in punch or grog.[4] What could have been more welcoming to a sailor who had just ridden out a storm or householders sheltering from miserable winter weather?

Thanks to the scale and efficiency with which the Dutch organized the trade, brandy became widely available in a range of grades and different price points. Furthermore, the success of brandy stimulated demand for alcohols distilled from other substances – gin (grain alcohol flavored with juniper

[1]   Rod Phillips, *A Short History of Wine* (London: Penguin, 2000), pp. 124–125. For a general account on the impact of the Dutch in the Bordelaise and western France, see Roger Dion, *Histoire de la vigne et du vin en France: des origines au XIXe siècle* (Paris: Flammarion, 1977), pp. 423–460.

[2]   Phillips, *A Short History of Wine*, p. 125.

[3]   Ibid., p. 124.

[4]   Ibid.

berries), rum (made from molasses, a by-product of sugar refining), various forms of aquavit or vodka (from grain or potatoes, with various flavorings), fruit-based *eau-de-vie* (kirsch from cherries, quetsch from plums, framboise from raspberries, calvados from apples), and marc (from the pressings left from the winemaking process).[5] Even whiskey – a localized and very rustic product made in Scotland and Ireland – seems to have benefited from the generalized demand for fiery booze in the wake of the brandy revolution. Many of these spirits beat even the cheapest brandy on price, at least in their native markets. Thus distilled alcohol entered the lives of millions of Europeans.

While brandy and other spirits offered consumers a more intoxicating alternative to wine, the so-called colonial beverages – coffee, tea, and chocolate[6] – provided liquid refreshment that imparted a sense of energy and alertness. Whereas spirits, wine, and beer numbed the mind with alcohol, coffee, chocolate, and tea were stimulants containing caffeine. Europeans learned to drink them heavily sweetened with sugar (a commodity that was available in ever greater supplies, thanks to the plantations of the Caribbean basin and Brazil), thus magnifying the effects of the caffeine.[7] Coffee, in particular, earned a reputation as the drink *par excellence* for scholars, writers, merchants, and professional men, all of whom needed clear heads to go about their business. It was not a coincidence that Lloyds of London, the famous insurance company, got its start (and its name) from a coffeehouse where the founders met. Jules Michelet, the great nineteenth-century historian, argued that coffee was the font of Enlightenment and progressive politics in eighteenth-century France: it was "the drink of the Revolution."[8]

---

5   Braudel, *The Structures of Everyday Life*, p. 246.
6   Strictly speaking, neither coffee nor tea was "colonial" in origin, as the former is native to Ethiopia and the latter to China. Chocolate, however, was a New World product, made from the bean of the cacao tree that is native to Mexico and Central America. Chocolate seems to have been the first of the three beverages to arrive in Europe. In 1544 some chocolate was presented as a gift to the Spanish court, and some specimens may have made the trans-Atlantic trip even earlier, right after the conquest of Mexico. From Spain, chocolate spread to Italy, which had several zones of Spanish rule or influence at the time, and thus to France and northern Europe. For details on the history of the reception of chocolate in Europe, see Sophie D. Coe and Michael D. Coe, *The True History of Chocolate* (London: Thames & Hudson, 1996), pp. 125–178.
7   On the deep affinity between sugar and the rise of colonial beverages in Europe, see the classic study by Sidney W. Mintz, *Sweetness and Power*, pp. 6, 8, 108–118, 121–122, 125, 127, 137–138, 141, 148–149, 153, 177, 182, and 187.
8   Quoted in Braudel, *The Structures of Everyday Life*, p. 261.

The precise paths and dates by which the colonial beverages reached France are not known.[9] Tea, which never became as popular there as coffee and chocolate, seems to have been known in the early 1600s, having been introduced to Europe by the Dutch in the first years of the century. Chocolate probably arrived next. There has been speculation that Anne of Austria brought chocolate with her from Spain when she arrived to marry Louis XIII in 1615 or that Spanish monks sent cacao to their French counterparts, but no hard evidence has emerged in support of either theory. However, we do know that by 1642 Alphonse de Richelieu, a prominent churchman and a relative of the famous minister of state, was advised by his physician to drink chocolate as a medicine for his spleen.[10] In 1659, the crown granted an exclusive privilege to manufacture and sell chocolate as liquor, as tablets, and in boxes (*boëttes*) to one David Chaliou, and thereafter chocolate seems to have caught on quickly among the French elite.[11] By 1670 or so elite Parisiennes were already substituting chocolate flavored with sugar, vanilla, and cinnamon for the traditional breakfast of porridge or soup and a little well-watered wine. Recipes for "Spanish style" chocolate that used chilies in addition to the other seasonings, such as sugar, vanilla, and cinnamon, also circulated at the time. Interestingly, in light of the contemporary shift away from spicy seasonings in cooking, such preparations were characterized as having a "high taste, for those with no fear of overeating."[12] By 1700 or so, chocolate of the sugar-and-vanilla variety, accompanied by bread, brioche, or other pastries, became the standard breakfast in aristocratic and aspiring bourgeois circles (coffee with hot milk and sugar became a common breakfast drink at a slightly later date). French artisans created a special pot for making and serving chocolate. Unlike earlier vessels based on Spanish models, the *chocolatière* was designed with a slot in the lid that

---

[9]   Chocolate was available in commercial quantities in Spain by the 1590s, although specimens of cocoa beans had been presented to the court much earlier. Coffee entered Western Europe from the Middle East around the same time, with Venice as its likely portal; the first commercial shipment to northern Europe arrived in Amsterdam in 1637. Tea was introduced by the Dutch in the early 1600s. See "Cacao," "Coffee," and "Tea" in vol. 1 of Kiple and Ornelas, eds., *Cambridge World History of Food*, pp. 638–639, 642–643, and 716–717; Wheaton, *Savoring the Past*, pp. 90–92; and Alfred Franklin, *Le Café, le thé et le chocolat*, vol. 3 of *La Vie privée d'autrefois: Arts et métiers, usages parisiens du XIIe au XVIIIe siècle d'après des documents originaux et inédits*, 27 vols. (Paris: E. Plon, Nourrit et cie, 1887–1902), pp. 33–38.

[10]   Coe and Coe, *The True History of Chocolate*, pp. 155–156.

[11]   Ibid., pp. 157–159.

[12]   Ibid., p. 163. Chili and vanilla were traditional Mexican seasonings for chocolate, which was sometimes sweetened with honey prior to the introduction of sugar by the Spanish.

accommodated the carved wooden swizzle stick used to froth the chocolate. They were manufactured in fine china, silver, earthenware, and pewter to attract buyers at many different price points – a sure sign that chocolate consumption was trickling down from the rich to the middling classes in ancien régime society.[13]

Although coffee came to France as early as 1644 (when a shipment arrived in Marseille from Venice), it only became a regular part of life in Paris some fifteen years later.[14] In 1669, the Turkish ambassador began serving it at diplomatic receptions, which attracted the interest of the court and high society. The first café in the city was opened a few years later by an Armenian merchant who had previously sold coffee from a stall at the annual fair sponsored by the abbey of St.-Germain-des-Prés. This establishment was short-lived. However, one of the waiters, an Italian named Francesco-Procopio dei Coltelli, joined the guild of lemonade sellers. Duly licensed, he made a success out of a string of several shops that sold coffee along with other non-alcoholic beverages, biscuits, and ices (another novel item on the Paris scene). At least one of these, which stood across from the Théâtre-Française (then located on the Left Bank in the street now called the rue de l'Ancienne Comédie), pioneered the elegant décor of mirrors and small marble-topped tables that would become identified with the Parisian café and somewhat later with the restaurant.[15] Procope's formula was a huge success and was soon imitated in all quarters of the city.

Books dedicated to explaining how to brew and serve all of the colonial beverages at home began to appear in France in the 1680s.[16] In 1692, both Audiger and Massialot incorporated discussions of coffee, tea, and chocolate into works that focused on the preparation of sweet dishes.[17] Black, sweetened coffee was often served as a digestive tonic after the dessert course. It become fashionable to serve a late afternoon snack of coffee, tea, or both accompanied by biscuits, petits fours, and other elegant tidbits made with sugar. The gastronome Brillat-Savarin pointed out that having dined only a couple of hours earlier, guests were rarely hungry or thirsty at tea time, which therefore became an occasion for pure indulgence in the sweet things of life.[18]

---

[13] Ibid., pp. 160–162.

[14] Jean Leclant, "Coffee and Cafés in Paris," p. 87.

[15] Ibid., pp. 88–92, and Wheaton, *Savoring the Past*, pp. 91–92.

[16] Ibid., p. 90.

[17] Ibid., pp. 90–91. Also Audiger, *Le Maison reglée*, pp. 563–564; and Massialot, *Nouvelle instruction pour les confitures*, pp. 270–272.

[18] Brillat-Savarin, *Physiologie du goût*, p. 276.

The principal consumers of coffee, tea, and chocolate and the better grades of brandy were precisely those upper- and upper-middle-income customers who were also critical to the quality end of the wine trade. Although such people continued to drink large quantities of wine by modern standards, their habits and preferences began to change as spirits and colonial beverages became part of their ordinary patterns of consumption. Whereas wine had formerly been the obvious choice for mid-day refreshment or a relaxing tipple between supper and bed, it now lost out to coffee in the daytime and spirits at night.

By the early 1700s, these new patterns had become sufficiently established to cause concern among physicians: people were drinking spirits and stimulating beverages in such quantity that it had an impact on health. For example, George Cheyne argued that distilled liquors were never meant to be consumed as beverages – they were properly the stuff of apothecaries, an ingredient in certain medicines, not a drink.[19] Whether they were distilled from wine, sugar, or grain, spirits were full of high concentrations of salts and oils, which formed gluey particles, clogging the circulation, heating the blood, and burning tissues.[20] They also led to drunkenness on an unprecedented scale, inflaming passions and inciting quarrels, blasphemy, and murder.[21] Punch and fortified wines such as port were dangerous for the same reasons.[22] A cup or two of coffee with milk was permissible for people who lived in cold climates, he thought, but taken in larger amounts or in the heat, it made people "stupid, feeble, and paralytic."[23] Chocolate, made from the oily nuts of the cacao tree, was impossible to digest and in any case was "too hot and heavy for valetudinary persons and those of weak nerves."[24] Black tea contained dangerously high concentrations of solar rays, and it was often flavored with unknown additives that created heaviness in the stomach. However, he declared that "the natural simplicity of green tea," which was nothing but the tender, young leaves of the plant in dried form, made a healthy drink when brewed weak and drunk with milk or a slice of lemon or orange.[25] Other approved beverages included spring water, cider or perry, and vinegar thinned with water (recommended for hot climates). Laborers and mechanics could drink beer. For healthy members

---

[19]   George Cheyne, *An Essay of Health and Long Life*, p. 43.
[20]   Ibid., p. 56.
[21]   Ibid., pp. 44 and 52–55.
[22]   Ibid., p. 55.
[23]   Ibid., p. 61.
[24]   Ibid., pp. 64–65.
[25]   Ibid., pp. 62–64.

of the genteel classes, Cheyne renewed his prescription of a pint of wine a day.[26]

NEW PATTERNS IN WINEMAKING AND CONSUMPTION

Even as the popularity of the new distilled and caffeinated beverages grew among elite consumers, the French wine business was undergoing substantial changes due to demographic, commercial, and technological developments. It is to these issues that we now turn.

For the most part, wine in medieval and early modern France was a bulk commodity, an ordinary staple of daily life that was characterized in generic terms as sweet or sour, full bodied or thin, powerful or weak. Quality was synonymous with sweetness and with a high alcohol content (the result of fully ripe, sugar-laden grapes), which retarded spoilage in addition to its other, obvious advantages. Such wines were difficult to produce north of the Mediterranean zone, where in many years the frosts came before the grapes were fully ripe and alcohol percentages languished in the single digits. Hence the enduring demand in northern Europe for the sweet wines of Greece, Sicily, and other southern lands, in spite of the huge premiums they commanded. Northern vineyards that were capable of producing strong, sweet wines – for example, those along the middle Rhine and the Moselle – also sold at prices high enough to offset the cost of transport to Paris, London, other parts of Germany, the Low Countries, Scandinavia, and even the Baltic as far as Russia. Otherwise, long-distance carriage was limited to regions where no grapes would grow (Scotland and Ireland, Scandinavia, the Baltic, etc.) or those where harvests were insufficient to meet the minimum demand for sacramental purposes and elite consumption and where beer constituted the everyday drink of the people (England, the Low Countries). At an early date, these markets were supplied with wine produced on the west coast of France from the mouth of the Loire south to Bordeaux, a region that for much of the Middle Ages was subject to the English crown.

With these exceptions, wine rarely traveled very far from its vineyard of origin to its point of consumption. The *vin ordinaire* of Paris was grown in the immediate hinterlands of the city. It was thin and sour in most years, but the short distance it had to travel made it cheap enough for daily use. Additional supplies of everyday wine flowed into the city from the central Loire, transported by bargemen based in Orléans or Blois, a trade

---

[26]   Ibid., pp. 42 and 60.

that was enhanced after 1577, when an act of the Paris *parlement* prohibited Parisian wine merchants from buying wine within fifty miles of the city, in deference to the bourgeois of Paris who owned land in that area and typically imported the wine grown on their estates for use in their city households.[27] In 1698, Paris consumed 100,000 barrels of wine from Orléans.[28] Because most varieties of the grapes under cultivation were red skinned, most wine was red, too, or the rosy hue known in western France as *clairet* or the blush color known in Champagne as *oeil de perdrix*. (A winepress could be used to separate the clear juice from the pigment-laden grape skins, but it was an expensive piece of equipment beyond the means of most winemakers.) Interestingly, early recipes rarely call for wine of a particular color, grape variety, or place of origin. It was assumed that the cook would use whatever was on hand, and because the primary function of wine in cooking was to add some bracing acidity to sauces or soups, the nuances of bouquet, taste, or hue were not considered critically important.

The high end of the Parisian market was dominated by the wines of lower (that is, northern) Burgundy (mostly whites, including many based on the Chardonnay grape or pinot blanc) and those of Champagne (mostly still pale reds and pinks composed of pinot noir and a mélange of other grapes, as well as a small amount of *vin gris*, white wine pressed from red grapes).[29] Both provinces shipped their casks to Paris via water routes (the burgundy was sent down the Yonne and Seine from Auxerre, whereas the champagne came down the Marne from Epernay), a factor that made the wines affordable luxuries for bourgeois households as well as staples of the royal cellar. In contrast, the lack of a water route or improved roads from upper Burgundy made the distribution of wines from Beaune or the Rhone valley much more difficult. The Côte d'Or and Beaune lie to the south of the line that divides the watershed of the north Atlantic from that of the Mediterranean. Although it was relatively easy to ship wine down the Rhone to Avignon (where it was much appreciated by the papal court in the fourteenth century) and Marseille, it was complicated and expensive to transport Beaune wines to Paris prior to the improvement of roads linking the Saône to the upper Loire in the middle of the eighteenth century. Thomas Brennan has pointed out that because Beaune was so isolated from northern markets, producers were virtually forced to create premium

---

[27]   Thomas Brennan, *Burgundy to Champagne: The Wine Trade in Early Modern France* (Baltimore, MD: Johns Hopkins University Press, 1997), p. 5.

[28]   Braudel, *The Structures of Everyday Life*, p. 235.

[29]   All of these wines are discussed by Bonnefons in *Les Délices de la campagne*, pp. 49–50. On the supplying of the Paris market from Burgundy and Champagne, see also Brennan, *Burgundy to Champagne*, pp. 2–8.

wines to bear the cost of transportation. A few casks of these high-quality wines traveled overland (and over hills) to Auxerre, where local merchants forwarded them to Paris.[30]

Whatever its provenance, wine was meant to be drunk promptly, usually within months of the fall harvest. Even wine that had been carefully and cleanly made was subject to a host of flaws that affected its taste, smell, and fundamental wholesomeness. The best barrels inevitably leaked a little, allowing wine to evaporate and air to seep inside. This created the conditions for oxidization and also encouraged the growth of bacteria that quickly turned wine into vinegar. Although these dangers could be minimized by keeping barrels topped up and storing them in deep, cold cellars, these methods were by no means universally applied, nor were they always effective. In warm autumns, wine could start to spoil within a few weeks of the harvest. Wine from grapes that were harvested in September was already considered "old" by the New Year. Balmy spring weather brought more trouble in the form of off-odors, discolorations, and sometimes bubbles caused by a renewal of fermentation. The wines of Champagne were especially prone to this last flaw, as we shall see. By Easter, many wines had already turned into vinegar, which helps to explain the prominence of vinegar as an ingredient in traditional cooking. Taillevent advised his readers to seek out strong southern wines to serve from Easter until the new wine was ready in the fall: higher concentrations of alcohol kept these wines stable over a longer period, by which he meant twelve to eighteen months. Wines that survived into their third or fourth years were singled out as truly extraordinary.[31]

For all these reasons, making and selling wines were businesses that traditionally took the short view: the goal was to ship the new vintage quickly, before it went bad. This began to change thanks to the growth of the brandy trade, which allowed perishable wine to be turned into stable spirits. Brandy could also be used to doctor wines, upping their alcohol content to the point at which spoilage was less likely. Although this practice was, technically, an adulteration of the natural wine, it became a very widespread practice among respectable winegrowers and merchants.[32] These factors, in turn, created an incentive to expand the area under vines in regions where

---

[30] Brennan, *Burgundy to Champagne*, p. 11.

[31] Hugh Johnson, *Vintage: The Story of Wine* (New York: Simon and Schuster, 1989), p. 127.

[32] Other preservatives promoted by Dutch traders included burning sulfur matches inside barrels prior to filling (a technique that originated in Germany), racking wine off the lees, and fining it with egg whites or fish bladder (isinglass) to remove impurities. Phillips, *A Short History of Wine*, p. 194.

distilling became established: a pattern already visible in the Charente and in the Languedoc by the 1660s.

In addition to importing huge quantities of brandy from western France, both for home consumption and redistribution abroad, Dutch merchants were also big customers in the Bordeaux wine market. In order to satisfy their demand for aromatic whites with some residual sweetness (which were popular in Holland and in the northern German and Baltic markets the Dutch supplied), producers switched from red grapes to white in several districts, the most famous of which was Sauternes.[33] When Dutch engineers drained the marshes at the confluence of the Dordogne and Garonne rivers, it was found that the wines made from grapes grown on the reclaimed land were much more robust and darker in color than the old-fashioned *clairets* of the region. Although these so-called palus wines were some-what coarse, they were well suited to the emerging taste for more pow-erful, assertive wines, and, by the late 1640s, they commanded higher prices from Dutch merchants than the lighter, more traditional reds of the region.[34]

Although the commercial expansion of wine production succeeded along the Atlantic seaboard on a scale unequaled elsewhere in France, we do find similar trends in other areas. Everywhere, there was an increase in the number of acres under vines. This was testimony to increased demand and rising prices, due to the growth of the export trade, distillation, and the French population itself, which increased by about 30 percent between 1700 and 1789. The trend of converting fields to vineyards was especially marked in the decade after the disastrous winter of 1708–1709, when vines were killed by cold weather from Marseilles to Champagne and a large por-tion of the 1708 vintage froze in its casks. The destruction of much of the 1708 vintage pushed prices on surviving stocks to record levels. Replanted vineyards took several years to begin producing grapes, so prices remained artificially high. Although the destroyed vineyards were again producing wine by 1720 or so, growers continued to plant. In Bordeaux and a few other places, the new vineyards were planted on drained or otherwise reclaimed land; elsewhere they stood on land that had formerly been used for field crops. Indeed, so many fields were converted from grain to grapes that local parliaments in Metz, Bordeaux, Besançon, and Dijon either considered passing or passed laws forbidding further conversions and commanding the destruction of vines recently planted in places where they had not grown before. In 1731, the crown imposed a similar edict on all of France, citing

---

[33]   Ibid., pp. 127–128.
[34]   Ibid., p. 128.

the primary importance of producing adequate amounts of grain. The laws, both local and kingdom-wide, were mostly ignored.[35]

Much of the expansion of vine cultivation was the work of peasant farmers. Vines offered peasants whose holdings were too small to support a family through subsistence agriculture a means of getting by from year to year.[36] Of course, when wine prices dropped – as they inevitably did when supplies increased – or when the vintage was destroyed by the weather, peasant winegrowers were faced with a terrible situation and were frequently reduced from mere poverty to indigence. But such were the risks of the eighteenth-century economy of makeshifts that many were willing to take the gamble.[37] Obviously, expensive equipment, such as new barrels or a wine press, was beyond the means of such growers. They favored high yields and early harvests out of sheer necessity, and, as a result, the wine they made was mediocre to bad, depending on the year. The last decades of the ancien régime were awash in plonk. Cheap wine was probably the one item of the popular diet that became more accessible to the working-class population of town and city in the course of the eighteenth century. On the eve of the Revolution, consumption in Paris was at the rate of 120 liters per person per year (including women and children, who drank much less than adult males). As Braudel observed, low-quality wine had become a cheap foodstuff, a source of calories when bread was in short supply and at all times a means of escape from the misery of poverty.[38]

Wine of low-to-middling quality was able to bear the cost of transport to city markets thanks to improvements in transportation sponsored by the monarchy beginning in the time of Louis XIV and continuing in the reigns of his successors. Canals were built and roads extended and improved, creating access to markets for areas that had previously been too isolated to consider commercial production. In the 1770s, internal tariffs were reduced, further encouraging the domestic wine trade at all price points. These developments had a noticeable effect on the drinking habits of Parisians, who gained access to wines from new sources, in addition to the traditional ones. In 1702–1704, 12 percent of all the wine received in Parisian ports came from Chablis and Auxerre; by 1788–1789, these parts of northern Burgundy accounted for only 6 percent of the Paris market. Imports to the capital from Champagne also dropped sharply during the same period, despite the popularity of a new product, sparkling champagne, among elite consumers. *Vins du table*

---

[35]   Phillips, *A Short History of Wine*, pp. 180–181; and Dion, *Histoire de la vigne et du vin en France*, pp. 595–600.

[36]   Ibid.

[37]   Hufton, *The Poor of Eighteenth-Century France*, p. 16.

[38]   Braudel, *The Structures of Everyday Life*, p. 237.

from the region of Orléans and Blois plummeted, too, falling from a market share of 57 to 24 percent.[39]

Meanwhile, Parisians were drinking much more wine, especially red wine, that originated south and west of the city's traditional provisioning crown, that is, in the Côte d'Or, the Maconnais, the Beaujolais, the Rhone, Anjou, Sancerre, and Touraine.[40] Whereas these regions had accounted for only 10 percent of the wine that arrived at Paris ports at the beginning of the century, they supplied almost 60 percent of the total on the eve of the Revolution. The Côte des Nuits (the section of the Côte d'Or directly south of Dijon) dominated the prestige end of this trade, with reinforcements from the region of Beaune, which produced somewhat lighter, but still substantial red wines. Other regions filled the demand for more ordinary red wines that were nevertheless full bodied and full flavored. By the 1760s, the region between Tours and Saumur, which formerly had been almost invisible in the Paris market, sent some 22,500 barrels of red wine to the city. A few years later, the Beaujolais was supplying Paris with about 80,000 barrels, or about one-quarter of all the wine the city drew from beyond its immediate neighborhood, a trend that would hold through the end of the century.[41] A newly expanded system of canals along the Loire and improvements in the land routes between the Saône and the Loire facilitated this enormous trade.[42] Premium wines from the Côte d'Or and Beaune benefited, but so too did cheaper wines from less prestigious districts. Interestingly, red wines from Burgundy and the Beaujolais also flowed in other directions: down the Saône to Lyon and the Mediterranean and up the Rhone to the frontiers of Switzerland. For example, when Voltaire, the ultimate Parisian, moved to the vicinity of Geneva in 1754, he stocked his cellar with burgundy and beaujolais, which supplanted champagne as the favorite wine of his old age.[43]

PREMIUM WINES: QUALITY, *TERROIR*, AND BOTTLE AGING

These shifts in traditional patterns of distribution and consumption and the general expansion of the market created problems as well as opportunities for producers of high-quality wines. Formerly, their products were the only ones that traveled very far, but now they faced competition from a host of cheaper wines. Furthermore, as palates adjusted to the fragrant aromas, bittersweet flavors, and slightly viscous, mouth-filling textures of

---

[39]   Brennan, *Burgundy to Champagne*, p. 197.
[40]   Ibid.
[41]   Ibid., pp. 198–200.
[42]   Ibid.
[43]   Wheaton, *Savoring the Past*, p. 216.

coffee, chocolate, brandy, and fortified wines, tastes began to change. Many wines seemed thin, watery, and unpleasantly sharp in comparison with the new beverages.[44] Residual sweetness, which had been generally prized as a compliment to spicy foods, now became associated with the dessert course. Starting as early as the 1660s, premium producers began to focus on developing wines that were full bodied, with concentrated, mellow flavors; luscious, rich textures; and deep, jewel-like colors.[45]

This trend for producing richer, full-bodied wines seems to have emerged first in the region of Bordeaux. Local Bordelaise landowners, many of whom were recently elevated members of the robe nobility with lots of capital to invest, were quick to see the opportunities offered by the expansion of trade stimulated by the Dutch and, after 1660, by the restoration of the Francophile Stuart dynasty in England, the oldest and one of the richest markets for their wine. More land was drained and planted with grapes in the following decades, including the Medoc, a peninsula to the northwest of the city, which eventually turned out to produce wines of great finesse. Interestingly, however, the first château to make fine wine that also had all the earmarks of the new, full-bodied style was an ancient vineyard close to the city called Haut-Brion. The perfectionist standards, deep pockets, and entrepreneurial skills of Haut-Brion's proprietor, Arnaud de Pontac, resulted in wines that were robust but suave.[46] Whereas traditional *clairets* were light in color and body, Haut-Brion was deep red, flavorful, and velvety on the palate. By the middle of the 1660s, it was selling for two to three times the price of other high-quality reds in the London market. A few years later, John Locke, who had become familiar with "Ho Bryan" at an upscale London tavern run by Pontac's son, made a detour on his tour of France to visit the vineyard that produced such delicious and memorable wine – a testament to how extraordinary it was.[47]

The techniques that Pontac used to get such stellar results were not new – many of them had been developed by monastic communities in the

44   Phillips, *A Short History of Wine*, pp. 186–187.
45   Ibid.
46   Ibid., pp. 142–143.
47   The tavern, called "Pontac's Head," was located near the meeting place of Parliament. It served food as well as wines from the family's estates (which included several properties in addition to Haut-Brion), and it quickly established itself as a favorite haunt of politicians and other well-connected members of London society. Historians have rightly stressed Pontac's genius in marketing his wine and given him credit for creating one of the first brand-name products in history. See Phillips, *A Short History of Wine*, p. 143; Johnson, *Vintage*, p. 203; and Clive Coates MW, *Grands Vins: The Finest Châteaux of Bordeaux and their Wines* (Berkeley and Los Angeles: University of California Press, 1995), p. 312.

Middle Ages – but he applied them systematically and rigorously to a site with great potential. Vines were pruned to reduce yields and concentrate flavor in the bunches that were allowed to mature. Whereas most vintners picked their grapes as early as the end of August, for fear of losing their crop to autumn rains or early frosts, at Haut-Brion harvests were postponed by a month or more. Laborers would be sent through the vineyard multiple times over a period of weeks with instructions to cut only the bunches that were ready on that particular day. Stems, leaves, and any moldy or rotten grapes were removed before the fruit was pressed. Such fully ripe grapes would have been intensely flavored and very sweet. Thanks to this concentration of sugar, the wine would have been higher in alcohol than the other wines of the region, entering the range of 9–12 percent, which became standard in the nineteenth century.[48] This higher alcohol content would have meant that Haut-Brion kept better than most wines of the day, and it would have contributed to the round "mouthfeel" that was characteristic of the new, richer style. It is likely that Pontac's wines were allowed extra time in the vat before being siphoned into barrels, a procedure that would have given the wine more color and a higher concentration of body-building tannins. The barrels themselves were renewed regularly, an expense that only a well-capitalized winemaker could afford.[49] The commercial success of Pontac's wine encouraged his well-heeled neighbors to adopt similar methods to increase quality. By the turn of the century, a whole class of so-called new clarets had entered the market, including the wines of Lafite, Latour, and Margaux.

One of the effects of more fastidious winemaking was that it eliminated flaws that could distort the perfume and flavor of the finished product. Carefully made premium wines tended to be not only more delicious but also more distinctive than ordinary ones, an effect that was heightened when the grapes came from a single, privileged site. Interestingly, when John Locke made his pilgrimage to Haut-Brion, he focused not on the techniques of vinification that Pontac had perfected but on the natural environment. Like the art of the *nouvelle cuisine*, the craft of winemaking remained invisible to amateurs. Locke, the physician and scientist, assumed that the particular, memorable taste of Haut-Brion had to stem from the specificity of its site, because the wine from the very next vineyard was universally acknowledged to be not as good. His brief meditation on the white sand and gravel of Haut-Brion and the oddly stunted vines that grew there is an early example of our modern fascination with *terroir*.

Traditionally, prime French vineyards had been described as possessing especially good *climat*, which encouraged full ripening of the grapes. To this

[48]   Flandrin, *Chronique de Platine*, p. 283.
[49]   Johnson, *Vintage*, p. 202.

emphasis on the sun exposure and weather, Locke added a focus on the soil and its composition.[50] Although systematic efforts to classify wines according to the geological and physical characteristics of vineyard sites would not appear in France until the nineteenth century, the belief that quality and distinctiveness were rooted in the soil and that the natural provenance of a wine was integral to its value were well established in the century before 1789. For example, Claude Arnoux observed in his *Dissertation sur la situation de la Bourgogne* (1728) that, although it was common for wine-makers to combine grapes grown on plots within the same general vicinity – a consequence of the subdivision of landholdings in the Côte de Beaune – it was acknowledged that the very best and most memorable wines came from individual sites with a pronounced individual character. "Those who wish to make excellent wines," he wrote, "only put in the vat the grapes of a single vineyard."[51] The price of such single-vineyard wines soared in the following decades, reaching sums of "400, 600, and even 950 *livres* per queue [double barrel] in the 1770s."[52] Such values attracted investments not only from the rich elites of Dijon, but even from so great a personage as the Prince de Conti, who bought the top property in Vosne-Romanée in 1760.

Because of the orientation of Bordeaux to the English and Dutch markets, very little of the new claret was shipped to Paris prior to the Revolution. However, Parisian tastes showed a similar shift toward a preference for full-bodied red wines, a taste that was satisfied through increasing access to the products of central and southern Burgundy and the Beaujolais. The still wines of Champagne, which traditionally had been highly regarded for their refreshing tartness and acidity, gradually lost ground to the more robust versions of pinot noir from the Côte d'Or and Beaune. In 1701, one old-fashioned connoisseur, the seigneur de Saint-Evremond, lamented that growers in Reims and Epernay were tinkering with their traditional methods and sacrificing the qualities that made champagne great in order to produce darker, more robust wines that catered to the new taste.[53] The

---

50   John Locke, *Travels in France, 1675–1679, as Related in His Journals, Correspondence and Other Papers*, edited with an introduction and notes by John Lough (Cambridge: Cambridge University Press, 1953), pp. 142–143.

51   Quoted in Johnson, *Vintage*, p. 271. Claude Arnoux (1695–1770) supplemented his earnings as a teacher of Latin and French in London with a second career as a promoter of wines from his Burgundian homeland. His *Dissertation sur la situation de Bourgogne, sur les vins quelle produit, sur la maniere de cultiver les vignes, de faire le vin & de l'éprover* (Londres: C. Jallason, 1728) is one of the most comprehensive and informative sources of the period.

52   Brennan, *Burgundy to Champagne*, p. 238.

53   Charles de Marguetel de Saint Denis, seigneur de Saint-Evremond, *The Letters of Saint-Evremond*, edited with an introduction and notes by John Hayward (New York: B. Blom, 1972), pp. 360–361.

wines of Champagne had sustained another blow a few years earlier, in 1694, when Louis XIV's doctor declared that champagne was too acidic for the royal digestion and ordered the king to henceforth drink nothing but burgundy.[54] Thus medical opinion seemed to validate the growing thirst for rich red wines. Seventy years later, physicians – not to mention partisans of the two regions – were still arguing about the relative merits of the wines with regard to health. In addition to defending champagne from charges of excessive acidity, champions of the region's *vins gris* and pale pinot noirs argued that deep red wines (that, is, burgundies) were composed of large, sticky particles that clogged the tubes of the body.[55] Although George Cheyne's works were not cited by name in this debate, it seems clear that his ideas about the dangers of viscous liquids and flame-colored foods contributed fresh ammunition to the old quarrel.

Even as these arguments continued to unfold, the fortunes of champagne were being revived, thanks to a purely contingent factor: the invention and diffusion of the modern wine bottle. Glass carafes had been used for serving wine in antiquity, a practice that was revived in Renaissance Italy, as glass technology became established first in Venice and then in other cities. However, these early glass vessels were fragile and precious, appropriate for dinner service but not for general household use. Glass bottles that were cheap and sturdy enough to be used for storage were invented in England in the 1630s.[56] The durability of the new bottles derived from a high proportion of sand in the molten glass, which was fired in a coal furnace that ran at a very high temperature thanks to the use of a wind tunnel, and from a design that left a deep punt or indentation on the bottom, which increased stability. Early bottles were sealed with ground glass stoppers (corks started to be used later in the century). In the 1660s, an investigation by the attorney-general confirmed that the credit for inventing this new kind of sturdy bottle belonged to Sir Kenelm Digby, a Catholic Royalist who was one of the founding Fellows of the Royal Society.[57] By

---

[54]   Gerard Sabatier, "Une révolution de Palais: le remplacement des vins de Champagne par ceux de Bourgogne à la table de Louis XIV en 1694" in *Boire et Manger au XVIIe Siècle au Temps de la Marquise de Sévigné*, papers from the second Symposium Vin et Histoire (Suze-la-Rousse: Université du Vin, 1998), pp. 43–59.

[55]   See the discussion in Abbé Tainturier, *Remarques sur la culture des vignes de Beaune et lieux circonvoisins (1763)*, foreword by André-Pierre Syren, preface, notes, and lexicon by Loïc Abric (Précy-sous-Thil: Editions de l'Armançon, 2000), p. 118–119.

[56]   On the development of the wine bottle and glass technology generally, see Eleanor S. Godfrey, *The Development of English Glassmaking, 1560–1640* (Chapel Hill: University of North Carolina Press, 1975), pp. 225–232.

[57]   Godfrey, *The Development of English Glassmaking*, pp. 228–229.

1670 wine bottles had caught on in Holland, where glassmaking technology was also advanced and where the port of Rotterdam had become the hub of the European wine and spirits trade. Bottles did not become common in France until the early decades of the eighteenth century, when they were still described as "in the English fashion."[58] The earliest facilities in France for making glass storage bottles on the English model opened in the vicinity of Bordeaux, at Sainte-Foy-la-Grande in 1723–1725 and in Libourne in 1750. The first bottle factory in Burgundy was established in 1752 by the noble family of Clermont-Tonnerre, the proprietors of several important vineyards.[59]

Wine bottles were attractive to merchants and consumers for a couple of reasons. Although wine was still typically shipped from the vineyard in barrels,[60] bottling it upon receipt at the warehouse or even after it arrived in the retail buyer's cellar allowed it to be stored in containers that were easy to transport to the kitchen and dining room without spilling. The traditional method was to draw wine from the cask into carafes, jugs, or buckets, a step that was eliminated when bottles were in use. More importantly, it turned out that sealing wine in bottles eliminated most of the spoilage that had so preoccupied merchants and their clients. Deprived of contact with the air, wine did not turn into vinegar, nor did it develop some of the off-flavors and funky tastes that were all too common in wine stored in casks. Although the bottles themselves and the labor it took to fill and seal them cost money, this was more than offset by the declining percentage of inventory that turned out to be undrinkable after a few months. So bottling made sense for any wine that one hoped to keep beyond Easter, provided that one had the means to afford the original outlay of funds. Well-to-do consumers who bought more expensive, better-quality wines were quick to see the long-term economy, as were merchants who anticipated holding stocks for any length of time or transshipping them to other locations.

Although consumers began bottling wine for purely utilitarian reasons, they soon discovered that the process could affect the taste, texture, and consistency of wine in interesting ways. The first major breakthrough in this area involved the transformation of champagne from a still wine into one that frothed with scintillating bubbles when the bottles were opened. Because of the northerly situation of Champagne and the chalk hillsides into which the deep, cold cellars were dug, newly pressed grape juice was routinely subject to very low temperatures in late autumn. As the temperatures

[58] Johnson, *Vintage*, p. 194.
[59] Jean-Robert Pitte, *Bordeaux Bourgogne: Les passions rivales* (Paris: Hachette, 2005), pp. 79–80.
[60] Phillips, *A Short History of Wine*, pp. 135–136.

dropped, the fermentation process slowed, often stopping completely before all the sugar in the grape must was consumed. When the weather warmed up in the spring, fermentation recommenced, causing the wine to froth and seethe with alarming vigor. The science behind this characteristic of champagne was not understood at the time, and it was widely considered to be a fault in otherwise excellent wines. Dom Pierre Pérignon (1638–1715), the famous cellar master of the Benedictine abbey of Hautvillers, one of the premier vineyards of the Marne valley, devoted much of his life to developing techniques for selecting grapes and vinifying them so as to eliminate the troublesome bubbles. He did not succeed in this endeavor, although the practices he put into place raised the quality of the abbey's wines by several notches, setting a new standard for the entire region.[61]

Although a bubbling barrel in the month of March was not a sight welcomed by any householder or merchant, the wine usually settled down into a drinkable state within a few weeks, as the sugar was consumed and the gas emitted by the fermentation process escaped through the seams in the cask. Bonnefons advised his readers to be patient: the bubbles would dissipate and the wine would taste better than ever by the end of Lent.[62] Bottling for storage before the secondary fermentation was complete changed the dynamics of this process by trapping the carbon dioxide and dispersing it in the liquid. If the bottles did not explode (and anywhere from 10 to 80 percent of champagne bottles did before the 1830s, when a device for measuring sugar content precisely was invented),[63] the result was wine that foamed into *mousse* when it was uncorked.

Historians now generally agree that the technique of making sparkling champagne was discovered by consumers rather than producers of the wine. Like the bottles that made it possible, *champagne mousseaux* appears to have been an English creation.[64] Champagne of the traditional, still sort had been known and prized in England for a long time – Henry VIII employed an agent in Ay, the village where some of the choicest Marne valley wines were made, in order to ensure that the royal cellars received regular shipments.[65] Imports flagged during the Civil War and Interregnum, but revived at the

---

[61]   Brennan, *Burgundy to Champagne*, pp. 248 and note 38, pp. 334–335. See also the discussion of contemporary evidence to which Brennan refers in François Bonal, *Livre d'or du champagne* (Lausanne: Grand Pont, 1985), pp. 26–36. And Eric Glatre, "Des vins de la Champagne aux vins de Champagne: Dom Pierre Pérignon, le vigneron méconnu" in *Boire et Manger au XVIIe Siècle*, pp. 91–110.

[62]   Bonnefons, *Les Délices de la campagne*, pp. 55–59.

[63]   André L. Simon, *The History of Champagne* (London: George Rainbird, 1962).

[64]   Brennan, *Burgundy to Champagne*, pp. 248–249.

[65]   Tainturier, *Remarques sue la culture des vignes de Beaune et lieux circonvoisins (1763)*, pp. 117–118; and Saint-Evremond, *The Letters of Saint-Evremond*, p. 153.

time of the restoration of the monarchy. The fashion for drinking champagne was encouraged by the seigneur de Saint-Evremond, a French soldier, man of letters, and political exile, who was warmly received at the English court in 1661. Saint-Evremond loved fine food and wine and was especially partial to the *vin gris* of Champagne (in his youth he and some gallant friends were dubbed the *"chevaliers des coteaux"* because they would only drink wines grown on the slopes or *coteaux* of Ay, Hautvillers, and Ambonnay).[66] He shared his enthusiasm and knowledge with his new English friends, who included many of the grandees of the court, and helped them to acquire large lots of the choicest wines.[67] For example, the Earl of Bedford placed an order for three tonneaux (about 750 gallons) of champagne Sillery 1664, a *vin gris* from the vicinity of Reims that Saint-Evremond held in high esteem.[68] Sometime in the mid-1660s, these aristocratic consumers – or their stewards or the London merchants who handled their orders – got the idea of bottling some of the wine for storage. When some of the bottles were uncorked a few months later, the wine frothed with scintillating bubbles. The Englishmen were delighted with the festive character of the fizzy wine, and the fashion for sparkling champagne was launched. Although it would remain a costly luxury (due to the high rate of exploding bottles), supplies of sparkling champagne soon became plentiful enough in London that the middle-class but aspiring Samuel Pepys bought two bottles to drink during a carriage ride through Hyde Park in 1679.[69]

Although French consumers seem to have begun experimenting with sparkling champagne in the 1680s, it did not catch on in Parisian society for another forty years.[70] As late as 1713, when the maréchal de Montesquiou d'Artagnan wrote to his wine broker in Epernay asking for bottled, sparkling

---

[66] Saint-Evremond, *The Letters of Saint-Evremond,* p. xxv.

[67] Brennan, *Burgundy to Champagne,* p. 248. André Simon claimed that Saint-Evremond not only helped his friends with their orders, but came up with the idea of bottling the wine, thus creating sparkling champagne. See André L. Simon, *The History of Champagne,* pp. 48–49. Phillips, *A Short History of Wine,* p. 138, suggests that Saint-Evremond brought bottles of champagne with him when he fled to England from France. However, because bottling was not yet a common practice in France, this seems unlikely. For yet another variation on the story of Saint-Evremond's involvement in the birth of sparkling champagne, see Gilbert Garrier, *Histoire social et culturelle du vin* (Paris: Larousse, 2005), pp. 153–155.

[68] Saint-Evremond, *The Letters of Saint-Evremond,* pp. 153–154.

[69] Dion, *Histoire de la vigne et du vin en France,* pp. 641–642. Phillips, *A Short History of Wine,* pp. 138–139.

[70] Brennan, *Burgundy to Champagne,* p. 249. Interestingly, Saint-Evremond, the godfather of sparkling champagne, seems to have preferred his wine *"tranquille,"* a taste that would survive among old-fashioned French gourmets until the age of Napoleon.

champagne, his request elicited a testy lecture from the merchant about the inferior nature of this product, for which fools were willing to spend fortunes.[71] The ultimate acceptance of *vin mousseux* owed much to the example of the Regent, the duke d'Orléans, whose patronage had already done so much to raise Massialot to preeminence in the culinary realm. Sparkling champagne was the duke's beverage of choice to accompany the intimate and festive suppers he hosted in the private quarters of the Palais Royal.[72] The wine would have matched the festivity of Massialot's elegantly constructed dishes and the fancy filled omelets that the Regent liked to concoct for his guests. Voltaire, whose rise to fame as a poet and dramatist dates from the Regency, described sparkling champagne as a feminine wine. Thanks to its delicacy, one could consume it in quantity without getting drunk, he thought. Indeed, it was "the only wine a woman can drink without becoming ugly."[73] With press like this, it was not surprising that sparkling champagne was in great demand and consequently cost much more that the still wines of Champagne.

By the 1720s, *negociants* in Reims and Epernay acknowledged the trend and began to focus increasingly on making and shipping sparkling wine in the bottle to Paris and beyond to international markets.[74] As early as 1728 the merchants of Reims petitioned for and received the right to export champagne in bottles (as opposed to barrels).[75] Throughout the eighteenth century, however, production of sparkling champagne remained small, never exceeding 500,000 bottles a year. Its scarcity in the face of demand placed it at the pinnacle of the luxury trade, with prices on the Paris market fluctuating between five and eight *livres* a bottle. Around 1750 the price for a bottle of sparkling champagne was seven *livres*, while imported sweet wines such as tokay and sherry sold for three *livres* and fine burgundies such as Montrachet *blanc* and Clos de Vougeot *rouge* went for only two.[76]

FROM SINCERITY TO AUTHENTICITY

The fact that bottling transformed still champagne into sparkling wine was immediately obvious to anyone who saw a bottle uncorked. With time and experience, it also became clear that storing wines of many kinds in

---

[71]   Quoted in André Simon, *The History of Champagne*, p. 61.
[72]   Ibid., pp. 55–58.
[73]   Garrier, *Histoire sociale et culturelle du vin*, p. 155.
[74]   Brennan, *Burgundy to Champagne*, pp. 269–270.
[75]   Simon, *The History of Champagne*, p. 59.
[76]   Garrier, *Histoire sociale et culturelle du vin*, pp. 155–156.

sealed bottles allowed them to mature, developing distinct flavors and aromas that were quite different from their younger incarnations. No one in the seventeenth century seems to have anticipated that this would be the case. Although it was known that the Romans buried sealed amphora of choice wines in the earth or stored them in cold cellars and that well-made wines improved as a result of this treatment, the fact that the *character* of wine changed as it aged came as a surprise. In particular, wines that had been cleanly and carefully made from grapes grown in good vineyard plots responded to aging not only by losing their raw edges but by developing a pronounced, unique, multilayered taste and bouquet within which individual notes could be distinguished.[77] Connoisseurship as we know it today, which owes so much to the appreciation of the mingling of *terroir* and grape variety over time, was unimaginable to early modern Europeans before the advent of bottle aging.

Interestingly, it took winemakers, merchants, and consumers decades to fully grasp the effects that bottle aging had on wine and to adjust their practices to take advantage of its potential. As late as the 1720s, when Claude Arnoux, a native of Beaune, first encountered aged burgundy in London, he was amazed by how the wine had been enlivened, its texture smoothed, and its color deepened to the most beautiful, velvety hue by six years of repose in glass.[78] If the quality measures taken by perfectionist winemakers such as the Pontacs enhanced the unique personalities of wine produced in prime vineyards, bottle aging took this identity to new heights of definition. Wines that had a pronounced *goût de terroir* (taste of the soil) came to be especially prized. Arnoux took his readers on a tour of the Côte d'Or, describing the changing landscape, the transition from limestone soils in the north to marl in the south, and the unique wines that captured the characteristics of each district, from intense, masculine Chambertin to delicate, violet-scented Volnay.[79] As authentic embodiments of the geology, topography, and climate of a particular place, such wines reflected the diversity of the natural world – that is, they were the oenological equivalents of cookery designed to capture *le goût naturel*. According to the modern aesthetic that emerged in ancien régime France, drink as well as food was supposed to taste of what it was.

This concern with the authenticity of wine – its status as a unique natural product that mirrored the land and weather from which it sprang – was new. Given the poor odds of preserving wine in casks for any length of time and the problems of "doctoring" and adulteration associated with

[77] Rod Phillips, *A Short History of Wine*, p. 141.
[78] Pitte, *Bordeaux Bourgogne*, p. 80.
[79] Arnoux, *Dissertation sur la situation de Bourgogne*, pp. 29, 36–37, and 42–43.

them, merchants and consumers had traditionally been more concerned with quality and wholesomeness than natural provenance. Was the wine pure? Was it spoiled? Had it been doctored in any way to cover up decay or to make it seem finer and more expensive than it really was? In a word, was the wine sincere?

As Lionel Trilling noted many years ago, *"sincère"* and *"sincérité"* are words of ancient usage in the French language, dating to at least 1475 and 1293, respectively.[80] Like their somewhat later counterparts in English, they were terms used to describe substances or, by analogy, persons, actions, or doctrines that were pure, wholesome, and free from corruption or adulteration. One of the early applications was in the wine trade, where judging the sincerity of a wine was a critical aspect of determining whether it could be sold and at what price.[81] Reputable wine merchants employed assistants whose special responsibility it was to taste wines and judge their sincerity before they were offered for sale and to monitor the condition of wines stored in the cellars. Like the protagonist of *Emile*, these guardians of *sincérité* retained the sensitive sense of smell and the unjaded palate of a child into adulthood. They were known in the trade as *"gourmets."* In 1384, the officers of the Burgundian court charged with tasting the duke's wine to test its purity were constituted as the *"Compagnie des courtiers gourmets piqueurs du vin."*[82]

Although the original job of the wine shop gourmet was to detect decay or adulteration, his sensitive palate also registered the nuances of flavor and bouquet that distinguished one wine from another – say a Chambertin from a Clos de Vougeot. This ability to discern fine gradations of aroma, texture, and taste was similar to the capacity for distinguishing the differences between varieties of pears, chickens reared on different diets, and butter from Meudon or Normandy cultivated by advocates of *le goût naturel*. As culinary aesthetics reoriented themselves around the identification and enjoyment of the unique flavors of natural foodstuffs, the appreciation of wine headed down a parallel path, gaining additional momentum thanks to the development of single-vineyard, bottle-aged premium wines. By the mid-1700s, the term *"gourmet"* had migrated from the wine shop into the culinary lexicon. Whereas *"gourmand"* referred to someone who reveled in eating with a slightly gluttonous enthusiasm, a *gourmet* was one whose gustatory pleasure was inseparable from the act of discriminating

[80]   Lionel Trilling, *Sincerity and Authenticity* (Cambridge, MA: Harvard University Press, 1971), p. 12.

[81]   Trilling, *Sincerity and Authenticity*, pp. 12–13.

[82]   Jean-Jacques Boutaud, *Le Sens gourmand: de la commensalité du goût – des ailments* (Paris: Jean-Paul Rocher, 2005), pp. 144–145.

one taste from another. In drawing the distinction between *"gourmand"* and *"gourmet,"* Jaucourt suggested, only half in jest, that a *gourmet* could taste the difference between specimens of sea bass caught in neighboring waters and preferred foie gras from geese fattened on fresh (as opposed to dried) figs.[83] At the table as in the wine shop, the *gourmet* was gifted with a keenly analytical sense of taste.

WINE AND FOOD IN *SERVICE À LA FRANÇAISE*

One of the unresolved issues of eighteenth-century cuisine was how to integrate fine wines with strong individual personalities into the aesthetics of the meal. The idea of structuring the menu as a series of two to seven courses, each consisting of a wine and a single *plat principal* chosen to be its perfect match, would come into its own around 1850. Although *service à la russe* got its name from the Russian ambassador, Prince Kourakine, who introduced it in 1810, it became closely associated with that quintessential bourgeois institution of the Second Empire, the gastronomic restaurant, whence it spread to private houses.[84] In the decades before and after the French Revolution, however, menus in most households continued to be structured around the principles of *service à la française,* just as in the age of Bonnefons and La Varenne, when choices in wine tended to be more limited.

Ordinary meals served *à la française* consisted of three courses, the *potage*, the roast, and the dessert, with additional courses added on festive occasions. Menus for dinner and supper were planned to ensure that everyone at the table would be able to find something to their taste. On special occasions, or when the group at table was large, it was common to offer two soups or different kinds of roasts, accompanied by an ample selection of entrées and hors d'oeuvres. This focus on the importance of variety was present even at intimate family meals. Although only one soup and one roast would be offered, the kitchen would invariably send out a choice of side dishes. For example, Brillat-Savarin described a family menu, circa

---

[83] *"Gourmandise"* in *Encyclopédie*, vol. 7, p. 754.

[84] Pitte, *French Gastronomy*, p. 105; Priscilla Parkhurst Ferguson, *Accounting for Taste: The Triumph of French Cuisine* (Chicago and London: The University of Chicago Press, 2004), p. 89; and Mennell, *All Manners of Food*, pp. 79 and 150. Mennell points out that some of the menus associated with the *nouvelle cuisine* begin to approach the idea of *service à la russe* by drastically reducing the number of dishes per course, while still offering at least two choices in each. In addition to creating a platform for perfect pairings of wine and food, *service à la russe* also reduced the workload of the kitchen, which surely contributed to its popularity in private households.

1740, in which the second course consisted of a roasted turkey, a salad, a vegetable dish, and a gratin or crème.[85] Even a simple menu *à la française*, such as Brillat-Savarin's turkey dinner, presented some challenges in terms of choosing a wine. Although the turkey itself would have been relatively versatile – unless it had a stuffing, as was chic at the time – the whole ensemble, including the tart salad, the unspecified vegetables, and the creamy side dish, would not necessarily make a brilliant match with any particular wine. American readers who have struggled to choose a wine for Thanksgiving dinner are familiar with the problem.

The solution that seems to have prevailed was not to attempt precise pairings of food and wine at all.[86] As late as the first decade of the nineteenth century, Grimod de la Reynière, a celebrated gourmet, recommended choosing wines for their innate interest and quality and offering both whites and reds on the same menu. The wines were to be served in the bottles in which they aged (Grimod thought that decanting wine dissipated the bouquet). In very hot weather, the bottles could be set on ice for an hour or less. After being opened, they were to be placed directly on the table, one of each kind within arm's reach of each guest. Despite the general preference for red wines, Grimod personally liked to serve two bottles of white wine for one of red. He particularly recommended a fine cru of Chablis produced by a grower named Chéron as an excellent choice for daily meals.[87] Unfortunately, he mentioned no reds by name. Although some of his contemporaries (including Brillat-Savarin) recommended a glass of Madeira with the soup, Grimod seems to have preferred dry French wines to accompany all the savory courses of the meal.

There seems to have been universal agreement that the dessert course called for a sweet wine. This was a category in which eighteenth-century consumers enjoyed an embarrassment of riches. Mellow, sweet Rhine wines were a traditional favorite that continued to have a following among Parisian gourmets. Although port, beloved in Georgian England, never caught on in France, French connoisseurs continued to favor fortified wines from the Mediterranean that had been prized for centuries. For example, Voltaire ordered fine Spanish Malaga by the cartload for his cellar at Ferney, even though he complained about the expense and pilferage by the men who delivered it.[88] Consumers could also experiment with sweet wines from Anjou (which were easy to come by in Paris in the second half of the eighteenth century) as well as Sauternes, Bergerac, and other southwestern

[85]   Brillat-Savarin, *Physiologie du goût*, p. 272.
[86]   Garrier, *Histoire sociale et culturelle du vin*, p. 228.
[87]   Grimod de la Reynière, *Manuel des Amphitryons*, pp. 227–229.
[88]   Wheaton, *Savoring the Past*, p. 216

wines that found their way to the city in small amounts. Finally, there was champagne *doux*, in which the level of bubbles, sweetness, and alcohol were discretely cranked up thanks to the addition of sugar and spirits during the bottling process.[89]

Any of these choices would have worked well enough with the array of wafers, biscuits, petits fours, and other cakes and pastries that appeared for dessert along with custards, sweet soufflés, fruits, and preserves. Fresh cream cheeses served with sugar and cream would have fit in, too. It would be interesting to know what people drank with the mature cheeses that were also a regular component of dessert: the sweet wine chosen for that course or perhaps more of the dry wines from the earlier part of the meal? That this was not the subject of much discussion at the time, even among fastidious gourmets, seems to underscore the relaxed attitude toward pairings of food and wine that prevailed in the era of *service à la française*.

[89] Simon, *The History of Champagne*, p. 61.

After the Revolution

By the 1780s, the transitions with which this book is concerned were complete. The ancient traditions that still shaped French habits of cooking, eating, and drinking when Louis XIV was a boy disappeared by the time Louis XVI ascended the throne, superseded by ideas and practices that form the basis of the modern food culture we know today. Traditional cooks understood their art as tempering the elemental properties of foodstuffs and transforming raw materials into objects of civilization. The modern cooks of the seventeenth and eighteenth centuries thought that their fundamental task was to preserve the qualities that made foods distinctive in their natural state. For millennia, strong seasonings had been used to create dietary balance and multi-dimensional layers of flavor, a culinary strategy rejected by the moderns, who developed new techniques and rich but mild sauces to highlight the true taste of principal ingredients. Wine had long been judged primarily according to its strength and purity, but, by the eighteenth century, the natural provenance of the wine was seen as intrinsic to quality, too. A culinary movement that originated in the Epicurean desire to bring seasonal variety to the table turned into something more – a means of communing with nature itself, in an era in which nature was seen as a source of the good, a refuge from the phoniness and corruption of aristocratic society. Dining without ceremony and a taste for *le goût naturel* were casual partners in 1650. A century later, thanks to the philosophes and above all to Rousseau, they had become fused in the pursuit of a simple and natural way of life. Food that tasted like what it was had become a symbol of freedom and authenticity.

The cult of natural simplicity had a profound appeal for members of the generation that came to maturity in the 1770s and 1780s – and not only in France. In a development that would have angered Rousseau (and whose irony Diderot and Voltaire would have relished), half-baked ideas about the virtue of a rustic life at one with nature inspired much theatrical posing in the decades before revolution overtook the ancien régime. The troubled protagonist of Goethe's great novel, *The Sorrows of Young Werther* (1775) rhapsodized about the joyful sense of wholeness he experienced while sitting at a crude table beneath the shade of a linden tree and eating sweet peas cooked in butter.[1] But the most bizarre example of theatrical rusticity was found at Versailles. Bored by the rituals of court life, the young queen, Marie-Antoinette, retreated into her private domain of the Petit Trianon. She became fascinated with Rousseau, even making a pilgrimage to his grave at Ermenonville in 1782.[2] A year later, she began building a faux peasant village on the Trianon grounds, where she and her friends (dressed in muslin gowns from Rose Bertin, the royal dressmaker) played at being milkmaids and supped on fruits, cheeses, and freshly churned butter. It did not occur to Marie-Antoinette that such contrivance was itself an affront to Rousseau's teachings or that the steep cost of her simple pleasures posed a burden on the genuine peasantry of France, who paid for them in the form of taxation.

Luckily, the ideal of simple food survived despite such grotesqueries. In the form of *cuisine bourgeoise,* the principles, techniques, and many of the recipes of Marin, Menon, Bonnefons, and La Varenne became established in Parisian kitchens as a kind of vernacular that continued to flourish into the nineteenth century. Dishes that first appeared in mid-eighteenth- or even seventeenth-century sources – for instance, *potage de santé* with seasonal herbs, veal ragout, chicken fricassee, fish with white butter sauce or *sauce rousse,* roasts with butter-thickened deglazing sauces, vegetables with cream, and *mirontons* – attained the status of classics, appearing in myriad versions. It is noteworthy that Menon's most popular book, *La Cuisinière bourgeoise,* continued to be reprinted into the 1840s. Just as important, we find cooks who were not yet born in 1789 creating new dishes on foundations laid in the kitchens of the ancien régime – the sure sign of a living tradition.

The enduring power of simplicity and its celebration by Brillat-Savarin and other gastronomes did not imply the demise of elaborate food in the mode of Massialot and La Chapelle. Rococo dishes had become the preferred

---

[1] After describing how he picked and cooked the peas himself, Werther continued in a tone straight from Rousseau: "How happy I am that my heart is open to the simple, innocent delight of the man who brings a head of cabbage to his table which he himself has grown, enjoying not only the cabbage but all the fine days, the lovely mornings when he planted it, the pleasant evenings when he watered it, so that, having experienced pleasure in its growth he may, at the end, again enjoy in one single moment all that has gone before." Johann Wolfgang von Goethe, *The Sorrows of Young Werther and Novella,* translated from the German by Elizabeth Meyer and Louise Bogan, poems translated by W. H. Auden, foreword by W. H. Auden (New York: Vintage, 1990), pp. 33–34.

[2] Simon Schama, *Citizens: A Chronicle of the French Revolution* (New York: Vintage, 1989), p. 156.

style at court in the reign of Louis XV, and they dominated the menus of the *grand couvert* right up to the end. (The last of these ceremonial dinners took place just days before a mob stormed the Tuileries palace on August 10, 1792, precipitating the fall of the constitutional monarchy established in 1789 and the institution of a republic.)[3]

After a hiatus in the peak years of revolutionary fervor, fancy food made a stunning comeback under the Directory (the government that succeeded the First Republic in 1794), the Consulate (1799–1804), and the First Empire (1804–1814/15). Lavish entertaining in private houses returned, a fashion led by the great diplomat Charles-Maurice de Talleyrand-Périgord (1754–1838), who served as foreign minister under the Directory and Napoleon and who negotiated on behalf of France at the Congress of Vienna (1814–1815). Talleyrand was a gourmet and a gourmand, the owner of the most prestigious vineyard in Bordeaux (Château de Haut-Brion), a great aristocrat of the old school, and also an architect of the new France. He understood the value of sumptuous food as a tool of diplomacy. (When asked what France needed to bolster its position in Vienna, he is said to have replied, "More saucepans.") From 1797 he employed a cook named Antonin Carême, who would turn out to be one of the culinary geniuses of the nineteenth century.

Carême picked up the project of codifying French cuisine where Massialot left off, and his influence remains decisive to this day. For example, it was he who devised what is still the standard classification of sauces into families, each descended from a mother recipe whose defining characteristics are perpetuated in the others. Carême's early training as a *pâtissier* encouraged his love of fanciful presentations. He became known for constructing elaborate structures of pastry and spun sugar (inspired by architectural drawings at the Bibliothèque Nationale) that stood several feet high and long. Such *pièces montées*, the most elaborate of which took a team of pastry cooks fifty-seven hours to complete, graced the center of immense buffet tables. This love of decoration and complex shapes also marked Carême's approach to savory dishes, which rivaled La Chapelle's in lavishness. To give one example, the recipe for Eggs Carême called for eggs to be baked in cylindrical molds with a garnish of truffles and pickled ox tongue until the whites were set. Each egg, unmolded, was nestled into a previously poached artichoke bottom; garnished with a ragout of lambs' sweetbreads, truffles, and mushrooms; topped with a brown sauce flavored with Madeira wine and cream; and garnished with a slice of tongue cut into a saw-tooth pattern.[4] After leaving Talleyrand's service, Carême cooked for Alexander I of Russia and the prince regent of England. In the late 1820s, he returned

[3]   Jousselin, *Au couvert du roi*, p. 59.
[4]   Recipe from *Larousse Gastronomique*, p. 195.

to France, where (for a huge salary) he directed the kitchen of James Meyer Rothschild, scion of the Jewish banking family. In 1814–1815, Carême's cuisine aided French efforts to be readmitted into the circle of great powers after the defeat of Napoleon; between 1829 and his death in 1833, it was an essential ingredient in the rise of the Rothschilds into the first rank of French society, despite their Jewish origin and faith.

Ironically, one of the most important vehicles for advancing the development of *grande cuisine* in the half-century after the Revolution was the restaurant, whose origins were linked to the rise of health food and the taste for Rousseauian simplicity. The form of service pioneered by early restaurants (a written menu card, fixed prices for individual portions, seating at private tables set within a public space) turned out to be so popular with the Parisian public that it spread to establishments that offered other, more voluptuous styles of cooking. Whereas there were perhaps a hundred eateries that called themselves restaurants in the 1780s, that number had increased to five or six hundred by the first decade of the 1800s and to three thousand or so in the 1820s.[5] Some of these establishments continued to feature bouillons and other light fare (indeed, a few restaurants calling themselves "bouillons" survive in Paris to this day). The majority probably offered dishes from the Parisian vernacular, *cuisine bourgeoise*, and at least one, *Les Trois Frères Provençaux*, introduced citizens of the capital to the specialties of the Midi. However, there were also restaurants that made elaborate cuisine of the sort formerly found only in grand private houses available to anyone who could pay, and it was this type of establishment that particularly became associated with post-Revolutionary Parisian life.[6]

The first gastronomic restaurants opened their doors to the public in the waning years of the ancien régime. Beauvillers, owned and operated by a former pastry cook in the household of the king's brother, the future Louis XVIII, moved to the Palais Royal in 1787, where its neighbors soon included the Grand Véfour, Véry, Méot, and the Boeuf-à-la-Mode. Under the Empire and Restoration, similar establishments spread to other parts of the Right Bank – to Les Halles (Le Rocher de Cancale), to the great boulevards (the Café Anglais, the Café Riche, the Café de Paris, the Cadran Bleu), and to the neighborhood of the Champs-Elysées (Ledoyen).[7] Parisians with money to spend – the remnants of the old nobility, successful generals, and growing ranks of nouveaux riches – flocked to these restaurants, where they could enjoy sumptuous food in a setting that was convivial but

5   Pitte, *French Gastronomy*, p. 120
6   Ferguson, *Accounting for Taste*, pp. 86–89.
7   Pitte, *French Gastronomy*, pp. 120–122.

discrete and unburdened by constraints that governed behavior at home. (The private dining room quickly emerged as a favorite rendezvous for lovers and mistresses.) Many of the memorable scenes of Balzac's *Comédie Humaine* were reflected in the mirrors of the city's palaces of gastronomic bliss.

Grand restaurants were profitable businesses, so much so that Carême was the last seminal figure of *haute cuisine* to work exclusively for private employers. For example, his pupil, Adolphe Dugléré (1804–1884), achieved culinary immortality as the chef of the Café Anglais. In addition to welcoming a free-spending, star-studded clientele (which on one occasion included Alexander II of Russia; his son, the future Alexander III; Wilhelm I of Prussia; and Bismarck, who shared an eight-course meal costing four hundred *francs* each), the restaurant provided Dugléré with a forum for experimentation. Some of his signature dishes, such as *sole à la Dugléré* and *soufflé à l'anglaise*, were created to showcase the creativity of the chef and his staff. Others, such as *potage Germiny* and *pommes Anna*, were invented to please regular clients (the soup was named for count de Germiny, a director of the Banque de France, whereas the potatoes were dedicated to Anna Deslions, a fashionable courtesan).[8] As the July Monarchy gave way to the Second Empire and then to the Third Republic, gastronomic restaurants replaced the kitchens of elite households as centers of culinary innovation.

Thus nineteenth-century France inherited both of the prominent strands of cuisine that emerged in the ancien régime – the rococo, which came down from Massialot and La Chapelle to Carême and his followers, and the *nouvelle cuisine* of the 1740s, which continued to flourish in the sphere of fine home cooking. Despite the obvious stylistic differences between these forms of cuisine – one fancy, the other simple – they were united in a fundamental commitment to the primacy of ingredients and to modes of preparation that allowed the character of those ingredients to dominate the effect on the palate. *Le goût naturel* reigned supreme. *Haute cuisine* and *cuisine bourgeoise* continued to explore the same culinary territory and to provide creative inspiration for each other – surely one of the factors that has encouraged the extraordinary vibrancy of French cuisine down to the present day.[9]

---

[8]   Ibid., pp. 123–124.
[9]   In comparison, Steven Mennell has pointed out that one of the weaknesses of English cuisine in the modern period is that the traditions of high and low cooking became separated around 1700, never to be reunited. "High" cooking followed French inspirations; middle-class kitchens, deprived of elite and distinctively English models, focused on thrift and convenience, shunned innovation, and gradually decayed. Mennell calls this "the decapitation of English cooking." See *All Manners of Food*, pp. 204–214.

During the Revolution and First Empire, when the old provinces were abolished in favor of new administrative units, the *départements*, there was a movement to recast the traditional identities of many towns and regions in terms of the foodstuffs they produced: Reims, formerly the coronation city of French monarchs, came to be symbolized on maps by bottles of champagne, Strasbourg by *pâte de fois gras*, Dijon by a pot of mustard, Normandy by apples, and so forth. Frenchmen were encouraged to think of their country as defined by what Grimod de la Reynière called its "alimentary topography."[10] Of course, regional products had been showing up in the Paris marketplace since time immemorial; but, thanks to the development of the railroads and other transportation networks (most of which centered on the capital), access to the foodstuffs of far-flung provinces became routine. By the time that Louis Napoleon (president of France, 1848–1851; emperor 1851–1870) and Hausmann (prefect of the Department of the Seine, 1853–1870) rebuilt Les Halles, the central market, in the 1850s, it was possible for Parisians to buy produce, cheese, meats, and specialty items from all corners of the country. In the seventeenth century, the delicate style of Parisian cooking had become identified with the realm as a whole, thanks to the social power and prestige of the capital's elite. Two hundred years later, the Parisian culinary vernacular attained the material basis of a truly national cuisine.

The revolution in transport and in other technical areas, such as preserving food in sterilized jars or cans (invented by Nicolas Appert in 1809), pasteurization (introduced in 1862), and commercial refrigeration (which became widespread in the 1870s), ushered in other changes in French habits of cooking, eating, and drinking. Many farmers and food artisans altered their priorities and methods in response to market demand. The uniform white rind on camembert cheeses is the result of one such effort to standardize a product so as to command a higher price.[11] As it became economical to transport *primeurs* from the Loire, fruit from the Rhone valley, *mesclun* from the backcountry of Nice, and oysters from the bay of Arcachon to Paris by rail, patterns of production in the city's old agricultural hinterland began to change, and the concept of what constituted the "season" for asparagus or melons or other fragile, short-lived items shifted, too. In this respect, the nationalization of the material basis for Parisian cooking coincided with

---

[10] See the discussion of patriotic gardens and gastronomical maps in Julia Csergo, "The Emergence of Regional Cuisines" in Flandrin and Montanari, eds. *Food*, pp. 502–506. Also Spang, *The Invention of the Restaurant*, pp. 167–169.

[11] The modification and standardization of camembert in light of market factors is one of the themes of Pierre Boisard, *Camembert: A National Myth*, translated by Richard Miller (Berkeley and Los Angeles: University of California Press, 2003).

the beginning of a new and ultimately global culinary regime in which vast distances are overcome by market forces that fill grocery shelves with a huge selection of foods that never seem to go out of season or vary much from place to place.

But all that is another story. The economic infrastructure of life has changed drastically since the eighteenth century, as have our ideas about nature and our relationship to it as human beings. Philosophy, science, and material culture have moved on. But the fact that many of us moderns still long to eat and drink in a manner that represents the variety of the natural world surely reflects our lasting attachment to the ideas of simplicity and authenticity that we find in the culinary revolution of ancien régime France.

APPENDIX

Recipes from the Early Modern French Kitchen

The recipes that follow are my reconstructions of dishes described in the French culinary literature of the seventeenth and eighteenth centuries. I have chosen recipes that illustrate the transition from the complex, spicy cooking of the Middle Ages and Renaissance to the modern preference for *le goût naturel* as well as the individual styles of cooks such as La Varenne, Bonnefons, Massialot, and Marin. Readers who are familiar with the techniques of French cooking as practiced today will recognize much that is familiar – but also some significant differences that reflect the methods and preferences of a time before the creation, in the nineteenth century, of canonical rules and recipes of *haute cuisine*. In the search for felicitous pairings of ingredients, early modern cooks came up with some unusual combinations, such as lamb with orange juice and chicken smothered with onions. The recipes that follow are refreshing in their simplicity and purity of taste, and they represent the efforts of several generations of French cooks to create dishes that highlighted the qualities of fine natural ingredients.

As readers of the previous chapters are well aware, early modern recipes often lacked precise proportions and step-by-step instructions on techniques. In writing up my versions of the following dishes, I have preserved whatever information of this sort was indicated in the original text and filled the gaps by drawing on my own experience as a cook – exactly the process that the culinary authors of the period expected their readers to follow. In some cases, I cooked a dish several times before settling on the way of making it described in the following, and readers who experiment with these recipes should feel free to modify them to suit their own tastes.

Do not be discouraged by the length of some of the recipes. In the interest of demystifying the techniques involved, I have opted for detailed explanations. Even recipes that involve several different operations are actually quite easy to execute. They require no unusual equipment or skills, but some of them require time and patience.

A note on staple ingredients used in these recipes: Eggs are grade A large, butter is unsalted, olive oil is extra virgin, and vinegar is made from wine, red or white. Early modern French cooking made much use of rendered pork fat, and, although I use it, I also note that in some cases olive or neutral vegetable oil may be substituted. The kind of uncured bacon that is used in France to make lardons is generally unavailable in the United States; Italian-style pancetta or regular American smoked bacon, blanched in water for about ten minutes, is used instead. Bitter Seville oranges, the only kind used in early modern French cooking, are almost unobtainable in American markets. Unless you are lucky enough to find some during their brief winter season, you may substitute a mixture of lemon juice and the juice of sweet oranges, as specified in the following. Verjuice is now available in some specialty stores and supermarkets; you may also substitute lemon juice in its place, as indicated in the individual recipes. Chicken figures prominently in these recipes, reflecting its popularity in early modern France. If you have a choice, buy birds that have been raised on pasture and have eaten a natural diet. Such chickens typically grow at a slower rate than chickens confined indoors and have greatly improved flavor and texture.

I: *FONDS DE CUISINE*, 1650–1800

BOUILLON OF BEEF WITH VEAL OR CHICKEN (MARIN)

Makes 2–3 quarts

High-quality bouillon was a cornerstone of fine cooking in early modern France, and it was especially critical to the success of the *nouvelle cuisine* that emerged in the 1730s. Marin singled out two of the several bouillon recipes he recorded in *Les Dons de Comus* as being particularly versatile.[1] One of these was given in the main section of the book, whereas the other was in the section on bourgeois economy. The first recipe called for veal shank or chicken in addition to beef (which would have upped the cost but also produced a lighter result), whereas the economy version made the chicken optional. Otherwise, the method and seasonings were the same. Marin argued that the key to excellent results in either case was meticulous care in skimming and degreasing and long cooking at a low temperature.

---

[1]   [Marin], *Les Dons de Comus*, vol. 1, pp. 2–3, and vol. 3, pp. 544–557.

He also pointed out that it was wise to avoid adding strongly flavored vegetables or herbs in any bouillon that was intended for general kitchen use. Such ingredients should be added later, only to the portion of the bouillon earmarked for the particular dish in which their flavors were desired. In this way, a clever cook could use a single batch of bouillon to prepare several meals, thus saving time, effort, and expense.

One of the problems with making bouillon at home in the United States today is that it is difficult to find a genuine stewing chicken – that is, a bird that is old and tough enough to impart body and deep flavor to the broth. If you want to serve poached chicken as a main course after the bouillon, you may add a regular fryer/roaster of 3–3½ pounds to the pot, removing it as soon as it is tender; however, it will not give much character to the bouillon. When the bouillon itself is the goal, it is better to add the equivalent weight of bony, cartilaginous parts – wings, backs, and necks for preference – which are cheap and easily available.

Remember that there is nothing shameful about buying good-quality canned or frozen stock at the grocery store. For the sake of convenience, eighteenth-century Parisian cooks often purchased bouillon from restaurateurs, and we should not feel compelled to be more perfect than they.

Equipment: A large stockpot or kettle with a lid, a skimmer or ladle, a fine strainer, a large bowl, and paper towels for final degreasing of the bouillon.

3 pounds beef shank (you may also use shin, chuck from the blade section, or even brisket, although the latter is usually sold in American markets without the bones, which give body to the stock; you may also use a combination of brisket and bones from other parts of the animal)
2 pounds veal shank or a stewing hen (about 2½–3 pounds) or the same weight of bony chicken parts (see previously)
Cold water
2 tsp salt
2 carrots, peeled
2 medium-sized onions, peeled
2 leeks, slit and washed to remove all dirt from the layers

1. Put the beef and veal or chicken in the stockpot and add enough cold water to cover the meat by 2 inches. Set the pot over moderate heat.

2.   As the water comes to the simmer, lots of gray scum will begin rising to the surface, a process that will continue for 5 minutes or more. (The scum is produced as certain proteins in the meat, bones, and cartilage dissolve in the hot liquid.) Use a skimmer or a ladle to remove all of the scum. Regulate the heat so that the liquid does not come to a boil during the skimming process, or else it will be impossible to spoon out all of the scum. This is a picky job, but, as Marin points out, it is essential to making bouillon that is clear and limpid.

3.   After the scum has all been removed, add the salt, carrots, onions, and leeks to the pot. Partly cover the pot with its lid, leaving room for steam to escape.

4.   Turn the heat down to low and maintain the liquid at a very slow simmer, with just the occasional, isolated bubble breaking the surface, for 4–5 hours. If the liquid evaporates below the level of the solid ingredients, add enough water to cover them again. *Do not, under any circumstances, allow the liquid to boil. If you do, fat and other impurities will be incorporated into the bouillon, making it cloudy and muddy tasting.*

5.   Taste the bouillon after 4 hours; if the flavor is not as full as you would like, let it simmer for an additional hour or so.

6.   When the stock is ready, strain it into the large bowl and set aside. By this point, the meats and vegetables will have lost most of their savor, having given their all to the bouillon. However, the meats may be served as a main course, moistened with a little bouillon and sprinkled with coarse salt, or used in preparations such as a *mironton* (see following) or, chilled and sliced, in a salad. The vegetables should be discarded. For vegetable soups, see the following variations.

7.   Degrease the bouillon. There are two ways to do this. Let the bowl of hot broth settle for a few minutes, allowing the fat to rise to the top. Remove as much of the fat as possible with a ladle or big spoon and then draw strips of paper towels across the surface to capture the last bits. Or you may chill the bouillon, uncovered, until the fat hardens on the surface. Scrape the congealed fat off with a spoon, cover the bowl, and refrigerate until needed.

Note: This bouillon is not very salty, a deliberate calculation, since bouillon is often reduced in the recipes in which it is used, increasing the concentration of salt.

Variation: Bouillon of Chicken and Veal: Follow the method in the preceding recipe, using 2 pounds of veal shank instead of the beef plus a stewing hen or 3 pounds of bony chicken parts.

COURT BOUILLON (MASSIALOT)

Makes about 1 quart

This is an acidic mixture, typically composed of some combination of water, vinegar, white wine, and lemon juice or verjuice that is flavored with aromatics such as onion, bay leaf, pepper, and cloves.[2] It is called *"court"* (short) because it simmers only briefly (and in some recipes not at all) before it is used to poach delicate items such as fish and seafood. Court bouillon was a staple of the fast-day kitchen inherited from medieval times. All of the culinary authors of our period used it, but they tended to be very casual in specifying proportions. The following is an adaptation of the court bouillon described by Massialot in his recipes for poached pike and carp (the ingredients are his, the proportions are mine). Interestingly, Massialot does not call for carrots, a standard ingredient in many more recent recipes for court bouillon

Equipment: A medium saucepan with a lid and a strainer for removing the solid ingredients at the end of the cooking process.

1 quart cold water
1 cup dry white wine
¼ cup white wine vinegar
1 Tb verjuice or lemon juice
2 small onions or 1 medium one stuck with 2 cloves
2 bay leaves
Zest of half of a lemon
Pinch of nutmeg
½ tsp black peppercorns
1½ tsp salt
Optional: drops of lemon juice, to taste

1. Combine all the ingredients in the saucepan. Bring to a boil over low heat, partly cover the pan with the lid, and turn the heat down to low. Simmer the court bouillon for about 20 minutes.
2. Strain the court bouillon to remove the onions and seasonings. The court bouillon may be used immediately or set aside and reheated for later use.

---

[2]   F. Massialot, *Le Nouveau cuisinier royal et bourgeois ou Cuisinier moderne,* unabridged facsimile of the edition published in 1748 by Joseph Saugrain, 3 vols. (Paris: Elibron, 2005), vol. 1, pp. 178–179 and 210.

JUS DE VEAU (MARIN)

Makes a little more than ½ cup

This recipe for *jus*, an intense flavoring for sauces and ragouts, appears in Marin's section on bourgeois cooking.[3] It calls for veal, but Marin notes that the basic method can be followed for any type of meat or poultry. This recipe is reminiscent of one given earlier by Massialot, but Marin, helpfully, specifies actual quantities, which are used here.

Equipment: A heavy saucepan or casserole with a tightly fitting lid, a wooden spoon, a strainer, and a bowl.

½ pound lean veal, very finely minced (Marin recommends meat cut
  from the *rouelle*, which is part of the shoulder, or *tranche*, the
  round, but any lean cut will do)
About 1 Tb suet (1 Tb oil may be substituted)
1 onion, sliced
1 carrot, chopped
1 parsnip, chopped
Bouillon or water

OPTIONAL, IF USING WATER INSTEAD OF BOUILLON:
2–3 parsley sprigs
A whole clove
Big pinch of salt

1. Line the bottom of the saucepan or casserole with the onion slices. Top with the minced veal. Dot the top of the veal with the fat (or drizzle with the oil, if using) and add the bits of carrot and parsnip. Pour in 1–2 Tb of bouillon or water.
2. Cover the casserole and set it over very low heat. The contents of the pan should sweat slowly, rendering their juices, which will eventually start to brown. The onions and veal will start to stick to the pan. This may take 40 minutes or more. Check the pan periodically and regulate the heat to make sure that the meat and vegetables do not burn.

---

3   [Marin], *Les Dons de Comus*, vol. 3, pp. 547–549.

3. When the contents of the pan have begun to brown and stick, add about ½ cup of additional bouillon or water. If using water, add the parsley sprigs, the clove, and a big pinch of salt to season. Bring to a boil, stirring and scraping to dissolve the coagulated juices on the bottom of the pan. Partly cover the pan and simmer the contents for half an hour.

4. Strain the *jus* into the bowl, pressing lightly on the solids to extract all the juice. However, be careful to avoid pushing any of the vegetables or meat through the strainer – you want clear liquid here without any purée. Skim off any fat that floats to the surface. The meat may be recycled in other recipes calling for cooked, minced veal.

5. The *jus* may be used immediately or stored in a covered container in the refrigerator for 3–5 days. It may also be frozen.

COULIS (MARIN)

Makes about 1½ cups

This recipe is the first cousin of the one for *jus* given previously.[4] It has a thicker texture, thanks to the addition of a little browned flour and the puréed veal and vegetables. Although Marin's master recipe for coulis specifies veal, the same method can be used for other meats and poultry, as he himself noted.

Equipment: A heavy saucepan or casserole with a tightly fitting lid, a wooden spoon, a food mill or a food processor, a bowl, and (optional) a sieve.

All of the ingredients for the *jus*, preceding recipe
1 Tb flour
If needed: 1 Tb oil, butter, or fat

1. Follow steps 1 and 2 of the preceding recipe for *jus*.
2. When the ingredients start to brown and stick to the pan, remove them and set aside. If there is less than a tablespoon of fat left behind in the pan, add some oil or butter. When the fat is hot, add the flour and stir over medium heat until the flour is golden.

---

[4] Ibid., vol. 3, pp. 549–550.

3. Add the bouillon or water and optional seasonings, as in the recipe for *jus*, and stir to deglaze the pan. Return the veal and vegetables to the casserole and simmer for at least half an hour (you want them to be very soft to facilitate puréeing in the next step).

4. Purée the contents of the casserole through the food mill. Alternatively, you may purée the meat and vegetables in a food processor. If the texture of the coulis does not seem fine enough, push it through a fine sieve.

5. The coulis may be used at once or stored in a covered container in the refrigerator for 3–5 days. It may also be frozen.

GREEN BUTTER WITH LEEK AND PARSLEY (MARIN)

Makes about 1 cup

Modern recipes for cold, flavored butters typically call for such things as minced herbs, anchovies, garlic, lemon juice, mustard, or shallots to be beaten into softened, creamed butter and then chilled prior to use. Marin's recipe is unusual in that it calls for leek and parsley to simmer in butter over very low heat, a process that enhances the flavor and aroma of the herbs in the finished product.[5] Because the butter and herbs are forced through a sieve or food mill or buzzed in a food processor, the leek and parsley form a fine purée suspended in the butter. Marin used *beurre vert*, as he called it, to finish a sauce for roasted chicken (see following recipe) and as a flavoring to be inserted between the skin and breast meat of chickens and other birds. He also noted that green butter adapted well in recipes for veal. For example, I have used green butter as the liaison in a simple deglazing sauce for sautéed veal chops and was delighted with the results. Green butter keeps well in a screw-top jar in the refrigerator, so you can always have some on hand with which to experiment. If the leek and parsley purée settles at the bottom of the jar, don't worry; just make sure that you include some of the herbs in each spoonful of the butter you use.

Marin specified blanching the leek and parsley in boiling salted water before mincing. You may do this, if you like, although I find it unnecessary – the long simmer in the butter releases the perfume of the herbs and softens them sufficiently for puréeing in the next step. Although the leek and parsley mixture is wonderful, you may want to experiment with other combinations of herbs, for variety.

------

[5] Ibid., vol. 2, pp. 192–193.

Equipment: A small saucepan, a sharp knife, a wooden spoon, a food processor or a sieve or a food mill, a small bowl, and a screw-top jar or other storage container.

**1 tender, young leek, root and tough greens trimmed, cleaned of all
    dirt and finely minced**
2–4 sprigs of parsley, finely minced
Pinch of salt
8 ounces (½ pound or 2 sticks) unsalted butter

1. Put the minced leek and parsley, the salt, and 1 Tb of the butter in a small saucepan. Cover and set over very low heat. The herbs should sweat in the butter without browning.
2. After 10 minutes, add the rest of the butter, cut into pieces, to the pan. Allow to melt slowly. Simmer the butter and herbs over low heat for 10–15 minutes or so.
3. Purée the butter, leek, and parsley mixture in the food processor or with the sieve or food mill, forcing though as many of the solids as possible (Marin instructed the reader to "use the force of your arms").
4. Pour the puréed butter into the jar and allow to cool completely before putting on the top. Store in the refrigerator until needed.

LIAISON DE FARINE OR ROUX (LA VARENNE)

Makes about ³⁄₄ cup

La Varenne included this recipe for *liaison de farine* in a special chapter on basic preparations.[6] It was designed to be made in advance and used to adjust the consistency of a wide variety of soups, sauces, and ragouts, to which it imparts a nutty, rich, slightly caramelized flavor. Thanks to the use of rendered fat instead of butter, the extended cooking time, and the use of minced vegetables, this roux is quite different from the versions one finds in more recent French cuisine, but it closely resembles the roux used in the Creole and Cajun cooking of southern Louisiana, where bell peppers and celery take the place of the mushrooms. This roux is delicious in sauces for poultry, fish, and shellfish as well as robust red meats, so do not hesitate to use it as an all-purpose thickener.

---

6   La Varenne, *Le Cuisinier françois*, 2001, pp. 125–126.

Equipment: A heavy-bottomed saucepan, a whisk, a wooden spoon, a food processor or a food mill or a sieve, and a screw-top jar or other storage container.

¾ **cup rendered pork fat (peanut oil or another neutral-tasting oil may be substituted)**
¾ **cup flour**
½ **cup onion, finely minced**
2 Tb meat or chicken broth
½ **cup mushrooms, minced**
½ **tsp wine vinegar, red or white**

1. Put the rendered pork fat or oil in the saucepan and set over medium-high heat. When the fat is hot, whisk in the flour a few tablespoons at a time. When all the flour is absorbed, turn the heat down to medium.

2. Continue cooking the flour and fat, stirring all the while, until the flour is mahogany brown. The texture of the flour will change as it cooks, and at some point you will find it easier to beat if you exchange the whisk for a wooden spoon. The important thing is to keep the roux moving in the pan in order to avoid sticking and burning. If the roux seems to be cooking unevenly or if you sense it is about to burn, lower the heat – the roux will take a little longer to get to the right color, but the risk of burning declines sharply when it is cooked over gentle heat. At higher temperatures, the roux will brown in 12–18 minutes; over low heat, the process might take half an hour.

3. When the roux has achieved the desired shade of brown, stir in the minced onion, turn down the heat (if you have not already done so), and continue to cook for about 5 minutes, until the onion is limp and translucent.

4. Add the broth, the minced mushrooms, and the vinegar. Allow the roux and its flavorings to simmer gently for several minutes until the mushrooms render their juices. This will thin out the roux a bit. Raise the heat and boil the roux gently to evaporate some of the liquids.

5. Remove the roux from the heat and allow to cool slightly. Purée the roux in the food processor or pass it through the food mill or sieve to make a silky paste.

6. Store the roux until needed in the refrigerator in a screw-top jar or other storage container. Before using, remove the amount you need for a specific recipe from the container and allow it to come to room temperature or warm it gently in a pan.

SAUCE À LA CRÈME (LA VARENNE AND BONNEFONS)

This is simplicity itself – nothing but fresh heavy cream thickened over heat and seasoned with salt and nutmeg.[7] The sauce may be made separately, or the cream can be added to sautéed or blanched, drained vegetables and allowed to thicken as the vegetables finish cooking (see the following section on vegetables). Depending on the butterfat content of the cream you use and how much you reduce it, this recipe will make about ½ to ⅔ cups of sauce.

Equipment: A saucepan and a wooden spoon.

1 cup heavy cream (avoid ultrapasturized cream if possible, because it often fails to thicken properly)
Pinch of salt
Pinch of nutmeg

1. Pour the cream into the pan and set over high heat to bring to a boil. Turn the heat down slightly and cook until the cream lightly coats a wooden spoon.
2. Remove the concentrated cream from the heat and season to taste with salt and nutmeg.

VARIATION: SAUCE À LA CRÈME ENRICHED WITH EGG YOLK

If your cream doesn't thicken as much as you would like, or if you want an especially rich sauce, try the following.[8]

Additional equipment: A small bowl and a whisk.

---

[7] Ibid., p. 118. La Varenne's description of how to make cream sauce is embedded in the first of two recipes he gives for asparagus *à la crème*. Bonnefons discusses the technique of making cream sauce with regard to many vegetables, including artichokes, asparagus, and peas; see *Les Délices de la campagne*, pp. 137–139 and 147–153.

[8] La Varenne explains how to use an egg yolk to enrich cream sauce and make it thicker in the second of his recipes for asparagus *à la crème*; *Le Cuisinier françois*, 2001, p. 238. Bonnefons's fullest description is in his recipe for Spanish salsify in *Les Délices de la campagne*, p. 104.

1 egg yolk per cup of cream in the recipe given previously

1. Beat the egg yolk with the whisk. A few drops at a time, beat in 2–3 Tb of the hot cream, gradually warming the egg yolk.
2. Scrape the egg yolk mixture into the saucepan and set it over low heat. Beat continually until the sauce is well blended and beginning to thicken up. Do not let the sauce come to a boil – this will curdle the egg yolk. Serve promptly.

SAUCE BLANCHE (LA VARENNE)

Makes about 2 cups

La Varenne paired this sauce with a variety of vegetables and fish.[9] However, in only one of these recipes, for *barbeau au court bouillon,* did he give proportions and information about technique, which I use here. Both the proportions and the method differ from modern sauces of the hollandaise family, which *sauce blanche* otherwise resembles. Modern recipes typically use a higher proportion of egg yolks to butter – between three and six yolks per ½ pound of butter, as opposed to the one or two yolks specified by La Varenne. Conventional wisdom is that sauces lower in egg yolks are fragile and liable to break down. Interestingly, I have not found this to be the case when using La Varenne's method. Modern recipes usually start by instructing you to stir the egg yolks, salt, and a small quantity of acidic liquid (lemon juice for hollandaise, a reduction of wine vinegar, tarragon, and shallot for béarnaise) over low heat and then to gradually beat in the butter (softened or melted, depending on the preference of the cook). La Varenne instructed his readers to start by heating the vinegar, salt, and butter, with the egg yolks added as the butter begins to melt. The egg yolks heat very gradually in the pool of melting butter, which minimizes the chance of scrambling (one of the common pitfalls of making emulsified sauces). If you want an especially luscious sauce, you may continue beating in additional butter by the spoonful.

Equipment: A heavy-bottomed saucepan and a whisk.

1 Tb white wine vinegar
¼ tsp salt
2 egg yolks (grade A large), lightly beaten with a fork

9 La Varenne, *Le Cuisinier françois,* 2001, pp. 187–188.

6–8 ounces (1½–2 sticks) unsalted butter, cold, cut into small cubes
Pepper, to taste

Note: The controls on my stove go down to 300 BTUs, which is perfect for this sauce, which requires very low heat. If your burners do not go that low (or if you are not sure if they do), use a heat diffusing pad – available at hardware stores – or do what La Varenne would have done at his *potager,* that is, lift the saucepan off the heat for a few seconds if it seems to be heating up too much. The traditional technique for monitoring the temperature is to stick a finger into the sauce; if it feels uncomfortably hot, remove the pan from the heat and beat the sauce vigorously to cool it down. Another warning sign of too much heat is steam rising out of the pan. The temperature must be kept below the simmering point throughout the cooking process.

1. Put the white wine vinegar, salt, and 1 stick of butter, cut into bits, in the saucepan. Set the pan over very low heat and stir with the whisk. Add the egg yolks. Keep beating. As the butter melts, it will gradually warm the egg yolks without curdling them.
2. When almost all of the butter is melted, begin adding the reserved pieces of butter, one at a time. La Varenne calls for a full ½ pound of butter, which makes for a delectable but very buttery sauce; depending on your taste and what you are serving with the sauce, you may wish to stop somewhere between 1½ and 2 sticks of butter.
3. Continue beating the yolk and butter mixture over very low heat until it begins to thicken into a creamy, silky mass. Resist the temptation to turn up the heat to hasten the process. Remove from the heat when the sauce is thickened to your taste.
4. Taste. Add some freshly ground pepper and more salt or drops of vinegar, if needed. Serve promptly.

VARIATIONS ON SAUCE BLANCHE

Other acidic liquids can be substituted for the white wine vinegar in *sauce blanche*: for example, verjuice (the juice of unripe grapes, a common ingredient in the seventeenth century, which is commercially available in some specialty shops today) or court bouillon (a mixture of water, aromatic seasonings, and white wine and/or vinegar that is used to poach fish and other delicate ingredients). La Varenne did not use lemon juice in *sauce blanche*, but substituting it for the vinegar or verjuice would create something close to a modern hollandaise sauce. If using the court bouillon, boil $^{1}/_{4}$ cup over high heat to reduce to 1 Tb. Cool, and then proceed with the preceding recipe.

For Marin's *sauce blanche* with mustard, see the recipe for poached leg of lamb *à l'Anglaise*, following.

SAUCE ROUSSE (LA VARENNE)

Makes about $^{3}/_{4}$ cup

This sauce, which La Varenne recommended for skate and other fish and for root vegetables, survives in French cooking today under the name of *beurre noir*.[10] Most modern recipes call for capers as an essential ingredient, but La Varenne's used parsley and green onion instead, with capers as an optional flavoring depending on the food with which the sauce was to be served.

Equipment: A small sauté pan and a wooden spoon.

6 ounces (1$^{1}/_{2}$ sticks) unsalted butter
1–2 sprigs parsley, minced
1 green onion or scallion, minced
1$^{1}/_{4}$ tsp wine vinegar, red or white, plus additional drops, to taste
Pinch of salt

1. Melt the butter in the sauté pan over medium-high heat. Add the parsley and green onion. Swirl the mixture around in the pan to distribute the heat. Lower the flame a little and continue to cook until the butter turns golden, then pale brown, and then a deep mahogany color. Do not allow the butter to burn – lower the heat or lift the pan off the burner if necessary.
2. Remove the pan from the heat and allow to cool for a minute or two (if you don't do this, the contents of the pan may boil over when you add the vinegar). Add the vinegar to the pan and return it to the heat, bringing the mixture to a boil. Add a pinch of salt and taste. You may wish to add more vinegar to the sauce, depending on what you are serving it with and your own preferences. Simmer the *sauce rousse* for another minute, swirling the pan by the handle to blend. Serve promptly.

---

[10] Ibid., pp. 198 (see instructions for *morue roti*) and 200–201 (for *raye fritte*).

SAUCE RAVIGOTTE/SAUCE RÉMOULADE (MARIN)

Makes about 1 cup

In the eighteenth century, *sauce rémoulade* and *sauce ravigotte* were closely related preparations that featured chopped herbs in a tangy dressing.[11] Marin gave two recipes for *ravigotte*. The first, meant to be served hot, featured veal stock in addition to mustard, anchovy, and a variety of green herbs. The second, a cold sauce, substituted oil and vinegar for the stock; the solid ingredients were pounded in a mortar. His *sauce rémoulade* called for the same ingredients as the cold *ravigotte*, but the herbs and anchovy were chopped instead of pounded, which produced quite a different texture. In the course of the nineteenth century in France (and also in the Creole cooking of New Orleans) the name "*rémoulade*" became associated with a mayonnaise-based mixture flavored with piquant, chopped seasonings. Marin's vinaigrette-based *ravigotte/rémoulade* is refreshing with roasted, grilled, and other plainly cooked fowl and meats, as recommended in his "simple and natural" menu of 1742. In addition to serving these sauces with cold chicken, try them with grilled squabs or Cornish hens as well as boiled veal or beef with coarse salt. They would also be delicious with boiled seafood.

Equipment: A small bowl and a whisk; for the *sauce ravigotte*, a mortar and pestle.

1–2 Tb wine vinegar, red or white
Pinch of salt
½ tsp dry mustard
⅔ cup olive oil
Big pinch of pepper
1 tsp salt-packed capers, rinsed
1 small salt anchovy, rinsed and filleted (or half of a larger one)
1 tsp finely minced green onions
1 small, tender inner stalk of celery
2 Tb finely minced mixed green herbs (use at least 1 Tb parsley, plus
    your choice of chives, chervil, or tarragon, depending on the
    seasonings in the dish the sauce will accompany and what you
    have on hand; all parsley is okay)

---

[11] [Marin], *Les Dons de Comus*, vol. 1, pp. 72–73 and 76.

1. Whisk the vinegar, salt, mustard, olive oil, and pepper together in the bowl or a measuring cup with a spout.

2. For *sauce ravigotte*: pound all the remaining ingredients in a mortar; when they have been ground to a paste, add the vinaigrette by drops and blend. For *sauce rémoulade*: mince the capers, anchovy, green onions, celery, parsley, and herbs and blend with the vinaigrette. Taste and correct seasoning.

II: SOUPS AND BISQUES

POTAGE AUX HERBES (MARIN)

Makes a little more than 2 quarts

This simple soup shows off fresh garden herbs and can be varied in many interesting ways, as the season and budget allow (see variations, following).[12] Although the recipe appeared in Marin's section on *cuisine bourgoise*, it resembles the *potages de santé* discussed by La Varenne and Bonnefons in its straightforward combination of seasonal produce and first-rate bouillon.

Equipment: A lidded pot or saucepan big enough to hold the bouillon and herbs; a wooden spoon, soup bowls, and a ladle.

3 Tb rendered fat or butter
A small handful of sorrel or chard, any tough stems removed, leaves washed, dried, and chopped
A head of lettuce or chicory, washed, dried, and chopped
A large stalk of celery, washed, dried, and chopped
2 quarts bouillon (see previous recipe) or store-bought bouillon or chicken stock
Salt
Slices of bread, slightly dried out or lightly toasted
Minced chervil or parsley

1. Warm the fat or butter in the pot over medium heat. Add the chopped herbs and sauté them for a few minutes, until their perfume is released. Sprinkle with a pinch of salt.

---

[12] Ibid., vol. 3, pp. 551–552.

2. Add the bouillon or stock and bring the pot to a simmer. Partly cover the pot, lower the heat, and simmer until the herbs are soft – about 25 minutes or so. Taste and add more salt, if necessary.

3. To serve, place a slice of bread in each individual soup bowl and add a ladleful of *potage aux herbes*. Top each bowl with a pinch of minced chervil or parsley.

VARIATIONS ON POTAGE AUX HERBES

Marin noted that many different vegetables could be combined with bouillon to make a variety of soups that were tasty, healthy, and economical. All of these variations were concocted along the same general lines as the preceding recipe. For example, he wrote that turnips could be peeled, cut into whatever shape one desired, and sautéed in fat until they were light brown. Seasoned with a pinch of salt, the turnips were then simmered in bouillon until tender, creating *potage aux navets*.[13] Leeks, onions, parsnips, carrots, cabbage, and cucumbers provide other possibilities and can be used alone or in combination: sauté them, moisten with bouillon, and simmer until tender. Marin advised readers to buy whatever vegetables were cheap and fresh on a given market day – a strategy that was sure to provide variety throughout the year.[14]

CHICKEN BISQUE (BONNEFONS)

Serves 4–6

Bisques were favorites in French kitchens in the seventeenth and eighteenth centuries. They could be made with a wide variety of ingredients, from pigeons to crawfish, but they always featured croutons simmered in bouillon until a tasty crust was formed on the bottom of the dish (croutons topped with cheese were known as *Jacobines*). This version, using chicken, is relatively simple to prepare, and it makes a warming supper on a cold night.[15] If you have some leftover roasted or poached chicken, you may use it in this recipe in lieu of the freshly cooked bird described in the following. Please note that the exact amounts of chicken, stock, bread, and cheese you need to make this dish will vary according to the size and shape of the baking

---

[13] Ibid., vol. 3, pp. 552–553.
[14] Ibid.
[15] Bonnefons, *Les Délices de la campagne*, pp. 223–224.

dish or casserole in which you cook it. Judging by sight works best, so have
a little extra of everything available when you start the recipe.

Equipment: A lidded stockpot or kettle for poaching the chicken, a shallow
baking dish or casserole for simmering the bisque, and a toaster.

A chicken, around 3–3½ pounds
Salt
Pepper
1 quart or more chicken stock, enough to cover the bird by 2 inches
Optional: an onion, peeled, stuck with 2 cloves
Optional: 2 carrots, peeled
Butter for the bottom and sides of the baking dish
Country-style bread for lining the bottom of the baking dish
1 cup or so freshly grated cheese (Bonnefons specified gruyère or
    "Holland" cheese – gouda would probably work well)
Thinly sliced lemon, for garnish

1. Wash and dry the chicken, season the cavity with salt and pepper, and
    truss it (see the instructions on trussing a chicken in the master recipe
    for roasted chicken, following).
2. Place the chicken in the stockpot and cover with stock or bouillon by
    2 inches (if you do not have enough stock, top up the pot with water).
    If you feel that the stock could use more flavor, add the optional onion
    and carrots. Bring the liquid to a boil, lower the heat to a simmer, and
    skim any scum that rises to the surface. Partly cover the pot with its
    lid and regulate the heat to maintain a lazy simmer. Do not boil, or the
    chicken will be tough.
3. Check the chicken after 50 minutes to see if it is done (cooking times
    vary depending on the exact size and shape of the chicken, the size of
    the pot in relation to the chicken, and the amount of broth used). You
    want the chicken to be thoroughly cooked (no pink joints or juices). The
    thickest part of the thighs should be tender when pressed and should
    move easily in their sockets. Remove the chicken from the pot as soon
    as it is done (overcooking will dry it out) and set aside until cool enough
    to handle. Discard the onion and carrots, if using, and set aside the stock
    to cool.
4. Meanwhile, preheat the oven to 350 degrees.
5. Cut slices of bread about ½-inch thick to line the bottom of the bak-
    ing dish or casserole. Toast the bread until it is light golden brown.
    (Bonnefons tells the reader to do this over the embers of a fire; you

may use a toaster or you may toast the bread in a low oven until it is dry and slightly brown.)

6. Butter the bottom and sides of the baking dish and line it with the pieces of toast. Put the pan in the oven and bake until the bread starts to stick to the pan (7–10 minutes). According to Bonnefons, this preliminary baking will promote formation of a crust on the bottom of the bisque, which improves the flavor. Make sure that the toast does not burn. Remove the baking dish from the oven.

7. When the chicken is cool enough to handle, remove the meat from the skin and bones and chop it into small dice (you may have more than is needed for the bisque). Spread a thin layer of chicken over the toasted bread. Sprinkle lightly with salt and pepper and top with one quarter of the cheese. Add a second layer of chicken, salt and pepper, and the rest of the cheese. Pour enough of the reserved chicken stock into the baking pan to come to within a $\frac{1}{2}$-inch of the top.

8. Place the casserole in the oven. Bake until most of the liquid has been absorbed by the bread and the top is crusty, about 45 minutes. (Check after 20 minutes; if the liquid is being absorbed quickly, add a little more and turn the heat down to 325 degrees.) Serve from the casserole, garnished with the lemon slices.

VARIATION: AN INFORMAL PIGEON BISQUE

Substitute 2–3 squabs (as we call pigeons in the United States) for the chicken in the preceding recipe. Bonnefons called for the pigeons in his bisque to be poached whole, heads intact, beaks resting on the edge of the basin in which the bisque is baked.[16] Alternatively, quarter the headless birds and simmer in a small quantity of well-flavored stock until tender; proceed with the recipe. Although the ragout of *béatilles* (cockscombs, truffles, and foie gras) recommended as a garnish for pigeon bisque in *Les Délices de la campagne* may be unrealistic in a modern kitchen, you could improvise in the same spirit by making a garnish of mushrooms sautéed with the pigeon livers (if available) or chicken livers, nicely seasoned with shallots and thyme, and deglazed with wine and butter. If pomegranates are available, add some of their colorful seeds to the garnish of lemon slices for a 1650s feast.

---

[16]   Ibid., pp. 248–253.

III: POULTRY AND MEAT

ROASTED CHICKEN WITH A CHOICE OF SAUCES FROM BONNEFONS, MASSIALOT, AND MARIN

Serves 4–6 or more, depending on the size of the chicken

Roasted chicken was a mainstay of fine cooking in early modern France. The *poularde* (a fattened hen of 4–5 pounds) or the somewhat larger *chapon* (a fattened, neutered male) were especially prized as ample sources of tender, juicy meat, although smaller birds (*poulets*) were also roasted on the spit. Bonnefons described the basic technique with his usual attention to detail: The cavity of the dressed bird was to be seasoned with salt, pepper, and a peeled onion stuck with 2–3 cloves. After being fixed on the spit, it should be rubbed with a little fresh butter or alternatively covered with bards of bacon to keep it moist during the first part of the cooking. After the bards were removed or the buttered chicken started to brown, it was important to baste the bird every few minutes, using drippings in the pan or drops of bitter orange or lemon juice. Once cooked to the perfect turn, the chicken would be presented at the table with a sauce, and it was in concocting the sauce that cooks showed their ingenuity. Here are three different sauces for roasted chicken, one each from Bonnefons, Massialot, and Marin, that illustrate their individual culinary styles. If you have a rotisserie, by all means use it to roast your chicken in the traditional manner, or follow these instructions for roasting in the oven.

Master Recipe for Roasted Chicken

Equipment: 3–5 feet of kitchen string (depending on the size of the bird) for trussing; a roasting pan just large enough to hold the chicken; a spoon or bulb baster; and a large, heated serving platter.

**A roasting chicken, 4–5 pounds, free-range and naturally fed, if
　　possible (if you use a smaller chicken in the range of 3–3½
　　pounds, decrease the roasting time by 10–15 minutes or so)**
Salt
Pepper
Optional: 1 small onion, peeled and studded with 2 cloves
1 Tb soft butter

1.　Preheat the oven to 425 degrees; rack in the lower middle position.
2.　Pull any visible fat out of the cavity of the chicken. Wash and dry inside and out. Season the cavity with salt and pepper and the optional onion and cloves.

3. Truss the chicken to keep it in shape while it roasts. Fold the wing tips under the neck of the chicken to hold them in place. Slide the kitchen string under the hips of the bird. Pull the string up over the legs and cross into an X; then draw the string down under the tips of the drumsticks. Run the strings along both sides of the bird; as you cross the wing joints, flip the chicken over and tie the strings in a double knot behind the neck.

4. Place the bird on its back in the roasting pan; sprinkle with salt and pepper and massage with 1 Tb of butter.

5. Put the chicken into the oven and roast for 30 minutes. Loosen the chicken with a wooden spoon (otherwise it will stick and be difficult to remove from the pan).

6. Turn the oven down to 400. Continue roasting for an additional 50–55 minutes, basting twice. (If your chicken is smaller, roast for an additional 40 minutes or so.) Test to see if the bird is done (tender breast and thigh meat, legs that move easily in their sockets, no pink juices draining from the vent). Remove from the oven when done and keep warm until serving time (all roasted chickens benefit from a rest of 10–15 minutes before carving).

ROASTED CHICKEN WITH BITTER ORANGE AND GARLIC DEGLAZING SAUCE (BONNEFONS)

This sauce marks the transition between medieval and modern sensibilities in French cooking.[17] In the late Middle Ages and the Renaissance, fowl were often served with acidic sauces of vinegar, verjuice, or citrus that were both sweetened and spiced. Bonnefons eliminated the spices and sugar and substituted garlic from his *potager* in their place; the texture and balance of the sauce is smoothed out with a little fresh butter.

Equipment: A wooden spoon and a deep, warm serving platter or individual plates, heated.

A chicken, see preceding recipe
Juice of 1 large lemon (about 3 Tb)
Orange juice – enough to measure ½ cup when combined with the lemon

[17] Ibid., p. 229.

1 large clove of garlic, pounded in a mortar with a few drops of water (if you don't have a mortar, mince the garlic very finely and mix with the water)
2–3 Tb butter

1. Roast the chicken as in the preceding master recipe.
2. Twenty minutes before the end of the estimated roasting time, baste the chicken with a little of the orange/lemon mixture. Baste again 10 minutes later, reserving most of the juice for step 4.
3. When the chicken is done, remove it from the roasting pan and keep warm.
4. If a lot of chicken fat has been rendered during the roasting process, spoon most of it out of the pan, leaving 1 Tb or so. Set the pan over high heat. Add the rest of the orange/lemon juice. Bring the liquids to a boil, scraping the bottom of the pan to dissolve the cooking juices. Reduce the liquids until they are slightly syrupy.
5. Turn off the heat. Add the garlic to the pan and stir. A gentle garlic aroma should fill the air. Swirl in 2–3 Tb of butter. Taste for seasoning, adding salt, pepper, drops of citrus juice, and/or butter as needed.
6. To serve: Pour the sauce into the warm platter or divide it among individual plates. Carve the chicken and arrange over the sauce.

Note: This combination of flavors is so great that I prefer to serve the chicken and sauce alone, without any accompaniment except some crusty bread. In Bonnefons's day, the chicken would have been accompanied by a variety of side dishes, at least one of which would have been a green salad. I like to follow the chicken with a green salad (no tomato or other additions) that is served on the same plate – the last drops of orange and garlic sauce are delicious with the greens.

───────────

ROASTED CHICKEN WITH OLIVES (MASSIALOT)

This recipe is typical of Massialot in that it pairs a simple roast with an elegant little sauce that is enriched with those intense flavoring elements, *jus* and coulis.[18] If you do not have these on hand (see the section on *fonds de cuisine* for recipes), you may use chicken bouillon only. Massialot does

───────────

[18] Massialot, *Le Cuisinier roïal et bourgeois*, pp. 338–339.

not specify whether the champagne or burgundy for the sauce is supposed to be red or white. I prefer the latter in this recipe. Any decent chardonnay will do, or substitute dry white vermouth. Massialot's trick of arranging the carved chicken on top of the sauce, allowing them to steep together for a few minutes, helps to blend the flavors. Note the use of fresh basil as a finishing touch. Basil (which I had associated primarily with *provençal* cooking prior to working on this book) was surprisingly popular in early modern Parisian cuisine.

Equipment: String to truss the chicken, a roasting pan, a saucepan, a wooden spoon, a whisk, and a deep, ovenproof serving platter, large enough to hold the sauce and the carved chicken in a single layer.

A chicken, see previous recipe
2 Tb olive oil
2 ounces pancetta or blanched bacon, diced small
Half of a small salt anchovy, filleted and minced
3 Tb flour
½ cup shallots, minced
¼ cup green onions with tops, minced
2 cups *jus* of chicken (made according to the previous recipe,
**   substituting chicken for the minced veal) or 2 cups chicken**
**   bouillon (homemade or store-bought)**
½ cup dry white wine
4–5 sprigs of parsley
1 bay leaf
Sprig of fresh thyme or about ½ tsp dried
¾ cup green olives, pitted unless very small
½ tsp capers, rinsed and chopped
Handful of fresh basil, torn into small bits (if not available, add ½ tsp
**   dried basil when you put in the rest of the herbs)**
Optional: one or two spoonfuls of coulis of chicken (follow the
**   previous coulis recipe, substituting chicken for veal)**

1. Roast the chicken as in the previous master recipe.
2. Make the sauce. Begin by browning the pancetta or blanched bacon over moderate heat in the saucepan in the olive oil until the lardons have rendered their fat and browned. Remove the lardons from the pan.
3. Stir the flour into the fat and cook slowly until it is a light, nutty brown and smells delicious. Turn down the heat, if necessary, to keep the roux from burning.

4. Add the minced shallots and green onions; sprinkle with a pinch of salt and sauté until tender.

5. Add the *jus* or chicken stock, wine, parsley, bay leaf, and thyme. Stir, scraping the bottom and sides of the pan to dissolve all the coagulated juices and browned bits. Bring to a boil, lower the heat, and simmer for at least twenty minutes while the chicken continues to roast.

6. While the sauce is simmering and the chicken is roasting, simmer $^3\!/_4$ cup of green olives in a saucepan of water for 15 minutes. This removes some of the bitterness from the olives. Drain.

7. When the chicken is done, remove it from the roasting pan to a carving board where you can keep it warm. Turn the oven off.

8. Pour any rendered fat out of the roasting pan. Set the pan over medium-high heat, deglaze with a little water, and add to the sauce.

9. Add the coulis (if using) or some additional chicken stock to adjust the consistency, as necessary. The sauce should lightly coat a wooden spoon. Add the parboiled, drained olives; the chopped capers; and some freshly ground black pepper. Lower the heat and allow to simmer for a few minutes. Taste to correct the seasoning – the sauce may need additional salt.

10. Carve the chicken into serving pieces.

11. Pour the finished sauce into the heated serving platter. Arrange the chicken on top of the sauce, pressing each piece down so as to partly submerge it in the sauce.

12. Put the platter in the turned-off oven and let sit for 5 minutes or so to allow the flavors to mingle. Serve piping hot, with the torn basil sprinkled on top just before you bring the chicken to the table.

ROASTED CHICKEN WITH GREEN BUTTER SAUCE (MARIN)

This recipe exemplifies the simplicity and finesse of Marin's cooking.[19] The recipe calls for a sauce that finished with a liaison of green herb butter. Substituting the herb butter for the sweet butter one would normally use infuses the sauce with subtle perfume and turns plain roasted chicken into a memorable treat. Serve with plenty of French bread to soak up the last delicious drops of sauce and follow with a green salad on the same plate.

Equipment: String to truss the chicken, a roasting pan, a wooden spoon, and a deep serving platter.

[19]   [Marin], *Les Dons de Comus,* vol. 2, pp. 192–193.

A chicken, see previous recipe
½ cup best-quality chicken bouillon or stock
2–3 Tb green herb butter with leek and parsley (see previous recipe
in the *fonds de cuisine* section)

1.   Roast the chicken as in the previous master recipe.
2.   When the chicken is done, remove it to the platter and keep warm.
3.   To make the sauce, deglaze the pan with the reduced chicken bouillon;
     boil down until it is slightly syrupy.
4.   Off the heat, swirl in 2–3 Tb of the green herb butter.
5.   Carve the chicken into serving pieces and serve with a little of the sauce
     under each piece.

CASSEROLE-POACHED CHICKEN WITH STUFFING AND AROMATIC VEGETABLES (BONNEFONS)

Serves 6 or more, depending on the rest of the menu

Bonnefons gave two variations on his recipe for casserole-poached chicken.[20] The first was for a young, tender, spring chicken prepared without a stuffing, served with a sauce composed of the cooking liquids thickened with an egg yolk, and garnished with spring vegetables, such as asparagus, peas, lettuce, and chicory. The other was for an older, larger bird that needed a longer cooking time and invited pairing with heartier flavors. Accordingly, it was stuffed with veal and herbs, garnished with leeks and parsley root that cooked with it in the casserole, and sauced with the cooking liquid, which was thickened with egg yolks (as in the first version) or, alternatively, with rice. These variations are significant because they illustrate Bonnefons's interest in adjusting recipes to fit the precise character of his principal ingredients and the vegetables available in different seasons. Because the recipe for the spring chicken is so simple (it is simmered in broth with only salt and pepper), you need a very flavorful bird to make the recipe worthwhile – not an easy thing to find in today's market. The recipe for the larger chicken is more forgiving, thanks to the stuffing and the aromatic vegetables that cook along with the bird, and it is well worth making today.

Equipment: String for trussing the chicken, a strainer, a saucepan, two bowls (one small, one medium-sized), a whisk, a wooden spoon, a small

---

[20]   Bonnefons, *Les Délices de la campagne*, pp. 123–125, 129–130, and 221–222.

frying pan, and a flameproof casserole with a lid just large enough to hold the chicken and vegetables. A heavy enameled oval casserole is ideal, but a Dutch oven or smallish covered roaster will do.

A chicken, 4½–5 pounds (free-range and naturally fed for preference)
Chicken stock, about 3½ cups in all
Salt
Pepper
1 parsley root, peeled and cut into cubes (if parsley root is
    unavailable, you may substitute celery root, but blanch the dice
    first before adding to the casserole to soften the strong taste of the
    celery)
3–4 leeks, roots trimmed, greens cut about 1 inch above where the
    white begins, cut in half lengthwise and carefully washed to
    remove all dirt
¾ cup onions, finely minced
2 Tb butter
1 cup fresh white bread crumbs
½ pound finely ground veal
¼ pound finely chopped beef suet or cold butter, cut into tiny bits
¼ cup parsley, minced
2 Tb chives, minced
1 Tb parsley, minced
Additional fines herbes, as your taste and the season dictate
1 egg (Bonnefons says to use 2, but I think that makes the stuffing too
    stiff unless you use small or medium eggs, which are hard to find
    nowadays)
2 egg yolks, lightly beaten
1 Tb verjuice (if not available, substitute lemon juice, freshly
    squeezed)

1. Pull any visible fat out of the chicken's cavity. Wash the chicken inside and out and dry it with paper towels. Sprinkle a pinch of salt in the cavity.
2. Sauté the minced onions in the 2 Tb of butter until they are soft and translucent. Set aside to cool.
3. Meanwhile, soak the bread crumbs in ½ cup of the chicken stock.
4. When the onions are room temperature, mix them into the bread crumbs and stock. Add the minced herbs, ½ tsp salt, and ¼ tsp pepper and mix. Then add the veal, the suet or ¼ pound of butter, and the beaten egg, and mix to blend.

5. Fry a spoonful of the stuffing mixture until cooked through. Taste for seasoning and correct, if necessary.

6. Fill the cavity of the chicken with the stuffing. Do not pack it tight – the stuffing will expand as it cooks.

7. Bonnefons tells his readers to self-truss the chicken by cutting a slit in the skin at the tip of the breastbone and pushing the tips of the drumsticks, crossed, through the slit. I find it easier to truss the chicken with a long piece of string (allow about 5 feet, as outlined in the previous master recipe for roasted chicken). Alternatively, fold the wings akimbo and tie the drumsticks together with kitchen string.

8. Place the chicken on its back in the casserole. Sprinkle lightly with salt and pepper. Pour the chicken stock around the bird, using more or less as necessary to submerge the legs and thighs, leaving the breast above the liquid. Top up the stock with water if needed.

9. On top of the stove, bring the contents of the casserole to a boil. Turn the heat down to very low, cover, and simmer. Alternatively, you may simmer the chicken in a 325-degree oven.

10. After the chicken has cooked for 30 minutes, add the parsley root to the casserole. Replace the cover and continue simmering.

11. Twenty minutes after adding the parsley root, add the leeks to the casserole, replace the cover, and continue simmering for another 40 minutes. Test the chicken to see if it is done. If not, return it to a simmer for another 10–15 minutes.

12. When the chicken is done, remove it and the vegetables to a large, deep serving platter and keep warm while you finish the sauce.

13. Strain the liquid into the saucepan and degrease it, as necessary. Place the saucepan over high heat and boil the liquid to reduce it to about 2 cups.

14. Beat the 2 egg yolks and the verjuice or lemon juice in the small bowl. Pour a spoonful of the hot poaching liquid into the egg yolks a few drops at a time and whisk vigorously; then add another spoonful and beat. Repeat until about a cup of the liquid has been beaten into the yolks. This process warms up the egg yolks gradually without scrambling them. Off the heat, pour the egg yolk mixture into the saucepan, beating as you do so. Then set the saucepan over very low heat and cook, beating constantly, until the sauce is slightly thickened. Taste for seasoning and correct, if necessary. Remove from the heat and set aside.

15. To serve, pour some of the sauce around the chicken and vegetables and present the rest in a warm sauce boat. When serving, remember to give each guest a spoonful of stuffing, in addition to a piece of chicken, some leek, and some parsley root.

―――――――

VARIATION: CASSEROLE-POACHED CHICKEN WITH
RICE-THICKENED SAUCE

Bonnefons mentions that the cooking juices of the casserole-poached chicken may be thickened with rice in lieu of the egg yolk liaison, but he does not explain how to do this. Here is my version of such a sauce, which is creamy in texture but fat-free or nearly so.

Additional equipment: A device for puréeing the rice – a hand-held immersion blender, a regular blender or food processor, a food mill, or a sieve and a wooden spoon.

ADDITIONAL INGREDIENTS:
2 Tb raw white rice
Optional: 1–2 Tb butter

1. Follow steps 1–12 from the preceding recipe.
2. Strain the liquid into the saucepan and degrease it, if necessary. Place the saucepan over high heat and boil the liquid to reduce it to about 2 cups (as in step 13 from the preceding recipe).
3. Turn the heat down to low. Add 2 Tb of raw rice to the chicken stock. Cover and simmer until the rice is very tender, about 30 minutes.
4. When the rice is very tender, purée it and mix it with the cooking liquid. The easiest way to do this is to use a hand-held immersion blender. Alternatively, you may purée the contents of the saucepan in a blender or food processor, pass it through the fine blade of a food mill, or push it through a sieve (the tried-and-true seventeenth-century technique).
5. Taste the rice-thickened sauce and correct the seasoning, if necessary. If you want a slightly richer taste, stir in a piece of butter.
6. Pour a little sauce around the chicken and vegetables and serve the rest in a warm sauce boat.

―――――――

CASSEROLE-ROASTED CHICKEN WITH ONIONS (MARIN)

Serves 6

This is one of the dishes Marin described in his section on *cuisine bourgeoise* and included in his menus for "simple and natural" meals.[21] Thanks to the

―――――――

[21]   [Marin], *Les Dons de Comus*, vol. 3, pp. 585–586.

casserole method, the chicken requires no special attention as it roasts, leaving the cook free to concentrate on other things. Easy to make, inexpensive, fragrant, and delectable, this recipe is eighteenth-century comfort food.

Equipment: A good sharp knife and a covered, flameproof casserole just large enough to hold the chicken (enameled cast-iron is ideal).

A roasting chicken, about 5 pounds (free-range and naturally fed for preference)
4 medium-large onions, to make about 4 cups when thinly sliced
Optional: 1 Tb butter, softened
1 herb bouquet (thyme, bay, plus other herbs of your choice; tarragon is delicious)
Salt
Pepper
Drops of lemon and orange juice to taste (Marin specifies the juice of a bitter Seville orange, but you may mix a few drops of regular orange juice into the lemon in an effort to approximate the Seville orange)

1. Preheat the oven to 375 degrees (rack in the lower middle position).
2. Pull any visible fat out of the chicken cavity. Wash and dry it inside and out. Season the cavity with salt and pepper. Truss, as in the master recipe for roasted chicken, or fold the wing tips under the bird's back and tie the drumsticks together with a piece of kitchen string.
3. Slice the onions paper-thin. Line the bottom of the casserole with all but a few of the onion slices. Sprinkle with a pinch of salt and pepper.
4. Place the chicken on its back on the bed of onions. Rub the breast and drumsticks with 1 Tb of the soft butter (if using) and sprinkle them with salt and pepper. Arrange the reserved onion slices on top of the chicken. Nestle the herb bouquet next to the chicken.
5. Cover the casserole and set it in the preheated oven. Roast, covered, for 1 hour.
6. After the chicken has cooked for an hour, uncover the casserole and baste the chicken with the accumulated pan juices.
7. Turn the temperature of the oven up to 400 degrees. Return the casserole, uncovered, to the oven and roast for another 30 minutes to finish cooking and to brown the bird. Test to see if the bird is done; if necessary, return it to the oven for a few more minutes.
8. Remove the cooked bird to a deep serving platter. Strain the cooking juices into a clean saucepan, pressing down on the onions to squeeze out all the juice. Remove the herb bouquet. Spoon the onions around the chicken and keep both warm while finishing the sauce.

9. Degrease the cooking juices, if needed. Boil the cooking juices down rapidly to concentrate a little. Taste for seasoning and correct, if necessary. Stir in drops of lemon juice, to taste.

Variation: Purée the onions into the degreased cooking liquid to form a slightly thickened sauce. You may use an immersion blender, a food processor, a food mill, or a sieve and a wooden spoon to do this.

VEAL RAGOUT (MARIN)

Serves 4

In his section on bourgeois cooking, Marin gave two methods of making veal ragouts.[22] The first used meat from the shoulder cut into pieces and larded; these were browned, floured, and moistened with water, bouillon, or wine, the juices forming a velouté sauce that was finished with an enrichment of egg yolk and verjuice. The second recipe called for a large piece of loin that was browned on a spit, braised in a sauce of bouillon and white wine, enriched with a liaison of egg yolk and verjuice, and finished with a garnish of mushrooms and other vegetables, as chosen by the cook. Recommended seasonings included parsley, chives, nutmeg, and a clove, although these, too, could be modified by the cook according to the season and to taste. Marin rolled the lardons in the herbs, salt, and pepper before inserting them into the meat, thus flavoring the veal from the inside. You may, of course, follow this instruction; however, I find it awkward (and unnecessary) to lard small pieces of meat cut for stew. As an alternative, I recommend browning the lardons with the veal and adding the herbs and other seasonings along with the bouillon and wine. Marin suggested that the cook exercise her own judgment in choosing other vegetables to join the mushrooms. I find that artichokes taste especially good with the tarragon and chives that flavor the sauce.

Equipment: A heavy casserole, sauté pan, or saucepan large enough to hold the meat and its vegetable garnish; a wooden spoon, two small bowls, a whisk, a stainless steel knife for trimming the artichokes, and a deep, hot serving platter.

2 pounds veal shoulder, cut into 3-inch chunks
1 Tb olive oil
1–2 ounces pancetta or blanched bacon, sliced into lardons

---

[22]   Ibid., vol. 3, pp. 581–582.

1 medium onion, chopped
1 heaping Tb flour
½ cup dry white wine
1 cup veal or chicken bouillon
1 Tb tarragon, minced (or 1½ tsp dried tarragon)
2 tsp chives, minced (or 1 tsp dried)
Speck of freshly grated nutmeg
Salt
Pepper
8 ounces fresh mushrooms
2 large artichokes, trimmed and quartered
A lemon
2 egg yolks
3–4 Tb parsley, chopped

1. Heat the olive oil in the casserole over medium-high heat. Add the lardons and sauté to brown and render their fat. Remove from the pan and set aside.
2. Add the veal and sauté to brown. Do not crowd the pan – it is important for the meat to take on a rich caramel color instead of just steaming in the fat. Remove the browned pieces and add others until the whole batch is brown. Remove all the veal and reserve.
3. Turn the heat down to low. Add the chopped onion and sauté until the onion is limp, translucent, and beginning to turn golden.
4. Add the flour to the pan and stir to brown, 3–4 minutes. This creates the foundation of an informal roux that will thicken the sauce.
5. Add the wine and bouillon to the pan. Stir and scrape to dissolve the coagulated juices in the pan.
6. Return the veal to the pan, along with any juices it has given off during its rest. Sprinkle with salt and pepper. Add the tarragon, chives, and a grating of nutmeg.
7. Bring the liquid in the casserole to a boil. Cover and turn the heat down to a low simmer. You want the meat to cook very slowly in liquid that gives off a gentle bubble now and then – cooking at a boil will toughen the fibers of the veal. Depending on your cooking equipment, you may find it easier to maintain this low temperature if you put the covered casserole in a preheated low oven, about 325 degrees.
8. Simmer the casserole for 1 hour. In the meantime, clean the mushrooms and artichokes. Rinse the mushrooms under running cold water to remove any dirt. Break the tough stems from the caps. If the caps are large, cut them in half or in quarters to make bite-sized pieces. Because the artichokes will discolor if exposed to oxygen, prepare an acidic bath

to keep them white by squeezing half a lemon into one of the small bowls and topping it up with cold water. To trim the artichokes, begin by breaking off the stem at the base of the artichoke. Pull the petals back and snap them off to discard, watching out for the thorns at the end of each leaf. When you are down to tender, yellow-green leaves, cut off the top of the cone where it joins the base. This will reveal the top of the thistle inside the artichoke. Cut the artichoke base into quarters and trim the white thistle out of each piece. Also, use your knife to remove any green skin from the outside of the base. Cut each quarter into two pieces and drop them in the lemon water as you go.

9. When the meat has cooked for an hour, add the mushrooms and the drained artichokes to the veal, stirring them well down into the sauce. Return the pan to a simmer, cover, and cook for another 30–40 minutes, until the veal is tender.

10. When the veal is done, remove the meat and vegetables to a deep serving platter. Keep it warm while you finish the sauce.

11. If the cooking liquid in the pan seems very thin, boil it, uncovered, for a few minutes to thicken it.

12. Make the egg yolk enrichment for the sauce. In a small bowl, beat the egg yolks until they are thick and sticky. By droplets, beat in a spoonful of the hot braising liquid. Continue beating in drops of liquid until you have added about $\frac{1}{2}$ a cup. This process warms the egg yolks without scrambling them. Off the heat, beat the warmed egg yolks into the rest of the braising liquid. Turn on the heat to very low and cook for several minutes, stirring constantly. Do not allow the sauce to boil or it will curdle. When the sauce has thickened and taken on a silky texture, remove from the heat and taste for seasoning. Add salt, pepper, and drops of lemon juice as needed.

13. Pour the sauce over the veal and vegetables, sprinkle with chopped parsley, and serve hot.

VARIATION FOR CHICKEN FRICASSEE

Marin's recipe for chicken fricassee follows exactly the same method: just cut the chicken into serving pieces and substitute them for the veal in the preceding recipe.[23] The simmering time for the chicken should be reduced to a total of about 30 minutes or so, depending on the size of the chicken. The breasts will be done a few minutes before the dark meat (remove them

[23]   Ibid., vol. 2, pp. 146–148.

to a platter and keep warm). Although Marin noted that it was possible to combine the chicken with all kinds of vegetable garnishes, he thought that a plain fricassee with mushrooms only was best. Add the mushrooms to the chicken at the beginning of the simmering period. Finish the sauce with egg yolk and lemon juice as in the veal recipe.

ROASTED RACK OF LAMB WITH BITTER ORANGE DEGLAZING SAUCE (BONNEFONS)

Serves 2 (can be doubled or tripled, as the size of your oven allows)

This sauce is a variation on the bitter orange and garlic sauce Bonnefons recommended for chicken.[24] Here he omits the garlic – a concession to the extremely delicate taste and texture of the whole baby lamb he specifies in the original recipe. The bitter orange sauce is delicious with ordinary lamb as well. Although I suggest pairing this sauce with a rack of lamb, it could easily accompany a roasted leg, too – just double or triple the ingredients for the sauce.

Equipment: A roasting pan just large enough to accommodate the lamb; a sharp knife for trimming the meat, if necessary; aluminum foil; a wooden spoon; and a warm serving platter or individual plates, heated.

A rack of lamb, about 1¼ pounds
Olive oil
Salt
Pepper
Juice of 1 lemon
Orange juice (enough to measure ½ cup when combined with the lemon juice)
Optional: 1 green onion, finely minced
3–4 Tb butter, cut into ½ Tb pieces

1. Preheat the oven to 450 degrees.
2. Trim all external fat from the lamb. This will probably mean removing the thin layer of fat that covers the chops, which most American markets leave in place when they weigh retail cuts. If the fatty membrane between the rib bones has not been cut away, do it yourself, using the blade of a sharp knife to scrape the membrane away from the bones.

---

[24] Bonnefons, *Les Délices de la campagne*, pp. 290–293.

Rub the trimmed rack of lamb with a little olive oil. Wrap the rib bones in a double thickness of aluminum foil to keep then from charring in the oven. Sprinkle with salt and pepper and place in a roasting pan just large enough to hold the lamb.

3.   When the oven is hot, roast the lamb for between 17–20 minutes, depending on how rare or well done you like your lamb. Seventeen minutes will yield rare lamb, 20 minutes, lamb that is a very pale pink.

4.   Remove the roasted lamb to a cutting board and keep warm while making the sauce.

5.   Spoon out any clear fat that has accumulated in the roasting pan. Set the pan over high heat. Add the combined lemon and orange juices and 2–3 Tb of water. Bring to a boil, stirring and scraping to dissolve the coagulated lamb juices in the roasting pan. Continue to boil until the liquid is syrupy. Turn off the heat. Stir in the cold butter piece-by-piece to blend. Add the optional minced green onion. Taste and correct the seasoning with salt, pepper, and extra drops of lemon or orange juice, as your palate indicates.

6.   To serve: carve the rack of lamb into individual chops and arrange on a warm platter or individual plates. Beat any lamb juices that have accumulated in the carving board into the sauce. Drizzle the lamb with the bitter orange deglazing sauce and serve piping hot.

POACHED LEG OF LAMB À L'ANGLAISE WITH TURNIPS AND MUSTARD-FLAVORED SAUCE BLANCHE (MARIN)

Serves 6–8

Mutton or lamb poached in salted water or bouillon, with or without aromatic vegetables, was a favorite dish in early modern French kitchens, and we find many recipes for it in the culinary literature of the time. Bonnefons called this mode of preparation "*à la Suisse,*" but, by the early 1700s, it had become known as "*à l'Anglaise*" (English-style), the name by which it has been known ever since.[25] It is a very easy and delicious way to cook lamb, producing a tender and juicy result. All you need is a stockpot or casserole big enough to hold the lamb covered by an inch or two of water and a heat source capable of maintaining a true simmer.

Because the meat cooks in water, there are no deglazing juices to form the basis of a sauce. Some cooks, including Menon, addressed this issue

25   [Marin], *Les Dons de Comus,* vol. 1, p. 326.

by cooking the lamb in bouillon instead of water and using this as the basis for a sauce. (His recipe called for a reduction of the cooking liquid boiled with anchovies, other seasonings, and hard-boiled egg yolks.) Marin, who recommended poaching the leg in plain salted water, called for sauces that were made separately. One option was a roux-thickened velouté made with meat bouillon, herbs, and a garnish of finely chopped egg yolks (see the following variation). His second suggestion called for a turnip garnish accompanied by a mustard-flavored *sauce blanche* – an utterly delectable combination that compliments the flavor of the rosy pink lamb.

Equipment: A stockpot or heavy casserole large enough to hold the meat; utensils for lifting the meat and turnips out of the pot (I use a big curved spatula and a wooden spoon); a carving board; a strainer or colander for draining the turnips; a large, deep platter for serving; a frying or sauté pan large enough to hold the turnips; a small saucepan; and a whisk.

A leg of lamb, 4–5 pounds, trimmed of all exterior fat (ask your butcher to cut or crack the end of the shank bone so that the lamb fits into the pot)

Water

Salt

1½–2 pounds turnips, peeled, quartered, and trimmed into large olive shapes

2 Tb butter or fat

Pepper

Chopped parsley

1 recipe *sauce blanche* made with white wine vinegar and 1½ sticks of butter (see previous *fonds de cuisine* section)

2–3 tsp (or to taste) Dijon-style mustard

Optional: ½ stick of butter (for additional enrichment to the sauce)

Optional: drops of lemon juice

1. Bring 5–6 quarts of water to a boil in the stockpot. Add 1½ Tb salt and the lamb. If there is not enough water to cover the lamb, add more. When the water returns to a boil, turn the heat down to maintain a low simmer. For medium-rare lamb, allow about 11–12 minutes per pound of simmering time or about 55–60 minutes for a 5-pound leg, starting from the point when the water returns to a boil. For rare lamb allow 10 minutes per pound.

2. Half an hour before you estimate that the lamb will be done, add the turnips to the pot and continue simmering.

3. At the end of the estimated poaching time, remove the meat from the pot and test with a meat thermometer. The reading for rare should be 125–130 degrees in the fleshiest part of the leg; for medium the reading should be 135–140 degrees.

4. When the lamb is cooked to your liking, remove it to a carving board and keep warm. It should rest for 20–30 minutes before carving.

5. Remove the turnips and drain. You may find a few flecks of scum clinging to some of them; if so, rinse under cold water and dry.

6. While the lamb is resting, make the *sauce blanche* following the directions in the *fonds de cuisine* section. My advice is to add a total of 1½ sticks of butter, rather than 2 sticks, at least initially. Off the heat, beat in the Dijon mustard and a little finely ground pepper. Taste. Correct for salt and pepper. If you would like a richer sauce, add more butter, bit-by-bit; if you think the sauce needs a little more acid, add drops of lemon juice. Set the sauce aside in a warm place or over a pan of hot but not boiling water while you carve the lamb and finish the turnips.

7. Melt the 2 Tb of butter in a sauté pan over high heat. Add the turnips to warm and brown them. Sprinkle with salt, pepper, and the chopped parsley.

8. Carve the lamb and arrange on the warm platter surrounded by the turnips. Serve the sauce in a warm sauce boat.

VARIATION: CAPER SAUCE FOR POACHED LEG OF LAMB À L'ANGLAISE

Marin's other recommendation to accompany the poached leg is a roux-thickened sauce garnished with hard-boiled egg yolks and capers.[26]

Equipment: Two medium saucepans (one for heating the bouillon, the other for making the sauce), a wooden spoon, and a whisk.

2 Tb butter
3 Tb flour
2 cups of good-quality bouillon or stock brought to a boil
Salt
Pepper
Nutmeg

[26]   Ibid.

1 Tb wine vinegar
6 hard-boiled egg yolks, minced
1 Tb capers

1. Melt the butter in the saucepan over medium heat. Add the flour and stir for a couple of minutes until the flour has turned a pale golden color. Remove from the heat.
2. Add the hot bouillon to the roux all at once. Return the pan to the heat and bring it to a boil, stirring constantly with the whisk to prevent lumps.
3. When the sauce comes to a boil, turn down the heat to low in order to maintain a simmer. Add salt to taste (depending on the saltiness of the bouillon), pepper, nutmeg, and vinegar and stir to blend. Simmer the sauce for 20 minutes to develop the texture.
4. When ready to serve, fold in the minced egg yolks and the capers and bring to the table hot.

MIRONTON OF LAMB (MASSIALOT)

Serves 2 (can be doubled or tripled)

Modern recipes for *mironton*, a popular dish in French home cooking, inevitably call for beef (typically cooked brisket or another stewing cut left over from making soup) and sauce flavored with onions and capers. Massialot published one of the first recipes of this type in *Le Cuisinier roïal et bourgeois*.[27] However, he also noted that the method of reheating thin slices of cooked meat in a small quantity of sauce associated with the name "*mironton*" could be adapted to other meats. His recipe for *mironton* of mutton has been adapted here for lamb and calls for ordinary cultivated mushrooms instead of the truffles and *mousserons* mentioned in the original. Although Madeira was not yet much used in France in Massialot's time, I think its flavor nicely compliments the other ingredients, so I recommend it, in the spirit of Massialot's remarks on improvisation. However, dry white wine also works and is more authentic to the period.

Equipment: A saucepan, a wooden spoon, and a gratin dish, pie plate, or shallow, ovenproof casserole big enough to accommodate the meat in a single, slightly overlapping layer.

---

[27]   Massialot, *Le nouveau Cuisinier royal et bourgeois*, vol. 1, pp. 432–433.

3 Tb butter, plus a little more for the gratin dish
⅓ cup finely diced ham
⅓ cup finely diced shallots
4 large mushrooms (or 6 medium ones), finely diced
1 cup bouillon (meat stock with lamb or mutton would be ideal;
  chicken will do)
¼ cup dry white wine or dry Madeira
1 heaping Tb flour
1 Tb chopped chives
1 Tb chopped parsley
Salt
Pepper
Handful of bread crumbs
½ pound (more or less) cooked lamb (leftover roasted leg or another
  cut), all fat and gristle removed, sliced as thin as possible

1. Preheat the oven to 400 degrees.
2. Melt 2 Tb of the butter in a saucepan over medium heat. Add the diced ham and sauté until it is nicely browned. Remove ham from the pan.
3. Add the shallot and sauté for a minute or so. Add the diced mushrooms and a pinch of salt. After a minute or two, the mushrooms will exude some juices. Keep sautéing until this evaporates.
4. Sprinkle the flour over the vegetables and sauté until lightly browned. Add the bouillon and wine. Stir and scrape the bottom of the pan to loosen the browned bits. Bring to a boil and then lower the heat to a lazy simmer.
5. Add the ham, chives, and parsley. Simmer, partly covered, for about 20 minutes to develop the silky texture of the sauce and blend the flavors.
6. While the sauce is simmering, cut the meat into thin slices, trimming off all fat and gristle.
7. Lightly butter the gratin dish.
8. Remove the sauce from the heat and taste for seasoning. Depending on the saltiness of the bouillon and the ham, it may need a pinch of salt. Add freshly ground pepper to taste.
9. Spoon a thin layer of sauce over the bottom of the gratin dish. Arrange the slices of lamb over the sauce in a single, slightly overlapping layer. Top the lamb with the rest of the sauce. Sprinkle with the bread crumbs and dot with the remaining 1 Tb of butter, cut into tiny pieces.
10. Put the *mironton* into the oven. Immediately turn the temperature down to 350 degrees and bake for 20 minutes, until the bread crumbs

are light brown and the sauce is bubbling around the edges of the pan. (Starting the oven at the higher temperature helps the top of the *mironton* to brown; turning the heat down to 350 allows the lamb to warm up without drying out.)

11. Serve directly from the gratin dish. Massialot suggests peas as a vegetable garnish; *petits pois à l'anglaise* (very tender young peas blanched and tossed in butter) work very well.

BOEUF À LA GLACE (MARIN)

Serves 8–10

This recipe is an excellent example of the *nouvelle cuisine* circa 1740.[28] It is elegant but understated, full of flavor but refined. Marin's veal bouillon, made with gelatinous cuts of meat and strongly reduced, would have gelled naturally when chilled. If you have made your bouillon from scratch and are confident of its gelling properties, you can omit the unflavored powdered gelatin in the following recipe. Whether your stock is homemade or store bought, it is important to choose bouillon that is well flavored but not tricked out with too many herbs and other extraneous seasonings, because these tend to be magnified in the cold jelly. This dish can be made a day ahead or in stages, with the meat braised and chilled on the first day and then sliced and iced with glaze on the morning of the day you wish to serve it. You may halve the recipe to make an elegant summer dinner for a smaller group. Note: Even if you do an immaculate job of degreasing the braising juices, a few impurities will remain, resulting in slightly cloudy aspic. (Jewel-bright and absolutely clear aspic is made with clarified bouillon, but Marin's recipe did not call for this.)

Equipment: A covered casserole just large enough to hold the meat (an oval casserole of enameled cast-iron is ideal), a wooden spoon, a saucepan, a saucer, a small ladle, and a deep serving platter sufficiently large to hold the meat in a single, slightly overlapping layer.

FOR THE BRAISED BEEF:

A beef tenderloin, 3½–4 pounds, trimmed and tied
1 Tb olive oil
2 ounces pancetta or blanched bacon, chopped

---

[28] [Marin], *Les Dons de Comus*, vol. 1, pp. 181–182.

1 thin slice of ham, chopped
½ cup minced onions
½ cup minced carrots
¼ cup minced parsnips
2 bay leaves
½ tsp thyme
2½ cups of beef or veal bouillon
Salt
Pepper

1. Preheat the oven to 375 degrees.
2. Put the olive oil, ham, and pancetta or blanched bacon into the casserole and set over medium heat. Sauté until the bits of meat are crisp and their fat is rendered; remove them and reserve.
3. Brown the tenderloin in the hot fat in the casserole, moderating the heat so that it does not burn. Remove the meat and keep warm.
4. Turn the heat down to low. Add the minced onions, carrots, and parsnips and cook until the onion is translucent but not brown.
5. Pour the stock into the casserole. Stir and scrape to deglaze the coagulated juices. Return the tenderloin, the ham, and pancetta to the pan. Sprinkle with salt and pepper. Add the bay leaf and thyme. Bring the liquids to a boil. Cover.
6. Place the covered casserole in the oven and roast for 15 minutes. Turn and baste the meat. Replace the cover and roast for 20 minutes more.
7. Thirty-five minutes after the meat has gone into the oven, check its internal temperature with a meat thermometer. The reading for rare is 120 degrees; medium rare is 125–130 degrees. The traditional way to check is to prod the meat with your finger: rare beef will feel slightly squashy in the center, whereas medium-rare meat will be springy. If the meat is not yet done to your liking, return it to the oven for a few more minutes.
8. When the beef is done, remove it from the casserole and set aside to cool.

FOR THE ASPIC GLAZE:

The degreased braising juices from the meat (pour the vegetables and juices into a sieve and set over a small bowl; push with a wooden spoon to extract all the juice; chill and lift any fat off the top of the coagulated juices)

½ cup of beef or veal stock or bouillon, more or less (to make a total of 3 cups with the reserved braising juices)
2 envelopes of powdered, unflavored gelatin

1. Sprinkle the gelatin into 1 cup of the cold stock or bouillon in the saucepan. Let the gelatin soften for 5 minutes or so. Then blend in the deglazing juices and the rest of the stock.
2. Set the saucepan over medium heat and stir until the gelatin has completely dissolved. This will take several minutes.
3. Test the aspic. Pour a small ladleful into a chilled saucer and refrigerate for 10 minutes or until set. Remove from the refrigerator. Cut the aspic up with the side of a spoon and leave at room temperature for 10 minutes. The jelly bits should hold their shape without being rubbery or tough. If the aspic seems too soft, return the saucepan to the heat, add half of an additional package of gelatin, and heat and stir to dissolve. If the jelly is rubbery and tough, return the pan to the heat to melt the aspic, add a little more stock or water, and stir to heat and blend. Then repeat the test.

TO ASSEMBLE THE DISH:
The braised beef
The aspic
Minced shallots, parsley, and other herbs, as you like
Cracked black pepper

1. Pour about ⅛ inch of the aspic into the serving platter and chill until set. Reserve the rest of the jelly for step 3.
2. Carve the meat into thin slices and arrange, slightly overlapping, on the layer of jelly on the cold platter. Sprinkle with the cracked pepper and minced herbs.
3. If, in the meantime, the aspic has set, put the saucepan over low heat to melt the jelly. Stir the liquid aspic over a bowl of ice until it is syrupy and on the point of setting. Spoon a little bit over each slice of meat, encouraging it to run down between the overlaps by lifting the slices with a fork. Chill for 10 minutes. Repeat with 2 or 3 more thin coats of just-about-to-set jelly, chilling between each application of glaze. Set the platter in the refrigerator and chill until the aspic is set.
4. About 10 minutes before serving time, remove the platter from the refrigerator and sprinkle with some additional shallots, herbs, and pepper, if you like. To serve, slide a meat fork in between the slices of meat and serve with a bit of glaze and seasoning on each piece.

IV: FISH AND SEAFOOD

Along with vegetables, dishes of fish and seafood bear the most dramatic witness to the revolution in taste that overtook elite Parisian kitchens in the seventeenth century. With a few exceptions, La Varenne and Bonnefons eliminated preparations that called for spices (other than pepper) and other strong seasonings in favor of delicate, butter-based sauces that allowed the infinite variety of the fish to shine through. Here are three master recipes from *Le Cuisinier françois* and suggestions about variations for similar presentations for many kinds of fish and shellfish.

MUSSELS SAUTÉED WITH HERBS, SAUCE BLANCHE (LA VARENNE)

Serves 4

Mussels and *sauce blanche* make a delectable and unusual combination in this recipe by La Varenne.[29]

Equipment: A large pot or kettle for steaming the mussels, a colander, a frying pan, a small saucepan, and a whisk, a serving platter, and a sauceboat.

4 quarts of fresh mussels in their shells
Water or fish stock
A bouquet of herbs of your choice
1 recipe *sauce blanche* (see the previous *fonds de cuisine* section)
    made with verjuice (if available) or lemon juice
2 Tb butter
Salt
Pepper
2 Tb green onions, minced
2 Tb parsley, minced

1. Clean the mussels by scrubbing each one with a stiff brush under cold running water. Using a small knife, scrape off the beard or wiry hairs that cling to the seams of the shells.
2. Put the mussels in the pot, add about 2 cups of water or stock, and turn the heat on to high. Cover the pot tightly and steam the mussels for about 4–5 minutes, until the shells start to open. Remove the mussels to the colander. Throw out any mussels whose shells failed to open

---

[29] La Varenne, *Le Cuisinier françois*, 2001, p. 200, recipe for *moules de poisson*.

3. When the mussels are cool enough to handle, remove each one from its shell, using a small knife, if necessary. Set aside.

4. Make the *sauce blanche*, using verjuice or lemon juice instead of the vinegar called for in the master recipe. Pour into a warm sauceboat and set aside while finishing the mussels.

5. Melt 1 Tb of butter in the frying pan and sauté the mussels for a minute or two over medium-high heat. Sprinkle with the chopped herbs and serve accompanied by the *sauce blanche.*

Other fish and shellfish recommended by La Varenne for serving with sauce blanche: Catfish – a cousin of the European barbel (poached in white wine or court bouillon), fresh cod (poached or roasted), langoustine (boiled), lobster (boiled), or tenche (poached in white wine).

―――――――――

ROASTED COD WITH SAUCE ROUSSE (LA VARENNE)

Serves 4

The mild taste of fresh cod is enlivened by La Varenne's *sauce rousse,* an ancestor of the *beurre noir* that is still popular in French cooking today.[30]

Equipment: A baking pan large enough to hold the cod, a sauté or frying pan for making the sauce, a wooden spoon, and a serving platter.

1¾ pounds of fresh filet of cod (choose the thickest piece available)
4 Tb melted butter
Large pinch of salt mixed with a small pinch of ground cloves
1 recipe of *sauce rousse* (see the previous *fonds de cuisine* section)
1 tsp capers, rinsed, dried, and minced
Optional: Dijon mustard, to taste

1. Preheat the oven to 400 degrees.

2. Cut the cod into four equal pieces (I find that the cod roasts more evenly if you divide it into individual servings prior to roasting). Rinse, pat dry, and arrange in the baking dish. Paint the fish on all sides with the melted butter. Sprinkle with the mixture of salt and cloves.

3. Roast the fish for about 9–10 minutes per inch of thickness. You don't want the fish to be flaky or dry, so test it a minute or so before you estimate that it will be done. (Remove the pan from the oven and press the fish with your finger; if the fish is springy instead of squashy in

―――

[30] Ibid., p. 198, recipe for *morue frais rostie, en ragoust.*

the center, it is ready.) Remove the fish to the serving platter and keep warm while making the sauce.

4. Following the previous instructions, make the *sauce rousse*. Beat in the mustard, if using. To serve, dribble the sauce over the warm fish and sprinkle with the minced capers.

Other fish recommended by La Varenne for serving with sauce rousse: Salmon (roasted or grilled, whole or in filets), shad (grilled), skate (poached or sautéed), and tuna (marinated with drops of wine vinegar, salt, pepper, cloves, bay leaves, and wine before braising or grilling).

MONKFISH WITH WHITE WINE BUTTER SAUCE (LA VARENNE)

Serves 4

This method of poaching fish in white wine, butter, and aromatic seasonings is still a staple of French cooking today. It is usually associated with delicate saltwater fish such as sole or flounder. La Varenne, however, recommended this method for a wide variety of fish, including monkfish and barbel.[31] La Varenne wrote that sauce of this sort should be *"bien liée"* (well-thickened), or even *"fort courte & bien liée"* (strongly reduced and well-thickened) to set it apart from the thin butter glazes he used in other recipes. Because he failed to spell out the technique he used to achieve this result, the recipe that follows is my best attempt to approximate the results he described. The method bears a family resemblance to that of making a modern *beurre blanc*, but uses somewhat less butter than many modern recipes. See also the following recipe for beets with *beurre blanc*, also from La Varenne.

Equipment: A sauté pan or shallow casserole with a tight-fitting lid that is just large enough to hold the fish; a slotted spatula, a serving platter, and a wooden spoon.

1¾ pounds of monkfish filet, cut into 4 equal serving pieces
Salt
Pepper
¼ cup onions, finely minced
2 Tb of cold butter, cut into dice (additional butter is called for later)
1 cup dry white wine (or a mixture of wine and water)

------

[31]　Ibid., p. 187; see also the recipe for *brochet* (pike) *en ragoust*, p. 178.

1 tsp capers, finely minced

8 Tb cold butter or more, according to taste, cut into ½-tablespoon-sized pieces.

1. Rinse the pieces of monkfish, pat them dry, sprinkle lightly with salt and pepper, and arrange in the sauté pan on a bed of minced onion. Add the 2 Tb of diced butter and the wine.
2. Place the sauté pan over medium-high heat and bring the liquids to a boil. Cover the pan and turn the heat down to very low to maintain a simmer. Cook for about 8 minutes and then test to see if the fish is done (it should be springy rather than squashy when you poke it with your finger). Remove the fish to a serving dish and keep warm while finishing the sauce.
3. Raise the heat under the sauté pan to high. Boil the juices rapidly to reduce them to about 1 Tb. Off the heat, swirl in 1 Tb of the cold butter and stir with a wooden spoon until the butter is almost melted. Add a second piece and keep beating until it, too, is melted. Turn the heat down to very low and return the pan to the heat. Add another piece of butter, beating vigorously as it melts, and keep going, piece-by-piece, until you think the sauce is thick enough. Taste and correct seasoning for salt and pepper.
4. To serve, dribble the white wine butter sauce over the fish and top with the minced capers.

Variation: Catfish Poached in Court Bouillon and White Wine: Because catfish are plentiful and cheap in the United States, Americans tend to think of them as plebian food. However, their sweet flesh is perfectly suited to the deluxe recipes that La Varenne devised for barbel, a related European species.[32] In addition to pairing barbel with *sauce blanche*, he cooked it in a manner similar to the preceding monkfish recipe. Omit the minced onion and substitute 1¾ pounds of catfish filets for the monkfish, ½ cup of court bouillon (or fish stock, clam juice, or even good-quality chicken stock) plus ½ cup of dry white wine for the cooking liquid, and ½ Tb each minced parsley and green onions for the capers. Check the fish after 7 minutes of simmering to see if it is done (the thinner catfish filets require less cooking time than the thicker monkfish).

Note: Other varieties of fish and seafood that received similar treatment in *Le Cuisinier françois* include carp (substitute minced onion for the other

---

[32] Ibid., p. 187, for *barbeau au demy court bouillon.*

herbs), eel (parsley and capers), flounder (onion and parsley with a drop of vinegar), oysters (poached in their own liquor and white wine with parsley and green onions), pike (poached in white wine with capers and mushrooms), and salmon (poached in either red or white wine with minced onion – a *beurre rouge*, perhaps?), so feel free to experiment.

V: VEGETABLES

More that any other element in the menu, vegetables introduce seasonal variety to the table, and finding ways of preparing them that highlighted their natural characteristics was one of the objectives of the delicate style of cooking that emerged in seventeenth-century France. The typical solution proposed by Bonnefons and La Varenne was to blanch vegetables briefly in salted water until barely tender and to pair them with mildly flavored sauces that had a high fat content, the better to magnify the taste of the principal ingredients. Cream sauces, with and without enriching egg yolks; La Varenne's *sauce blanche*; simple butter glazes; and even vinaigrettes seasoned with garden herbs all fit into this pattern.

Below I list suggestions derived from *Les Délices de la campagne* and *Le Cuisinier françois* for pairings of vegetables with the cream and butter sauces described previously in the section on *fonds de cuisine*. Thanks to the success of delicate cookery in redefining French cuisine, there is no longer anything revolutionary about creamed peas or asparagus with *sauce blanche*; however, the combination of *sauce rousse* with root vegetables is delicious and less expected. I conclude with two other dishes that seemed worth recounting in detail: beets with *beurre blanc* from La Varenne and, to mark the transition from the medieval tradition of spicy vegetable cookery, spinach with raisins and aromatic spices from Bonnefons.

To serve with sauce à la crème, plain or enriched with an egg yolk: Artichoke bottoms (blanched), asparagus (peeled, cut into short lengths, and sautéed in butter prior to adding the cream), cardoons (blanched), cauliflower (blanched), fava beans (young ones peeled and blanched, older ones braised with lettuce, savory added to the cream in both cases), mushrooms (morilles, *mousserons*, or cultivated mushrooms blanched or previously sautéed in butter), peas (tender new peas blanched; older, mealier ones braised with a lettuce heart prior to adding the cream), and salsify (blanched).[33]

[33] Bonnefons, *Les Délices de la campagne*, pp. 100–155; and La Varenne, *Le Cuisinier françois*, 2001, pp. 118, 120–121, 238, and 307.

To serve with sauce blanche: Artichoke bottoms or hearts, asparagus (whole, peeled and blanched), carrots (cut into rounds and blanched), cauliflower, parsnips, salsify, and skirret (blanched).[34]

To serve with sauce rousse: Beets, carrots, and parsnips.[35]

BEETS WITH BEURRE BLANC (LA VARENNE)

Serves 4

In his list of dishes suitable for Good Friday, the strictest fast day of the church year, La Varenne mentions *"bette-raves au beurre blanc"* (beets in white butter).[36] Sadly, no recipe is included with the listing. However, in an earlier chapter on entremets suitable for fast days, he described a dish of beets sauced with vinegar and fresh butter that suggested the thickened butter sauces that he used for fish. Pairing such a luscious sauce with the earthy beet seems slightly odd nowadays, but it is delicious. Because beets kept well through the winter, they would have been a welcome addition to the Lenten table, when the growing season was just beginning in the region of Paris. The rich, elegant sauce, creamy but balanced by the acidity of the vinegar, would have provided relief from the general austerity of the fast day menu. Note: If you use red beets (as La Varenne recommends), their powerful color will turn the portion of the *beurre blanc* with which they come into contact into *beurre rose*!

Equipment: A large pot for boiling the beets or, alternatively, a shallow pan in which to roast them; a colander (if boiling the beets); a small, sharp knife; a saucepan; a whisk; and a serving dish. For peeling the beets: some cooks use rubber gloves because red beets stain skin.

1½ pounds beets without their tops, well scrubbed and trimmed
Olive oil or neutral vegetable oil (if roasting the beets)
2 Tb finely minced onion
8 ounces (2 sticks) butter, cut into tablespoon-sized pieces
¼ cup wine vinegar
Salt
Pepper

---

[34] La Varenne, *Le Cuisinier françois*, 2001, pp. 95, 111–112, and 117.
[35] Ibid., pp. 306–307.
[36] Ibid., pp. 245 and 306.

1. La Varenne says that the beets may be boiled or roasted on the fire. To boil the beets, bring a large pot of salted water to a boil; add the beets and cook for about 15–20 minutes (depending on their size) after the water returns to a boil. Test to see if they are tender when pieced with a sharp knife; if not, return to the heat for a little longer, and then drain. To roast the beets, preheat the oven to 450 degrees. Rub the scrubbed beets with a little oil, put them in the roasting pan, and roast 30–40 minutes until tender. Remove from the oven and set aside.

2. As soon as the beets are cool enough to handle, peel them, using a small, sharp knife. Slice the peeled beets into rounds, sprinkle with salt and pepper, and keep warm in the serving dish while making the *beurre blanc*.

3. Over a medium flame, heat 2 Tb of the butter in the saucepan, add the minced onion, and sauté for a minute or two until the onion is translucent and tender. Add the vinegar and boil until the liquid is reduced by half to 2 Tb.

4. Remove the pan from the heat. Stir in 2 pieces of butter until they are almost entirely melted. Return the pan to very low heat and continue beating in the butter one piece at a time. If you sense that the sauce is getting too hot, lift it off the heat for a minute and whisk vigorously. As you add more and more butter, the texture of the sauce should become dense and creamy. Taste and beat in salt and pepper, if needed.

5. To serve: top the warm beets with the *beurre blanc* and serve at once.

SPINACH WITH RAISINS AND AROMATIC SPICES (BONNEFONS)

Serves 4

This dish, which combines spinach with sweet raisins and aromatic spices in a buttery sauce, is an example of the more traditional elements that persisted in the French kitchen of the 1650s.[37]

Equipment: A large pot for blanching the spinach, a colander, a sauté or frying pan large enough to hold the spinach, a wooden spoon, and a serving dish.

1½ pounds spinach, tough stems removed, meticulously washed in several changes of cold water to remove all sand and grit

[37] Bonnefons, *Les Délices de la campagne*, p. 145.

6 Tb butter
1½ Tb raisins, plumped in hot water and drained
1 Tb verjuice or the juice of half a lemon
Salt
Pepper
Ground cinnamon
Ground cloves

1. Blanch the spinach in boiling, salted water for about 2 minutes, until wilted and tender. Drain at once. Run cold water over the spinach in its colander to cool and stop the cooking process.
2. When the spinach is cool enough to handle, squeeze out the extra water, a handful at a time.
3. Heat the butter in the sauté pan over medium-high heat. Add the raisins and sauté for a minute. Add the verjuice or lemon juice and boil rapidly to reduce slightly. Then begin adding the spinach one handful at a time, stirring with the wooden spoon to coat the spinach with sauce, until all the spinach has been added and most of the liquid has been absorbed. Sprinkle with salt, pepper, and pinches of cinnamon and cloves to taste and stir to blend. Serve immediately.

Variation: Bonnefons's recipe is similar to one published a century earlier by Scappi (discussed in Chapter 2), the major difference being that Bonnefons called for spinach that had been blanched and squeezed dry, whereas Scappi simply tossed his spinach in a pan with fat and seasonings until it wilted. I have found the Scappi method to be excellent with young, tender spinach or chard.

Bibliography

Ackerknecht, Erwin H., "The End of the Greek Diet" in *The Bulletin of the History of Medicine*, vol. 45 (1971), pp. 243–249.

Amouretti, Marie-Claire, "Urban and Rural Diets in Greece" in Jean-Louis Flandrin and Massimo Montanari, eds., *Food: A Culinary History*, English edition by Albert Sonnenfeld (New York: Columbia University Press, 1999).

Andrews, Jean, "Chili Peppers" in Kenneth F. Kiple and Kriemhild Coneè Ornelas, eds., *The Cambridge World History of Food*, 2 vols. (Cambridge and New York: Cambridge University Press, 2000).

Ariès, Philippe, and Georges Duby, eds., *A History of Private Life*, translated by Arhur Goldhammer, 5 vols. (Cambridge, MA: Harvard University Press, 1987–1991).

Arnoux, Claude, *Dissertation sur la situation de Bourgogne, sur les vins quelle produit, sur la maniere de cultiver les vignes, de faire le vin & de l'éprover* (Londen: C. Jallason, 1728).

Aronson, Nicole, *Mme de Rambouillet ou la magicienne de la Chambre bleue* (Paris: Fayard, 1988).

Audiger, N., *La Maison réglée et l'art de diriger la maison d'un grand seigneur tant à la ville qu'à la campagne* in Gilles and Laurence Laurendon, eds., *L'Art de la cuisine française au XVIIe siècle* (Paris: Editions Payot & Rivages, 1995).

Auerbach, Erich, "La Cour et la Ville" in *Scenes from the Drama of European Literature: Six Essays* (New York: Meridian, 1959).

Berg, Maxine, and Elizabeth Eger, eds., *Luxury in the Eighteenth Century: Debates, Desires and Delectable Goods* (New York: Palgrave Macmillan, 2003).

Berry, Christopher J., *The Idea of Luxury: A Conceptual and Historical Investigation* (Cambridge: Cambridge University Press, 1994).

Bienvenu, Marcelle, Carl A. Brasseaux, and Ryan Brasseaux, *Stir the Pot: The History of Cajun Cooking* (New York: Hippocrene, 2005).

Bober, Phyllis Pray, *Arts, Culture, and Cuisine: Ancient and Medieval Gastronomy* (Chicago and London: The University of Chicago Press, 1991).

Boire et Manger au XVIIe Siècle au Temps de la Marquise de Sévigné, papers from the second Symposium Vin et Histoire (Suze-la-Rousse: Université du Vin, 1998).

Boisard, Pierre, *Camembert: A National Myth*, translated by Richard Miller (Berkeley and Los Angeles: University of California Press, 2003).

Bonal, François, *Livre d'or du champagne* (Lausanne: Grand Pont, 1985).

[Bonnefons, Nicolas de], *Les Délices de la campagne*, dedicated to mistresses of households, augmented by the author, 2nd ed. (Paris: Pierre des Hayes, 1656).

———, *The French Gardener*, transplanted into English by John Evelyn, 3rd ed. (London: Benjamin Tooke, 1672).

———, *Le Jardinier français que enseigne à cultiver les arbres & herbes potagères avec la manière de conserver les fruits et faire toutes sortes de confitures, conserves & massepains* (Paris: Pierre Des Hayes, 1651).

———, *Le Jardinier français qui enseigne à cultiver les arbres & herbes potagères avec le manière de conserver les fruits & faire toutes sortes de confitures, conserves & massepains*, dedicated to the ladies, with a commentary by François-Xavier Bognard (Paris: Ramsay, 2001).

Bonnet, Jean-Claude, "The Culinary System of the *Encyclopédie*" in Robert Forster and Orest Ranum, eds., *Food and Drink in History: Selections from the Annales Economies, Sociétés, Civilisations*, translated by Elborg Forster and Patricia M. Ranum (Baltimore, MD, and London: Johns Hopkins University Press, 1979).

———, "Le Système de la cuisine et du repas chez Rousseau" in Serge A. Thériault, *Jean-Jacques Rousseau et la Médecine naturelle* (St. Denis, Montréal, and Québec: Les Editions Univers, 1979).

Bordieu, Pierre, *Distinction: A Social Critique of the Judgement of Taste*, translated by Richard Nice (Cambridge, MA: Harvard University Press, 1984).

Boutaud, Jean-Jacques, *Le Sens gourmand: de la commensalité du goût – des ailments* (Paris: Jean-Paul Rocher, 2005).

Braudel, Fernand, *The Mediterranean and the Mediterranean World in the Age of Philip II*, translated by Siân Reynolds, 2 vols. (Berkeley: University of California Press, 1995).

———, *The Structures of Everyday Life*, translated by Siân Reynolds, vol. 1 of *Civilization and Capitalism, 15th–18th Century* (New York: Harper & Row, 1981).

Brennan, Thomas, *Burgundy to Champagne: The Wine Trade in Early Modern France* (Baltimore, MD: Johns Hopkins University Press, 1997).

———, *Public Drinking and Popular Culture in Eighteenth-Century Paris* (Princeton, NJ: Princeton University Press, 1988).

Brillat-Savarin, J.-A., *Physiologie de Goût*, with an introduction by Jean-François Revel (Paris: Flammarion, 1982).

———, *The Physiology of Taste or Meditations on Transcendental Gastronomy*, translated by M. F. K. Fisher (Washington, DC: Counterpoint, 1994).

Brockliss, L. W. B., "The Medico-Religious Universe of an Early Eighteenth-Century Parisian Doctor: The Case of Philippe Hecquet" in Roger French and Andrew Wear, eds., *The Medical Revolution of the Seventeenth Century* (Cambridge: Cambridge University Press, 1989).

Brown, Theodore M., "The College of Physicians and the Acceptance of Iatro-Mechanism in England, 1665–1695" in *The Bulletin of the History of Medicine*, vol. 44 (1970), pp. 12–30.

Buisseret, David, *Henry IV* (London: Allen and Unwin, 1984).

Burke, Peter, *The Art of Conversation* (Ithaca, NY, and New York: Cornell University Press, 1993).

Bury, Emmanuel, "Le monde de l'honnête homme': aspects de la notion de 'monde' dans esthétique du savoir-vivre" in *La Notion du "monde" au XVIIe siècle*, vol. 22 (autumn 1994) of *Littératures classiques*, pp. 191–202.

Capatti, Alberto, and Massimo Montanari, *La Cuisine italienne: histoire d'une culture* (Paris: Seuil, 2002).

———, *Italian Cuisine: A Cultural History*, translated by Aine O'Healy (New York: Columbia University Press, 2003).

Cassirer, Ernst, *The Philosophy of the Enlightenment*, translated by Fritz C. A. Koelln and James P. Pettegrove (Princeton, NJ: Princeton University Press, 1951).

Cheyne, George, *The English Malady or a Treatise on Nervous Diseases of All Kinds*, 2nd ed. (London: G. Strahan, 1734).

_____, *An Essay of Health and Long Life*, 10th ed. (London: G. Strahan, 1745).

_____, *An Essay on Regimen, Together with Five Discourses, Medical, Moral, and Philosophical* (London: for C. Rivington; Bath: J. Leake, 1740).

Child, Julia, Louisette Bertholle, and Simone Beck, *Mastering the Art of French Cooking*, 2 vols., updated (New York: Alfred A. Knopf, 1983).

Clark, Kenneth, *The Nude: A Study in Ideal Form* (Princeton, NJ: Princeton University Press, 1956).

Coates, Clive, MW, *Grands Vins: The Finest Châteaux of Bordeaux and Their Wines* (Berkeley and Los Angeles: University of California Press, 1995).

Coe, Sophie D., and Michael D. Coe, *The True History of Chocolate* (London: Thames & Hudson, 1996).

Cohen, Edgar H., *Mademoiselle Libertine: A Portrait of Ninon de Lanclos* (Boston: Houghton Mifflin, 1970).

Collingham, Lizzie, *Curry: A Tale of Cooks and Conquerors* (Oxford: Oxford University Press, 2006).

Collins, James B., *From Tribes to Nation: The Making of France, 500–1799* (Toronto: Wadsworth Thompson Learning, 2002).

Comrie, John D., ed., *Selected Works of Thomas Sydenham MD with a Short Biography and Explanatory Notes* (London: John Bayle Sons & Danielson, 1922).

Cook, Harold J., "Physicians and Natural History" in N. Jardine, J. A. Secord, and E. C. Spary, eds., *Cultures of Natural History* (Cambridge: Cambridge University Press, 1996).

Corbier, Mireille, "The Broad Bean and the Moray: Social Hierarchies and Food in Rome" in Jean-Louis Flandrin and Massimo Montanari, eds., *Food: A Culinary History*, English edition by Albert Sonnenfeld (New York: Columbia University Press, 1999).

Craveri, Benedetta, *The Age of Conversation*, translated by Teresa Waugh (New York: New York Review Books, 2005).

Crosby, Alfred W., Jr., *The Columbian Exchange: Biological and Cultural Consequences of 1492*, 30th anniversary ed., forewords by J. R. McNeill and Otto von Mering (Westport, CT, and London: Praeger, 2003).

Csergo, Julia, "The Emergence of Regional Cuisines" in Jean-Louis Flandrin and Massimo Montanari, eds., *Food: A Culinary History*, English edition by Albert Sonnenfeld (New York: Columbia University Press, 1999).

Le Cuisinier Gascon, reprint of the 1740 edition (Pau: ICN, 1999).

Cunningham, Andrew, "The Culture of Gardens" in N. Jardine, J. A. Secord, and E. C. Spary, eds., *Cultures of Natural History* (Cambridge: Cambridge University Press, 1996).

Damrosch, Leo, *Jean-Jacques Rousseau: Restless Genius* (Boston: Houghton Mifflin, 2005).

Darnton, Robert, "Philosophers Trim the Tree of Knowledge: The Epistemological Strategy of the *Encyclopédie*" in *The Great Cat Massacre and Other Episodes in French Cultural History* (New York: Basic Books, 1984).

_____, "Readers Respond to Rousseau" in *The Great Cat Massacre and Other Episodes in French Cultural History* (New York: Basic Books, 1984).

David, Elizabeth, *French Provincial Cooking* (London: Penguin, 1970).

———, *The Harvest of the Cold Months: The Social History of Ice and Ices* (New York: Viking, 1995).

———, *Is There a Nutmeg in the House? Essays on Practical Cooking with More than 150 Recipes*, compiled by Jill Norman (New York: Viking, 2000).

———, *Italian Food* (New York: Smithmark, 1996).

———, *Spices, Salt and Aromatics in the English Kitchen: English Cooking, Ancient and Modern*, vol. 1 (London: Penguin, 1970).

Davidson, Alan, *The Oxford Companion to Food* (Oxford and New York: Oxford University Press, 1999).

Da Vinha, Mathieu, *Les Valets de Chambre de Louis XIV* (Paris: Perrin, 2004).

Davis, Audrey D., "Some Implications of the Circulation Theory for Disease Theory and Treatment in the Seventeenth Century" in *The Journal of the History of Medicine and Allied Sciences*, vol. 26 (1971), pp. 28–39.

Debus, Allen G., *The Chemical Philosophy: Paracelsian Science and Medicine in the Sixteenth and Seventeenth Centuries*, 2 vols. (New York: Science History Publications, 1977).

———, *The French Paracelsians* (Cambridge and New York: Cambridge University Press, 1993).

———, *Man and Nature in the Renaissance* (Cambridge and New York: Cambridge University Press, 1978).

Denuzière, Jacqueline, and Charles Henri Brandt, *Cuisine de Louisiane: Histoire et recettes* (Paris: Editions Denoël, 1989).

Dewald, Jonathan, *Aristocratic Experience and the Origins of Modern Culture: France, 1570–1715* (Berkeley and Los Angeles: University of California Press, 1993).

Dion, Roger, *Histoire de la vigne et du vin en France: des origins au XIXe siècle* (Paris: Flammarion, 1977).

Duby, Georges, *The Early Growth of the European Economy: Warriors and Peasants from the Seventh to the Twelfth Century*, translated by Howard B. Clarke (London: Weidenfeld and Nicolson, 1974).

———, *France in the Middle Ages, 987–1460*, translated by Juliet Vale (Oxford: Blackwell, 1991).

Dumas, Alexandre, *Mon dictionnaire de cuisine* (Paris: U. G. E. Poche, 1998).

Ehrard, Jean, *L'Idée de nature en France dans la première moitié du XVIIIe siècle* (Paris: Albin Michel, 1994).

Elias, Norbert, *The Civilizing Process: The History of Manners and State Formation and Civilization*, translated by Edmund Jephcot (Oxford and Cambridge, MA: Blackwell, 1994).

Encyclopédie, ou Dictionnaire raisonné des sciences, des arts et des métiers, par une société de gens de lettres, edited by M. Diderot and, for the part on mathematics, M. d'Alembert, 28 vols. (Geneva [Paris and Neufchastel], 1772).

Escoffier, Auguste, *The Escoffier Cookbook: A Guide to the Fine Art of French Cuisine* (New York: Crown, 1969).

Evelyn, John, *Acetaria: A Discourse of Sallets* (Brooklyn, NY: Brooklyn Botanic Garden, 1937).

———, *John Evelyn, Cook: The Manuscript Receipt Book of John Evelyn* (Totnes and Devon: Prospect Books, 1997).

Fairchilds, Cissie, *Domestic Enemies: Servants and Their Masters in Old Regime France* (Baltimore, MD: Johns Hopkins University Press, 1984).

Feibleman, Peter S., *American Cooking: Creole and Acadian* (New York: Time-Life Books, 1971).

Ferguson, Priscilla Parkhurst, *Accounting for Taste: The Triumph of French Cuisine* (Chicago and London: The University of Chicago Press, 2004).

Fernández-Armesto, Felipe, *Food: A History* (London: Macmillan, 2001).

Fiddes, Nick, *Meat: A Natural Symbol* (London and New York: Routledge, 1991).

Findlen, Paula, "Courting Nature" in N. Jardine, J. A. Secord, and E. C. Spary, eds., *Cultures of Natural History* (Cambridge and New York: Cambridge University Press, 1996).

Fink, Beatrice, "Saint-John de Crèvecoeur's Tale of a Tuber" in *Eighteenth-Century Life*, vol. 25, no. 2 (spring 2001), pp. 225–238.

Flandrin, Jean-Louis, *Chronique de Platine: pour une gastronomie historique* (Paris: Editions Odile Jacob, 1992).

———, "Dietary Choices and Culinary Technique, 1500–1800" in Jean-Louis Flandrin and Massimo Montanari, eds., *Food: A Culinary History*, English edition by Albert Sonnenfeld (New York: Columbia University Press, 1999).

———, "From Dietetics to Gastronomy: The Liberation of the Gourmet" in Jean-Louis Flandrin and Massimo Montanari, eds., *Food: A Culinary History*, English edition by Albert Sonnenfeld (New York: Columbia University Press, 1999).

———, "*Le goût et la nécessité: Sur l'usage des graisses dans les cuisines d'Europe occidentale*" in *L'Annales ESC* 39 (1983).

———, "Introduction: The Early Modern Period" in Jean-Louis Flandrin and Massimo Montanari, eds., *Food: A Culinary History*, English edition by Albert Sonnenfeld (New York: Columbia University Press, 1999).

———, *L'Ordre des mets* (Paris: Editions Odile Jacob, 2002).

———, "Seasoning, Cooking, and Dietetics in the Late Middle Ages" in Jean-Louis Flandrin and Massimo Montanari, eds., *Food: A Culinary History*, English edition by Albert Sonnenfeld (New York: Columbia University Press, 1999).

Flandrin, Jean-Louis, and Jane Cobbi, *Tables d'hier, tables d'ailleurs* (Paris: Editions Odile Jacob, 1999).

Flandrin, Jean-Louis, and Massimo Montanari, eds., *Food: A Culinary History*, English edition by Albert Sonnenfeld (New York: Columbia University Press, 1999).

Forster, Robert, and Orest Ranum, eds., *Food and Drink in History: Selections from the Annales Economies, Sociétés, Civilisations*, translated by Elborg Forster and Patricia M. Ranum (Baltimore, MD, and London: Johns Hopkins University Press, 1979).

———, *Medicine and Society in France: Selections from the Annales, Economies, Sociétés, Civilisations*, translated by Elborg Forster and Patricia M. Ranum, vol. 6 (Baltimore, MD, and London: Johns Hopkins University Press, 1980).

Franklin, Alfred, *Le Café, le thé et le chocolat*, vol. 3 of *La Vie privée d'autrefois: Arts et métiers, usages parisiens du XIIe au XVIIIe siècle d'après des documents originaux et inédits*, 27 vols. (Paris, E. Plon, Nourrit et cie, 1887–1902).

French, Roger, and Andrew Wear, eds., *The Medical Revolution of the Seventeenth Century* (Cambridge: Cambridge University Press, 1989).

Fried, Michael, *Absorption and Theatricality: Painting and the Beholder in the Age of Diderot* (Berkeley and Los Angeles: University of California Press, 1980).

Fumeroli, Marc, "Premier témoin du parisianisme: le 'monde' et la 'mode' chez les moralists du XVIIe siècle" in *La Notion du "monde" au XVIIe siècle*, vol. 22 (autumn 1994) of *Littératures classiques*, pp. 165–190.

Furet, François, *Revolutionary France, 1770–1880,* translated by Antonia Nevill (Oxford and Cambridge, MA: Blackwell, 1992)

Galloway, J. H., "The Mediterranean Sugar Industry" in *Geographical Review,* vol. 67, no. 2, pp. 177–192.

Garrier, Gilbert, *Histoire social et culturelle du vin* (Paris: Larousse, 2005).

Gay, Peter, *The Enlightenment: An Interpretation,* 2 vols. (New York: W. W. Norton, 1966).

Gillet, Philippe, *Par mets et par vins: Voyages et gastronomie en Europe 16e–18e siècles* (Paris: Payot, 1985).

[Glasse, Hannah], *The Compleat Confectioner, or, the Whole Art of Confectionary* (London: printed and sold at Mrs Ashburner's, Yewd's, Kirk's and Deard's, I. Pottinger, and J. Williams, 1760).

———, *First Catch Your Hare: The Art of Cookery Made Plain and Easy by a Lady (1747),* a facsimile of the first edition, supplemented by the recipes that the author added up to the fifth edition and furnished with a preface, introductory essays by Jennifer Stead and Priscilla Bain, a glossary by Alan Davidson, notes, and an index (Totnes: Prospect Books, 2004).

Glatre, Eric, "Des vins de la Champagne aux vins de Champagne: Dom Pierre Pérignon, le vigneron méconnu" in *Boire et Manger au XVIIe Siècle: Au Temps de la Marquise de Sévigné,* papers from the second Symposium Vin et Histoire (Suze-la-Rousse: l'Université du Vin, 1998).

Glotz, Marguerite, and Madeleine Marie, *Salons du XVIIIe siècle* (Paris: Nouvelle Editions Latines, 1949).

Godfrey, Eleanor S., *The Development of English Glassmaking, 1560–1640* (Chapel Hill: University of North Carolina Press, 1975).

Goethe, Johann Wolfgang von, *The Sorrows of Young Werther and Novella,* translated from the German by Elizabeth Meyer and Louise Bogan, poems translated by W. H. Auden, foreword by W. H. Auden (New York: Vintage, 1990).

Goldman, Elizabeth C., *Exclusive Conversations: The Art of Interaction in 17th-Century France* (Philadelphia: University of Pennsylvania Press, 1988).

Goodman, Dena, *The Republic of Letters: A Cultural History of the French Enlightenment* (Ithaca, NY, and London: Cornell University Press, 1994).

Gordon, Daniel, *Citizens without Sovereignty: Equality and Sociability in French Thought, 1616–1789* (Princeton, NJ: Princeton University Press, 1994).

Green, Peter, *Alexander to Actium: The Historical Evolution of the Hellenistic Age* (Berkeley and Los Angeles: University of California Press, 1990).

Greico, Allen J., "Food and Social Classes in Late Medieval and Renaissance Italy" in Jean-Louis Flandrin and Massimo Montanari, eds., *Food: A Culinary History,* English edition by Albert Sonnenfeld (New York: Columbia University Press, 1999).

Grimod de la Reynière, Alexandre-Balthazar-Laurent, *Almanach des gourmands, hiutième année (1812),* selections chosen and with a preface by Allen S. Weiss (Paris: Mercure de France, 2003).

———, *Manuel des Amphitryons,* edited by Misette Godard. (Paris: Editions A. M. Métailié, 1983).

Guerrini, Anita, *Obesity and Depression in the Enlightenment: The Life and Times of George Cheyne* (Norman: University of Oklahoma Press, 2000).

Hazan, Marcella, *Marcella's Italian Kitchen* (New York: Alfred A. Knopf, 1986).

Hesser, Amanda, *The Cook and the Gardener: A Year of Recipes and Writings from the French Countryside* (New York: W. W. Norton, 1999).

Höfler, Manfred, *Dictionnaire de l'art Culinaire français: Etymologie et histoire* (Paris: Edisud, 1996).

Hufton, Olwen H., *The Poor of Eighteenth-Century France, 1750–1789* (Oxford: Oxford University Press, 1974).

———, *The Prospect Before Her: A History of Women in Western Europe, 1500–1800* (New York: Alfred A. Knopf, 1996).

Hulliung, Mark, *The Autocritique of the Enlightenment: Rousseau and the Philosophes* (Cambridge, MA: Harvard University Press, 1998).

Hundert, Edward, "Mandeville, Rousseau and the Political Economy of Fantasy" in Maxine Berg and Elizabeth Eger, eds., *Luxury in the Eighteenth Century: Debates, Desires and Delectable Goods* (New York: Palgrave Macmillan, 2003).

Hyman, Philip, and Mary Hyman, "La Chapelle and Massialot: An Eighteenth-Century Feud" in *Petits Propos Culinaires*, vol. 2 (August 1979), pp. 44–54.

———, "Printing the Kitchen: French Cookbooks, 1480–1800" in Jean-Louis Flandrin and Massimo Montanari, eds., *Food: A Culinary History*, English edition by Albert Sonnenfeld (New York: Columbia University Press, 1999).

Israel, Jonathan I., *Dutch Primacy in World Trade, 1585–1740* (Oxford: Clarendon Press, 1989).

Jackson, Ralph, *Doctors and Diseases in the Roman Empire* (Norman, OK, and London: University of Oklahoma Press, 1988).

Jardine, N., J. A. Secord, and E. C. Spary, eds., *Cultures of Natural History* (Cambridge: Cambridge University Press, 1996).

Johnson, Hugh, *Modern Encyclopedia of Wine* (New York: Simon and Schuster, 1998).

———, *Vintage: The Story of Wine* (New York: Simon and Schuster, 1989).

Jones, Colin, *Paris: Biography of a City* (New York: Viking, 2004).

Jousselin, Roland, *Au couvert du roi: XVIIe–XVIII siècles* (Paris: Editions Christian, 1998).

Kantorowicz, Ernst, *The King's Two Bodies*, reprint ed. (Princeton, NJ, and New York: Princeton University Press, 1997).

Kaplan, Laurence, "Beans, Peas, and Lentils" in Kenneth F. Kiple and Kriemhild Coneè Ornelas, eds., *The Cambridge World History of Food*, 2 vols. (Cambridge and New York: Cambridge University Press, 2000).

Kaplan, Steven Laurence, *Provisioning Paris: Merchants and Millers in the Grain and Flour Trade during the Eighteenth Century* (Ithaca, NY, and London: Cornell University Press, 1984).

Kiple, Kenneth F., and Kriemhild Coneè Ornelas, eds., *The Cambridge World History of Food*, 2 vols. (Cambridge and New York: Cambridge University Press, 2000).

L. S. R., *L'Art de bien traiter (1674)* in Gilles and Laurence Laurendon, eds., *L'Art de la cuisine française au XVIIe siècle* (Paris: Editions Payot & Rivages, 1995).

Lacey, Richard W., *Hard to Swallow: A Brief History of Food* (Cambridge: Cambridge University Press, 1994).

La Chapelle, Vincent, *The Modern Cook*, 3 vols., 3rd ed. (London: T. Osborne, 1744).

Lamb, Patrick, *Royal Cookery: Or, the Compleat Court-Cook. Containing the Choicest Receipts in All the Several Branches of Cookery, to Which Are Added Bills of Fare for Every Month of the Year*, 2nd ed. (London: A Nutt and J. Roper, 1716).

La Quintinie, Jean-Baptiste de, *The Compleat Gardener or Directions for Cultivating and Right Ordering of Fruit-Gardens and Kitchen-Gardens with Diverse Reflections on Several Parts of Husbandry*, in six books to which is added his *Treatise of Orange-Trees, with the Raising of Melons*, omitted in the French Editions. Translated by John Evelyn, Esq. (London: Matthew Gillyflower, 1699).

———, *Instruction pour les jardins fruitiers et potagers avec un Traité de la culture des orangers, suivi de quelques Réflexions sur l'agriculture* (Paris: Actes Sud, 1999).

Larousse Gastronomique, edited by Jennifer Harvey Lang (New York: Crown, 1988).

Laurendon, Gilles, and Laurence Laurendon, eds., *L'Art de la cuisine française au XVIIe siècle* (Paris: Editions Payot & Rivages, 1995).

Laurioux, Bruno, *Manger au moyen âge: pratiques et discours alimentaires en Europe aux XIVe et XVe siècles* (Paris: Hachette, 2002).

———, "Medieval Cooking" in Jean-Louis Flandrin and Massimo Montanari, eds., *Food: A Culinary History*, English edition by Albert Sonnenfeld (New York: Columbia University Press, 1999).

———, "Spices in the Medieval Diet" in *Food and Foodways I* (1985), pp. 43–76.

La Varenne,[François Pierre], *Le Cuisinier françois*, edited by Jean-Louis Flandrin and Philip and Mary Hyman (Paris: Montalba, 1981).

———, *Le Cuisinier françois*, edited by Philip and Mary Hyman (Paris: Manucius, 2001).

———, *The French Cook*, translated into English in 1653 by I. D. G., with an introduction by Philip and Mary Hyman (Lewes: Southover Press, 2001).

Leclant, Jean, "Coffee and Cafés in Paris, 1644–1693" in Robert Forster and Orest Ranum, eds., *Food and Drink in History: Selections from the Annales Economies, Sociétés, Civilisations*, translated by Elborg Forster and Patricia M. Ranum, vol. 5 (Baltimore, MD, and London: Johns Hopkins University Press, 1979).

Le Grand d'Aussy, P.-B.-J., *Histoire de la vie privée des français depuis l'origine de la nation jusqu'a nos jours (1782)*, 2 vols. (Paris: Sens Editions, 1999).

Le Roy Ladurie, Emmanuel, *The Ancien Régime: A History of France, 1610–1774*, translated by Mark Greengrass (Oxford: Blackwell, 1998).

———, *The Peasants of Languedoc*, translated with an introduction by John Day (Urbana, Chicago, and London: University of Illinois Press, 1974).

———, *Saint-Simon and the Court of Louis XIV*, with the collaboration of Jean-François Fitou, translated by Arthur Goldhammer (Chicago and London: The University of Chicago Press, 2001).

Lespinasse, René de, *Histoire générale de Paris: Les Métiers et corporations de la ville de Paris* (Paris: Imprimerie Nationale, 1886).

Levine, Joseph M., *The Battle of the Books: History and Literature in the Augustan Age* (Ithaca, NY, and London: Cornell University Press, 1991).

Levy, M., *Early Arabic Pharmacology* (Leiden: Brill, 1973).

Lewis, Archibald, *Naval Power and Trade in the Mediterranean, A. D. 500–1100* (Princeton, NJ: Princeton University Press, 1952).

Lewis, W. H., *The Splendid Century: Life in the France of Louis XIV* (New York: William Morrow, 1954).

Lilti, Antoine, *Le Monde des salons: Sociabilité et mondanité à Paris au XVIIIe siècle* (Paris: Broché, 2005).

Lloyd, G. E. R., ed., *Hippocratic Writings*, translated by J. Chadwick, W. N. Mann, I. M. Lonie, and E. T. Withington (London: Penguin, 1983).

Locke, John, *Travels in France, 1675–1679, as Related in His Journals, Correspondence and Other Papers*, edited with an introduction and notes by John Lough (Cambridge: Cambridge University Press, 1953).

Long, Janet, "Tomatoes" in Kenneth F. Kiple and Kriemhild Coneè Ornelas, eds., *Cambridge World History of Food*, 2 vols. (Cambridge and New York: Cambridge University Press, 2000).

Lopez, Robert, *The Commercial Revolution of the Middle Ages, 950–1350* (Cambridge and New York: Cambridge University Press, 1976).

———, "The Trade of Medieval Europe: The South" in *The Cambridge Economic History of Europe*, translated by M. M. Postan and H. J. Habakkuk, vol. 2 (Cambridge: Cambridge University Press, 1952).

Lougee, Carolyn C., *"Le Paradis des Femmes": Women, Salons, and Social Stratification in 17th-Century France* (Princeton, NJ: Princeton University Press, 1976).

Lough, John, *An Introduction to Eighteenth-Century France* (London: Longmans, 1960).

———, *An Introduction to Seventeenth-Century France* (New York: MaKay, 1961).

Marie, Jean-Pierre, *La Cuisine des lumières ou le ménage des champs et de la ville* (Paris: Editions E. D. K., 2003).

[Marin, François], *Les Dons de Comus d'après l'édition de 1742*, 3 vols., preface by Silvano Serventi (Paris: Editions Manucius, 2001).

Martino, Maestro, *The Art of Cooking: The First Modern Cookery Book/Composed by the Eminent Maestro Martino of Como*, edited with an introduction by Luigi Ballerini, translated and annotated by Jeremy Parzen, and with fifty modern recipes by Stefania Marzini (Berkeley and Los Angeles: University of California Press, 2005).

Massialot, François, *Le Nouveau cuisinier royal et bourgeois ou Cuisinier moderne*, unabridged facsimile of the edition published in 1748 by Joseph Saugrain, 3 vols. (Paris: Elibron, 2005).

[Massialot, François], *The Court and Country Cook: Giving New and Plain Directions How to Order All Manner of Entertainments, Together with New Instructions for Confectioners*, faithfully translated out of French into English by J. K. (London: A. and J. Churchill and M. Gillyflower, 1702).

———, *Le Cuisinier roïal et bourgeois qui apprend à ordonner toute sorte de repas & la meilleure manière des ragoûts les plus à la mode & les plus exquis*, corrected and augmented, with illustrations, 3rd ed. (Paris: Charles de Sercy, 1698).

———, *Nouvelle instruction pour les confitures* (Paris: Charles de Sercy, 1692).

Maza, Sarah, "Luxury, Morality, and Social Change: Why Was There No Middle-Class Consciousness in Prerevolutionary France?" in *The Journal of Modern History*, vol. 69, no. 2 (June 1997), pp. 199–229.

Mazzini, Innocenzo, "Diet and Medicine in the Ancient World" in Jean-Louis Flandrin and Massimo Montanari, eds., *Food: A Culinary History*, English edition by Albert Sonnenfeld (New York: Columbia University Press, 1999).

McGee, Harold, *The Curious Cook: More Kitchen Science and Lore* (New York: Hungry Minds, 1990).

———, *On Food and Cooking: The Science and Lore of the Kitchen* (New York: Simon and Schuster, 1997).

McGovern, Patrick E., *Ancient Wine: The Search for the Origins of Viniculture* (Princeton, NJ: Princeton University Press, 2003).

McGovern, Patrick E., Stuart J. Flemming, and Solomon Katz, eds., *The Origins and Ancient History of Wine* (London and New York: Routledge, 2004).

McNeill, J. R., and William H. McNeill, *The Human Web: A Bird's-Eye View of World History* (New York: W. W. Norton, 2003).

McNeill, William H., *The Rise of the West: A History of the Human Community* (Chicago and London: The University of Chicago Press, 1963).

Mennell, Stephen, *All Manners of Food: Eating and Taste in England and France from the Middle Ages to the Present* (Urbana and Chicago: University of Illinois Press, 1996).

————, ed., *Letter d'un pâtissier anglois et autres contributions à une polémique gastronomique du XVIIIème siècle* (Exeter: University of Exeter Press, 1981).

[Menon, François], *La Cuisinière bourgeoise*, new ed. (Paris: Guillyn, 1762).

————, *Le Nouveau Traité de cuisine* (Paris: Saugrain Fils, 1739).

————, *La Science du maître-d'hôtel cuisinier* (Paris: Chez les libraires associés, 1749; reprint Paris, 1982).

Le Ménagier de Paris, edited by Georgine E. Brereton and Janet M. Ferrier (Oxford: Clarendon Press, 1981).

Michel, Dominique, *Vatel et la naissance de la gastronomie* (Paris: Fayard, 1999).

Mille et une bouches: Cuisines et identities culturelles, edited by Sophie Bessis (Paris: Editions Autrement, 1995).

Miller, Judith, *Mastering the Market: The State and the Grain Trade in Northern France, 1700–1860* (Cambridge and New York: Cambridge University Press, 1999).

Mintz, Sidney W., *Sweetness and Power: The Place of Sugar in Modern History* (London and New York: Penguin, 1985).

Mongrédien, Georges, *La Vie de société aux XVIIe et XVIIIe siècles* (Paris: Hachette, 1950).

Montanari, Massimo, *The Culture of Food*, translated by Carl Ipsen (Oxford: Blackwell, 1994).

————, "Peasants, Warriors, Priests: Images of Society and Styles of Diet" in Jean-Louis Flandrin and Massimo Montanari, eds., *Food: A Culinary History*, English edition by Albert Sonnenfeld (New York: Columbia University Press, 1999).

————, "Production Structures and Food Systems in the Early Middle Ages" in Jean-Louis Flandrin and Massimo Montanari, eds., *Food: A Culinary History*, English edition by Albert Sonnenfeld (New York: Columbia University Press, 1999).

Morineau, Michel, "The Potato in the Eighteenth Century" in Robert Forster and Orest Ranum, eds., *Food and Drink in History: Selections from the Annales Economies, Sociétés, Civilisations*, translated by Elborg Forster and Patricia M. Ranum, vol. 5 (Baltimore, MD, and London: Johns Hopkins University Press, 1979).

Mousnier, Roland, *Paris au XVIIeme siècle* (Paris: CDU, 1961).

Mustel,[Nicolas-Alexandre] de, *Mémoire sur les pommes de terre et sur le pain économique* (Rouen: Besongne, 1767).

Olney, Richard, *Simple French Food*, new introduction by Patricia Wells, foreword by James Beard (New York: Collier, 1992).

Pagel, Walter, *Paracelsus: An Introduction to Philosophical Medicine in the Era of the Renaissance* (Basel: S. Kaerger, 1958).

Palmer, R. R., *The School of the French Revolution: A Documentary History of the College of Louis-le-Grand and Its Director, Jean-François Champagne, 1762–1814* (Princeton, NJ: Princeton University Press, 1975).

Parmentier, Antoine Augustin, *Manière de faire le pain de pommes de terre, sans mélange de farine* (Paris: Imprimerie Royale, 1779).

————, *Recherches sur les végétaux nourrissans* (Paris: Imprimerie Royale, 1781).

Perry, Charles, A. J. Arberry, and Maxime Rodinson, *Medieval Arab Cookery: Papers by Maxime Rodinson and Charles Perry with a Reprint of a Baghdad Cookery Book* (Totnes: Prospect Books, 1998).

Peterson, T. Sarah, *Acquired Taste: The French Origin of Modern Cooking* (Ithaca, NY, and London: Cornell University Press, 1994).

Phillips, E. D., *Aspects of Greek Medicine* (New York: St. Martin's Press, 1973).

Phillips, Rod, *A Short History of Wine* (London: Penguin, 2000).

Picard, Roger, *Les Salons littéraires et la société française, 1610–1789* (Paris: Brenato, 1943).

Piponnier, François, "From Hearth to Table: Late Medieval Cooking Equipment" in Jean-Louis Flandrin and Massimo Montanari, eds., *Food: A Culinary History*, English edition by Albert Sonnenfeld (New York: Columbia University Press, 1999).

Pitte, Jean-Robert, *Bordeaux Bourgogne: Les passions rivales* (Paris: Hachette, 2005).

———, *French Gastronomy, the History and Geography of a Passion*, translated by Jody Gladding (New York: Columbia University Press, 2002).

Platina,[Bartolomeo Sacchi], *Le Platine en françois: de honesta voluptate et valetudine*, following the edition of 1505, preface by Silvano Serventi and Jean-Louis Flandrin, transcription by Mathilde Ribot (Paris: Editions Manucius, 2003).

Pomiane, Edouard de, *Cooking with Pomiane*, introduction by Elizabeth David (New York: The Modern Library, 2001).

Porter, Roy, and G. S. Rousseau, *Gout: The Patrician Malady* (New Haven, CT, and London: Yale University Press, 1998).

Porter, Roy, *The Greatest Benefit to Mankind: A Medical History of Humanity* (New York: W. W. Norton, 1997).

Prudhomme, Paul, *Chef Prudhomme's Louisiana Kitchen* (New York: William Morrow, 1984).

Ranum, Orest, *Paris in the Age of Absolutism: An Essay*, revised and expanded ed. (University Park: Pennsylvania State University Press, 2002).

Rebora, Giovanni, *The Culture of the Fork: A Brief History of Food in Europe*, translated by Albert Sonnenfeld (New York: Columbia University Press, 2001).

Redon, Odile, Françoise Sabban, and Silvano Serventi, *The Medieval Kitchen: Recipes from France and Italy*, translated by Edward Schneider (Chicago and London: The University of Chicago Press, 1998).

Revel, Jean-François, *Culture and Cuisine: A Journey Through the History of Food*, translated from the French by Helen R. Lane (New York: Doubleday, 1982).

Riera-Melis, Antoni, "Society, Food, and Feudalism" in Jean-Louis Flandrin and Massimo Montanari, eds., *Food: A Culinary History*, English edition by Albert Sonnenfeld (New York: Columbia University Press, 1999).

Robinson, Jancis, ed., *The Oxford Companion to Wine* (Oxford: Oxford University Press, 1999).

Roche, Daniel, *A History of Everyday Things: The Birth of Consumption in France, 1600–1800*, translated by Brian Pearce (Cambridge: Cambridge University Press, 2000).

———, *The People of Paris: An Essay in Popular Culture in the 18th Century*, translated by Marie Evans in association with Gwynne Lewis (Leamington Spa, Hamburg, and New York: Berg, 1987).

Rock, Judith, *Terpsichore at Louis-le-Grand: Baroque Dance on the Jesuit Stage in Paris* (Saint Louis, MO: The Institute of Jesuit Sources, 1996).

Rodinson, Maxime, "Recheches sur les documents Arabes relatifs à la cuisine" in *Revue des Etudes Islamiques*, (1949), pp. 96–165.

———, "*Romania* and Other Arab Words in Italian" in *Petits Propos Culinaire*, vol. 34 (March 1990), pp. 31–44.

Roger, Delphine, "The Middle East and South Asia" in Kenneth F. Kiple and Kriemhild Coneè Ornelas, eds., *The Cambridge World History of Food*, 2 vols. (Cambridge and New York: Cambridge University Press, 2000).

Root, Waverley, *Food: An Authoritative and Visual History and Dictionary of the Foods of the World* (New York: Simon and Schuster, 1980).

———, *The Food of France* (New York: Vintage, 1977).

———, *The Food of Italy* (New York: Vintage, 1992).

Rosenberger, Bernard, "Arab Cuisine and Its Contribution to European Culture" in Jean-Louis Flandrin and Massimo Montanari, eds., *Food: A Culinary History*, English edition by Albert Sonnenfeld (New York: Columbia University Press, 1999).

Rousseau, Jean-Jacques, *Emile or On Education*, introduction, translation, and notes by Allan Bloom (New York: Basic Books, 1979).

———, *The Reveries of the Solitary Walker*, translated with a preface, notes, and an interpretative essay by Charles Butterworth (New York: Harper, 1982).

Rumohr, Karl Friedrich von, *The Essence of Cookery*, translated by Barbara Yeomans (London: Prospect Books, 1993).

Sabatier, Gerard, "Une révolution de Palais: le remplacement des vins de Champagne par ceux de Bourgogne à la table de Louis XIV en 1694" in *Boire et Manger au XVIIe Siècle au Temps de la Marquise de Sévigné*, papers from the second Symposium Vin et Histoire (Suze-la-Rousse: Université du Vin, 1998).

Sabban, Françoise, and Silvano Serventi, *La Gastronomie à la Renaissance: 100 recettes de France et d'Italie* (Paris: Editions Stock, 1997).

———, *La Gastronomie au Grand Siècle: 100 recettes de France et d'Italie* (Paris: Editions Stock, 1998).

Saint-Evremond, Charles de Marguetel de Saint Denis, seigneur de, *The Letters of Saint-Evremond*, edited with an introduction and notes by John Hayward (New York: B. Blom, 1972).

Saint-Simon, Louis de Rouvroy, duke de, *Mémoires de duc de Saint-Simon*, edited by G. Truc, 7 vols. (Paris: Gallimard, 1947–1966).

Salaman, Redcliffe N., *The History and Social Influence of the Potato* with a chapter on industrial uses by W. G. Burton (Cambridge: Cambridge University Press, 1949, reprinted 1970).

Sassatelli, Giuseppe, "The Diet of the Etruscans" in Jean-Louis Flandrin and Massimo Montanari, eds., *Food: A Culinary History*, English edition by Albert Sonnenfeld (New York: Columbia University Press, 1999).

Saule, Béatrix, "Tables à Versailles 1682–1789" in *Versailles et les tables royals en Europe XVIIème-XIXème siècle* (Versailles: Musée National des Châteaux de Versailles et de Trianon, 1993–1994).

Schama, Simon, *Citizens: A Chronicle of the French Revolution* (New York: Vintage, 1989).

———, *The Embarrassment of Riches: An Interpretation of Dutch Culture in the Golden Age* (Berkeley and Los Angeles: University of California Press, 1988).

Schivelbusch, Wolfgang, *Tastes of Paradise: A Social History of Spices, Stimulants, and Intoxicants*, translated from the German by David Jacobson (New York: Vintage, 1992).

Schofield, Robert E., *Mechanism and Materialism: British Natural Philosophy in an Age of Reason* (Princeton, NJ: Princeton University Press, 1970).

Schorger, A. W., *The Wild Turkey, Its History and Domestication* (Norman: University of Oklahoma Press, 1966).

Scully, D. Eleanor, and Terence Scully, *Early French Cookery: Sources, History, Original Recipes and Modern Adaptations* (Ann Arbor: University of Michigan Press, 1995).

Serres, Olivier de, *Le Théâtre d'agriculture et mesnage des champs*, introduction by Pierre Lieutaghi (Paris: Actes Sud, 2001).

Sévigne, Marie de Rabutin-Chantal, marquise de, *Selected Letters*, translated and with an introduction by Leonard Tancock (London: Penguin, 1982).

Shand, P. Morton, *A Book of French Wines* (London: Jonathan Cape, 1963).

Shapin, Steven, "Trusting George Cheyne: Scientific Expertise, Common Sense, and Moral Authority in Early Eighteenth-Century Dietetic Medicine" in *The Bulletin of the History of Medicine*, vol. 77 (2003), pp. 270–271.

Shovlin, John, *The Political Economy of Virtue: Luxury, Patriotism, and the Origins of the French Revolution* (Ithaca, NY, and London: Cornell University Press, 2006).

Sigerist, Henry E., *A History of Medicine*, 2 vols. (New York: Oxford University Press, 1961).

Simon, André L., *The History of Champagne* (London: George Rainbird, 1962).

Siraisi, Nancy, *Medieval and Early Renaissance Medicine: An Introduction to Knowledge and Practice* (Chicago and London: The University of Chicago Press, 1990).

Sokolov, Robert, *The Saucier's Apprentice* (New York: Alfred A. Knopf, 1976).

Soniat, Leon, Jr., *La Bouche Creole* (Gretna, LA: Pelican, 2006).

Spang, Rebecca L., *The Invention of the Restaurant: Paris and Modern Gastronomic Culture* (Cambridge, MA: Harvard University Press, 2000).

Spencer, Colin, *British Food: An Extraordinary Thousand Years of History* (New York: Columbia University Press, 2002).

Strong, Roy, *Feast: A History of Grand Eating* (New York: Harcourt, 2002).

Symons, Michael, *A History of Cooks and Cooking* (Urbana and Chicago: University of Illinois Press, 1998).

Taillevent, *Le Viandier, d'après l'edition de 1468*, preface by Mary and Philip Hyman (Paris: Editions Manucius, 2001).

Tainturier, Abbé, *Remarques sur la culture des vignes de Beaune et lieux circonvoisins (1763)*, foreword by André-Pierre Syren, preface, notes, and lexicon by Loïc Abric (Précy-sous-Thil: Editions de l'Armançon, 2000).

Takats, Sean, trans., "Cuisine" in *The Encyclopedia of Diderot and D'Alembert Collective Translation Project* at http://www.hti.umich.edu/d/did/

Tannahill, Reay, *Food in History* (New York: Crown, 1988).

Temkin, Owsei, *Galenism: Rise and Decline of a Medical Philosophy* (Ithaca, NY, and London: Cornell University Press, 1973).

Thériault, Serge A., *Jean-Jacques Rousseau et la Médecine naturelle* (St. Denis, Montréal, and Québec: Les Editions Univers, 1979).

Therman, Paul H., and Karen Hunger Parshall, eds., *Experiencing Nature: Proceedings of a Conference in Honor of Allen G. Debus* (Dordrecht, Boston, and London: Kluwer, 1997).

Thomas, Keith, *Man and the Natural World: Changing Attitudes in England, 1500–1800* (New York and Oxford: Oxford University Press, 1984).

Toussaint-Samat, Maguelonne, *History of Food,* translated by Anthea Bell (Cambridge and Oxford: Blackwell, 1992).

Trilling, Lionel, *Sincerity and Authenticity* (Cambridge, MA: Harvard University Press, 1971).

Turner, Jack, *Spice: The History of Temptation* (New York: Alfred A. Knopf, 2004).

Vehling, Joseph Dommers, ed. and trans., *Apicius: Cooking and Dining in Imperial Rome,* with an introduction by Frederick Starr (New York: Dover, 1977).

Verral, William, *A Compleat System of Cookery in Which Is Set Forth a Variety of Genuine Receipts Collected from Several Years Experience under the Celebrated Mr. de St. Clouet, Sometime since Cook to His Grace the Duke of Newcastle* (London: printed for the author, 1759).

_____, *The Cook's Paradise or A Compleat System of Cookery* (London: Sylvan Press, 1948).

Watson, Andrew, *Agricultural Innovation in the Early Islamic World: The Diffusion of Crops and Farming Techniques, 700–1100* (Cambridge and New York: Cambridge University Press, 1983).

Wear, A., R. K. French, and I. M. Lonie, eds., *The Medical Renaissance of the Sixteenth Century* (Cambridge: Cambridge University Press, 1985).

Wear, Andrew, "Medical Practice in Late Seventeenth- and Early Eighteenth-Century England: Continuity and Union" in Roger French and Andrew Wear, eds., *The Medical Revolution of the Seventeenth Century* (Cambridge and New York: Cambridge University Press, 1989).

Wellman, Kathleen, "Nature and Culture in the *Discourses of the Virtuosi of France*" in Paul H. Therman and Karen Hunger Parshall, eds., *Experiencing Nature: Proceedings of a Conference in Honor of Allen G. Debus* (Dordrecht, Boston, and London: Kluwer, 1997).

Wheaton, Barbara Ketchum, *Savoring the Past: The French Kitchen and Table from 1300–1789* (New York: Simon and Schuster, 1983).

Willan, Anne, *Great Cooks and Their Recipes from Taillevent to Escoffier* (Boston: Little, Brown, 1990).

Wilson, Arthur M., *Diderot* (New York: Oxford University Press, 1972).

Wolfert, Paula, *The Cooking of South-West France* (New York: Harper & Row, 1988).

Wright, Clifford A., *A Mediterranean Feast* (New York: Morrow, 1999).

Young, Arthur, *Travels in France during the Years 1787, 1788, and 1789,* edited with an introduction by Jeffry Kaplow (Gloucester, MA: Peter Smith, 1976).

Index